BREAKING
BARRIERS

BOOKS BY CARL T. ROWAN

South of Freedom
The Pitiful and the Proud
Go South to Sorrow
Wait Till Next Year
Just Between Us Blacks
Breaking Barriers

BREAKING BARRIERS

A MEMOIR

CARL T. ROWAN

LITTLE, BROWN AND COMPANY
BOSTON   TORONTO   LONDON

First Edition

Library of Congress Cataloging-in-Publication Data

Rowan, Carl Thomas
   Breaking barriers : a memoir / Carl T. Rowan. — 1st ed.
     p.   cm.
   ISBN 0-316-73977-3
   1. Rowan, Carl Thomas. 2. Journalists — United States — Biography.
3. Afro-Americans — Biography. 4. United States — Race relations —
Social conditions. 5. Race discrimination — United States.
I. Title.
PN4874.R74A3   1991
070'.92 — dc20
[B]   90-42827

10 9 8 7 6 5

RRD-VA

*Published simultaneously in Canada
by Little, Brown & Company (Canada) Limited*

Printed in the United States of America

To that small, brave group of white Americans
who still chase dreams of racial justice,
believing that only a fair sharing of opportunities
can keep America healthy and free

Contents

Foreword

AS THE LIGHTS of freedom go on again, from Berlin to Tallinn, we Americans watch with smugness and sanctimony. We act as though it is only in distant places like Bucharest and the Baltics, Panama and Prague, that ordinary people have a terrible time finding hope and happiness.

I know better. Even in the "most enlightened" reaches of my own society, such as my old home state Minnesota, bigotry has found an easy home and racial-social justice has been an outcast.

During my blessed lifetime I have had the good fortune of being thrust onto the ramparts where freedom was challenged by tyranny, so I have been infused with the belief that my life's experiences say something meaningful, even profound, about the course we ought now take in a very dangerous world.

I have been emboldened by the comment that "There is no history; only biography," and discouraged by a friend's observation that "There are no autobiographies; only lies." But I am confident that my disadvantaged and then privileged life offers a bit of the driftwood of wisdom that comes with the deluge of times glorious and god-awful, sensational and sad.

I have been, in my early days in Tennessee, Richard Wright's *Black Boy;* and in my late teens a Booker T. Washington coming *Up from Slavery;* and in my thirties and forties a black Horatio Alger in the minds of some whites. But I have never been Ralph Ellison's *Invisible Man.*

America has changed remarkably since I began to climb out of the Great Depression. So this memoir is about the mutual climb to self-respect of a nation that once wallowed in fear and a black kid who was almost trapped in hopelessness.

Breaking barriers! Just as no man is an island in the sea of human hopes and hatreds, so no man is capable of bashing alone the roadblocks to justice and human freedom. That is why this memoir is not entirely about the life of Carl Rowan; it is about the lives of Rosa Parks, Gus Courts, Martin Luther King, Jr., Whitney Young — all of them black — and Hubert Humphrey, Harry Truman, Lyndon B. Johnson, the white heroes of eras in which courageous people risked a lot to try to prove that Homo sapiens is intelligent enough to realize that survival requires ignoring meaningless differences in the human species.

I have spent almost five years trying to give accuracy, meaningfulness, humanity, to this memoir. In all three respects, I have had the indispensable support of my wife, Vivien, who has never read a chapter; and of Judith Plunkett, who sublimated her personal conservatism and did research that matched my admonition, "Just give me the facts, ma'am"; of David Mazie, my close colleague of more than two decades, who provided invaluable research and insights; and of Jeanne Bowers, my former colleague in the production of prize-winning television specials, who thought foolishly that getting married and having a baby was an escape from this endeavor. And then Kristine Bock, a young lawyer-to-be from Minnesota, who came to me at a time of my great need and said emphatically, "We will finish this book." She committed an incredible number of hours to proving that a promise is a promise.

But no promise comes to happy fruition in the world of book publishing without the author having an editor who really cares. It took almost five years for me to complete this book because Little, Brown's executive editor Fredrica Friedman read every paragraph and page enough times to ensure that I was telling Americans all that they needed to know, in ways that they could understand fully and relate to personally. However proper or improper it is for an author to say this, *Breaking Barriers* is partly the product of an editor who has matched the pages to the needs, concerns, fears, and prejudices of likely readers.

I also would like to acknowledge associate editor Colleen

Mohyde, to whom I owe a great debt, and copyeditors Sue Betz-Keating and Peggy Freudenthal, who brought perceptive eyes to their reading of the manuscript.

I thank my "home newspaper," the *Chicago Sun-Times*, and my radio show sponsor, K mart, for helping to finance travels and research leading to columns and broadcasts that pumped many facts and insights into these pages. I salute the Joint Center for Political and Economic Studies in Washington, D.C., for the information it has provided over the years. I acknowledge most of all the reality that no one breaks barriers without strong people helping them to push the ramrod, so I thank the late John and Betty Cowles and their family, and other editors and friends at the *Minneapolis Tribune*, who literally pushed me into the role of pioneer. Many of my great supporters, such as Bill and Lucy Steven, are mentioned at length in pages of this book.

Over five years my staff has called hundreds of public information offices in every federal bureau and agency and offices of most senators and congressmen, seeking a bit of information here, a kernel of truth there. I thank this oft-maligned group of very dedicated public servants who man those offices.

Finally, I cannot thank appropriately all those who have been so much a part of my life, but who also have helped me recall portions of it in ways that describe how a great nation "grew up" as I did and now struggles for greater glories, as I do.

Carl T. Rowan
Washington, D.C.
August 11, 1990

BREAKING
BARRIERS

CHAPTER ONE

Days of Hopelessness and Fear

I T WAS A FEW MINUTES before 2:00 A.M. on June 14, 1988, that I was awakened by the noise of someone tampering with my bedroom window.

I lay almost paralyzed with the primeval fear I had as a child sleeping on the floor of a wretched house in Tennessee and being awakened by the screams of a sister who had been bitten on the ear by a large and menacing rat.

That dark June morning of 1988, my paralysis was broken by a woman's scream that was not unlike the biting outcry of my little sister, a cry I have never forgotten.

I sat up in bed and said to myself, "That's on your property!" I knew that one or more persons had scaled my ten-foot fence and that one of them was brazen enough to try to enter my house.

My mind was suddenly clogged with memories of telephoned threats to kill me, and of an FBI warning that one hate group that was harassing my wife and me was operating out of a gun store in Virginia. Because of those threats my son Carl Jr., a former FBI agent, had come to the house with a gun and spent the night waiting for the assailants who never showed up. He had left an exempt-from-registration revolver at my house for protection.

If you are lucky enough never to have been mugged, raped, or had your home burglarized in your presence, you will not understand the fear that I felt, especially when the woman screamed a second time. I ran in nothing but my nightshirt to a window at the far corner of the house and, in the dim glow of a streetlight some fifty yards away, saw a tall naked woman with huge breasts flopping up and down as she ran from a man. I saw cigarettes light up, reminding me that druggies had scaled my fence before, leaving butts that police said were laced with PCP, the drug some called the angel of death.

I telephoned 911, awakened my wife, and, during the interminable wait for the police, remembered the gun that my son had left. I got it without telling my wife, took off the trigger lock, and loaded it.

When we saw the first police cruiser, I sneaked outside my patio door into the darkness near my bedroom, 175 feet from the Jacuzzi, to try to open a gate so the police could dash in and arrest what I assumed was a dangerous bunch of druggies.

I never got to the gate because, in almost pitch darkness, I suddenly was confronted by a six-foot-four-inch nineteen-year-old who was puffing on a cigarette of some type as he ran toward me and the open patio door to my house. I jumped back inside and warned the man to halt — that I had a gun. He ran toward me recklessly, knocking over a garden light. I, a marksman in my Navy days, said to myself: "This sonofabitch isn't going to stop." I would shoot him in the foot. But as I decided to pull the trigger, he lunged at me and began to fall on his face. His wrist caught the bullet that was intended for his foot.

United States Attorney Jay Stephens's office investigated immediately and found, press stories to the contrary, that the man I shot was four feet from my family room door, far from and out of sight of the swimming pool and Jacuzzi, when he was wounded. There would be no federal prosecution.

I soon learned that I had a problem, not with white Republicans, but with a black Democratic mayor, Marion Barry. I had written about the rank corruption in the Barry administration. I had told Barry to his face that his apparent addictions to alcohol and drugs and his sexual escapades outside marriage made him "a disgrace, a betrayer of black children."

Now Barry could strike back by prosecuting me on the technical misdemeanor charge that the gun I used to protect my home was "unregistered." Barry told some newsmen privately to "come to the courthouse and watch the fall of the great Carl Rowan." Then he telephoned my son Carl Jr. and suggested that the case might be dropped if I would "lighten up" in my criticism of his sleazy administration.

"Drop dead," my son said, and I confirmed that I would make no such deal.

The media staked out my house, hounding me everywhere, as though I suddenly had become some grotesque criminal. It was as though no one remembered, or gave a damn, that a few months earlier I was hosting the Ronald Reagans as president of the Gridiron Club, or presiding over a dinner at which I handed out a quarter of a million dollars to black high school seniors who aspired to excellence.

Finally I convinced myself that the story was not how a few punks could invade my property and wreck my life and reputation, it was how I got from the rat-bite days to a point where so many thousands of people telephoned, wrote, sent telegrams to say that they cared about what was happening to me. I gave myself feeble consolation by drifting back to a happier time and place — February 28, 1964, in the East Room of the White House.

It was full of distinguished Americans, many black, many white, including my beloved friend Hubert H. Humphrey, Secretary of State Dean Rusk and his wife, Virginia, and Senator Ernest Gruening of Alaska. The president of the United States was speaking:

> This is a very delightful and happy moment for me. . . . It is always cheerful when a man of intelligence, courage, and capability accepts a position of great responsibility in his government. Carl Rowan's whole life has been spent in preparation for this extremely important assignment. . . .
>
> I think it is good for our country at this time and at this point in the history of the world that Carl Rowan takes over the sensitive post of director of the United States Information Agency. He succeeds a very able man [Edward R. Murrow]. He has a very difficult job, telling the people of the world about the *good* things and the *bad* things in our country.
>
> My wish to you, Carl, is that you may serve your country in the future as you have in the past. If you do that, the nation will be the principal beneficiary.

Lyndon Baines Johnson of Texas was talking about me, and my family and friends were applauding gustily. I was still almost in a state of disbelief that the president of the United States had called me from my post as ambassador to Finland to take over the agency that spoke for him and the rest of America to the world.

I strained for a modicum of humility. I told President Johnson and that supportive throng how I had gone from State Department official to UN representative to ambassador to Finland to USIA chief, and that my mother thought I was having a lot of trouble holding a job. Emboldened by applause, I then told the president of a Tennessee relative who telephoned to say, "Only in America, Cuz, could a poor colored guy from Middle Tennessee rise to such a high position. By the way, could you spare three hundred bucks?"

I said that I had replied, "You are absolutely right. Only in America could a poor colored guy leave an embassy with 120 employees, take over an agency with 12,120 employees, and take a fifteen-hundred-dollar pay cut. Could *you* spare three hundred bucks?"

Johnson guffawed, as did the other guests.

I went on to make some very serious comments about my guarantee that I would serve not only America but the cause of truth and freedom. Then I rode home asking myself a lot of provocative questions.

How did an impoverished black boy from Jim Crow* Tennessee wind up in a job where he would sit in the president's cabinet meetings and in the deliberations of the National Security Council? How did I get a job where I would report only to the president of the United States? And how was I going to survive financially, given the pay cut and the fact that I already was at the brink of insolvency?

That night, on the "CBS Evening News," Walter Cronkite related the story about my cousin wanting three hundred bucks, and me, the old pay-cut bureaucrat, needing it more.

Later, *Reader's Digest* printed the Cronkite version of this exchange and sent him a check for three hundred dollars. Cronkite, ever the sensitive gentleman, endorsed the check over and sent it to me.

---

* "Jim Crow" describes a practice or policy of segregation or discrimination against Negroes in public places, public vehicles, employment, schools, etc. The term derives from a song sung by Thomas Rice in a mid-1800s Negro minstrel show.

"Rowan, how did you get here?" I asked myself. "You just can't get here from there!"

I thought about it for a few moments and then, in newfound contact with reality, said to my wife: "Deposit this check!"

What and where was the "there"? I have no trouble remembering.

Burrowed into my mind is the memory of a dark night in McMinnville, Tennessee, in 1933. My brother, Charles, my sister Ella, and I, with a couple of cousins, were sleeping on a pallet on the splintery floor of an old frame house alongside the Louisville & Nashville railroad tracks. We were jarred awake by Ella's screams. My father, Tom, rushed in with a lighted match, which he quickly put to the kerosene lamp. He held it close to Ella, and we saw that her ear was bleeding. She had been bitten by a rat.

This was traumatic enough for me, eight years old at the time, but what followed was even more devastating. My mother was almost hysterical, shouting to my father that he had to get out and earn some money, because we couldn't go on living like that. She didn't want her children going to bed hungry, especially when bed was just a pallet on a dirty floor in a room infested by roaches.

"How do you expect the children to get any sleep when they lie awake listening to the rats gnaw holes through the wall?" she screamed.

I shared my mother's fear of the rats, her disgust over having her children hungry, but the male part of me sympathized with my father.

"I'm working every day I can to find any kind of job," he would say. "Times are hard."

That was no excuse for my mother. She would reel off the names of a few black men who had jobs and say, "Their children aren't being bitten by rats every night."

My father's response was to borrow a big steel trap. Just before bedtime he set it in the corner of the room in which we slept, admonishing us: "If any of you have to go out in the yard to pee tonight, don't stumble over here, 'cause this trap is big enough to snap off the leg of a goddammed grizzly bear."

In the wee hours we heard the trap spring, then a bloodcurdling cry from what turned out to be one of the biggest rats I had ever seen. My father ran in. We saw that this rodent was as tough as a grizzly, snarling at us, struggling to get free, even as blood oozed out of its mouth.

"Get me a broom, boy!" my daddy shouted.

I got it and watched him break the handle over his knee, then beat the rat to death with the broomstick. This scene, this noise, the sight of this awful creature, provoked another outburst from my mother.

I lay awake on that pallet for another few dark hours, hearing the gnawing of other rats. Then I heard my father get up and go to the kitchen to make his breakfast and indulge in the one thing that gave him a genuine sense of manhood: his memories of his stint in Europe as a soldier in World War I. He was frying thick slices of white salt pork, which he would eat with corn bread and molasses over which he had poured the grease from the fatback. Butter was a very rare commodity in our house.

Over the noise of that fat pork frying (also called Hoover's ham, in honor of the president blamed for bringing on hard times), I heard my father singing: "Stars and stripes gonna wave over yonder some sweet day-ay."

It seemed that on a million mornings I heard that sound of frying fatback, my father singing that line, telling us all that there had been another bruising nighttime argument.

With so many talkative kids sleeping on the same pallet, word of the rat bite rushed through the little black community, and probably through maids and yardmen in the white community as well. But embarrassment was no factor compared with fear and misery, because we knew that most blacks in McMinnville were poor, and often hungry, and had to fight off rats, mice, roaches, and other vermin. Some of my buddies teased me, yet one offered some advice whose worth I am not still sure of, though I followed it.

"Get yourself a pet white rat," my pal Bill Hogan said. "Ain't no regular rat ever gonna come near a white rat."

I thought he was nuts, or pulling my leg, but I got a pet white rat, which I took to the pallet every night — after Ella and the girl cousins were asleep (even a white rat would have terrified them). Many nights I heard gnawing, but to my amazement nobody ever was bitten again.

In 1962, when I had my tail in a sling because of an outspoken speech that I had given in late 1961 in Philadelphia about the Congo, Moise Tshombe, and Union Minière, Edward R. Murrow said to me: "Great speech. Now I hope you have a way to protect your ass."

"I have," I said. "I've got me a white rat."

"What?" asked the befuddled Murrow. He laughed so as to expose large teeth when I told him of the rat-bite episode in McMinnville and suggested that I had "a white rat protector" in the White House.

We finally fled that wretched house, but not to get away from rodents. We were avoiding the landlord and other bill collectors.

"Mama, there's a white man coming," I would say.

She would peek out and say, "That's the man with our insurance policy. I don't have the twenty cents to pay him. You go up to the screen door, but don't unhook it, and tell him there's nobody at home."

Obediently, I started for the door, hearing my mother's final whisper: "Son, be sure to call that white man 'mister.'"

It is impossible for Americans under age fifty to understand the times about which I write. I was born four years before the great stock market crash of 1929 in a dying little coal-mining town called Ravenscroft, Tennessee. I was an infant when my father, with a fifth-grade education, and my mother, who had completed eleven grades, decided that McMinnville, with its nurseries, lumberyards, and livery stables, offered greater opportunities.

My parents never expected an economic calamity that would make life miserable for most people everywhere, especially black people in brutally racist communities, which is what McMinnville was. But they lapsed into poverty that was so bad that my children wince when I talk about it. It is as though they cannot believe that in that rat-infested house we had not a single clock or watch. We told time by the arrival of the train from Tullahoma to Sparta, and if it was late then I was late for school. We had no electricity, no running water, and, for most of the time, no toothbrushes. Many a time a sister would say, "Your breath smells," and I would run a finger across a bar of Octagon soap and massage my teeth and gums until I could no longer stand the foul taste of the laundry soap. Toilet paper was a luxury we did not know when second-hand newspapers were good enough for our outhouse. I remember almost never having more than one pair of socks at a time, and I had to wear those socks to school for five straight days. In between weekly baths in the tin laundry tub, the sweat and dirt gathered on my feet so that between my toes there was an abundance of what we called toe jam.

We just accepted it as our fate in life that we had no telephone, no radio, and no regular inflow of money.

My father tried hard for work and sometimes got a job stacking lumber at twenty-five cents an hour. On days when his back was killing him, he still went if a messenger said there was work. Breakfast was supposed to be the big meal before such heavy labor, and my father loved the rare days when, through hook or crook, he could have fried chicken, fried apples, and fried corn before going to the lumberyard. But those days were so rare that lunch became the meal of survival, and that always meant navy beans, pinto beans, black-eyed peas, butter beans (dried limas), whippoorwill peas, each boiled with a slab of Hoover's ham on alternate days. A baked sweet potato and a glass of buttermilk were cherished additions, even though everyone knew that the combination created so much gas that no two humans could sleep comfortably on the same pallet.

I don't think my father ever earned as much as three hundred dollars in a single year. When he worked and earned a little money, this became another reason for marital conflict. My daddy never stopped thinking that he could bolster his ego, his self-respect, his reputation as a breadwinner, by going down to the banks of the river to play poker. Black people had to go to such weedy hideouts because, while white folk played poker and shot craps in their homes with impunity, the cops waited eagerly to pounce upon any black gambling activity and seize and keep whatever money the black gamblers had.

I could tell by the way my father strutted home from the river that he was a winner. He would say to me, "Boy, we're gonna have a good dinner tonight. You go to Piggly Wiggly's and get five pounds of jack salmon [at ten cents a pound] and then go by the courthouse and pick the biggest, sweetest watermelon you can buy for a nickel. And you can even buy a box of Kellogg's Cornflakes and go by the dairy and get a half a gallon of milk. We're gonna have a good dinner tonight, 'cause I just won eighteen dollars."

My mother always believed that if he said he had won eighteen dollars, he really had won twenty-eight dollars or more. So she would go through his pockets at night. And the happiness of "a good dinner" would deteriorate into another brawl.

But not the kind of brawl that ensued the many times that my father came away from the riverbank a loser. He would be in a foul mood, as all losing gamblers are. She would be incensed that she couldn't even pay the paperboy (she would resubscribe every time a boy we owed quit and a new one took our route) or buy one of the kids a badly needed pair of shoes. No child goes unaffected by the quarrels emanating from such an atmosphere. I believed my mother when she accused my father of leaving his children in an environment that caused whooping cough, diphtheria, diabetes, tuberculosis, and a host of other diseases. Yet I hated the arguments with all my heart.

"Why can't my daddy get a good job?" I asked over and over again.

When there was no lumber to stack, when times were really rough, my father would ask me to go hunting with him. He would bring two shells for his shotgun, which was all he could afford. They called him Two-Shot Rowan because it was legend that Tom Rowan might miss a rabbit with the first barrel, but never with the second.

I survived the depression eating fried rabbit, rabbits and dumplings, broiled rabbit, rabbit stew, and a host of similar dishes made possible because Two-Shot Rowan so often came home with a rabbit or two draining blood down his pants leg.

What an irony of life that, during the Lyndon Johnson presidency, I walked into the then-famous Sans Souci restaurant in Washington and the maître d', the late Paul Delisle, said to me: "Mr. Rowan, I have something very special for you today: *civet de lapin*."

"Paul, *civet de lapin*?" I said, smiling. "In every language I know, that's rabbit, and in my boyhood I ate all the rabbit I ever intend to eat."

Delisle bent over in laughter. "I was in the French resistance," he said, "and I'd have starved to death but for the rabbits. I don't touch rabbit either. Would you settle for some filet of sole?"

When we couldn't afford shells or didn't spot rabbits, my daddy would wait for a big rain and ask me to go fishing with him on the banks of the Barren Forks River. We would catch a good fish, which we called a sucker, and that made for a heavenly meal. But more often we would drag out carp, lazy ugly fish that lay in the mud on the bottom of the river, sucking up vulture fare. On hungry days a carp got a kiss in my house.

Beside our house we grew tomatoes, lettuce, and pole beans in the summer. Not many yards away there was a sty with four pigs in it. It was my job to slop the pigs, but slop was hard to come by when there rarely was leftover food.

Many a day I would be playing baseball in the nearby cottage lot with my buddies when I would bend over to hold my aching stomach.

"Hell, you ain't got nothing but hunger colic, and everybody gits that. Throw the fuckin' ball!" one of my buddies would say.

To avoid hunger colic, some days I would take the box of salt and go sit among the tomato plants, eating one hot tomato after another. After days of doing this, sores broke out on my legs. I was told that eating too many tomatoes had put too much acid in my blood.

The great days, relatively speaking, were in the fall when it got cold enough to be hog-killing time. I would hold the pigs while my father cut off their testicles and smeared the bleeding wound with turpentine. He would eat the fruits of these castrations, goodies we delicately called mountain oysters. I said I would die of hunger first.

At slaughter time, I wanted no part of the job of hitting the hog in the head with an ax. Instead, I would make sure that the water in the big black pot was boiling hot. Once they strung that hog up, slit its belly, and began to clean it with the steaming water, I watched with apprehension, knowing what my next job would be: cleaning the crap out of the hog's intestines. We would boil these innards in the big black pot, rendering them fit for several feasts of boiled chitlins, fried chitlins — any way one could cook hog guts.

Waste not, want not, was a rule of life, so it was almost miraculous the ways in which almost every inch of that hog was used. On the night of the killing we'd eat the pork tenderloin — a real delicacy. The chitlins had to be cooked soon or only the flies and rats would touch them. As we devoured them, I kept wondering how anything that smelled so bad could taste so good. We had no refrigerator, so my father quickly disposed of the hog's brain by eating it mixed with scrambled eggs. Then came time for a supper of pig's feet, we hoped with some black-eyed peas and turnip greens on the side. Lord knows how I hated those fat and sticky pig's feet, but hunger doesn't entertain much squeamishness.

The hams and shoulders had been taken to some friend's little shack for smoking. Long before we laid a tongue on them, we would have to eat the hog's head, a fat monstrosity that I would eat out of desperation and then vomit.

The hog's ears, snout, tail, and leftovers from the head would be turned into a gruesome little delicacy called souse. Someone told me it was a curse the Germans had bequeathed upon us as a penalty for our winning World War I.

Hogs also deliver a lot of fat, which my family was not about to waste. It was put in that all-purpose black pot in the yard and rendered of lard with which we would fry things for weeks. The pieces of fat with all the grease rendered out were called crack-lins — and these were dropped into cornmeal batter to make the famous cracklin bread. Just one pone of cracklin bread and a glass of buttermilk made for a belly-quietening, nutritious dinner on many an evening when nothing else was available.

My mother taught me which free-growing plants were edible, so I spent a lot of days picking dryland watercress and lamb's-quarter and other plants that tasted marvelous when boiled with a little piece of Hoover's ham. And most days of summer meant picking blackberries growing along public roads until the chigger bites forced me to stop. There were times when my mother made water pies — just water, sugar, and a little butter inside a crust — so those summer days of free blackberries were heaven.

I went to the movies almost every weekend, getting the ten cents for entry through ingenious ways that included selling a junk dealer items he already owned. I was in the grip of *The Black Ace*, Bob Steele, and Ken Maynard and Hoot Gibson and Tarzan as played by Johnny Weissmuller. But, oh God, how I was entranced by a Saturday serial in which Clyde Beatty maneuvered safely through *The Lost Jungle*.

I went into the fields to make my own bows and arrows for our games of cowboys and Indians. But I needed a store-bought six-shooter with caps to give realism to my life. Living in poverty to me will always mean hearing my mother say angrily to my father, "You can't even provide thirty-five cents for me to buy our son a god-dammed cap gun for Christmas!"

Christmas usually is the best time of childhood, but it so often was the worst time of mine. It was, however, one of the few times we got oranges in my house. If we got sick and needed castor oil, our mother somehow found some oranges that we could suck as a chaser. But Christmas was a feast of oranges and apples, pecans, English walnuts, and "nigger toes" (Brazil nuts). Whatever the depth of poverty, my mother found a way to bake a white cake with coconut icing, a yellow cake with caramel icing (my father's favorite), and a chocolate cake with chocolate icing. But she tolerated no gluttony. Each member of the family got a generous slice first time around, then she locked the three cakes in a trunk. The next servings were at her discretion.

My mother knew that even after we fled the home by the railroad tracks for other rental units, her children were in trouble. We had never lived in a house whose walls were not infested with chinches, or bedbugs, that would awaken us in the night. I remember lighting a lamp on many nights to find the sheet red-spotted by my blood, sucked out by chinches.

I would help my mother on Saturdays and Sundays by taking the mattresses outdoors where we would beat them like rugs. Then we would rub the mattress buttons with kerosene, having learned that somehow the bedbugs found a way to hide inside these buttons.

But myriad chinches would also get out of the walls during the darkness and climb the bedposts to do their biting. I didn't patent the idea, so I have no way of proving that I had an original idea when I got four empty tin cans, put the bedposts in them, then filled them with kerosene. No bedbug swam its way to our mattress again.

Every time I read the arrogant opinions of some white male about the weaknesses and sins of black men, I think back to the 1930s and a father who was a damned smart guy, except that he had been denied formal education and had no way to become "a good provider."

Seared into my mind is the day that Thomas David Rowan, veteran of the last great war to save democracy, got his bonus of four hundred dollars. We normally put only wood in the kitchen stove, saving the coal for the potbelly in the living room. But Pops made one hell of a fire in the kitchen stove, using kindling, wood, bark, and some hustled anthracite that I figured wouldn't light up under a blowtorch. He put Mom's little black irons on the eyes of the kitchen stove until they began to glow. Then he pressed four hundred one-dollar bills to a beautiful crispness and stood before his family with pride.

My beleaguered mother was not overwhelmed. "No poker," she said. "No buying bootleg booze from Redwheels. Just use that money to buy us some housing with no rats, roaches, and chinches." She and we were sick of fleeing landlords we couldn't pay.

So, on a little piece of land on what the city would later name Congo Street, across from Old Man Cope's junkyard, my daddy spent four hundred dollars to build a little four-room frame house in which he and my mother had a bedroom, Charles and I had a place to sleep, our three sisters could go to bed alone, and there was a living room–kitchen area. There was no running water, no electricity, and no indoor plumbing, but we were what someone might have called an "upwardly mobile" family.

The remarkable thing about this country is that even in an era of grotesque bigotry there were roads of escape. I have never believed that any American boy can be president; that is jingoistic self-deception. But I do now believe that some of us, allied with a pet white rat or two, can beat the system to a satisfying degree.

The first time I can remember thinking that I could be someone special was when I was seven or eight. I was hurrying home to have some butter beans with my mother and father when, on East Main Street near the school, Mrs. Malone walked to the little picket fence around her house and said, "Little Rhau-wen, boy, can you spell 'boh-lown-uh' for me?"

B-o-l-o-g-n-a, I said proudly. "Remarkable," she said.

"Spell 'sand-wich,' " Mrs. Malone requested, and I ticked off the right letters with a growing sense of pride and achievement.

I squeezed myself and danced from foot to foot as she asked for four or five other words before dismissing me with the declaration, "You are really a smart little boy."

This triumph was dampened by the reality of hot liquid running down my left leg as I turned onto Edgefield Street to run home. How could I ever explain to my mother and father that being such a good speller had caused me to wet my pants?

My mother understood a lot more than I imagined in those days. She told me in many simple ways that trained intelligence could be a passport away from misery. She wanted me to make it to college.

"And hard work pays," she would always add, and then put her hands, feet, and knees where her mouth was. She would go clean some white family's house for a dollar a day. Then on some nights, she would go to another white home to cook, serve food, do the dishes at a dinner party. As the oldest child, I was the "man of the house" during the long hours when both parents were away. When our mother came back around 11:00 P.M. we all were awake or quickly jumped out of bed. We knew that she would have a bagful of leftovers from the dinner party. And if she got a decent tip, she would stop en route home and buy each of us a nickel Chilly Bear, a paper cup of pineapple or orange sherbert. Few moments were so joyful as those late-night feasts.

Many weeks, my mother did her dollar-a-day cleaning and her dinner party jobs and still let white families bring laundry to our house. She boiled the dirtiest clothes in that same big black pot in the yard where we boiled chitlins, rendered lard, made cracklins, and, of course, cleaned our own laundry.

When a white person drove up on a Saturday morning and gave my mother $1.50 for doing the laundry, I would watch her count the money with the same pride shown by my father after he had won $18 in riverbank gambling.

"Carl, first you go to the McMinnville Grocery Store and get a dime's worth of mixed sausage, and a dozen eggs [ten cents], and a nickel's worth of white beans, and a nickel's worth of Hoover's ham — now you get the leanest chunk meat they've got.

"And, boy," my mother would continue, "on your way home you stop at Stiles's Bridge Store and get a nickel's worth of coal oil [kerosene]. Can you remember all that?"

"I can remember, Mama."

I recall the first time I told her that I was "saving money" from these purchases at the Bridge Store so I wouldn't have to pawn her fruit jars to get Saturday movie money.

"Saving money?" she asked.

"Yes, ma'am. Mr. Stiles gives me the same amount of coal oil for four cents as he gives me for a nickel, and the same amount of Irish potatoes for nine cents that he gives me for a dime. So if I buy four cents' worth or nine cents' worth, I'm two cents on my way to the movies on Saturday."

I doubt that Stiles gave me an extra penny's worth of anything. In later years, I complained that he could slice cheese so thin you could see through it. But at age nine I wanted to believe that I wasn't cheating my mother by chopping a penny off the purchase of kerosene.

I shall never forget her looking at me with raised eyebrows when I revealed my money-saving scheme, then patting me on the head as she said: "You really *are* a smart little boy!"

Families buying precious food by the penny, the nickel, the dime, do not buy best-selling books or costly magazines. The only books my parents struggled to pay for were schoolbooks. I bless the memory of my mother sitting in a drafty and cold, or hot and humid, "living room" night after night, squinting by a flickering kerosene lamp, commanding me to "read this," "spell that," or "tell me what four times three is."

She displayed an innate understanding that parental support and praise are wonderful stimulators of the self-respect, the yearning for knowledge, the willingness to work, of children at all levels of ability. I loved it beyond explanation or understanding when she would call off the words in my spelling book and, after I had spelled each correctly, would say to me: "There can't be anybody in that school smarter than you."

The following morning it might be raining midget alligators, but I would be up early with the scissors, cutting a piece of linoleum as an inner sole for my shoe (I had learned that cardboard didn't last long), hoping that it would keep the water out until I got to school and back. That linoleum never did the job any better than the cardboard; but the praise endured a lifetime of storms.

*   *   *

No matter how sensitive and supportive a parent may be, kids living in deprived environments are in peril from before the moment they are born; mental retardation and other afflictions come with being conceived in the womb of a woman of poverty; whooping cough, diphtheria, diabetes, German measles, meningitis, and polio hit hard in areas where children live in want and filth. But the perils I recall personally went far beyond diseases.

I remember that a cousin, Walter Keel, was accused of stealing a monkey wrench at the very time he was sitting on the railroad tracks with me. They sent my cousin to a reform school, and he got sucked up in an environment of rage and crime, and his life was wrecked.

I remember this injustice with special pain, because it tells me how outside the criminal justice system the black people of America were in those days. There were no black lawyers within scores of miles. The courts were not appointing *pro bono* white lawyers to defend blacks accused of crimes of any sort. There was no Miranda ruling to protect any black against self-incrimination because of browbeating by a cop. Blacks were scared to death of the police, the judges, the courts. "Go up there and try to defend Cousin Walter and they'll cook up a reason to put *you* in jail," a buddy would say.

Black people in Tennessee in the 1930s accepted meekly whatever the cops, lawyers, and judges did. God, how I shudder when I recall the many times I could have lost my future for something I really did wrong.

In the summers my close buddy Bill Hogan and I would climb into Old Man Cope's junkyard and help ourselves to the incredibly sweet peaches on a tree that grew there. Other times, we would go into that junkyard and cut copper wiring out of the wrecked cars, then sell that copper back to Old Man Cope. When the winter got bad (and the temperature could drop to near zero), my parents would give me a tow sack and ask me to go over to the depression-stilled lumber mill to pick up the driest bark that was lying around. Then I was to walk up the railroad tracks to pick up any coal that had fallen off a car of the L & N railroad. My buddy Bill and I scrounged all the bark we could find, but there was almost no coal that had fallen off the railroad cars that some other needy family had not already picked. Bill and I would look at a loaded car sitting in the dusk, waiting to be taken somewhere by the next day's train.

"Hell," I would say, "I ain't gonna freeze tonight while all this goddam coal is sitting here. Let's just fill our tow sacks with enough to get us through the night."

Bootlegging booze that the white guy called Redwheels drove out of the Cumberland Mountains in a Model T Ford with red spokes was "economic survival" for some unemployed blacks in McMinnville. Warren County was dry. And while the white folk could bring in all the whiskey they wanted from Davidson County (Nashville), the cops preyed on the black community. My uncle Wilbur drove them crazy. I remember laughing after a search of his house, in which the cops found no illegal booze, when he showed me that he had hidden gallons in the stovepipes in his kitchen. I laughed even more when, after an apparent tip, the cops rushed back and tore the stovepipes apart. They found nothing because my uncle had buried the booze under the pile of firewood in the yard.

My buddy Bill Hogan and I got tired of pawning our mothers' fruit jars to get money to see cowboy star Tim McCoy. We were tired of scrounging the worn-out zinc covers of washboards, the aluminum from broken dippers, to sell to Old Man Cope. So we started tailing the known bootleggers. We saw them buy from Redwheels and bury, say, three half gallons in the weeds along the railroad track.

We would lift one of the three bottles buried by one bootlegger (after all, we left him two!) and sell it cut-rate to another bootlegger. We were in about the same danger as someone crossing a Mafia cocaine peddler these days.

The lures to disaster are always endless for poor kids, which partly explains why America's reform schools and penitentiaries are so overcrowded with males who are poorly educated and jobless.

White kids had whites-only skating rinks, a swimming pool, and other recreational outlets in McMinnville; black kids could go to the Slobbery Rock Café, the adjacent pool hall, or swim in the wretchedly muddy and dirty Barren Forks River.

I was a teenage pool shark. I could bank a ball "cross side" into the side pocket as surely as I could spell b-o-l-o-g-n-a. I was damned near unerring in banking a ball off two cushions into a corner pocket. Some days I would go to the pool hall, having lost twenty cents or so matching pennies, and just wait until some truck-driving stranger would walk in. He would say that he could beat anybody in the house, and an old-school hustler leaning against the fly-specked wall would say: "Shit, I got fifty cents to your dollar that you can't even beat that scrawny little asshole of a boy sitting over there."

After a few pleasantries about the morality of each other's mothers, the bet was on for a game of eight ball. Naturally, I won, or I wouldn't be telling this story. When the truck driver paid his dollar and saw the old corner hustler throw me fifty cents, he would say something like, "Why, you little motherfucker."

And I would stand to all of my five feet three inches and say, "Mister, *I* do not play the dozens."

Getting away with this kind of bravado made it seem so simple to use a wire loop to reach through a fence to snatch an ear of corn off a farmer's stalk; or, on an especially hungry morning, to go into the Hugheses' grazing area and suck hot milk from the teats of a cow; or to appropriate a watermelon from some stranger's farm. "Crime" and the jailhouse beckoned almost every moment of my life.

Probably the luckiest thing that ever happened to me was when my grandmother Ella Johnigan talked me into coming to Nashville to live with her during my seventh and eighth grades. She was a devout Seventh-Day Adventist, and at first dragged me to worship with her every Saturday. And, of course, I went to the Seventh-Day Adventist school. I know from those days why some people want prayer and religion in the public classrooms: if you want to indoctrinate young-sters, get them when they are young and gullible. I became an example of the mesmerizing impact of Saturday sermons, the effect of tent revivals, on young minds. I shivered when Elder Warmack interpreted the Bible to say that a Great Bear would one day rule the world. I was ecstatic when his wife sang "Jerusalem, Jerusalem."

I soon was on Jefferson Street, arguing with others, especially Church of Christ zealots, that "since Sunday is the first day of the week, Saturday is the seventh, so by God's decree Saturday is the Sabbath." I accepted no argument that the God who in Genesis said "And on the seventh day shall thou rest" had never heard of our calendar.

I could recite the eleventh chapter of Leviticus by rote, noting that the Lord had specifically told Moses and Aaron which beasts of the earth and creatures of the sea they could eat. "Whatever parts the hoof and is cloven-footed and chews the cud, among the animals, you may eat."

So in my grandmother's house there was, just to be safe, no rabbit, no catfish, no shrimp. In fact, we only ate meat made of soybeans, except for what was sneaked in by Grandfather Cecil Johnigan, who worked at the State Tuberculosis Hospital a few miles outside Nashville and came home every weekend. He would show up with a gallon tin of mincemeat, another gallon of cherry preserves, and assorted goodies the author of Leviticus never heard of. He even brought me a little crystal radio set on which I listened to the "Grand Ole Opry" and to the baseball games of the Nashville Vols.

One helluva fellow, I thought of my grandfather, wondering how he got so much food, so many other items, out of that hospital every week. I later understood that he had "totin' privileges" in lieu of a decent salary. The white folks had told him that he would get forty dollars a month and everything he could tote home.

The Seventh-Day Adventist church did not run a high school, so my grandmother told me I had the option of going to huge Pearl High in Nashville or back to Bernard High in McMinnville. I opted to rejoin my buddies, to go to a tiny, ill-equipped school that probably would not even have existed but for the generosity of the Julius Rosenwald family.

Remember that until well after 1900, many states and communities frowned on teaching Negroes to read and write, and some made it a crime to do so. Southern states were allocating little or nothing for the education of blacks. It was in 1913 that a Jew named Julius Rosenwald set up the Julius Rosenwald Fund to provide grants for the construction of schools for Negro children. By 1932 more than five thousand schools, including Bernard, had been built with Rosenwald money in almost nine hundred counties in fifteen states. I had gotten into some fierce arguments on the corner by observing openly that it was mostly the Jews — at King's Department Store and a few other places — who would extend desperately needed credit to colored families that were devastated by the depression.

I was thirteen when I went back to McMinnville to begin the ninth grade. I was appalled that late summer of 1938 over a fact that I should not have forgotten: there were no jobs, no recreational facilities, nothing for young blacks that was uplifting, unless you were willing to suffer through a sermon at a tent revival on a Sunday afternoon just to grab a piece of fried chicken and brown-sugar pie that the faithful sisters would cook and bring in a supply so abundant as to belie their poverty. Obviously, they were exercising totin' privileges from the white homes in which they did day labor.

I figured I didn't need to go to any revivals. After all, I could give chapter and verse of so much of the Bible that the school's principal, J. E. Wood, told me that the ninth-grade Bible class teacher didn't want me in the room embarrassing her.

Everyone talked of my becoming a preacher. But when I went to the Slobbery Rock Café and danced with Evelyn Hobbs to "Tuxedo Junction," or into the pool hall to restore my reputation as "the colored Willie Hoppe," I knew that I was not going to be a minister. First of all, I was too angry at too many things to be a loving man of God. Before that freshman year began, I was "sophisticated" enough to think about the cynicism with which Americans greeted all politicians, but especially the occupant of the White House, Franklin Delano Roosevelt.

Those late-August days I would stand on the corner of Main and Spring streets with my buddies, "holding up" the First National Bank in an architectural sense, hoping to land a job mowing lawns, unloading a railcar of one-hundred-pound cement bags, digging a basement under an existing house.

"Hallelujah!" one funny guy in my circle would say. "Mr. Rooooo-se-velt gonna rescue us from all this with his NRA [National Recovery Administration]."

"NRA? What's that stand for?" a straight man would ask.

"Nigger's Raggedy Ass!"

"Hah, hah, hah!"

Every time I read any of the appalling 1980s statistics about teenage pregnancies and births out of wedlock, I remember those months and years leaning against that bank building, listening to a few truths, a lot of lies, and some incredible fantasies poured forth by teenage black guys trying to prove their manhood. My buddies were a generation ahead of the people who conceived of *Penthouse* magazine's "Forum," in which dreamers relate stories of fanciful sexual exploits. Every black teenager on that corner allegedly had his "Lady Chatterley" — or two, or three. After each outlandish story, Franklin Woodley or someone would say, "Shiiiit!"

But the storytelling made everybody so horny that we would take another gamble on going to reform school. Half a block from that bank corner, where Police Chief Jap Bain and his assistants would hang out many nights, there was a car repair garage. One of the guys told us that the best whore in McMinnville had a bedroom on the second floor across from the garage. So we would climb the tree behind that garage, leap onto the roof, then lie watching her.

We were occasionally wide-eyed and incredulous to see one of the town's most prominent men show up. One night the boss of one of my Peeping Tom buddies entered the bedroom and proceeded to engage in cunnilingus (a word none of us had heard of at that time).

"I can't believe my *boss* is doing that. I could get rich blackmailing that cocksucker."

"What you can get is your ass killed. Fact is, *we* gonna kill your ass if you don't shut up that kind of talk."

The tales of sexual exploits, especially of tasting the "forbidden fruit," of having intercourse with a white girl, were entrancing because every male on that corner had had just enough temptation to believe that anything was possible. In my first book, *South of Freedom*, I told a story about the white girl on my newspaper route.

Almost daily this girl, whose name I never asked, would meet me in front of her house. She smiled and talked sweetly, and I would give her a paper whether I had an extra or not. After I quit the newsboy route, I would pass her on the street, and she would pause for a few sentences of chatter about nothing in particular. That fall I saw her working in Piggly Wiggly on a few Saturday mornings when I went in to buy candy, grapes, or fig bars. She always tried to wait on me, chatting much too much for me to feel secure. My colored buddies soon began teasing that "the little pop-eyed clerk in Piggly Wiggly's has got hot pants for Carl!"

I was concerned about this banter, but not alarmed until one summer afternoon in 1941 when we were standing on the First National Bank corner. This girl, whose eyes were not the only well-developed parts of her body, walked by and stopped to tell me that she thought she would get to go to college the fall after next.

The guys were silent until she walked away. Then one asked, amid laughter: "What the hell are you, Rowan, her counselor?"

I answered by joining in the laughter, hoping to silence them by appearing unaffected. Then one rhyming character started singing:

> *The whites caught Rastus the other night*
> *Bending over a damsel white;*
> *They pinned old Rastus 'gainst the wall,*
> *Now Rastus got no balls at all.*

There was a roar of laughter, and I participated as heartily as the rest. But I was frightened. I had heard grown-ups talk about one Negro citizen who had never married. They swore that he had been caught with a white girl near Sparta, Tennessee, and that four white men whipped and castrated him. After that, the story went, he had no need for a wife. I also heard the street-corner know-it-alls talking about venereal diseases. A mixed case of syphilis — that is, syphilis acquired through intercourse with a person of another race — was supposed to be the most deadly kind of all. I turned these things over in my mind and concluded that I would have absolutely nothing to do with that babe. Jumping Jehoshaphat, *no!*

"Hell, fellows, I don't even know the girl's name," I pleaded when the laughter died down.

"Naw, but you sure seem to have her number," snapped a young wit, who promptly was rewarded with more laughter.

I knew that they would continue until all aspects of the subject were exhausted.

One of my buddies decided that if I didn't want the pop-eyed girl, he did. She went with him to the bank of the Barren Forks River, with me secretly shadowing them. They had just begun to fornicate when, in jealousy and excitement, I caused a bush to make a noise.

"Rape!" the Piggly Wiggly clerk shouted. "He's raping me!"

My buddy ripped up more bushes than a city housing developer as he got out of there. I wasn't far behind him.

We later sat, wet with sweat, in the Slobbery Rock, listening to the Charlie Barnet band's version of "Cherokee," and I said to him, "Have you learned a lesson, you disloyal asshole?"

I would learn that where women and sex, especially outlawed sex, were concerned, virile young men, black or white, rarely learned the right lesson.

Probably the worst reward of being a "nice boy" turned out to be the best reward. Some white health officials visited Bernard to say that too many black kids were sneaking into the clinic with gonorrhea and syphilis, and health workers were having a special problem getting their sexual contacts to come in for medical treatment. (In those days, treatment of syphilis involved a long and miserable series of lead injections, because penicillin and other wonder drugs had not been discovered.)

The health officials wanted a responsible student to take over some pamphlets and put on an anti-VD program. Principal Wood decided that Rowan was the one to head this program. I walked into his office to meet with a white man and a very young white woman who began to explain the pictures of penises that seemed to be falling off, of women's labia with grotesque sores on them, of guys with what they called blue balls, and of people infested with crabs.

Till then I knew about crabs only from the most vulgar of insults when two guys were playing the dozens, a "game" in which young men would match wits at insulting each other's mother, sister, or other relatives.

"Your momma's pussy ain't got but one hair on it, and the crabs are using that for a diving board."

In my deprived world it was a measure of manhood to be creatively vulgar, an art that has made Richard Pryor "Richard the Rich." A couple of my buddies who would rather die before reading a literature assignment would stand on that corner and recite, or compose spontaneously, some of the funniest, dirtiest limericks imaginable. Only in 1963, when I saw a book called *Erotic Poetry*, did I realize that my street-corner cronies were in the tradition of Baudelaire, Ezra Pound, John Dryden, Keats, and Yeats.

I knew that no student said no to "Professor Wood." So I became the Bernard High VD officer. It took me only a few days to realize that the guys paid no attention to me (and, of course, if I had shown any of the "dirty" pictures to a girl, I would have been suspended from school). The pamphlets and pictures scared the hell out of me but were totally ignored by my classmates. Some paid a price. One day my buddy Bill Hogan said to me: "Your favorite cuz is in terrible trouble."

"Jesus Christ, what did he steal now?"

"A piece of pussy."

"Aw, c'mon."

"No kidding. He done knocked up that little bitch from out near Leesburg, and her daddy says he gonna marry her or die."

"Jesus Christ!"

"You ain't heard the worst, pal. The dumb sonofabitch is gonna have to drop out of school, and he's the best fuckin' runnin' back we got."

"Jesus Christ!" I said, with emphasis.

Early one sultry July night, an older friend said he was going to take me where we could have some real fun. He lured me into walking three miles to a small rural community where he said we'd find two sisters who'd just love to stroll through the woods and "listen to you imitate the Ink Spots." By the time we'd finished the walk, it was well past 8:00 P.M., and virtually everyone in this country enclave was in bed. My mentor said: "The mother of these two girls knows that you're a nice boy. She admires you. So you go in and ask her if Silly and Billy can come out for a stroll."

Out of a combination of foolishness and horniness, I went in and sat on the edge of the mother's bed while she told her daughters that it was OK to go out with me. I don't remember if I told her that another rascal was waiting.

Only moments outside the house, the younger daughter said, "Sis is with your buddy, and I'm yours. And do you know where we gonna do it?"

"Do what?" I asked, my knees turning a trifle weak.

"Do *it*," she said. "We gonna do it on the swinging bridge."

To get to her house, my buddy and I had crossed a rickety suspended wooden bridge that swung frighteningly over a gorge and a little stream.

"Why," I asked, "do we hafta do it on the swinging bridge?"

"Because my daddy don't trust you like my momma does, and he gonna come checkin' up. But we'll know he's on the way soon as he takes two steps on that swinging bridge. Then we can stop doing it and look like we just going for a stroll."

It was a long walk back from that bridge to McMinnville. My buddy said, "We pulled off a beaut tonight, old pal." But I barely heard him. I couldn't rejoice. My old job as anti-VD officer was torturing me. "It can't be," I said to myself, "that tonight is the first time that girl was swinging on her back on that bridge," and a lot of water passed under that swinging bridge before I felt secure in my mind that this girl hadn't given me anything other than a good time.

I remember, not with pride, the first time I shot craps. I had gotten a dollar-a-week job at the home of Mr. and Mrs. Tittle, the part owners of the hardware store. I went by after school every day to wash the dishes left over from lunch, to free the lawn of bulb grass, to mow it whenever necessary, and to do whatever handyman chores needed to be done. I knew that what the Tittles were paying me was ridiculously low, but they were part of my dream. I figured that Tittle was making fifty dollars a week, and his Dodge couldn't be more than three years old. His house was in one of the best parts of town, in fact, next door to the Magnesses, the rich family whose name was on the town library, where I was forbidden to study.

"Dear God," I would say, "let me grow up to earn fifty dollars a week like Mr. Tittle, own a Dodge like that, and have a nice house with a green lawn and flowers."

I was ecstatic when Tittle told me that he didn't like getting up in the winter cold to make a fire or to get that Dodge out of the crampy garage. He said he would pay me another seventy-five cents a week if I would come by *before* school to make a fire and back the car out for him.

"I can't drive, and I have no license," I said. This was 1939, when I was fourteen.

"You can do it," he said.

So I took on the added responsibilities knowing that earning $1.75 a week might enable me to save enough to buy a nice Christmas gift for the girl I adored. All went well until one morning when I backed the Dodge into a massive maple tree, knocking off a lot of bark, destroying the car's right taillight, and bashing in a fender. Tittle paid more to repair that Dodge than he would pay me over three years.

He didn't dock my pay, so by Christmas of 1939 I had about ten dollars saved up, surely enough to buy a gift for the girl I so much wanted to impress — and get to. It turned out that I loved myself more than this girl. I went by the Federated Store and spotted a red, white, and blue angora sweater that I just had to have. I needed shoes, and I wanted a pair of pants that would look sharp. So I bought them. I walked out of the Federated Store with only a nickel left. And I was asking myself how I would ever buy the forty-nine-cent Cashmere Bouquet set in the J. C. Penney's store window that I now had planned to get for my heartthrob.

The "preacher-to-be" soon found the devil behind him pushing. A buddy told me that a few kids were having a small crap game on the riverbank behind the cattle slaughter pen. No biblical admonition against gambling could stop me. I ran that nickel up to two dollars and quit, and went to J. C. Penney's and bought the Cashmere Bouquet set.

It almost crushed my heart when I learned that the object of my affection was not impressed. A man several years older had shown up with a bracelet for her that had cost seven dollars. I almost made a destructive decision that shooting craps, playing the numbers, bootlegging, and stealing were all justified if you got the money, because getting the money was the sure way of getting the girl.

But I never could accept the idea that I was a failure at anything. No one told me then to never look back; I just never looked back. Triumphs were where I found them. Like the day that the Roosevelt administration threw a crumb to Bernard High in the form of a piddling amount of National Youth Administration (NYA) funds. Principal Wood called me to his office to say that he had a nice job for me. I would get three dollars a month to come in early and come back late to raise and lower the flag every day.

McMinnville had no "welfare program" that I ever heard of. No community chest or United Way ever gave us anything. There was no food stamp program. But a year or so before I graduated from Bernard the federal government did send into our town truckloads of surplus food, and some of the cheese, the cans of pork and beans, the other victuals, trickled down to our black school. Principal Wood would occasionally authorize me to take a few cans of something to my family, but I was way ahead of him because I had learned about totin' privileges from Grandpa Cecil. Some afternoons I would waddle home, weighted down by huge mounds of cheddar cheese, cans of pork and beans, tins of fruit, jellies, and jams. I never worried about it, because I was sure that Professor Wood had stored in his own home a hundred times what I had grabbed.

The question of the early 1940s is still the question of today. How do deprived, poorly educated kids escape temptation and deprivation, survive foolish and often unlawful escapades, and get anyplace close to an even chance in the race that privileged Americans like to call "the pursuit of happiness"?

We have yet to find a meaningful answer.

CHAPTER TWO

My Rescue — by Teachers and a Grisly War

I T WAS SO DIFFICULT in those depression years to focus on much other than getting enough to eat, and girls, and whupping Lynchburg or Gallatin on the gridiron. I shall be forever grateful that one marvelous teacher forced me to focus on some other things.

She was only an inch or so above five feet tall and probably never weighed more than 110 pounds in her eighty-five years, but she was the only woman tough enough to make me read *Beowulf* and think for a few foolish days that I liked it.

I refer to Miss Bessie — Mrs. Bessie Taylor Gwynn — the woman who taught me English, literature, history, civics, and a lot more than I realized when I attended Bernard High from 1938 to 1942.

I shall never forget the day she scolded me, insisting that I wasn't reading enough of the things she wanted me to read.

"But, Miss Bessie," I complained, "I ain't much interested in *Beowulf*."

She fastened on me large brown eyes that became daggerish slits and said, "Boy, *I* am your *English* teacher, and I know I've taught you better than this. How dare you talk to me with 'I ain't' this and 'I ain't' that?"

"Miss Bessie," I said, "I'm trying to make first-string end on the football team. If I go around saying 'it isn't' and 'they aren't' the guys are gonna laugh me off the squad."

"Boy," she said, "you'll make first string only because you have guts and can play football. But do you know what *really* takes guts?

Refusing to lower your standards to those of the dumb crowd. It takes guts to say to yourself that you've got to live and be somebody fifty years after these football games are over."

I started saying "we aren't" and "if I were," and I still made first-string left end and class valedictorian without losing the respect of my buddies. I remembered that with a special sense of tragedy when I read recently that many black kids were afraid to display knowledge or scholarship for fear that their peers would accuse them of acting white.

Miss Bessie died in 1980 after a remarkable forty-seven years in which she taught my mother, me, my brother and sisters, and hundreds of other black youngsters who were deprived economically, in terms of family backgrounds, and in almost every other measurement of disadvantage. She would be *unforgettable* to most of her pupils under any circumstance, but I remember her with special gratitude and affection in this era when Americans are so wrought up about a "rising tide of mediocrity" in public education and are worrying about finding competent, caring teachers to help their children to cope in an increasingly technological, sophisticated, and dangerous world.

Mrs. Gwynn was an example of an aphorism we must accept: An informed, dedicated teacher is a blessing to children and an asset to the nation — values not even remotely reflected in what most of our teachers are paid.

Miss Bessie had a bearing of dignity — an unpretentious pride that told anyone who met her she was educated in the best sense of that word. There was never a discipline problem in her classes. We knew instinctively that you didn't mess around with a woman who knew all about the Battle of Hastings, the Magna Charta and Runnymede, the Bill of Rights, the Kellogg-Briand Pact outlawing war, the Emancipation Proclamation — and could also play the piano.

This frail-looking woman, who could make sense of the writings of Shakespeare, Milton, Voltaire, and bring to life Booker T. Washington and W. E. B. Du Bois, was a towering presence in our classrooms. We students memorized the names of members of the Supreme Court and the president's cabinet, having learned early that it could be very embarrassing to be unprepared when Miss

Bessie said, "Get up and tell the class who Frances Perkins is and what you know and think about her."

I wonder how many teachers today make their students learn the names of officials who spend the public's money and make policies that affect us all so profoundly.

Miss Bessie knew that my family, like so many in those hard days of the Great Depression, couldn't pay rent regularly, let alone maintain a subscription to a newspaper. She knew that my family didn't even own a radio. Still, she prodded me to "look out for your future and find some way to keep up with what's going on in the world." So I became a delivery boy for the *Chattanooga Times*, rarely making a dollar a week because most of my subscribers never paid. But I got to read a newspaper every day.

Miss Bessie noticed and heard things that had nothing to do with schoolwork but were so important to the well-being and development of a youngster. There was a time when a few of my classmates, especially her daughter, Ennys, made fun of my frayed, hand-me-down overcoat, calling it "strings." As I was leaving school one day Miss Bessie patted me on the back of that old overcoat and said, "Carl, never waste time fretting about what you *don't* have. Just make the most of what you *do* have — a brain."

Like millions of youngsters in today's ghettos and barrios, I needed the push and inspiration of a teacher who truly cared. Miss Bessie gave plenty of both as she immersed me in a wonderful world of similes, metaphors, alliteration, hyperbole, and even onomatopoeia. She acquainted me with dactylic verse, with the meter and scan of ballads, and set me to believing that I could write sonnets as good as any ever penned by Shakespeare, or iambic pentameter that would put Alexander Pope to shame.

You can't understand what a rare person Mrs. Gwynn was among black women, or even black men, in the 1930s and 1940s unless you know that in that era less than 1 percent of black women and even fewer black men went to college. Miss Bessie had gone to Fisk University in Nashville from 1909 to 1911, attending only the normal school; there she learned a lot about Shakespeare, but most of all about the profound importance of trained intelligence — especially for a people trying to move up from slavery.

"What you put in your head, boy," she said to me one day, "can never be pulled out by the Ku Klux Klan, the Congress, or any-body."

Poor black children in rigidly Jim Crow McMinnville didn't have much of an opportunity to put a lot in their heads in the 1930s and 1940s. Our little school was "no frills" to say the least.

Not only was our high school library outrageously inadequate, but blacks were not allowed to enter the town's Magness Memorial Library except to mop floors, dust tables, or do windows. But, through one of those Old South arrangements secretly arrived at by whites of good conscience and blacks of the stature of Miss Bessie, my teacher kept getting books smuggled out of the white library.

"If you don't read, you can't write, and if you can't write, you can stop dreaming," Miss Bessie told me.

So I read whatever she told me to read and tried to remember what she insisted that I store away.

The night of our graduation, May 25, 1942, three buddies and I walked near the persimmon tree, one guy toting a paper bag that turned out to contain a bottle of corncob wine that someone had gotten from my uncle McKinley Rowan. This product of fermented corncobs looked like horse liniment, tasted worse, and had the kick of a mule, so I grimaced at the prospect of my buddies proposing a toast. After each of us took a throat-burning swig from the bottle, Hogan announced that the three of them had decided to join the Navy the next day.

"You gonna join us and go help fight this war?" he asked me.

"Nope," I replied. "In the Navy a Negro can't be nothing but a cook or a mess attendant. I can't cook, and I don't want to tend mess. I'm going to college so that, when they draft me, I'll have a chance to become an officer."

There was a painful silence, then a soft, "OK, motherfucker." The bottle was passed around again, fists were rammed into shoulders as gestures of farewell, and we went home.

While my buddies went off to the Navy, I went back to the corner of the First National Bank building, waiting for someone to offer the jobs that would earn me enough money to go to college. The ranks of job seekers dwindled rapidly as the draft board swooped up able-bodied blacks, and others volunteered out of a belief that life in the military would have to be better.

So I had plenty of lawns to mow. When I came in from work around sundown I would notice how rapidly the war had become *the reality* in my town. Soldiers from Camp Forrest in Tullahoma seemed everywhere, and the girls of McMinnville were going GI crazy. I considered these guys to be poachers on my territory, so I would go to a movie and then the Slobbery Rock every night just to protect my turf. After playing the big spender one Saturday night, I went home and decided to take inventory of my cash before going to bed.

"My God," I said to myself, "I blew fifty-five cents on that chick tonight!"

But I didn't, or couldn't, change my lifestyle, so I woke up one July morning virtually broke. I had seventy-seven cents left of my go-to-college money. I felt sick just realizing that kids would be entering college in less than two months, and there I lay without even bus fare to Nashville. I told myself, scoldingly, that I'd have been better off joining the Navy with my buddies.

I washed up, made my hair look good with an application of Tuxedo-brand pomade, put on the best clothes I owned and put the rest into a cardboard box. I wrote a note to my parents, who were at work, saying "I've gone to Nashville for college" and went to the McBroom Lines trucking company. I asked a young woman which driver had the run to Nashville; she pointed to him without mumbling a word.

"I need a ride to Nashville real bad," I said to him.

"What's your problem?"

"I just woke up and realized I've been spending all my pay to take girls to movies and the honky-tonk, and I'm left with seventy-seven cents to get me to school."

"Hell, I'll give you a ride. But what school is going to let you in for seventy-seven cents?"

"I'm hoping to get a scholarship at Fisk. The rich boys there play lousy football. I play a helluva left end. Once I get the football scholarship, I'll work and save the money."

The driver looked me over with obvious skepticism. I wasn't sure whether he disbelieved that I played a helluva left end at my modest weight or doubted my vow not to blow my wages next time.

I already had met enough courageous, truly decent white people to know that I could never become an embittered racist. This truck driver reemphasized the rule of life that you judge and value people where and how you find them. He and I had a great conversation en route to Nashville, and not long after we passed Murfreesboro he said: "Hell, with just seventy-seven cents you don't need to hire any taxis or pay streetcar fare. If you can tell me how to get to Fisk, I'll drop you off there."

But that stop at Fisk was a quick and bitter disappointment. I only got to see some low-level guy who almost laughed when I told him I played a helluva left end. "You'd never make it here," he said and just waited for me to pick up my box of clothes and go.

I walked the mile or so to Grandmother Johnigan's house and was relieved somewhat by her warm embrace. My aunts Katie and Dixie, my mother's half sisters, expressed joy to see me again. I told them what a fool I had been all summer and how the guy at Fisk had almost spat in my face.

"You'll make it," my grandmother said in a tone that left no room for doubt. "Your grandfather has a job for you at the hospital — at one dollar a day."

The next morning I took the long journey out to the State Tuberculosis Hospital and got a job mopping floors, delivering food to patients, and getting my face mask incredibly dirty when I brushed down the screens around the porch wards where many patients were placed.

One day a young doctor said to me: "I've been talking with your grandfather, whom we admire very much. I'd like to give you a few things you might find helpful when you enter Tennessee State next month."

"What?"

We walked over to his Ford and he pulled out a couple of suits and a sport coat, all close to brand-new.

"You can't wear these?" I asked.

"Not with this expanding butt and belly. They're yours if you want them."

"God, do I want them! Thank you, sir!"

Later, I told my grandfather that this doctor didn't weigh a pound more than I did. "Do you think he just wanted to give me something decent to wear?"

"We don't know, and if I ever find out I won't tell *you*. Just wear them in ways that would make the doctor proud."

That doctor, whose name I wish I could remember, sure made me proud to be one of the best-dressed freshmen at Tennessee State, no small achievement considering the competition of studs from Pearl High in Nashville. I would have been a bit ashamed to wear my "strings" onto campus, and this, added to the insecurities arising from my small-school background, would have put terrible pressures on me. But when I showed up in the light gray suit that the doctor had given me, a few coeds looked at me in ways that I interpreted to say, "*You* are *welcome*, Mister."

My new sense of security vanished fast when I learned of the high schools from which my classmates had graduated. But I had no doubts about my abilities regarding algebra and soon found classmates seeking me out for help on tough problems. This alone made me popular enough to get nominated for vice president of the freshman class, a post to which I was elected without opposition.

I was shocked to get A's in every course except algebra and to find that a couple of girls I tutored got A's while I got a B. But I took it philosophically, telling one of the girls, "I'm not coming back next quarter anyhow, 'cause I'm broke, so what the hell difference does it make?"

A few days later I stood on the steps of the administration building, saying good-bye to my buddy Joe Bates, laughing with him about how we had struggled through the first quarter with one guy buying a bottle of milk and the other a day-old cake and making it lunch for two.

"I'm so sad to see you go," Joe said. "Before you go, walk with me to the Greasy Spoon so I can get a pack of cigarettes."

"The Greasy Spoon doesn't open till eleven."

"I gotta check, 'cause I'm dying for a smoke."

We walked down to the little campus restaurant, and, as I predicted, it was padlocked. Bates and I walked away across the dirt circle where the Dinky Bus made its U-turn, discharging students who would throw their green bus transfers to the ground. The litterbugs seemed to have spread a zillion transfers around.

We had taken a few steps up the sidewalk when something said to me, "Carl Rowan, one of those wads you just passed in the weeds was not a bus transfer." I went back and reached into the weeds.

"Joe," I half shouted, "I just found a bill, and it doesn't look like a one!" I opened the wad to find that it was a twenty-dollar bill.

"Joe," I said, "I just pray to God that whoever lost this money doesn't need it as badly as I do."

I walked straight to the administration building, where I paid my tuition for the second quarter — for three months during which two teachers would give me blessed help.

I was stunned to learn that I was being put in Art 101, An Introduction to Art. Art was hardly heard of at Bernard High. I couldn't draw a box, let alone an apple.

"Jesus," I said to Bates, "if I had known they would sandbag me with this class I'd have gone home to tote bags at Brown's Hotel." I didn't mean it, of course, so I went to Art 101 to find that my teacher was a soft-spoken woman with a lovely brown face, Miss Frances Thompson.

I hated her when, as her first gesture, she asked the students to take a piece of paper and write the grade they expected to get in her class. This art illiterate summoned up a lot of courage and wrote a *C* on his paper. Miss Thompson collected the papers and studied each for a few seconds. "Would Carl Roe-ann from McMinnville please raise his hand?" she asked, mispronouncing my name.

I stuck up a trembling hand.

"Would you please stay after class for a few seconds to talk with me?"

"Ye . . . ye . . . yes, ma'am."

When the other students fled the classroom, she opened up an agonizing dialogue.

"Were you surprised that I knew you were from McMinnville?"

"No, ma'am."

"Will it surprise you if I tell you I know every grade you got in high school and at Tennessee State last quarter, and I know you never got a C? Why did you put a C on this piece of paper?"

"I don't know, ma'am."

I sat there paralyzed, like a bunny in a Ferrari's headlights, as she stared at me, finally saying to my relief, "I want to read you something."

Miss Thompson reached into her desk drawer and pulled out a piece of paper containing a quote from Daniel Burnham, a Chicago architect and city planner — words he spoke in 1925, the year of my birth. I listened intently as Miss Thompson quoted Burnham:

> Make no little plans, they have no magic to stir men's blood and probably themselves will not be realized. Make big plans; aim high in hope and work, remembering that a noble, logical diagram once recorded will never die, but long after we are gone will be a living thing, asserting itself with evergrowing insistency. Remember that our sons and grandsons are going to do things that would stagger us. Let your watchword be order and your beacon beauty.

Miss Thompson handed me a clean piece of paper. I looked into her eyes once, then wrote a big *A* on it. I still doubt that any teacher in history ever worked harder to help a kid to earn an A in art.

That woman had given me a gift far beyond the two suits and the sport coat from the doctor. She had made me believe in myself. She had given me a new measure of self-esteem.

More than thirty years later, I gave a speech in which I mentioned that Frances Thompson had given me something that I needed desperately, something money could not have bought even if I had had some money. A newspaper printed the story, and someone mailed a clipping to this beloved teacher. She wrote me a note that brings tears to my wife's eyes till this day:

> You have no idea what that newspaper story meant to me, so long in retirement. For a lot of years I endured my brother's arguments that I had wasted my life. That I should have gotten married and had a family. When I read that newspaper article in which you gave me credit for helping to launch a marvelous career, I put the clipping in front of my brother. When he had read it I said, "You see, I didn't really waste my life, did I?"

If Frances Thompson was sweet and quietly helpful, history professor Merle Eppse was just the opposite. During the first quarter I had learned that his History of Civilization class was an exercise in avoiding insults. Eppse wanted achievement, scholarship, hard work, and study, and he brooked no excuses. In letting a student know what he expected, he probably went beyond the bounds of professorial behavior that any college should allow.

A McMinnville friend of mine, Vera Sims, and her family had moved to Nashville a couple of years earlier. She was in my class. One day, when she had no answer for an orally proffered Eppse question, he lit into her with a monologue: "I knew you would show up today, sleepy and ignorant, no sign of doing any homework, because I was driving down Jefferson Street last night and saw you out there leaning into some dummy's car. Now you can try to please some no-good jerk and get pregnant, or you can come to class ready to please me and go on to be somebody important. . . . Mr. Roe-ann, tell her the answer to my question."

"My family pronounces it Rhau-wen, sir."

"Oh, goddammit, Roe-ann or Rhau-wen, the question is whether you're trying not to embarrass your old McMinnville buddy. No use you playing a dummy, 'cause her favors will still go to that punk who was driving the car she was leaning in. Do you know the answer to my question?"

"I do, sir." I gave the answer to the man who had given me an A in the first quarter and would give me A's in the second and third quarters. Little did I know that this man, hated by so many and loved by a few, would also give me a chance to make history, to live a life I never thought possible.

One morning in the spring of '43 I sat in his class wondering why he was late. Suddenly, Eppse burst into the room, asked a favorite student to take over the class for a few minutes, and said: "Mr. Roe-en, come with me to the dean's office!"

Fear hit me with such force that my heart creased my scalp. In 1943, when a student went to the dean's office, the *student* was in trouble, not the *dean*. We walked to the office of Dean George W. Gore with Eppse saying nary a word.

When we entered, Eppse said to this man who would distinguish himself as an educator: "Here's the boy who's volunteering to join the Navy."

"Muh . . . muh . . . me?" I stammered. "I'm not volunteering to join the Navy."

"Yes, you are, boy," Eppse insisted.

Dean Gore raised his hand and said, "Just a minute, Professor Eppse." Then he turned to me and said calmly: "Are you aware that in the entire history of the United States there has never been a Negro officer in the Navy?"

"Yes, sir," I said proudly, "I read the *Pittsburgh Courier*." (This was the leading, nationally circulated black newspaper.)

"Are you also aware that here at all-Negro Tennessee State we often get messages from the government that are intended for the all-white University of Tennessee in Knoxville?"

"No, sir, I didn't know that."

"Well, let me show you a series of telegrams between the Navy Department and Tennessee State."

Gore read one from the Navy asking that Tennessee State have students take a national examination for admission to the Navy V-12 program to send officer candidates to reserve midshipman schools. Then he showed me his telegram asking the Navy, "Do you really mean *us*?" And he handed me the Navy's reply, "Yes, we mean *you*."

Gore gave me a solemn look and explained, "We don't want Tennessee State embarrassed. Someone here has got to pass this exam. So I've asked Professors Eppse and Boswell to pick out a half-dozen young men who might pass that exam, and Professor Eppse has chosen you. That is a wonderful endorsement from your professor. So I know that out of your loyalty to Professor Eppse, and to Tennessee State, and to your race, you are going to —"

"Yes, sir," I interrupted, "I volunteer to join the Navy!"

I went on to get all A's that third quarter at Tennessee State — and to pass the Navy exam. Meanwhile, part of my world was falling in around me.

My father had gambled himself into a hole and taken loans against the home he had bought with his World War I bonus. I understood why I had, in a year, received from my parents only three dollars to sustain me in college, but I had no idea that my mother was taking extra work as a domestic, sending my brother, Charles, down the railroad tracks to drum up extra laundry business, hoping to earn enough to save the home. She failed, and in desperation began to drink more and more.

Not that I could have stopped it, since I had no money, but the sheriff held an auction at which that little frame house was stripped away from my family without anyone telling me until years later, when my sister Jewel said, "You know, we're just renting this place now." Soon after Jewel spoke to me they were thrown out for failing to pay the rent.

My family had no telephone, so letters were the only way to stay in touch. I didn't write often, because I was so dedicated to succeeding. When I wrote, it might be a month before I got a reply, which invariably was full of bad news about which parent was getting drunk, who hurt whom in a marital brawl, how economically desperate the whole family was. I would become so depressed that for a day or two I could not concentrate on my studies. Subconsciously, I opted for an "out of sight, out of mind" existence. In pursuit of a dream, I was leaving my family behind.

Meanwhile, Grandmother Ella became sick from what the doctor told me was elephantiasis. He complained that "she hasn't always taken her medicine."

"I know," I said. "I now am convinced that she used her medicine money to keep me in college and in the running for a Navy commission."

Passing the written examination provided no sure entry into V-12 and midshipman's school. I had to get past two white Navy interviewers in Nashville, and then a physical exam.

"If one of 'em doesn't get you, the other will," said a skeptical professor.

"You will make it, son," my grandmother said the day I left for the interviews and the physical. She died a few days before I was notified that I had passed all exams and was to await assignment to a V-12 program.

At summer quarter's end, I went back to McMinnville, to the Edgefield Street house into which my family had moved after losing our Congo Street place. I had a card showing that I was in the Naval Reserve, awaiting assignment — a card that gave me protection from many local cops and military policemen who sometimes asked openly what "an able-bodied nigger is doing walking the streets."

That summer of '43 I ceased being a "black boy" and came to think of myself as a man.

By 1943, the local draft board had almost cleared the town of able-bodied Negroes (even though the Marines didn't want any blacks, the Navy wanted very few, and the Army wanted only so many as could fit into all-black units). The drafters of McMinnville figured they could not send white boys to war while black bucks were to be seen leaning against the bank building at Spring Street and Main.

But I was undraftable, with the Navy having a claim on me. So a lot of whites figured that I would handle a greater-than-normal share of their dirty work. They had no way of knowing that my status as a potential Navy officer, my year at college in an environment drastically different from McMinnville, had created revulsion in me for all the economic and social rules of my hometown. Even I did not realize that a year away from this little red-clay town had given me an air of haughtiness that would antagonize the white citizens for whom I had worked for years.

When a white person drove up to my little house on Edgefield Street and said he or she wanted someone to mow a lawn or serve food or wash dishes at a party, I did not take the easy way out, saying, "I have another job." I laced on the sarcasm of refusal by saying, "I'm giving a dinner tonight. You know anybody who might work for me?"

I was what the barber for whom I once worked called "a rebellious little sonofabitch." Rebellious I was. I flaunted my naval exemption every time a military policeman or local cop stopped me to inquire why I was strolling Main Street at midday in a suit and tie.

It was late October when I received orders to report to Washburn Municipal University of Topeka, Kansas. I had never heard of Washburn and thought how ironic it was that I could not go to the public library to learn something about it. I had only a general idea of the route to Topeka, since I still had never been out of Tennessee except for the time our football-team bus got lost and accidentally crossed into Alabama. But I had Navy travel orders that made it clear which trains I should take from where to where.

It has been said — correctly — that war is hell. This war turned out to be the great liberator, for it gave me a national mission of honor that would open up new horizons of opportunity and potential achievement.

CHAPTER THREE

Breaking
the Navy's Barriers

I WAS A BABE in a dreamworld that late-October day in 1943 when I went to the L & N station in McMinnville to take the train to Tullahoma and onward to Nashville, where I was supposed to crawl into my first Pullman-car berth and snooze my way to St. Louis, my way station to Topeka. I had learned from other blacks that the train station clerks didn't assign sleeping-car berths, either upper or lower, to Negroes. They would *die* at the thought of a black Pullman porter drawing a curtain on an area where a black man got one berth and a white woman accidentally got the berth above or below him. But this was war. And I was off to help the Navy deliver a fatal blow to Adolf Hitler.

I should have known that neither the power brokers nor the rail station clerks of Tennessee would care a damn about what I was off to do to Hitler. Many whites of McMinnville in those days shared Hitler's hatred of Jews, and as for blacks, they would go Hitler one better by never giving a Negro the opportunity to embarrass them the way Jesse Owens embarrassed *der Führer* at the 1936 Olympics.

I learned at every window of every train station that the white people there (no blacks worked in any of these white-collar railway jobs) put their prejudices far above my idealistic notions about why I was going to war.

So I rode from McMinnville to Tullahoma to Nashville in the smoky, dirty Jim Crow car, right behind the engine, like other blacks had done for decades.

I didn't know a lot about the Missouri Compromise, the Mason-

Dixon line, or anything else that set the boundaries of Jim Crow. But I was fascinated to discover that Navy travel vouchers for first-class Pullman-berth accommodations were honored in St. Louis, even for blacks.

On that crowded train to Topeka, I thought a lot about what I might be journeying into. I had been so brainwashed by the first years of my life that I just assumed Washburn, where I was ordered, must be a black college. Then the rational part of me would say, "Christ, if the Navy never has let a Negro become an officer, why and where would they embrace enough Negroes to create a whole class of colored candidates to study in Topeka, or go to mid-shipman's school?"

It was almost dusk that Sunday afternoon when I gathered my luggage at the Topeka train station. I took a taxi to Washburn for some shocking discoveries. The taxicab driver stopped at a tree-lined driveway to the university buildings and said, "This is as far as I can go." I paid him, then stared up at a sight that seemed straight out of the movies. Sailors and their girls lined that roadway like the old Burma Shave signs, and their smooching sent a message that a whole lot of romancing was going on. But there was a more serious message for me: all sailors and girls were white, so either I had come to the wrong college or the taxicab driver had failed to take me to the entrance for Negroes.

I went into the nearest building and, holding my Navy orders in my hand, asked a cluster of white sailors: "This is Washburn University?"

It was probably only a couple of seconds, but seemed an eternity, before one of them said, "Sure is."

"I'm looking for the administration building," I said, and one sailor walked to the door with me to point the direction. I looked back just long enough to note a what-the-hell-is-he-doing-here? look on some faces.

I went into the administration building, where a chief petty officer named Pappas and a Lieutenant Beuhler gave me an extra-warm welcome. The Navy obviously had sent them a guess-who's-coming-to-your-unit message, and they were prepared. Pappas gave me a slip of paper with my house, room, and bunk numbers on it and asked a sailor to take me to House 5-B. As I started out of the building, Pappas grasped me by the elbow in a firm but friendly way and whispered, "I don't think you'll be lonely here."

Lonely? That word keyed me to the reality that I had seen only white sailors and white girls along the driveway. I knew there wouldn't be many blacks around.

I reported officially on November 1, 1943, and was surprised that the first thing I had to do was sign an affidavit saying: "I hereby certify that I have never had fits, head injury, asthma, venereal disease, that I am not a bed wetter, do not walk in my sleep, and that I am not concealing any disease or disability. I understand that concealing any of the above defects makes my enlistment fraudulent, and subjects me to trial by a military court."

"I'm gonna love the Navy," I said to myself.

What a shock to discover that I was in a unit of 335 sailors, 334 of them white! But these were not just 334 *white* boys. They were the *honors* guys from high schools and colleges far better than Bernard High and Tennessee State. My first concerns were not about how the white guys would treat a Negro; I assumed that, despite its reputation for bigotry, the Navy would not let its experiment with racial change be undermined by some bigot. My uneasiness arose from learning in the first days that I was competing with guys who had had high school courses, like analytical geometry and spherical trigonometry, that I hadn't even heard of even after a year of college as a math major. Having missed a Head Start, I was badly in need of some compensatory education.

These white guys were born in, had grown up in, levels of education far above anything that ever was available to me. I knew that I either worked and studied hard to catch up, or I would fail.

A years-later look at my Navy records made it clear to me what I had walked into at Topeka, and later during a V-12 semester at Oberlin College and then midshipman school. Those Navy records say that I was valedictorian at Bernard High with a grade point average of 2.95 out of a possible 3.0. At Tennessee State I got 12 A's and 3 B's, earning 84 grade points out of a possible 90.

But I was so far behind my competitors in terms of family educational background, family income, quality of high school, access to libraries, availability of courses and laboratories, that I became a C-plus student that first semester at Washburn. I knew I was catching up when I got a B in calculus and wound up my two semesters at Washburn one grade point above a B average.

But the drama of those months at Washburn was not in any classroom. It was in the mealtime, evening, social, and other relationships with 334 white guys, many of whom had never known a Negro on anything close to an equal footing. The tension was in the Navy staff, where a couple of guys went out of their way to help me, and a couple of chief petty officers from Mississippi tried in flagrant ways to drum me out of the program. The excitement was in the determination of several white sailors to wipe out Jim Crow in Topeka and make it clear to drugstores, theaters, and whatever that where they went, I could go. (None of us imagined that Topeka would become home to one of the great Supreme Court cases in the nation's history, *Brown* v. *Board of Education*.)

Branch Rickey's Brooklyn Dodgers and every other barrier-breaking sports team would come up against the "problem" the Navy faced at Washburn: Who would be the Negro's roommate? I never learned how Charley Van Horn of Coffeyville, Kansas, wound up as my roommate, but I do know that I felt good when he quipped, "I'll be too damned busy trying to memorize Ohm's law and pass this physics course to count the pigment in your skin." And so it was that we became good friends, too.

There were a couple of guys in House 5-B, the former sorority house where I was billeted, who were racists to the core. How remarkable, I thought, that black Americans, like other oppressed peoples, had developed special antennae for detecting bigots — even the ones who tried to cloak their hatred in pseudofriendly talk.

But most of the guys in House 5-B simply discovered early that we had so many things in common that skin color ought not dominate any relationship. We all hated the guy who would run through the house in the winter morning darkness shouting, "Off your ass and on your feet, and down the stairs and in the street" — some mornings driving us out into seventeen-below temperatures to do *calisthenics*! We all hated the Friday afternoon drills and the Saturday inspections. We found we could detest Chief Petty Officer Montgomery without regard to our race, class, or color, because he was mean.

Some white faculty members and some members of the black community in Topeka said that they felt sorry for me, being put "under all that racial pressure" and "facing all that emotional strain day after day." I suppose they never believed me when I told them that I felt no overweening pressure or strain that arose solely from my being a lone Negro in a white world. The reality was that *I* felt sorry for the decent young white men who were straining not to commit any racial faux pas that might get them in trouble with Chief Pappas or Lieutenant Beuhler.

One evening after dinner when we were lounging around griping and swapping lies, one sailor was telling his roommate about his troubles with his fiancée.

"She didn't write for days. When I got a rumor she might be dating someone else, I telephoned. She said it's nothing more than her being real busy. But I think there's a nigger in the woodpile somewhere." I ignored that as a meaningless cliché. But it seemed to embolden one of the real racists, who began telling a few guys how they "kept niggers in their place" in his hometown, Oxford, Ohio.

A chilly silence enveloped his corner of the room as several guys stole a peek at me. I took a couple of steps across the room and gave the bigot a long, icy stare. The apprehensive faces of some of these young men seemed to ask, "Is this where the racial brawl begins?" But I broke the chill by yelling to Noah Brannon of Brownsville, Texas, "Let's hit the piano. Wanna begin with 'Star Eyes' or 'My Ideal'?"

Quickly this man from the town of one of America's worst race riots (in 1906) was at the piano, and I was above him singing . . .

> *All my life I've felt content to star-gaze at the skies;*
> *Now I only want to melt the star-dust in your eyes. . . .*

Soon other sailors drifted to the piano, and joined us in song . . .

> *A tinkling piano in the next apartment,*
> *Those stumbling words that told you what my heart meant . . .*

The things we hated were not the only things that bound us together. We all loved the idea that we soon would . . .

find the girl in my mind
The one who is My Ideal. . . .

Then there was the spirit of camaraderie that just rises up naturally among Navy guys who wind up singing "The Whiffenpoof Song."

The following day, the commander of the V-12 unit, Lieutenant Bontrager, called me to his office where he said he was sending a letter to Washington "commending you for the way you handled that racial incident last night. I personally commend you for not punching that little snot in the nose, or creating a bad scene in any way. But you seem to understand very well that a lot more is riding on your behavior than the fate or feelings of one man."

I knew what he meant. I also knew that this and other reports that Bontrager sent to Washington would give backing and bravery to those who were arguing that Navy Jim Crow was unnecessary and destructive of both the esprit de corps and efficiency of ships and other units.

Ah, if only the commander could have known what was going on when Brannon stopped playing the piano and I stopped singing! We got engrossed in conversations that enlightened us about why racial separation was so doggedly defended by so many white Americans, including Noah Brannon, who considered himself a devout Christian and said he planned to be a missionary.

I was the first Negro whom Brannon had ever known so closely. He had seen yardmen, porters, cooks, and maids, but surely had never sat in a classroom next to a black person, let alone joined one at the piano. So one evening, like a man awakening in the darkness and sensing that he is in bed with a stranger, Brannon said to me: "Carl, where is that overpowering odor they told me all Negroes have?"

I could have become defensive, even angry, but I found Brannon's first racial question to me exceedingly funny, so I laughed heartily.

But he wasn't laughing. I sensed that he wanted a serious reply.

"If I don't have such an odor, Noah," I said, "I must have lost it in the shower room. I'll bet that could happen to anybody — of any race."

Brannon shook his head as if to say, "Boy, have I been dumb."

"Until I met you, Carl, I didn't even know Negroes had last

names," he said. I furrowed my brow to show disbelief, causing him to add: "Honestly! We always called them 'Aunt Susie' and 'Uncle Charlie.' "

I explained to Brannon that this dated back to slavery, when white owners recognized no marital and family bonds among blacks.

This missionary-to-be expressed amazement when I told him that in McMinnville I could not get a drink of water in any drugstore unless the fountain clerk could find a paper cup.

"It was all right there before my eyes, but I never saw it," he said. "You probably can't get a drink of water at a Brownsville drugstore either."

Late one afternoon in June 1944, nearly eight months after I first met Noah Brannon, we were singing some farewell songs because I had been ordered to the V-12 unit at Oberlin College. Brannon stopped playing "I'll Be Seeing You" abruptly and motioned me over to a sofa. He said, in a breaking voice: "You plan to be a writer after the war. Sometime, why don't you just sit down and tell all the little things it means to be a Negro in the South, or anyplace where being a Negro makes a difference. If you're a Southern white person, you see these things and you don't. You're taught not to care. Don't preach, but tell it all, for there must be many people in the South with big hearts but so little knowledge of this thing."

Brannon, Van Horn, Pappas, Beuhler, and a lot of people at Washburn did not know it, but they were instrumental not only in changing America's military, but in mobilizing this country's first groping steps to find its conscience, its heart and soul, in terms of racial and social justice.

But no social change of the magnitude that the Navy was trying could go forward without some traditionalists attempting to sabotage it. I knew in my first days at Washburn that Chief Montgomery recoiled at the idea of having Negro officers, whom he would have to salute and call "sir." So I became wary of doing anything that would give him an excuse to "get" me. But I made what could have been a fateful goof one afternoon.

In physical education, the unit had been split into two groups, one to box, the other to wrestle. I drew a scrawny kid named Knudson as my wrestling opponent. He whispered to me that every time he wrestled seriously his shoulder would pop out of joint, and he didn't want Montgomery and others to see that or they might disqualify him for further study and midshipman's school.

"Let's just put on a good show without jeopardizing your shoulder," I said. As we went through our pretense, I could hear some boxers throwing heavy leather, and I just had to take a peek. No sooner had I glanced up at the boxers than Montgomery's voice boomed out for all to hear.

"Goddammit, Rowan, if you prefer boxing, you can have boxing." He ordered that someone go get a sailor whom I'd never met but had been "the champion in his weight at Stanford," according to the whispers of my housemates.

I hated boxing. About all I knew of that manly art was what I had gleaned from watching Joe Louis, Max Schmeling, and others in theater newsreels. But I knew that I had to defend myself in this environment. In fact, Montgomery had thrown me into a fight with a tough House B-5 kid named Brady a few days earlier, and when it became a flailing brawl Montgomery just forgot to ring the bell to end the round. I still had a lot of sore spots from that encounter.

The guy from Stanford arrived and started jumping up and down and throwing shadow punches in staccato fashion. Montgomery glowered at me and said, "Get your ass in there."

I entered the ring and my opponent circled to his left. I circled to mine. He danced right and I skipped to my right. He poked out a left jab that was at least a foot short. I swung a left hook that missed him by a yard. He swung a right; I ducked under it and rushed into a clinch. Someone should have played a waltz, the way we danced in each other's arms for several seconds. We backed out of the clinch, and the circling, ducking, and dodging began anew. Hardly two decent blows had been landed by either of us when the round ended. A furious Montgomery walked up to the kid from Stanford and said, "That's enough. This is a damned disgrace. . . ."

When I got back to House 5-B, some of the guys shouted, "Hail to the champ! The champ! The champ!"

"Champ, hell," I said. "I'm really lucky that I didn't get my butt beat to a pulp."

"Right," someone said. "You might have if old Brady hadn't gone over to tell the guy from Stanford he'd better watch his ass, 'cause you were the champion in your weight class at Tennessee State."

I laughed so hard my stomach ached. Then I asked Brannon to play the piano so Brady and I could sing a song. It broke up the guys in 5-B when we did an out-of-harmony version of "My Buddy."

I was surprised to learn, at the end of the March term at Washburn, that the Navy was transferring me to the V-12 unit at Northwestern University in Evanston, Illinois. Had Lieutenant Bontrager or Beuhler or someone convinced Washington that it was unfair to me to keep me in Topeka's Jim Crow environment? Had someone told Washington that I'd be less "lonely" in a unit with at least one other Negro in it?

The bitter irony in 1944 was that word came from Washington to my V-12 unit at Washburn that Northwestern would not permit a Negro to live in campus housing. So I was retransferred to Oberlin College in Ohio, one of those little quirks of fate that turned out to be so important in my development.

I had access to a good library at Washburn, so I could learn a lot about Oberlin before going there. I was pleased to read that it was the first college in America to admit both blacks and women on an equal basis with white men. Oberlin had been an important link in the Underground Railway that carried slaves to freedom. It was considered by many to be the premier small liberal arts college in the land, with a renowned conservatory of music.

The first thing that struck me when I reached this citadel of liberalism was that two black guys, Al Fairbanks, Jr., of St. Louis, and Samuel L. Dean of Washington, D.C., were in the Oberlin V-12 unit — and *we were assigned to be roommates.*

That summer semester at Oberlin was uneventful, except that I realized that some extremely smart students from great high schools had driven up the curve on which everyone was graded, and suddenly I was a C-plus student again. I learned something else that would be of great value in later years of chasing success. Where my grade was based on objective criteria, as in my integral calculus and analytical statistics classes, my grades were good; but in classes where grades were based on the teachers' subjective judgments (Background of the Present War, Naval History and Elementary Strategy, and Introduction to Sociology), I was an average student because I did nothing to forge a personal relationship with my teachers so as to help convince them that I was above average.

That summer at Oberlin was tough academically. I later realized that it was stifling socially. I never got close to the white Navy guys at Oberlin because, in putting us three black sailors together, the Navy created the impression of "two separate worlds," and the two groups wound up going separate ways. Dean, Fairbanks, and I got to know a lot of black students and girls in the black communities of Oberlin and Cleveland, but not much happened to broaden our abilities to function in a predominantly white world or on a warship with an interracial crew.

I was greatly relieved to learn that I had done well enough at Oberlin to receive orders to the Naval Reserve Midshipman School at Fort Schuyler in the Bronx. There I met two more black "guinea pigs" — Theodore Chambers and Clarence P. McIntosh. We were pleased that no one tried to put us together, either out of racial animosity or of a misguided notion that we had to be kept from feeling lonely. Everything was strictly alphabetical in the billeting at Fort Schuyler, with the result that the midshipman in the bunk above mine was a white fellow from Pascagoula, Mississippi.

My bunkmate and I commiserated with each other throughout the early, tension-filled days of close order drills, meticulous bunk inspections, almost inhuman tests of our physical endurance, *running* from one class to the next, and frantic cramming for tests in navigation, gunnery, aircraft recognition, and more. Fort Schuyler was tough — so difficult that midshipmen at other schools called it "The Laundry," a reference to the high percentage of commission candidates who were washed out.

It soon became obvious to me that my Mississippi bunkmate was about to flunk out. He had virtually given up studying and sat around munching on Hershey bars during periods when the rest of us were cramming for an important exam. One night, as my company studied gunnery problems, he offered me half a candy bar. I shook my head to decline, then a sixth sense told me that the Mississippian was making a sort of parting gesture.

"Rowan, you know — *hell, everybody knows* — that I'm flunking out of this heah goddammed rat race," he said. "But there's one thing I gotta git off my chest, just sort of one Southern boy to another."

Nearby midshipmen stopped studying to roll their eyes uneasily in our direction.

"Just wanna tell you," he continued, "that a little while back, down yonder in Pascagoula, if somebody had told me I'd be sitting beside a Nigra tonight I'da called him a damn liar. If they'da told me I'd be sitting beside one and not minding it — I mean *liking* it, *appreciating* it — I'da knocked somebody's teeth out. But here I am, and before I go I just wanna tell you that, and wish you luck."

As my bunkmate left, so did some of my bitterest feelings about my native South.

My qualifications ratings at Fort Schuyler were all better than "good," and I got scores of 3.5 for general attitude and 3.4 for maturity out of a possible 4.0. I thought it wasn't too bad. Especially considering the competition in my battalion from guys like Howard Baker of Tennessee, who would become Senate majority leader and White House chief of staff. It still ranks as one of the glorious moments of my life when, at age nineteen, I was commissioned as an officer and a gentleman in the United States Navy.

John Stuart Mill wrote that "The despotism of custom is everywhere a standing hindrance to human advancement." Never could this have been more obvious than during the World War II efforts to take racism out of the American military. Blacks had fought with valor in the American Revolution, even though they were less than wanted at first. When George Washington took command of the Continental Army in 1775, he ordered recruiters not to enlist "any stroller, negro or vagabond." But when Lord Dunmore, the governor of Virginia, started recruiting both free and slave Negroes to fight on the British side, Washington changed his tune. Some five thousand of the three hundred thousand men who fought for United States independence were black, and two were with Washington when he crossed the Delaware on Christmas Day of 1776.

Still, America's fighting men were racially segregated at this stage of World War II. Dwight D. Eisenhower had expressed fears about integrating the Army. One admiral had warned that if black officers were sent aboard ships, "Race conflict will greatly impair morale and hurt our war effort."

But by 1944 the National Association for the Advancement of

Colored People (NAACP), the National Urban League, Eleanor Roosevelt, and a lot of other groups and individuals had laid on such pressure that the U.S. Air Force could not go on with a segregated group of fighter pilots at Tuskegee, Alabama, the U.S. Army with a segregated division at Fort Huachuca, Arizona, and the U.S. Navy with nothing but a bunch of black cooks and mess attendants. So, under intense pressure, the Navy commissioned directly thirteen Negroes at the Great Lakes Naval Training Center. But the three of us from Fort Schuyler, along with Ensign Samuel L. Gravely from the reserve midshipman school at Columbia University, were the first Negro Navy officers with the training that qualified us for duty anywhere, including on oceangoing vessels.

As we blacks graduated, we had no doubt what the next phase of "Operation Integration" would be. Yet the despotism of custom caused the Navy to move with great caution. I overheard one officer at Fort Schuyler say, "This integration scheme will blow up the first day a Negro officer walks into a ship's wardroom or into an officer's club." So many people doubted the ability of a democracy to change.

So the people in Washington who sensed that integration was inevitable, who believed that it had to come if there was real justification for fighting Hitler, mostly yielded to the cowards. For the first experiments with integration at sea, they picked auxiliary craft — fleet tankers, troop transports — for mixing black signalmen, electricians, boatswain's mates, with white counterparts. The fighting ships were declared off-limits for "social experimentation."

The Navy wanted to be sure, and I now think correctly so, that every Negro officer sent aboard ship where he might be commanding whites would carry with him the best of training and credentials. So I was sent to Great Lakes for fire fighter training, and then to Miami for intense training in antisubmarine warfare, the usages of the latest radar and sonar, the actuality of commanding a vessel at sea.

After almost two years of training, the Navy finally assigned me to a seagoing vessel, an old tanker, the USS *Mattole*, where I was, in less than two months, named assistant first division officer, assistant cargo officer, assistant communications officer, third division officer, and then communications officer. The ship's commanding officer, Commander George H. Chapman, Jr., said in my first fitness report, "The officer's services have been satisfactory." To the questions of what duties he recommended me for, he said that ashore I should be "administrator of colored personnel" and that at sea I should be on a "ship manned by colored personnel."

Considering Chapman's mentality, I was gleeful that, after only two months under his command, the Navy transferred me to a newer, faster, bigger tanker, AO-30, the USS *Chemung*. I was given deputy command of the communications division, a group of about thirty-five men of whom only two were Negroes. Several of my white men, including the chief petty officer, were southerners.

What the Navy obviously wanted to know was whether white southerners would take orders from a Negro officer. They did, and they executed them without protest or even the slightest hesitation; but most of the credit here must go to the two commanding officers of the *Chemung*.

As a communications officer, I saw every message coming aboard that ship before the captain saw it. I also rummaged back through the files to read messages from the Bureau of Personnel advising the captain that a Negro officer was coming aboard. There were suggestions that he might want to "prepare the crew." Yet there were no indications that the skipper had done any preparing.

One icy, windy night in the North Atlantic as I stood the midnight to 4:00 A.M. watch, the skipper came to the bridge. For some reason, he uttered the first and last sentence about race that I ever heard him say.

"I guess you've wondered why I never called a meeting of the crew to explain that you were coming, or anything like that," he said. "Well, I'm a Navy man, and we're in a war. To me, it's that stripe that counts — and the training and leadership that it's supposed to symbolize. I didn't want any member of my crew to think you were any different from any other officer coming aboard; therefore I figured I'd better not call any meetings about you that I didn't call for other officers."

I appreciated that remark, for without any do-gooder lectures, the skipper had shown an acute understanding of what I — and other Negroes — wanted: no special restrictions and no special favors; just the right to rise or fall on merit.

I felt that I had run for six touchdowns and been named to the all-American team when Commander C. K. Holzer showed me his report to Washington saying: "This officer is colored, but has been outstanding in preventing any adverse criticism of this fact, by his performance of duty. . . . This officer has demonstrated a marked willingness to learn his assigned duties, and a good perception of his particular tasks. With more experience he will be an able communications officer. Recommend promotion."

Having heard other crew members (white) bitch vehemently about Holzer, I felt this was high praise. Weeks later they told me with glee that Holzer was leaving and that we were getting "a real Navy man" as a skipper. I wasn't rejoicing, because I learned that the new commanding officer was to be Philip H. Ross, an old-line graduate of the Naval Academy. I had serious misgivings about what he would think of having a racial "experiment" taking place on his ship.

But as far as I could determine, Ross never paid official, public, or private notice of the fact that I was a Negro. We were carrying high-octane gasoline for the refueling of aircraft carriers, and he simply took it for granted that I knew what I was doing during refueling and that I would know what I was doing while standing watch as officer of the deck. It occurred to me that he probably lost a hell of a lot more sleep over the fact that I was only nineteen than he did over the color of my skin. I was happy to see that in his report to Washington he said he would be "pleased" to have me under his command anywhere, and if only 30 percent of those under him were to be promoted, I should be one of them. He commented: "This officer has performed his assigned duties diligently and efficiently. He has manifested a marked willingness to learn."

It would be nice if I could report here some heroic roles in naval battles that earned me a chestful of ribbons. But policy decided at the presidential level still dictated that blacks were not to be assigned to combat ships until it became clear that their presence did not endanger the morale of white fighting men. So the closest I came to getting killed was during those days near the end of the war in Europe when we were hauling gasoline into the North Atlantic. I was always wary of slipping and tumbling into the sea during the very delicate operations of refueling a huge aircraft carrier, and we worried like hell about being hit by a torpedo from a German submarine, but I have since concluded that by the time of my most dangerous seagoing, the Nazi subs had mostly been chased away.

I didn't concoct any heroic stories that my family could spread around McMinnville, primarily because contact with my family dwindled to close to nothing. I had ordered an allotment to be taken from my pay to ensure that my sister Jewel could go to college, but I rarely got a letter from her except when she wanted to scold me for not making the allotment larger. My parents had sunk so deeply into the muck of drinking and personal conflict that a letter from them was rare — and, when a short one came, it was from my mother. My father's functional illiteracy wiped out any inclination to write letters.

What had happened, I realized, was that my family and I now lived in separate worlds. I had, as some say pejoratively, "outgrown my raisings" and was in a world of education, racial freedom, and opportunity, albeit limited; social integration, of a sort; and rising expectations for the future — a world that required me to devote every waking moment to ensuring that no opportunity went unrecognized. My family was still imprisoned in that special hell that we Americans reserve for those who get trapped by racism, booze, drugs . . . and hopelessness.

I have never spent a week of my adult life when I did not at some time ask myself whether, during those years in college, in V-12, at midshipman's school, aboard ships, I could not have done more to liberate my parents, my brother and sisters, from their social incarceration. This is not a guilt trip. I still do not know how I could have made much of a difference. I do know that the pressures on me were always so great that I rarely got a chance to think about much other than my need to succeed — to beat back those who hoped that I would become proof that integration in the Navy could never work.

I have not told the full story of those marvelous Navy days. I have slipped over some things and people that were very important to my growing up. A man is not made by algebra tests, calisthenics, and North Atlantic deck watches alone. Racial slurs, commendations for ignoring them, perfect refuelings at sea — these are at the fringes of life.

. Boys of eighteen become men-going-on-twenty-eight according to the women they meet. Because of my unique spot in the Navy, I met more than my share. I had not understood why the girls in McMinnville were soldier crazy when the GIs from Camp Forrest rolled into town in their jeeps. But I learned the magic of having one Topeka girl pass the word to others that "There's a colored guy in that V-12 unit at Washburn!" In New York, that midshipman's uniform attracted women more than a Swiss bank account ever could. Lord, how the gold braid of an ensign wowed girls!

I was a male chauvinist in those days, exploiting my midshipman's and ensign's uniforms from the Stagedoor Canteen to Chicago, to Miami, to Norfolk. I knew that most Americans had never seen a black Navy officer, so I strutted in my uniforms like a peacock. I met some women who wanted to pluck me feather-by-feather.

My game produced no serious fumbles until the *Chemung* pulled into Norfolk on a summer day in 1944. I didn't know anyone in Norfolk, so I hired a taxi and asked the driver to "take me to a neighborhood where I can meet some nice people."

We reached an area that I remember as very nice. I asked the driver to let me out, paid him, and began to stroll in a black neighborhood of houses that were most imposing by the standard of my daddy's domicile — houses with neat lawns and pretty shrubs and flowers around them.

I was wearing my Navy whites on which that stripe of gold braid was matched only by the splendiferous cap of a Navy officer. I walked along until I spotted a marvelously sculptured young woman trimming a hedge. I went over and introduced myself.

We chatted, and I got the sense for the first time since I joined the Navy that it was not my uniform that impressed a woman. This woman acted as though she had not seen the Navy whites, the gold braid, the cap, but that she was interested only in me. She had just gotten a math degree and planned to do postgraduate study.

She went inside and cleared it with her parents, then invited me to join them for dinner. I went in and came to know a part of the rising black middle class that did not exist in the McMinnvilles of America. Her daddy worked at the Norfolk Navy Yard, so he in his way, like me, was a beneficiary of a god-awful war.

After dinner, I learned that my accidental date played the piano and sang beautifully. We joined in a couple of tunes to her parents' delight. I relished doing a little teaser that I now sing to my grand-daughters:

> *Aw, gimme a little kiss, Will ya, huh?*
> *And I'll give it right back to you.*

Thus began a torrid and beautiful romance — so hot that it wouldn't cool down even when at age twenty, with no college degree and no certain notion of a future, I asked her to marry me. And, still impoverished, bought her a costly engagement ring.

My romanticism, naked passion, the virility of youth that ought to be bestowed on men of my current wisdom, had brought me to a fateful fork in the road of life. At the time, lust stirred up enough rosy clouds to blind me to any peril.

CHAPTER FOUR

Romance, Fear, Anger — at War's End

ON THE MORNING of June 18, 1946, less than two months short of my twenty-first birthday, Navy officials in Norfolk gave me $27.60 in final pay and $100 in mustering-out pay and told me that I was honorably released from active duty. I was free to go back to McMinnville. They gave me a white scroll with the White House seal on it just over my name and rank, and Harry Truman's signature below the following words:

> We now look to you for leadership and example in further exalting our country in peace.

I should have been happy to be free, proud of that message from my president, but I was a jumble of contradictions. I wasn't sure that I wanted to be "free" after almost three years in the Navy. After all, I had never held a civilian job except for the stint washing dishes and mowing lawns for the Tittles, the month at the TB hospital, and other menial chores. Where would I get a job now, especially if I wanted to be a writer? Sure as hell not in McMinnville or anywhere else in the South.

I had looked around at Norfolk, still relentlessly Jim Crow, and at black families, still carrying the scars of the Great Depression, still mired in unemployment, and I realized that I was angry. "We fought for nothing," I told myself again and again.

That was no twenty-year-old ex-sailor who journeyed from Norfolk to McMinnville that June day in 1946. When you are plucked out of a totally Jim Crow environment at age seventeen and thrown into a totally white environment where more is at stake than your personal life, you mature rapidly. When, at nineteen, you are standing the deck watch in the late night on a tanker carrying high-octane gasoline, you age fast. When you have gotten deeply enough involved with a brilliant and mature young woman to ask her to marry you, the attributes of adulthood pop up everywhere. I was an old twenty as I went home.

"Where you goin', boy?" the bus driver asked me, sending my blood vessels bulging. I wanted to say to him, "Listen, Buster, where I'm coming from white boys saluted and called me 'Mister.' " I just ignored him, knowing that racial violence was epidemic in the South.

I tried to think only pleasant thoughts — of the girl I was leaving behind. I reached into a bag in which I carried photographs of her along with copies of some of the sentimental things that I had written for her or about her. I didn't feel very good about myself, because I knew that hour by hour I was talking myself out of getting married. In order to feel less like a rat, I thought back to the time when we had quarreled and she had stunned me by writing that she was thinking of marrying someone else. The North Atlantic had not been large enough to swallow up my grief.

I got off the bus to stretch my legs at a rest stop in Murfreesboro, Tennessee, and was infuriated by the signs: WHITE WAITING ROOM / COLORED WAITING ROOM. And on the toilet doors: WHITE LADIES / COLORED WOMEN. I said to myself, "Pull yourself together, man; you've got some hard work to do."

In Norfolk I had bought copies of the *Norfolk Journal and Guide*, the *Pittsburgh Courier*, the *Baltimore Afro-American*, and the *Chicago Defender*, newspapers that black Americans counted on to tell them what was going on that affected the lives of black people.

The black newspapers carried story after story of a mob action here, of police brutality against a black war veteran there, of egregious acts of racial discrimination in the nation's capital.

"Dear God," I thought, "history is repeating itself."

My father had tried to tell me that "the white folks got real mean" when he and other black doughboys came home from Europe after World War I. "Seems they was gonna make sure that the nigger remembered his place," he had added.

Only later, at college and during the war when I got to read a lot of things they didn't have at Bernard High, did I understand the resurgence of the Ku Klux Klan, the rash of lynchings of blacks, the naked campaigns against Jews and Catholics. . . . I remembered reading of the searing rift in black opinion over the obligation of Negroes to fight that war. It had been the "militant" W. E. B. Du Bois, not the accommodationist Booker T. Washington, who had written in *The Crisis*, official publication of the NAACP:

> This is Our Country. . . . Our country is at war. The war is critical, dangerous and world-wide. If this is our country, then this is our war. We must fight it with every ounce of blood and treasure. . . . We will not bargain with our loyalty. We will not profiteer with our country's blood. . . .

But that was 1918. In 1919 Du Bois would write:

> We return from the slavery of uniform which the world's madness demanded us don to the freedom of civil garb. We stand again to look America squarely in the face and call a spade a spade. We sing: This country of ours, despite all its better souls have done and dreamed, is yet a shameful land.
>
> It lynches . . . it disfranchises its own citizens . . . it encourages ignorances . . . it insults us. . . .

But the shame did not diminish. Instead, the racial atrocities became so commonplace that in 1922 the NAACP ran ads in the *New York Times* and other newspapers decrying the fact that in 1918 through 1921, 28 people had been burned publicly by American mobs, and in the years 1889 through 1921, 3,436 people had been lynched.

There had been many villains during this dark and ugly chapter of American life, and I had been surprised to read that foremost among them had been the president of the United States, Woodrow Wilson. Yes, Wilson, the Virginia intellectual and president of Princeton who defeated William Howard Taft and Theodore Roosevelt partly on the strength of votes he won by promising blacks "absolute fair dealing."

Wilson wasted little time rewarding black voters by sanctioning the segregation of the federal government. First the U.S. Postal

Service separated black and white workers. Next the Treasury Department and the Bureau of Engraving and Printing ordered Jim Crow work arrangements. Then the Navy Department, headed by Josephus Daniels, went Jim Crow. Some historians say that the segregation campaign began because Wilson's Georgia-born first wife was offended when she saw white women and black men working in the same room at the post office.

Black leaders were outraged. In 1914 a delegation of Negroes went to Wilson to protest. Wilson said to them:

> The white people of the country, as well as I, wish to see the colored people progress, and admire the progress they have already made, and want to see them continue along independent lines. There is, however, a great prejudice against the colored people. . . . It will take one hundred years to eradicate this prejudice, and we must deal with it as practical men. Segregation is not humiliating but a benefit, and ought to be so regarded by you gentlemen. If your organization goes out and tells the colored people of the country that it is a humiliation, they will so regard it, but if you do not tell them so, and regard it as a benefit, they will regard it the same. The only harm will be if you cause them to think it is a humiliation.

That June day in '46 I thought of Wilson's record and wondered about Harry Truman. "Is he just a redneck from racist Missouri who's gonna let history repeat itself?" I wondered.

One of the most atrocious of postwar racial incidents, during Truman's presidency, involved Isaac Woodard, a black U.S. Army sergeant who had served three years, fifteen months of it in the South Pacific.

Upon discharge at Fort Gordon, Georgia, in 1946, Woodard, still in uniform, caught a bus to his home in North Carolina. At a stop in South Carolina, Woodard went to the "colored only" men's toilet. When he came out the bus driver cursed him for taking too long. At the next town, the driver summoned lawmen and convinced them to arrest Woodard on charges of drunkenness (the record would show that Woodard did not even drink alcoholic beverages). During the arrest, the lawmen beat Woodard with a blackjack, and one of them poked him in his eyes with a nightstick.

Woodard was denied medical care, locked in a cell overnight, then found guilty and fined fifty dollars the next day. When the ex-serviceman finally reached an Army hospital in Spartanburg, South Carolina, medical examiners found his corneas so badly damaged that he was permanently blind.

The NAACP and its leader Walter White screamed in outrage, inspiring Orson Welles and many other celebrities to condemn publicly the assault on this war veteran.

Truman said to White: "My God! I had no idea it was as terrible as that. We've got to do something."

The president, much of the nation, and I watched with burning passion when Sheriff Linwood L. Shull of Batesburg, South Carolina, went on trial before U.S. District Judge J. Waties Waring, scion of eight generations of Charleston aristocracy and son of a Confederate veteran. When it had become obvious that South Carolina authorities were not going to prosecute the lawmen who beat and blinded Woodard, federal officials claimed jurisdiction on grounds that Woodard was riding an interstate bus at the time of the crime. But a trial before a born-and-bred southern elitist like Waring? There was hope in that Waring had divorced his wife of thirty-two years and married a Detroit divorcée who was fifteen years his junior. Charleston society shunned Elizabeth Waring, and she rejected their social custom of racial segregation, calling them "sick, confused and decadent . . . full of pride and complacency, morally weak and low."

Whatever Waring's intentions were regarding Sheriff Shull, he soon found that there would be no justice within his court. Shull admitted that he struck Woodard with a blackjack — in self-defense when the Negro attacked him, he said — but he denied blinding him. Waring noted with dismay that the United States attorney had not even tried to find witnesses who might substantiate Woodard's version of the incident. FBI agents claimed they had not turned up any evidence against the policemen involved.

When the jurors declared Shull not guilty, the white courtroom spectators (segregated) cheered loudly. Waring would later tell me that it made him sick at his stomach.

So Truman had no idea it was that bad. "Hell," I thought, "most white Americans don't know how bad it is because the newspapers, magazines, and radio stations do not tell them the truth about the brutalities waged against Negroes in general and black ex-GIs in particular. White people never will know until we get some Negroes on the white newspapers and magazines." The white daily newspapers carried almost nothing about blacks except for an item about someone stealing a chicken or being accused of rape or robbery. That Woodard case, as much as any event, steeled my resolve to be a writer, to bust open the lily-white journalistic establishment in America.

In my anger over the Woodard case, I succumbed to a measure of prejudice myself. I cursed Harry Truman, believing that because he was white and southern he would do nothing to stop the assaults on Negroes. I blamed Truman for the shockingly weak performance of the U.S. attorney, for the ineptitude of the FBI.

Truman, I would learn, was indelibly angered by the Woodard case. He wrote one of his World War I buddies to say: "When a Mayor and a City Marshal can take a Negro sergeant off a bus in South Carolina, beat him and put out one of his eyes [*sic*], and nothing is done about it by State Authorities, then something is radically wrong with the system."

I soon stopped castigating Truman. On December 5, 1946, he issued an executive order creating the President's Committee on Civil Rights, which was to tell him how America could prevent other outrages.

Lynchings were the ultimate terror tactic generations before Americans would come to regard "terrorists" as the bane of civilized societies. When I came home from the war, not many white Americans seemed to understand, or care about, the dimensions of the terror imposed by lynch mobs or brutal policemen.

In my town there were no black policemen or deputy sheriffs, no blacks patrolling Tennessee's highways, no black bailiffs or judges in the courtroom. We used the terms "the Law" and "the Man," and both terms meant white. When "Here come the Man" was shouted, every black person knew that potential trouble was on the way. We just didn't know who that day's victim might be.

President Truman's Committee on Civil Rights would report to him:

The devastating consequences of lynchings go far beyond what is shown by counting victims. When a person is lynched and the lynchers go unpunished, thousands wonder where the evil will appear again and what mischance may produce another victim. And every time lynchers go unpunished, Negroes have learned to expect other forms of violence at the hands of private citizens or public officials. In describing the thwarted efforts of the Department of Justice to identify those responsible for one lynching, J. Edgar Hoover stated to the committee: "The arrogance of most of the population of that county was unbelievable, and the fear of the Negroes was almost unbelievable."

I was especially troubled to find that white political demagogues were encouraging lynchings and other racial atrocities. In Georgia, Eugene Talmadge said that when elected governor he would assign to every sheriff an assistant "to take care of nigger trouble." I was outraged to read, again and again, that crimes of race were not the business of the FBI or any other part of the federal government because states' rights under the Constitution precluded any federal jurisdiction.

I took a little heart when I saw that the mobs and the racist politicians were alienating a lot of white Americans, provoking them to abandon acceptance of the doctrine of states' rights.

I found the parallels between 1946 and 1919 dismayingly striking. At the start of World War II, the leaders of the war mobilization effort had seen no places of consequence for black workers. Rosie the Riveter could not have fat lips, curly hair, and a brown or black skin. Most of the unions of the American Federation of Labor (AFL) and the Congress of Industrial Organizations (CIO) either barred Negroes or admitted them only on a segregated basis.

Black hopes for economic justice had risen when Franklin D. Roosevelt was elected president in 1932. But while his wife, Eleanor, became active in pressing for racial and social justice, FDR would not go beyond making a few inconspicuous appointments of blacks to federal jobs, setting up an informal kitchen cabinet of black advisers, and occasionally speaking up publicly against lynchings and police brutality. He insisted to Eleanor that his programs of general national economic recovery were "great civil rights laws that will benefit Negroes." But FDR was loath to do anything that he thought would diminish national unity behind the effort to prepare for possible U.S. entry into the war in Europe. He was unwilling to face the issue of racism in either the industrial mobilization or the buildup of military forces.

But blacks were learning how to force the hand of even a very popular president. In mid-1941 the black union leader A. Philip Randolph, NAACP head Walter White, and others threatened a demonstration of fifty thousand blacks in Washington. Seeking to avoid the demonstration, Roosevelt invited the angry blacks to Washington, where they demanded that he issue an executive order decreeing the end of racial discrimination in America's defense industries. Roosevelt issued his historic Executive Order 8802, in which he also created the national Fair Employment Practices Committee (FEPC).

The idea of any kind of FEPC was controversial beyond explanation in the context of 1941. A southern "liberal," Mark Ethridge, who became a member of the committee, said angrily that "No power in the world — not even all the mechanized armies of the earth, Allied and Axis — could force the southern white people to the abandonment of the principle of social segregation."

Social segregation. Social equality. Miscegenation. Intermarriage. The "mongrelization" of the white race. These were the compelling issues of the postwar 1940s, not just in the minds of demagogues like Talmadge or the Ku Klux Klansmen, but in the heads of elitists such as Ethridge.

Many black leaders had ducked these issues of social equality and intermarriage for decades, figuring that it was not prudent to tell the whole truth about the kind of society blacks really wanted. I told myself in 1946 and 1947 that when I became a real journalist, I would face those issues head-on. But in those postwar days I had doubts about the wisdom of my pursuing a career in journalism. This was, after all, one of the most discriminatory professions in America.

In 1947 Louis R. Lautier, black correspondent for the only black daily newspaper in the land, was trying to get admittance into the press galleries of Congress. He was rejected by the Standing Committee of Newspaper Correspondents on grounds that while he did indeed report for one daily newspaper, the *Atlanta Daily World*, he also represented thirty-six weeklies of the Negro Newspaper Publishers Association, and this technically made him ineligible for the daily press gallery. His barring made headlines in *Time* magazine, *Commonweal*, and other serious publications in America. The *Chicago Sun's* Griffing Bancroft, who cast the only vote to admit Lautier, called his fellow correspondents' decision "nothing short of outrageous." The Senate Rules Committee overrode the journalists and let Lautier in.

"*This is the profession I'm joining?*" I asked myself. But no professions in America were truly open to black people. Blacks could teach (but only black children), preach (but only in black churches), practice medicine (on black patients), or, with considerable rarity, practice law, but only in certain jurisdictions.

But I couldn't feel sorry for myself, because day after day the newspapers reminded me that blacks were finding it very difficult to get good training in any profession. Negroes had sued to get into the University of Missouri law school, but state officials set up a "separate but equal" school for blacks. The *St. Louis Post-Dispatch* found that, to preserve Jim Crow, the state was paying $807 a year to educate a black law student, but only $228 a year for a white student, and that the black student still was getting an inferior education.

The University of Arkansas had refused to admit a Negro law student, but under legal pressure said that if he reapplied he could use the law library and study under the regular white faculty — but he would have to use a separate classroom.

A few other southern states were paying relative fortunes to send blacks to northern professional schools rather than admit them to universities in their home states.

Harry Truman's blue-ribbon committee would say to him, in its historic report, "To Secure These Rights," that Americans had "four essential rights," those being the right to safety and security of the person, the right to citizenship and its privileges, the right to freedom of conscience and expression, and the right to equality of opportunity. During those violent, troubled years of 1946 and 1947 I was a war veteran who knew that I did not enjoy a single one of those rights. This realization told me that I absolutely had to go into journalism.

*   *   *

Postwar McMinnville was depressing beyond belief. I saw some of my old buddies, guys with fine minds who had gotten grades in the 90s, toting bags at Brown's Hotel. Others were still "holding up" the First National Bank building, telling old lies and waiting for odd jobs. The cousin who had "knocked up that little bitch from out near Leesburg" was still married and producing more babies. I still couldn't get a drink of water in the drugstore unless the fountain clerk could find a paper cup.

An "officer and a gentleman" of the United States Navy could not go back to mowing lawns and unloading boxcars of cement, so there was just no work for me. I was nursing carefully that one hundred dollars of mustering-out pay along with the small amount of money that I had saved.

"I've got to get the hell out of here," I said one day, and I took the bus to Nashville, where a cousin let me sleep on a cot for the few weeks before I would go back to Oberlin.

For a while the letters from my fiancée came often and full of passion. Then we both sensed the ardor waning. I know I wrote more and more about my excitement at going back to Oberlin, my decision to take a degree in math, and my intention to then do postgraduate work in journalism. I said less and less about getting married soon.

Whoever said "Absence makes the heart grow fonder" never knew the temptations that caused some wag to add, "Yeah, for somebody else." My unique status as a black naval officer was still attracting women, and I had more than ordinary popularity among the girls at Tennessee State and Fisk University.

One day a former college classmate introduced me to her beautiful cousin, Edith. I soon was strolling through Centennial Park with her on gorgeous summer nights, crooning her favorite song, "As Time Goes By," and some of my favorites like "Moonlight Becomes You."

"Before we get too involved," I would say, "you must know that I'm engaged to a lovely girl in Norfolk." Then I would do my damnedest to get *too involved.*

One night we sat on the grass under a tree, watching the lightning bugs put on a firework display, when Edith said to me: "I'd like to write to your fiancée."

"Jeeesus Christ," I thought, "how can any woman be so beautiful and so dumb?"

"It's obvious," Edith continued, "that Cheerye has a lock on your heart. I just want to tell her how lucky she is to be getting such a nice, loyal guy."

I almost let the word "shit" slip through my clenched teeth. But then the devil got to me. I knew that I could not tell the fiancée, whom I called Cheerye, that the engagement was off. I wanted her to be the one to break it off. I knew that if Edith wrote her she would say something that would make my fiancée furious at me. When we got back to the house I wrote the Norfolk address on a piece of envelope and gave it to Edith. That still ranks in my mind as one of the most unconscionable things I ever did.

As I expected, the engagement quickly went up in the smoke of one Norfolk woman's anger. I drank almost no alcohol in those days, but when it was clear that I no longer was committed to marriage, I went by a friend's house on Jefferson Street in Nashville and drank a huge rum and Coke.

I was liberated! A few days later I caught a train for Oberlin College. I could pursue my dream of becoming a newspaperman.

CHAPTER FIVE

The Long Road Toward Wisdom

M Y TRIP from Nashville back to Oberlin was only a few hundred miles, but intellectually, socially, politically, it turned out to be the longest voyage I would ever take.

It was a journey fraught with many doubts — about myself, my walking away from marriage, my decision to go back to Oberlin, my abilities as a writer, my chances of finding a good job once out of journalism school.

There were virtually no Negro role models in any field of communications for a black youngster in 1946. No more than a handful of Negroes worked as reporters on white daily newspapers, and none was close to being a household name. The great magazines had no Negro staff editors and rarely ran anything written by a black person. Richard Wright had made a monumental breakthrough six years earlier when his *Native Son* was published and again in 1945 when *Black Boy* came out. Still, most publishers were not clamoring for black authors. *White* writers such as Lillian Smith, Jonathan Daniels, Gunnar Myrdal, Ralph McGill, Harry Golden, Margaret Halsey, and Ashley Montagu were professing to express the frustrations and hopes of black people. Aside from the print media, there were no black broadcasters. No black screenwriters in Hollywood. Even a public relations job in a white corporation was beyond the reasonable hopes of a black. It was as though nature had handed down a rule that black people were not to earn a living using the English language.

So what was I doing on this journey? I believed that I could

change things. I felt that publishers and editors could not possibly
be as steeped in bigotry as some of the people whom I had
confronted in the Navy. Those experiences in helping to beat down
racism aboard Navy ships had multiplied the ambitions instilled in
me by my mother and by Grandmother Ella, who had worn my ear
off telling me, "Where there's a will, there's a way." So there just had
to be a place for me in the whole broad spectrum of journalism if I
got the proper credentials.

People asked why I didn't just go straight to journalism school
and why I was going to Oberlin. I told a partial truth: that in V-12
and midshipman school I had piled up so many hours of math and
science that it was easier to take a bachelor's degree in math and do
a year of graduate work in journalism than to get a bachelor's in
journalism.

I never talked about the other reason: I figured that Oberlin
would permit me to study in a special oasis, sheltered from the
hurts, the anger, the rage, that all victims of racism experience.

Oberlin in a postwar autumn setting was remarkably different
from the college that I had seen during that summer semester as a
Navy student. Whereas the Navy had assigned me to room with the
only other black V-12 students, Oberlin put me with eleven white
guys.

So at the outset, that autumn of '46, I began to see why Oberlin,
founded in 1833, was renowned for its egalitarianism. I could not
wait to learn more about the fabled stories of underground
abolitionist planning, of Oberliners harboring runaway slaves, of
literally snatching black fugitives away from federal agents who
were trying to return them to their southern "owners."

What I first learned about Oberlin was shocking. The school had
a unique system in which men students did not eat in their
dormitories. Each man was assigned to one of the women's dorms
for all meals, someone having decided that this socializing process
was a vital part of getting a liberal education. I was assigned to Pyle
Inn where forty women dined with me and thirty-nine other guys. I
was the only black in the place.

My first concerns had nothing to do with social equality. Eating at
Pyle Inn generally was just the preliminary to bull sessions in which
students argued about the burning issues of the day. It took me only

one evening to realize that my deprivation involved much more than money or formal education. I was woefully deprived in the sense that there was little in my background to prepare me for the discussions that were taking place.

One of the first postdinner sessions was about the newly founded United Nations and whether it was really "man's last best hope for peace," or just another pipe dream to tide the militarists over until the next war. A pretty blonde from Scarsdale, New York, went into a little soliloquy about who held the right to veto actions in the UN Security Council, then asked me if I thought it right for a few Great Powers to be able "to frustrate the will of the majority of mankind."

"Jee-sus!" I said to myself, then mumbled aloud, "Doesn't seem right to me."

I hustled out of Pyle Inn at the first opportunity, knowing that I was in over my head. I listened to students from all over the country, and it was obvious that they came from homes where political, economic, and social issues were discussed daily. None of *my* relatives sat around talking about whether it was right for the United States to turn against its ally, the Soviet Union, or arguing about whether the military or civilians ought to be given control of atomic energy.

"You can't go to Pyle Inn and be embarrassed every night," I told myself. "You've got some reading to do."

Thus did those very bright young women provoke me into doing what was absolutely essential for a young man aspiring to be a journalist: to read newspapers and magazines every day and to give up hearing Nat King Cole sing "I Love You for Sentimental Reasons" once or twice a day so I could listen to the news on the radio.

As I read and listened, more and more, I could feel my self-assurance increasing. When the discussion was about President Truman's proposal for national compulsory health insurance, and a young man began to rail against socialized medicine, I dared to ask, "How many doctors in your family?" Then I paraphrased Truman's argument that the people against a federal health plan always seemed to be the ones rich enough not to need it.

I learned the art of cloaking ambivalence in fancy rhetoric when issues arose about which I wasn't sure where I stood — such as the Taft-Hartley Act. Some students spoke eloquently of a "repressive, antiunion law that is an outrage against the workingman." This appealed to me, since working people were all I had known. But none of them had had any jobs good enough for a union to care about. In fact, I knew the unions had been powerful barriers to blacks getting decent jobs during the great mobilization for World War II. So, in my ambivalence, I talked about the arrogance of old John L. Lewis and how some of the unions provoked the Congress into passing a stringent law to cut them down to size.

No discussions got hotter, or caused me more mental anguish, than those about "the Palestine problem," about the future of Jewish refugees still in Germany and Austria, about Zionism, about the Balfour Declaration and talk of partitioning Palestine.

But when the discussion came around to interracial dating or marriage, I said with all the profundity I could muster, "People don't marry races; they marry individuals."

"You don't practice what you preach," a blonde from Binghamton, New York, said to me at the session's end. "You've never invited me to a movie."

I did — and suddenly the postdinner rap sessions seemed a lot more interesting.

Dating, however, was not my preoccupation at Oberlin. I was having a tough time, partly because during my last year in the Navy I had forgotten a lot of math. Also because I knew, as did my professor and adviser, that math was simply my major of convenience. I would get grades good enough to graduate and then go on to journalism.

The trouble was that Oberlin was not helping much, in any formal way, to prepare me to be a reporter or editor. The *Oberlin Review* was run by students who reflected the prejudices of the professional journalism community: they didn't believe any black student had the smarts to analyze an important issue, to dig up vital information, or to write it for a community of white readers. The most I got from the editors of the college newspaper was the right to show up in the office occasionally and claim that I was a reporter.

Classes were large in those postwar days, my English class numbering well over one hundred students. For weeks I sat in this throng as the new invisible man, with the teacher, Miss Foster, unaware that I existed.

I was frustrated, and one day admitted it to myself. I gave myself a lecture about how timidity never bestowed success on anyone. I decided to confront Miss Foster at the end of the next class.

This prim and proper woman looked nonplussed when I said to her: "I'm sitting back there in the crowd, and I feel helpless that I can't get the help I need from you."

"Help?" she said, as if fearful that I was going to ask for a ten-dollar loan.

"I intend to be a journalist," I said, "and I've already written several things. Would you just critique one of them for me?"

"Of course," she said, but her tone told me she was worried about what she was committing herself to. I gave her a copy of "A Conqueror's Plea," an angry bit of prose that I wrote as I returned from a war that I knew had not given me freedom.

At the next English class, Miss Foster asked me to speak with her afterward. My knees were shaking as I awaited her critique. She picked up my writing and said, "Whew! I think you'll make it."

That put forty years of wind under my wings. No matter that she then suggested a few changes of punctuation here, the change of a verb or noun there. It was the breakthrough that I needed. She called upon me often. She asked me to stay late for chats. I was no longer the invisible student.

Word spreads fast among a faculty at a college such as Oberlin, and Miss Foster soon spread the word that she had a young black ex-GI in her class who just might have a future. That didn't help me in my vector analysis class, but it sure did with other professors and the president's office.

But nothing did more than those sessions at Pyle Inn to push me toward wisdom, to force me to develop concepts of justice and take stands, even unpopular ones.

It is remarkable how many great decisions of life are made not by preference but because of financial or other uncontrollable circumstances.

I left Oberlin that summer of '47 wanting very much to go to the Columbia University graduate school of journalism, but I was not accepted. I was approved by Syracuse, Indiana University, and the University of Minnesota. How to make a choice?

The Baltimore Afro-American chain of "Negro newspapers" actually made the decision for me without knowing it. During the summer and early fall of '47 the *Afro* paid me ten to fifteen dollars for each free-lance article that I wrote, so that kept me from going back to McMinnville. I talked a Tennessee State University official into letting me stay in a room in one of the empty dormitories — to sort of make the dormitory there my base while I traveled from one racial trouble spot to another. Meanwhile, I was getting my GI Bill eligibility for graduate school straightened away, knowing that without this marvelous federal "welfare program" I could never get a graduate degree in journalism.

This process led me to the stark reality that I needed a few bucks more than the GI Bill provided. I would need desperately those ten- and fifteen-dollar checks from the *Afro*. When editor Bill Gibson said, "We have no correspondent in Minnesota or neighboring states," I knew that Minnesota was where I was going.

Aside from having become a pretty good student, I wanted to be known as a good citizen. I was encouraged to engage in Minneapolis's political life by my political science teacher, Max Kampelman, who later would become a noted Washington lawyer and Ronald Reagan's chief arms control negotiator with the Soviet Union.

I was introduced to Bill Leland, head of one of the first city human rights commissions in America. Leland took me in that fall of '47 to meet Minneapolis's Mayor Hubert Humphrey. I also was introduced to one of the great and unsung black journalists in the land, Cecil Newman, who used his *Minneapolis Spokesman* and *St. Paul Recorder* to hold a sizzling fire to the feet of Humphrey and other Minnesota officials. Newman taught me that age twenty-two was not too early to make a commitment to the NAACP, the Urban League, or other black groups trying to wipe out bigotry.

So by the time I got my master's degree in August of 1948, I was no stranger to the black people of the Twin Cities, or to white power-wielders like Mrs. F. Peavey Heffelfinger and the other grandes dames who worked so hard to erase Minneapolis's reputation as the capital of anti-Semitism in America and a bastion of hostility toward blacks.

Just before graduation, I asked two of my professors what I

should do to get a job. Both laid out the advantages and disadvantages of starting with a small newspaper rather than being a fly on the wall of a major journal. But both knew that because of racism Carl Rowan had no option of applying at a newspaper in Paducah or Pascagoula. In effect, they said, "What the hell, try the Minneapolis newspapers" — the morning *Tribune* and the afternoon *Star.*

So one August morning I walked into the personnel office of the Minneapolis newspapers, bearing the scars of myriad rejections.

"Great grades," the personnel woman said as she perused the other materials that I had brought along. "Would you mind taking some tests?"

Then she gave me verbal tests, manual dexterity tests — everything imaginable. When the tests were over she said, "Well, we have no jobs available now, but if anything opens up, we'll call you."

I said thank you with a chill that would have made June in Acapulco seem like January in Bemidji. "They've done it to me again," I told myself.

I caught the University Avenue streetcar to St. Paul, where I was renting a room on Avon Street. The Veterans Administration had screwed up, and I was late getting my money. The *Afro* had sent checks for my articles to the University of Minnesota, but nobody could find them. A white grocer had given me credit for purchases of raisin bread and peanut butter, and Mrs. Roberta Davis, my landlady, had on occasion forced me to eat her family's food.

As I walked the blocks from the streetcar to my room, angry and depressed, Mrs. Davis was down on Avon Street to meet me.

"Thank God you came straight home," she said. "A Mr. Gideon Seymour of the Minneapolis papers has called three times for you. He wants you to come back to Minneapolis right away. I think he may have a job for you."

"Good Lord," I replied. "If he calls again, tell him I'm on my way back."

I would not learn for many years that the Minneapolis papers had a great man as owner, John Cowles, Sr., and that he had laid the law down to Scymour and other editors. He had told them that he did not believe that in all of America they could not find a single black man or woman capable of being a reporter on his newspapers. And I had no idea that Seymour had, to protect his job, told the personnel department to tell him if "one of them showed up." That woman in personnel obviously had telephoned Seymour the moment I walked out of her office.

Seymour was cool. "Twelve A's and three B's in journalism didn't catch my attention," he said. "But the fact that you were a Navy officer, and the captain let you decode those messages, did. I figure you're the right man for us. But I don't have a job."

"Sir, I don't understand," I said, feeling uneasy.

"I have just laid off seven members of the Newspaper Guild," Seymour explained. "The guild would probably strike if I hired you at this time. But if you can find work until the storm blows over, I'll hire you at sixty dollars a week."

Incredibly, the following day I got a call from Carl Murphy, publisher of the *Afro-American* newspapers, offering to pay me eighty dollars a week to come to Baltimore and do public opinion surveying of the presidential contest among Harry Truman, Henry Wallace, and Thomas Dewey. After negotiating all expenses, plus the eighty bucks a week, I accepted as though it were manna from heaven.

I knew almost no one in Baltimore. I spent my first lonely Sunday just strolling the streets and then back to my room to try to construct my polling questions to get the most honest and meaningful answers. I knew that the *Afro* was interested only in how Negroes planned to vote, but I knew that out of curiosity I would also ask questions of many whites for a clue to how the overall campaign was going.

I started out assuming that most blacks would support the uncompromisingly liberal Wallace, a large number would back Truman out of party loyalty, and only a handful would vote for Republican Dewey. I was amazed during my first day in the *Afro*'s offices to have a young woman whisper, "Mr. Carl has made a deal to support Dewey."

"You've got to be joking," I said as I got ready for trips to Richmond and Washington, D.C., to do polls.

I was surprised at the strength of Truman, who was running well ahead of Wallace among blacks, and even ahead of Dewey among the whites who would talk to me. Therefore, I was stunned when I picked up a copy of the *Washington Afro* and saw a headline over my byline indicating that black voters favored Dewey. Outraged, I telephoned the top *Afro* editor in Baltimore and asked, "What illiterate wrote that headline?"

"There was a problem with the headline, but your copy wasn't changed," he said. "I'll ask the copydesk to be more careful."

Believing it was an honest mistake, I went to Philadelphia, where I found astonishing support for Truman, and only a small number of people saying they would vote for Dewey. I wrote this, but when I picked up a copy of the *Afro* I saw a headline blaring: PHILLY VOTERS SWEET ON DEWEY. This over my byline!

I called editor Bill Gibson in a rage. This fine man said, "I've got to level with you. Mr. Carl gave orders that he and only he would write the headlines for your reports."

With the rage and impetuosity of a recent journalism school graduate, steeped in lectures about ethics, I said: "Well, you tell Mr. Carl that this Carl just quit." I prayed that Seymour was ready to hire me.

The following day I got a call from the *Afro*'s personnel manager, Furman Templeton. "Mr. Carl says you can quit," he related, "but we'll have to dock your pay for the price of airfare from Minneapolis and back."

Smoke started oozing from my eyeballs, but my brain stayed cool enough to enable me to lie effectively. I said Mrs. Davis had listened in when Mr. Carl telephoned me, and knew everything that he promised. I threatened to sue.

A couple of days later I got a check for travel and pay with nothing deducted. I wrote my last article for the *Afro* saying that Truman would get so many black votes that he had a chance of catching Dewey, who had been declared a certain winner by most of the polls.

I stayed in Baltimore until election night, and into the next day, when it was decided that, the famous *Chicago Tribune* headline notwithstanding, the little haberdasher from Missouri had won his own term as president of the United States.

When I got back to Minneapolis, Seymour told me that he was ready to hire me to work for the morning *Tribune*, but further comments and developments convinced me that they were not giving me a fair shot. He called in William P. Steven, the rotund managing editor who was fresh from Oklahoma and looked to me like the classic redneck that I had seen in the movies.

My suspicions were heightened when Steven asked, "What would happen if I asked you to cover a meeting of the Kiwanis or Rotary clubs?"

"Sir," I said, trying to mute my high umbrage, "if there is a story there, I'll bring it back."

"But suppose Rotary or Kiwanis calls me and says they don't want a colored reporter?" Steven continued.

I misjudged Steven's mind-set and intentions, and a hard little knot grew in my gut, but my journalistic training prevailed. "Sir," I said, "if I work for you we must have an understanding that when I go out I will not be a 'colored' reporter, but the representative of the *Minneapolis Tribune*. If the Kiwanians or Rotarians know that I am your representative and that either I write the story or there will be no story, you'll never have a problem. But if the word gets out that groups can call in and say they only want a white reporter, you are going to have problems from now to doomsday."

Steven gave a smile that I would not know for years was his seal of approval.

Still, I was disappointed to learn that it would be a long time before I covered any meetings of Kiwanis, Rotary, or anything else. Seymour or someone had made a decision — cowardly, I thought — that I needed to begin on the copydesk, editing wire stories, writing headlines, learning the city. I would be working nights on a copydesk run by a man named Lou Greene, who was described by other Tribuners as a bloody tyrant. Paranoia washed over me.

Then I got word that a couple of old-timers on the copydesk had marched into Seymour's office and declared that they "ain't going to work on any copydesk with a nigger."

Seymour simply looked them in the eyes, pausing for effect, and said: "When are you two picking up your final paychecks?" The two slinked back to the copydesk.

But the lingo of newspapering, like Navy life and sailing, is replete with racial references. I remember the night when the first edition of the *Tribune* came up with a long black mark on page one. Instinctively, someone on the copydesk shouted through the intercom, *"Nigger on page one!"*

For generations printers had referred to this black aberration as a "nigger," which I knew from journalism school. But that shout from the copydesk almost paralyzed the nearby reporters and editors. Or so some told me, because I made it a point not to look up, just to continue editing the one-paragraph story that Lou Greene had entrusted to me.

The first edition completed, a couple of reporters and a few junior editors asked me to join them for dinner at the nearby Commerce Club. I accepted, only to walk into an ugly situation when the restaurant said flatly that it did not serve Negroes, and my *Tribune* colleagues, many of whose names I didn't know, raised one hell of a stink. A few days later the Commerce Club burned down.

I arrived at work at 2:00 P.M. the day after the fire to hear one of my intended dinnermates say, "Goddam, you play rough, don't you?"

I spent almost two years on that copydesk, and I shall forever be grateful for what I learned from that magnificent old curmudgeon Lou Greene. "Goddammit, commas come in pairs," he would shout to my embarrassment. "Your subject in 'a group of whores' is singular, goddammit, so what school told you to make the verb plural?" he would ask. "You sure never won any goddam spelling bee, because you keep putting an extra *e* in the word *judgment*." "Goddammit, when are you going to learn that nobody rapes anybody in this newspaper? Guys assault women, but they don't 'rape' 'em!"

Lou Greene was a foulmouthed, ill-tempered guy when anyone on the copydesk screwed up — or when he was distraught about some "anti-Israel" editorial that had been run in the *Tribune* or *Star*. But he taught me so much about journalism that I almost cried the day that I was told that I was ready to become a reporter.

One of the most important things I learned during those copydesk days at the *Tribune* was that I would have a bleak future as a journalist if I did not move in the same social and other circles as my fellow staff members. That is why I was so pleased when star reporter Geri Hoffner (later Mrs. Geri Joseph, Minnesota's Democratic national chairperson) asked me to join her and others for dinner and to play golf at her exclusive, no-Negro-members country club.

It now seems hard for me to believe that naked racism was practiced in restaurants, in housing, in so many other areas of life in northern cities like Minneapolis in 1948. But then, it was in 1946 that Minneapolis's Radisson Hotel accepted world-renowned contralto Marian Anderson as a guest only with the stipulation that she ride the freight elevator.

I still shake my head in near disbelief when I recall how a white couple who invited a black couple to dinner was scorned by their neighbors. I remember with lingering affection John and Inez McDonald, Roz and Dick Kleeman, Bob and Pat Smith, Monique and Dan Hafrey — colleagues whose many invitations showed that the social equality bugaboo meant nothing to them.

It surely did not hurt that our publisher, John Cowles, Sr., and his wife, Betty, set such a marvelous example of preaching and practicing racial equality. She was a powerful supporter of the Minneapolis Urban League. He was a man of intense intellectual curiosity, as I learned early in a rather shocking way. Butterflies as big as bats were flapping in my stomach the Sunday afternoon, only weeks after beginning work, that I went to his home to a reception (a wet-behind-the-ears twenty-three-year-old going to the publisher's home). I got there right on time and found that I was the first guest.

"Welcome to Minneapolis and the *Tribune*," Betty Cowles said.

"Thank you," I said, showing off one of the nice things nature gave me: a white set of teeth.

"I'm having a scotch," John said. "What can I get you?"

"I'll have the same," I said, thinking that I would have asked timidly for a Coke if he had not disclosed that he was consuming some hard stuff.

As he splashed the whiskey over ice cubes he said, apropos of nothing: "Carl, did you vote for Harry Truman or Henry Wallace?"

My mouth sagged in disbelief, which he must have noticed, for he added: "I'm assuming you didn't vote for Dewey, because I can't imagine that many Negroes did. But I'm really interested in what motivated Negroes to vote however they did."

"Well, I can sure talk about that, Mr. Cowles, because up till coming here I was doing public opinion surveying for the *Afro-American* newspapers."

"Yes, Gid Seymour told me that."

That launched a discussion about how, even though Henry Wallace seemed far more liberal than Truman, blacks developed a great admiration for Truman because he wouldn't knuckle under to Strom Thurmond and the Dixiecrats. "Many Negroes felt they had to be loyal to a man who would risk losing rather than turn his back on a commitment to racial justice," I said.

"Fascinating," Cowles said. "Let's have another scotch before the crowd arrives." I welcomed the idea, because it seemed that every swallow drowned one of those butterflies. I would later learn a word for what was happening — *potvaliance*, bravery under the influence of alcohol.

When one guest, a prominent banker, came in, Cowles introduced me as "a new member of our staff. He and I have had some extremely interesting discussions about the presidential election."

My feet hardly touched the sidewalk as I walked to Lake Street to catch a streetcar. "Boy, are you lucky!" I said to myself. "Talking politics man-to-man with the publisher!" I wondered how many other rookie journalists had been invited to the publisher's home so soon. "Did he invite me because I'm a Negro?" I wondered, then dismissed the question with the thought that when you've faced so many barriers because of race, why not take a special break here and there?

But something profoundly more important to my life than any party at the home of a publisher was happening at that time. I had fallen in love.

CHAPTER SIX

Love and Marriage

JOHN DRYDEN wrote:

> *All human things are subject to decay,*
> *And when fate summons, monarchs must obey.*

A hundred and sixty-six years after Dryden made that brilliant observation, I found fate being exceedingly kind to me.

On a foul late-fall day of 1948 in St. Paul, I peeked out my window and saw that a family was moving into the house next door. I watched for a while as the scraggly, beat-up furniture was carried in and then I went downstairs to urge Mrs. Davis to take a look.

"Lordy," said my landlady, a devout churchgoer who never took the deity's name in vain, "can you believe that he's got to cut some baling wire to open the car door so he can let his wife out?"

"I don't blame him," I said. "The way she looks, I'd wire her in too."

A few days later I read an account in the Negro newspaper, the *Minneapolis Spokesman*, of a speech by a new Urban League official in St. Paul that I considered especially wise and powerful. I decided immediately that I ought to interview this new number-two man, Whitney M. Young, and let readers of the *Afro-American* papers on the East Coast know his views. I could earn another badly needed ten to fifteen dollars with such an article. I telephoned Young, who suggested that I come by his home for an interview.

"Where do you live?"

"At 301 North Avon Street in St. Paul. . . . Do you know? . . ."

"Jesus Christ, you live next door to me! You just moved in, didn't you?"

I walked over, met his wife, Margaret, and realized these were two special human beings. That interview began a long friendship with Young, as I began to play poker with him, his boss, S. Vincent Owens, and a few other prominent young blacks.

Shortly after our first meeting — the last day of December 1948, to be exact — I got off the University Avenue streetcar and walked up Avon Street toward my residence. Just ahead of me leaving the streetcar was a young woman whose winter bundling did not hide her leanness or affect the athletic intensity of her stride. She turned her head just enough to see who was behind her, giving me a glimpse of a cheek that was the color of milk splashed with a dash of chocolate and strawberries.

It was one of those Minnesota days when a cloudless sky and a bright sun lulled walkers into forgetting that it really was colder than a witch's wand in the Klondike. I noticed that the sun gave her long brown hair a reddish glow. Then I wondered whether she was "colored or what," and "where, dear God, is she going?"

She was moving along at a brisker pace than I was accustomed to, so I hastened my steps to what seemed a half trot to keep within the distance of effective observation. As I crossed the street at the corner of the Davises' house, she turned to enter Young's house.

"Lord have mercy!" I mumbled to myself.

I went inside, where Mrs. Davis told me that two sisters on nearby Carroll Street had telephoned to insist that I come and help them welcome in the New Year. I groaned, remembering that the mother of the two girls seemed to be playing matchmaker. She had provoked her older daughter to say to me, "I thought I was what you wanted when you were hanging out at our house all fall. Now I know that it was because we have a TV set and you were really in love with Jackie Robinson and those goddam Brooklyn Dodgers."

"I'm not celebrating tonight," I told Mrs. Davis.

When she went into the kitchen, I dialed Young's house and was immensely relieved when he answered.

"Man, *who* is that *chick?*"

"That's no chick. That's my wife's best friend," he said to his own laughter.

He half whispered that he and Margaret couldn't afford a baby-sitter, and that the young woman I'd seen had volunteered to sit while they went to a New Year's Eve bash.

"She must be one hell of a friend," I said.

"Hell, come meet her and judge for yourself."

I ran upstairs to the bathroom, washed my face, ran the washcloth under each armpit and rubbed on deodorant, slapped a dab of Tuxedo-brand pomade on my hair and brushed like hell, slapped on some shaving lotion, put on a clean shirt — and cursed myself that I'd forgotten to brush my teeth. That done, I strolled to my neighbor's house.

Margaret did the introductions: "This is Vivien Louise Murphy from Buffalo, New York. She's studying public health nursing at the university. Vivien, Carl Rowan is our neighbor and an aspiring journalist at the *Minneapolis Tribune*."

I leaned toward her, hand out to shake, hoping some of my after-shave lotion would waft her way.

"How do you do?" she said, oh so damned cool and proper as to seem curt.

I noticed that she was wearing one of those stylish plaid dresses that I had seen in the window of Peck & Peck. It did not emphasize breasts, hips, or any part of her body. But her face aroused more than enough imagination. The cheekbones and eyes combined to give a slightly Oriental cast, which people would mention for years. I learned that night that the look was the product of Negro, Cherokee, and Caucasian lineage.

"Why'd you leave Buffalo to come to this god-awful climate?" I asked, fumbling for conversation.

"After Buffalo," she said, "there are no bad climates."

Young was noticeably sinking into an urge to play matchmaker.

"Before we go, how about a good, strong toast to the New Year?" he said.

I still rarely drank hard liquor at that time. The trauma of Red-wheels and his rotgut booze, and McMinnville's bootleggers, and my mother and father coming home drunk and then fighting, still held a terrible grip on me. But Young had thrown out a peer-pressure bomb.

"Yeah," I said. "You got a bourbon and ginger ale?"

"Got it," he replied, adding, "And you, Vivien?"

"Nothing, thank you."

"I've even got a bottle of champagne," Young cajoled her.

"*Nothing*, thank you," she repeated as she sat on a stained sofa.

"Goddam, she's strong willed," I thought in an air of disappointment.

Young lifted his eyebrows and winked at me as if to say that he was shifting to Game Plan Two. He put on a record of marvelously romantic music. I took the cue and said, "Would you like to dance?"

After a long pause and a look that I took to be condemnation, she simply stood. And we danced. She flowed so effortlessly with every beat of the music, but never treading on my lead, that I knew this was a woman who had exceptional control of her body.

As the song ended, she said: "You are about the freshest thing I ever met." She didn't mean it as a compliment.

Margaret and Whitney were dressing for their party. I took that moment of privacy to say, "I'm not going anywhere tonight. Could I help you baby-sit?"

"No, thank you."

"I may not be much of a dancer, but I'm great with babies."

"No, thank you."

I got up to leave, pressing my lips against each other so tightly that I knew my face would say, "God, how I wish she had said yes."

As I walked out the door, Vivien Murphy gave me a look that I thought was calculated devilishness and said: "You really *are* the freshest thing I've ever met."

I went to my room and listened alone on my radio to Guy Lombardo ushering in 1949. Every song that I heard that night reminded me of the baby-sitter next door.

"Classy lady," I thought, "but stubborn as a goddammed Tennessee mule."

I awakened on New Year's Day asking myself whether I should telephone her before I prostituted myself and went up to the house on Carroll Street to watch the football bowl games. I got her number at Powell Hall from Margaret, but it took me two days to get the nerve to dial it.

"I wondered if you'd call," she said.

"You knew I'd call," I replied. "Could we go out together?"

"Perhaps. What do you have in mind?"

I did not fully understand at the time how notions of class and caste sink into the psyches of human beings and dictate their social, business, political, and other behaviors. What I knew, from the New Year's Eve conversation, was that Vivien Murphy was not from wealth, but that her daddy was a postal supervisor in Buffalo, which was a long jump above my daddy. Her father and mother had gone to Fisk University. Her older brother was a physician, her older sister a social worker, her younger brother studying dentistry. I wanted to show that even though we came from different Negro worlds, this Navy officer and gentleman from McMinnville had some class, too.

"I have tickets for us to see Judith Anderson's performance in *Medea*," I said.

There was a silence that could have killed a cobra.

Then Viv said, "Oh, *Medea!* Well . . . OK."

"I'll be at Powell Hall at seven P.M. in a taxi," I said.

"No, you won't," she said. "You can't afford a taxi, so we'll take the streetcar."

I paused, then said, "OK." Hanging up, I said to myself, "This is the most practical female in the whole goddammed world!"

Getting ready for that theater date was close to a nightmare. Those suits given to me by the TB hospital doctor were long gone. I had been living hand to mouth on the GI Bill for so long that I didn't have a decent wardrobe. My best outfit was a pair of dark slacks and a corduroy sport jacket. With that I would either wear the grubby parka that had served me in the North Atlantic or my Navy trench coat. I had to wear the trench coat.

I walked into Powell Hall knowing that I was less than elegant. She walked down the stairs and I looked and knew that she was more than lovely.

She told me she was working on an important paper about curare-type drugs. She fascinated me with talk about how the hospitals were saving lives with the very thing Indians put on the tips of arrows to kill people.

"Maybe I could help on your paper," I said. "If you have the facts, I can type the words — and into pretty damn good sentences."

"Sounds great," she said.

Then I told her how I hoped to get off the dead-end assignment on the copydesk and become a real reporter. I felt good that she listened so sympathetically.

Medea was not meant for tired and sleepy students and news-papermen, not even with Judith Anderson in it. Vivien and I sat through an interminable period of neck-snapping nods, bleary-eyed awakenings to such asinine comments as "Isn't she great?"

Finally liberated, we walked out of that Minneapolis theater into seventeen-below-zero temperatures — *plus* a northwest wind that cut through my trench coat as though it were a piece of Viv's hospital gauze.

"Wouldn't you rather take a taxi?" I said.

"No, I'm fine," she said. I thought I could hear her teeth chatter.

We got back to Powell Hall and I moved for a good-night kiss. I got a peck that would have driven a rooster to anger. I didn't know whether the windchill had numbed my lips to the point where I felt nothing, or if my date had put me down.

But I noticed that Viv's greatest urge was to get into a warm room. So she gave me a cool "Good night" and disappeared into the sanctuary of her dormitory.

"Shit," I said to myself. "I've got to walk back to the goddammed streetcar in this brutal weather. How did I let that woman talk me out of taking a taxi?"

I awakened the next morning with my mind saying, "Disaster. Terrible date. Disastrous date. *Medea*? God, how could you do it?"

As has so often been the case in my life, music came to my rescue. A popular song of the day went, "My Darling, My Darling, I've wanted to call you 'My Darling' For many and many a day. . . ."

I waited until I knew Viv was out of the hospital and telephoned Powell Hall. I was relieved when she answered promptly.

I did not even say hello before I began singing: "Medea, Medea, I've wanted to call you 'Medea' For many and many a day. . . ."

She laughed raucously, and with an enthusiasm that surprised me.

"I *may* live long enough to forgive you," she said.

"Would a little down-home barbecue and a movie Saturday night help?"

"Let's try it," she said.

*   *   *

I left the Davises, learning for the first time that I could borrow money, and bought a tiny house in Minneapolis so I could bring my mother, now separated from my father, out of McMinnville and, truth be told, in the hope I could get closer to Viv.

I found it hard to believe, or accept, but this lovely young woman was just as stubborn as I was — and am. She revealed that she was the widow of a fighter pilot who had been sent to Europe months after their marriage and was shot down over Italy. Her first husband never saw the five-year-old daughter, who was in Buffalo with Viv's mother. I figured this had given her some steel and spunk. We found that we could argue over most anything, and after every squabble, days would go by before one of us found a face-saving way to resume communications. I remember one especially nasty quarrel that threatened to break off our relationship forever. I knew that I had been wrong, but didn't want to say it. But how to approach her? Something said to me, "Man, she's the biggest tightwad you ever met. Borrow some money from her and she'll never let you out of her sight."

I called Powell Hall and she answered with a curt, "Yes?"

"I've got a little problem. And even though you're angry at me, I figured you'd be a friend in a time of need."

"What need?"

"I need to borrow ten dollars."

"Of course you can," she said. "When will you come and get it?"

"I'll meet you in twenty minutes at our old place overlooking the Mississippi," I said.

"You what?"

"I'll be there," I said and hung up.

We had a joyful reunion, and, true enough, she never let me out of her sight as long as I owed her that ten dollars.

Then she jolted me. She told me that if she was to get her degree as a public health nurse, she had to do months of fieldwork, and she had decided to do hers in Buffalo, where she could be with daughter Barbara. I tried to talk her out of leaving, but she was just as strong willed on this as on every other issue. So near the end of 1949 she left, and I was sick at heart and terribly lonely.

There must be fifty ways to learn that you are in love. Mine was to realize that, with Viv gone, I didn't care about parties anymore. I was getting my kicks writing letters to, and wishing I could shuffle off to, Buffalo.

I was the writer, the poet, the romanticist. Viv was the very private person, reluctant to say openly or put on paper what was in her heart. So whereas I dropped my heart into my typewriter, she wrote back with a very subdued pen.

"I wonder if she's ever coming back," I asked myself over and over.

"She's never coming back," a young woman from Pittsburgh told me over and over, urging me to believe that she, not Viv, was the woman of my future.

Then, early in 1950, after more than six months' absence, Viv telephoned me to say, "I'll be back next week."

"You're staying with me?"

"No, no. I have my bachelor's, but I owe the hospital some hours of work. I'll be staying at the university."

"Damn!"

I picked her up at the airport and took her to my little house, where I had made spaghetti sauce with a recipe that she uses till this day. My mother made date bars.

As we began to eat that spaghetti dinner, with lettuce and blue-cheese dressing and some garlic bread, I let my lips do what my heart was doing: sing.

"Oh, I haven't seen a crocus or a rosebud, or a robin on the wing, But I feel so gay in a melancholy way that it might as well be spring. . . ."

Viv gave an embarrassed look, as she has every time I've sung over forty years.

There was no proposal that either of us can remember. We just knew that we were going to get married. I realized the sanctity of our commitment when she said to me that, in order to stop riding streetcars, she would go fifty-fifty with me in buying a car.

We got the cheapest stick-shift Ford that we could find, and I was so excited that, even though I had no driver's license, I drove it home. But shifting gears was killing me, because it kept killing the engine when I clutched improperly. Once it stalled where two policemen sat in a car watching school kids cross the street.

"Having trouble?" one cop asked.

My heart was racing a hundred miles a minute, but I kept my cool.

"I seem to have flooded this baby. Could you guys give me a push?"

The policemen swung their cruiser around behind me and gave me a push. When we got to what I thought was enough speed, I threw the gear out of neutral into first, and, just as I remembered from my high school days of watching an uncle drive, the motor started. I rolled off with a wave of thanks, telling myself, "Drive all the way home in first. Don't you dare try to shift gears." I could feel beads of sweat running from my armpits down to my waist.

I got that car to the little house I had bought for my mother.

Viv, who had a driver's license, arrived saying, "My God, you did drive it home. You are one nervy Oscar!"

"Isn't that why you're going to marry me?"

"But you broke the law! Suppose you had gotten caught?"

"Let me tell you how close I came to getting caught." I told her of getting the push from the police.

"You're joking?"

"Hell, no!"

I told her that I wanted her to drive me to a special place — Twenty-ninth and Portland. I instructed her to park the car on Twenty-ninth alongside the Milwaukee Railroad tracks (Portland was a very busy one-way street).

"What's going on?" she demanded.

"I want you to approve the first residence of Mr. and Mrs. Carl T. Rowan." (My mother had other relatives coming to her house, and we wanted to live alone.)

We went up to inspect the one-bedroom second-floor apartment, and, as I expected, she asked, "How much?"

"Seventy dollars a month."

"Well, not bad," she said as I thought, "Lord, please don't let a train come by now!"

I talked her into spending half that night watching me practice driving on the more-or-less empty streets, even though I didn't even have a beginner's license. The next day she drove me to St. Paul to take the driver's test, the written part of which I passed handsomely, but the driving part of which I failed. I had a wee bit of trouble with parallel parking.

Undaunted, I hit the streets again that night, and parked and parked until the next morning. Two days later I got my license.

A couple of Friday nights later we went to a party that lasted until about 2:00 A.M. I had had a few bourbons by this time and bravely suggested that she go to the apartment with me instead of to Powell Hall.

"No," she said. "That wouldn't look right, and it wouldn't be right. My roommate and all my friends at the hospital would know that I didn't come home, so I must have spent the night with you."

"So you care more about your damned friends than you do about me?"

"No, sweetie," she said. "But you've got a reputation to protect, and I've got a reputation to protect. So why risk our reputations for a few moments of passion?"

I was in a high dudgeon, although I knew in my heart that she was right. I drove her to Powell Hall and didn't linger for any one-foot-on-the-floor kisses. When I got to the apartment I didn't look for any safe parking place on Twenty-ninth. I put that darling little Ford right in front of the duplex and rushed upstairs and fell asleep.

About four hours later I was awakened by a thud and stepped out of bed in my birthday suit as I heard my landlady shouting, "Mr. Rowan! Mr. Rowan! They hit your car!"

It seemed to take forever for me to find my trousers, jump into them, and run downstairs. I stepped out to see a guy in a Hudson, front end smashed in like an accordion, gunning his motor, trying to make a fast getaway. My poor car was so crunched it looked as though the rear bumper were part of the steering wheel.

I ran to the Hudson and said, "Hold it, buddy. I've got your license number. So get your ass out — *now!*"

The guy was so drunk he couldn't find the door handle. I asked my landlady to call the police.

When the cops had collected all the data they needed, I went in to call Viv and tell her that "A goddammed drunk just totaled *our* car." Then, still acting like the rejected lover, I threw in a cheap shot. "If you'd come with me like I asked, the goddammed car wouldn't have been parked on Portland."

"Now that's unfair, and I know that the man I'm about to marry is not that unfair."

"I'm not," I said. "Please forgive me — and get over here right away to look at this heap of junk."

"Never again a stick shift," I said. We went back to the Ford dealer with our insurance money and bought an outrageous job called Crestliner by Ford, and the bumblebee by us — because it was black with chartreuse side panels.

Viv wanted me to meet her family, and I wanted to show off the new car. So we fried some chicken, boiled some eggs, and packed a loaf of bread, then jumped into the car and drove 1,010 miles to Buffalo, stopping only when we needed gas. And that was when there were no interstate highways!

I was tired as a dog when we rolled up to 50 Lyth Avenue, her parents' modest house in which they had lived for almost three decades. But I wouldn't admit that the long drive had tuckered me out.

"Oh, it was nothing," I boasted to her father, Benjamin Franklin Murphy, who was called Pat by everyone. "We could do another thousand miles if we had to," I boasted to Barbara.

I quickly sensed that Viv's mother was an extraordinarily strong person, as she made it clear that Pat Murphy always turned his paycheck over to her, and she doled out whatever spending money she thought the family could afford. Viv had told me that in all his life her daddy had never had more than one decent suit of clothes at a time.

Call it a matriarchal black family, but that was how this black woman from South Carolina and black man from Alabama nursed a trifling amount of money in such a way as to send all their children to college and postgraduate study, producing a family of honor and pride.

Our second day in Buffalo, I really got a chance to talk to Viv's father. He paid me the high honor of breaking out one of his bottles of homemade peach wine. Each of us bearing a brimming glass, we went to the swing on the front porch. He talked a bit about what a struggle it was for any black to get a decent job, and especially a promotion, in any part of the Postal Service. He counted himself a lucky man to be a railway postal supervisor.

"I'm gonna take real good care of your daughter, sir," I said. "When we get married next month I'll be making eighty dollars a week."

I knew that that was more than he was earning after a lifetime of work, and I hoped it would impress him that Viv had chosen someone who would never let her miss a meal.

We went back to Minneapolis to clean up her obligations to the University of Minnesota Hospital and to get me ensconced in my new job as a reporter instead of a headline writer. We decided that we would go back to Buffalo to be married in her childhood church on August 2, 1950.

Again we did the 1,010 miles nonstop, except for pauses at filling stations. Over what I don't recall, but we got into a big argument the day before the wedding. I was unrelenting and she was unyielding.

"How can we get married while fussing like this?" she asked.

"I guess we can't. Hell, I'll just drive back to Minneapolis."

She walked up real close, smiled, then asked: "Sweetie, are you taking my half of the car, too?"

"Damn," I said with a smile, "we never did agree as to who has the half with the motor."

We kissed passionately, and the wedding was on.

We said our vows, then, with Barbara, took a honeymoon boat trip across Lake Erie and proceeded to Minneapolis, where we moved into that Portland Avenue apartment that was furnished only with a bed.

Two days later we took delivery of our second piece of furniture, a Zenith combination television set, radio, and Cobra record player. That was 1950s state of the art. I shall never forget the two delivery-men looking around as they brought this $650 entertainment center into an apartment bearing absolutely nothing but a bed.

Viv got a job at Minneapolis General Hospital, across the street from the *Tribune*, making about the same amount of money that I did and working much the same hours. So at eleven o'clock each night we would meet, go to the apartment, sit in the chairs I had bought at an "estate" sale and refurbished, and eat smoked cheese and crackers while we watched whatever fare was on the tube.

We decided straight out that I didn't have "my money" and she didn't have "her money." She didn't have "her mail" and I didn't have "my mail." Every paycheck went into a pool to meet our obligations, which were many and at times overwhelming. Whoever picked up the mail opened and read everything. There were no secrets — a rule that has prevailed for more than forty years. I had no great career decisions to make, nor did she, but we made it a point, while riding home after work, to talk to each other about the problems of the day, the angers and anxieties, the special new hopes.

I had long before come to understand that what I first called pigheadedness and prudery in Viv was really integrity, class, and, most of all, character. I just knew that whether an assignment took me to Duluth or Damascus, I never had to worry about what my wife was doing.

I learned over the years that no man does better than to marry a woman whose advice he respects and, most of all, whom he trusts beyond any doubt. I accepted a lot of pigheadedness to get a lot of wisdom and character, and this has made me a very, very lucky man.

CHAPTER SEVEN

The Reporter

W HAT SHOULD BE the role of a black reporter in this Minneapolis environment?" I asked myself. I had set my heart and mind against ever becoming anyone's "black reporter" of "black events."

When Bill Steven raised questions about the breadth of my reportorial assignments, I said, "Let's make a deal: You will not assign me to any story simply because I'm a Negro; you will never deny me an assignment simply because I'm a Negro."

"You've got a deal," said Steven, now the executive editor.

But that did not end my anguish. I could have gone through the small but mostly sophisticated community of the Twin Cities boasting, "I'm the equal of the white reporters; I only write about white issues!" But I never got caught up in that absurdity. I knew that for all I might bring to "white" and international issues, I also wanted to contribute to whites' and blacks' understanding of the racial and social issues of the early 1950s. Many state legislatures were grappling with demands for fair employment laws. Blacks were trying to get into all-white colleges. A war was rising against Jim Crow in restaurants, theaters, streetcars — even cemeteries. Campaigns were raging to give black people meaningful suffrage.

I said to myself: "Your determination not to become a token Negro reporter must not deter you from telling decent, thoughtful Americans some truths that only you can tell them."

In 1950 no more than five blacks could claim to be general-assignment reporters, and few were writing anything serious about the American social, political, or economic scene. A sensitive editor in Pittsburgh had wondered what life must be like for a Negro in the segregated South, but he had no black reporter to go tell him; so he had a white reporter named Ray Sprigle stain himself with juice from the husks of walnuts and go to the South pretending to be a Negro.

"There has never been a white man created by God who can go feel, sense, understand, what happens to a real Negro in the South," I said, furious at my profession.

"What is your responsibility as a new, professionally trained journalist on one of the best newspapers in America?" I asked myself many times as I wrestled with my precondition that I not become "just a Negro reporter."

"You can still be 'just a reporter' and help change America," I said to myself. "You don't have to become a raving advocate; all you have to do is tell the American people some truths that they do not know, explain some things that they clearly do not understand, and you can fulfill every journalistic obligation that burdens any reporter of any race."

That is not as difficult a posture as it may seem at first reading. Remember that Minnesota was the possible home of every bigot in Laura Z. Hobson's *Gentleman's Agreement*, that classic book and movie about anti-Semitism. Minneapolis had been declared the capital of anti-Semitism in America. What's more, Minnesota was the site of egregious discrimination against American Indians.

But who was I to think I could "enlighten" the relatively rich, well-informed people of Minnesota, the people renowned for electing "great politicians"? I might never have tried but for the mistake of a secretary who handled reportorial assignments. I showed up for work and found no assignment in my box.

"Damn, I didn't know you were working today."

"No problem," I said, "unless you think I'm going home. I'm going to the morgue [the *Tribune*'s library] to do research on a good story."

I went to the morgue, but why was I there? I flicked through the latest unfiled clippings and saw story after story of racial violence in the South, of racial conflict in the Congress . . . and then it hit me! The request from V-12 buddy Noah Brannon! Why not spend the next six hours doing research on what it means to be black in postwar America?

I then wrote what I thought was a hell of a proposal. But would my racially protected city editor, Bower Hawthorne, or my Scandinavian white managing editor, Paul Swensson, or Executive Editor Steven grasp the importance?

The night of that memo, at 11:00 P.M., I met Viv at the hospital and said: "You cannot believe how audacious your husband was today."

"God, what did you do now?" — a question she would learn to ask hundreds of times.

"I suggested that they pay for me to tour the South and write a series of articles about what it means to be a Negro in the postwar South."

"You're pulling my leg."

"Not till we get home."

We got to our apartment, and, as we walked in, I handed her a copy of my memo.

"Read this while I get out the smoked cheese and crackers. And I'm celebrating my bravery with a beer."

I came out with a platter of cheese and saltines to hear Viv say, "Sounds like a great idea to me."

"Yeah, but you're not a white editor or publisher."

We sat up past 1:00 A.M. watching TV and downing that smoked cheese that we loved so much. I complained a couple of times that it was fattening me up, while nothing stuck to Viv's lean, athletic frame.

"You eat two Snickers and don't gain an ounce; I throw your wrappers away and gain two pounds."

And we talked about what I could write that would be shocking to Minnesotans.

"It's shocking to me, too," said Viv. "You forget that since my parents took me out of Texarkana, Arkansas, as a baby I haven't been back to the South."

"Come on, you went to Fisk in Nashville for a while. That's South."

"Not if you never left the campus."

"OK," I said, "tell me anything. I'll call this series 'The Education of My Sheltered Wife.' "

"Do you really think they'll send you?"

"Hell no."

*　　　*　　　*

I was especially punctual going to work the following day, arriving ten minutes before my scheduled time of 2:00 P.M. To my astonishment, Managing Editor Swensson was waiting at the elevator.

"I thought you'd never get here," he said.

"I'm not late," I said, looking fearfully at my watch.

"No, you're not late. I just couldn't wait to tell you that your memo has been approved. We all think you've proposed one helluva piece of journalism."

"Jee-sus Christ . . . er, I mean that's wonderful," I said.

"As soon as you get your coat off and are ready, come over and let's talk about where you want to go, an expense advance, and that sort of stuff," Swensson said.

"I'll be ready in a few minutes," I said, "but could I just go back out for a few minutes to check something?"

"Of course," said my smiling editor.

I rushed across the street to the hospital where Viv worked.

"What's up?" she inquired.

Ever the musician-comedian, I burst into song: "I'm Alabammy bound . . . !" Disbelief filled her face, and I said, "They've approved my trip to the South."

She gave me a big hug and a kiss, then I ran down the corridor and to the meeting at which I explained how I was going to change the face of American journalism.

Call it fate, God, or what you will, but someone somewhere had smiled upon me professionally, just as it or He had watched over me during those ugly days when I stayed only a step or two ahead of the people in Tennessee who dragged young blacks off to reform school.

But, to be truthful, I had ceased to believe totally in fates and gods. Miss Bessie had riveted into my mind words from Sallust's speech to Caesar: "Every man is the architect of his own fortune. . . ."

So I left Minneapolis feeling lucky to have an assignment that opened horizons far beyond the obituaries, the no-consequence stories, that I had been writing. I remembered how everyone thought it was a milestone for me to be assigned to the opening of a new Cadillac dealership, highlighting speeches by a big honcho, a vice president, from General Motors in Detroit.

At one point I asked the GM vice president if he would agree to an interview, and he accepted with pleasant enthusiasm. We sat on a zebra-striped sofa, and I was in the midst of my first question, when a black waiter leaned over to whisper to me: "You can't sit there."

"What the hell are you saying?" I whispered back in about two thousand decibels.

"We aren't supposed to sit down," he said.

"We who?"

"Aren't you one of the help?" he asked.

I got a lot of laughter from my reportorial colleagues by telling them of the perils of being a Negro reporter. I still believe today that this emboldened them, helped them to forget race in handing out assignments.

Now here I was going on a costly assignment that did involve racial issues that I hoped would touch the hearts and minds of the millions who read the *Tribune*. I left town knowing that while fate may have smiled upon me, I was the one who had to survive travel into my native Tennessee; into a brutally racist city, Birmingham, Alabama; into Gene Talmadge's Georgia; into a troubled New Orleans and a violent Monroe in Louisiana; and into a Southwest smoldering under the passions of legal assaults upon segregation in universities and other public facilities.

We gave this series of articles the provocative title "How Far From Slavery?" I knew that my mission was dangerous, but I realized also that if I faced those dangers bravely and reported events honestly, I could indeed be the architect of my own journalistic destiny.

So in January of 1951 I flew into Louisville. My blood began to boil when I went to the airport candy stand. One white soldier was there when I arrived. The attendant waited on him. Other whites arrived, so she passed me going up the counter to wait on them. Then she passed me going down the counter to wait on others. This was the old protocol system: blacks didn't get served until all whites had been served.

"Damned if I'll leave any money here," I mumbled and walked away.

I took a plane to Nashville, seventy-two miles from my hometown, remembering that I had not been at that airport since 1945, when there were no outward signs of racial segregation. So few blacks were flying out of Nashville in 1945 that officials didn't think about it. I was shocked in 1951 to see signs on two airport chairs proclaiming: FOR COLORED PASSENGERS ONLY. I was even more shocked to see four airport toilets marked WHITE MEN, COLORED MEN, then WHITE LADIES, and the last inviting COLORED WOMEN.

Back in my hometown, I learned of "progress": the town now had a clinic, and doctors operated on colored people there. One of my classmates had recently had an emergency appendectomy. But, operation performed, an ambulance had delivered her to her home. There were no overnight accommodations for blacks.

But more recently two blacks had died in the basement of the clinic while waiting for transportation home, so the clinic had designated a bed in a corner on the first floor for emergency Negro patients.

I wrote about these things with journalistic restraint, aware that neither whites nor blacks in McMinnville knew nor cared about journalistic ethics. Many whites and blacks resented my writing about things that embarrassed their town.

I just presumed it was a white person who wrote to me: "Come home again, nigger, and we'll have a delegation out to meet you, and it won't be no brass band."

I traveled six thousand miles in six weeks, looking at my hometown; at then all-white Crossville, Tennessee, where I saw a sign hanging from a tree at the city limits saying NIGGER, DON'T LET THE SUN SET ON YOU HERE; at Milledgeville and Macon, Georgia; at Birmingham; at Oklahoma, Texas, and other places where college segregation was being challenged. I put my life at risk many times, but I remember most poignantly facing peril simply by trying to spend a nickel for a newspaper.

In Miami, I had literally forced the agent for the Florida East Coast line to give me what the *Minneapolis Tribune* had reserved for me: seat 37, car 4, on the New Royal Palm. When the agent tried subtly to switch me to Jim Crow car 1, I raised a stink and won. So by the time I got to Macon I was feeling my oats.

As I approached the "colored" waiting room, a sleepy-eyed Negro said, "Taxi?"

"As soon as I get my bags."

"Where y'all goin'?"

"To Milledgeville. You can take me to the bus station?"

"I'll take you to Milledgeville — for fifteen dollars."

"Man, fifteen dollars is a lot of money," I said.

"OK, ten dollars?"

"No, thanks."

"OK, I won't even make breakfast money, but I'll make the trip for seven dollars and a half."

"I'll talk to you as soon as I buy a morning paper," I said, noticing that no papers were for sale in the waiting room for blacks. I walked into the "whites only" waiting room, picked up a paper, and held out a nickel for the female vendor.

Suddenly I heard a booming voice: "Boy, this ain't the colored waiting room!"

I looked over my shoulder and saw the stationmaster walking toward me.

"I know," I said, trying to sound cool and casual.

"Well, what the hell are you doing in here?"

"As you can see, I'm buying a newspaper." I again offered my nickel to the female vendor.

"Don't take his money," the stationmaster ordered.

The woman clenched her outstretched hand and shouted at me, "No, no, no. You've got no business in here."

I stepped toward the stationmaster to say, "According to your separate-but-equal theory, I should be able to buy anything in there that I can buy in here. There are no papers in the colored waiting room."

"Well, you'll have to go back in there and let the redcap come and buy you a paper," he said.

"He's darker than I am, and I've got the nickel. What's the logic there?" I demanded.

"He's in uniform."

"In uniform? Suppose I were in the uniform of the United States Navy?"

"You'd still have to go where niggers belong," he said, showing irritation that I dared to challenge his authority.

I swallowed hard at his use of the word "niggers," but retained enough composure to ask him: "If your segregation system or democracy had to fall, which would you uphold?"

"Goddammit, I just follow orders," he said, staring at the expensive camera hanging about my neck. "You ain't in New York," he snapped. "You're just another black nigger in Georgia."

Suddenly the rebuffs and humiliations of three weeks in the Deep South began to take their toll. I stepped into the stationmaster's face and said, "Only a low, un-American creature would 'just follow orders' which he is unable to explain to his own conscience."

The enraged stationmaster said, "I'll take care of you," and ran for what I figured was a gun or a telephone, either of which could have been lethal. "Follow him and see where he goes!" the stationmaster shouted to a redcap.

I told myself, "If he is calling policemen, I'll probably get beaten. If he is calling civilians, I may be in for worse."

I rushed over to the black taxi driver. "Buddy," I said, "you just made a quick seven dollars and a half." I said for all to hear, "*Take me to the bus station.*" Then I whispered, "But let me out in Milledgeville."

We jumped into his old Ford and he drove off toward the bus station with a Negro redcap running after us, trying to obey his boss. The driver soon lost the redcap, then made a couple of turns, and hit the open highway.

I looked back and was relieved that no police car was following us. Then I almost shouted to myself, above the rattle of the taxicab, "Georgia still is just a police state. And every white man is a policeman."

Even Macon did not prepare me for what I would find in Birmingham.

I remember peering into restaurants where my entry would have brought my arrest and noting that the waiters, waitresses, busboys, cooks, and dishwashers were all black. I got to the cook at one place, and she said: "Ain't it silly. I make the biscuits with my black hands. Colored waitresses drag their sleeves in the gravy and stick their fingers in the coffee. That's just mellow fine. But any one of us is too dirty or too something to sit in there and eat."

I was astonished one day to look up and see a sign on the building housing the Imperial Laundry: WE WASH WHITE FOLKS' CLOTHES ONLY. The only people washing and ironing clothes in that laundry were Negroes.

"Why do you work in a joint like this?" I asked one of the workers.

"Shucks, the joke's on the owner," the perspiring washerwoman replied. "They do wash *some* Negroes' clothes here, 'cause mine is in one of the tubs there."

My journey to Washington, D.C., brought an assortment of rebuffs and attempted insults, some of which were laughable. I went to a five-and-ten-cent store where, a black Washingtonian assured me, colored people were served. I sat at the counter and ordered two doughnuts and a glass of milk.

"Colored can't sit down," the waitress said, to my astonishment.

I knew exactly what she meant but pretended that she was telling me that colored people had pains in their derrieres.

She took that to mean that I was saying I was not colored.

"Do you have your foreign credentials?" she asked.

"What you ask," I said angrily, "is whether I am an American citizen or a foreigner. I am an American."

"Well, I am sorry, sir," she said apologetically, "but we are told that American Negroes must eat standing, or they are not to be served."

I gripped the edge of the counter so hard that beads of cold perspiration broke out on my arms and hands.

"Do you mean to tell me that in the nation's capital . . ." I began, then fell into silence. Why should I scold this waitress? Why berate a young woman who didn't set up the system and had no power to change it?

"I've lost my appetite," I said, and left that five-and-ten.

My eighteen articles on the South, printed in the *Minneapolis Tribune* in February and March of 1951, became a journalistic sensation. It would be years before I understood the real reason why. Sophisticated white people who bought books had read Richard Wright's *Native Son* and *Black Boy*; they had read Harriet Beecher Stowe's *Uncle Tom's Cabin* and Lillian Smith's *Strange Fruit*. But ordinary white newspaper readers had never read anything like my narrative of a six-week journey into the land of Jim Crow.

Time magazine called my articles "a perceptive, well-written series on segregation and prejudice in the South as only a Negro could know them." *Editor & Publisher* called the series "a significant, readable glimpse into the American race problem as only a Negro sees it." The *Minneapolis Spokesman* said, "Articles like 'How Far From Slavery?' make a contribution to helping make America free in truth as well as theory."

I savored the thought that I had broken new ground.

As I have said, one of the most important things that I learned during my early days at the *Minneapolis Tribune* was that I would have a bleak future as a journalist if I did not move in the same social and other circles as my fellow staff members. The hard psychological barrier to cross involved inviting editors and other bosses to our first house, a three-bedroom, one-bath (plus a toilet in the basement), brick and stucco place on a corner lot in a neat, previously all-white neighborhood. It cost $12,500. Viv and I were thrilled when I had the basement finished off to a rec room and we turned that naked toilet into a half bath. She said that all her years growing up in Buffalo she had always dreamed of the day when she would have more than one bath.

Now, I said, the time had come for me to invite some editors for dinner. The executive editor, Bill Steven, and wife, Lucy, had invited us to their home many times. So had Gretchen and Bill Elston, the editorial page editor. I knew that social reciprocity was extremely important. I had sensed that most of the great career decisions were not made in the office, but over drinks, lunch, dinner. So Viv and I did our social and professional duties. We invited the Stevens and the Elstons to "dinner at eight."

"What shall we serve?" asked Viv.

"What you cook when we really splurge."

I was referring to Viv's occasionally buying filet of beef, cutting it into bite-sized pieces, seasoning it with salt, pepper, garlic, and butter, and then browning it delicately under the broiler. Then she would take the juices from the meat and add tomato sauce and other seasonings. Just before going to the table she would put the beef in this sauce and heat it to tender perfection. This, served over a bed of rice, with a crisp green salad and French bread, was heavenly.

"How much beef should I buy?" Viv asked.

"Four pounds," I said.

"Two pounds," she said.

In more than forty years of marriage, I have always been the overdoer, the overbuyer, the overeater, the overdrinker, the overspender, and Viv the conservative opposite. Some men are terrified to know that their wives are at large with credit cards. I am constantly chastising my wife for going shopping for three hours and spending perhaps ten dollars.

I had no doubt that she would come home with two pounds of filet.

That venture into entertaining the bosses started out as a comedy of errors. At 7:00 P.M. I was in our one bathtub. Viv was in fading green pedal pushers, dashing about frantically, trying to ensure that no dust showed on the lamps, the silverware was placed properly, the china that we had gotten as a wedding gift was gleaming. Then the doorbell rang.

"God, who could that be?" I heard Viv say.

She opened the door and I recognized Gretchen's voice saying, "Hello, Vivien, so nice of you to invite us."

Now some white people may have some strange ideas about what black people wear when they entertain, but Gretchen and Bill knew that Vivien Rowan would not preside over a dinner party in faded pedal pushers.

"Did we come on the wrong night?" I heard Bill ask.

"No, this is the night," said Viv. "Please come in."

"We're early?" asked Gretchen.

"Only an hour, so please come in and be comfortable. Carl will be down shortly, then I'll get dressed."

By this time I had leaped out of that bathtub and, water dripping from me, begun to shave frantically.

"Goddammit," I mumbled as blood oozed from a sliced part of my chin. I didn't even know about styptic pencils then, so I tried to stanch the red flow by pasting on a dab of toilet paper.

I dressed in record time and rushed down to play host while Viv rushed up to try to beat my record at bathing and dressing.

When Viv came down the steps in a sleek black dress, pearls on her neck and ears, she looked stunning. I was so proud. I figured she could serve those editors sardines, or ham sandwiches, and they would extol the cuisine.

Dick and Jeanne Fox, our closest friends, and another black couple arrived. The scotch, gin, bourbon, flowed freely, and in turn the conversations, with just enough challenges and disagreements about the issues of the day to keep everyone's blood pressure from dropping. Then, having become ravenous, I gave Viv a couple of those for-God's-sake-when-do-we-eat looks, which she returned with one of her you're-drinking-and-hah-hahing looks. After what seemed to me an eternity, she said, "Dinner is served."

Lucy Steven took her position at the head of the buffet line without prodding. I looked at her heaping plate and thought, "Lucy is a good drinker, and that redhead can eat, too." Gretchen's and Bill's plates indicated that they weren't counting calories. I, the proper host, was waiting to go through the buffet line last.

I piled rice on my plate, almost drooling in hunger, then got to the pot with the beef filet and the tomato sauce. I saw one tiny piece of beef swimming in the sauce. I jerked my head toward Viv in that crude way in which spouses say, "Come quick." She walked near and I said, "Put the rest of the beef in here."

"That's all the beef," she said.

"What?"

"I'm sorry, honey, but that's all the beef."

"Jeee-sus Christ," I whispered. "Grab some hot dogs and cut 'em up and put 'em in here."

Fiercely proud, in or out of social crisis, Viv said: "I will not put any hot dogs in there."

I put that one piece of beef and a lot of liquid on my rice, covered it with a huge helping of salad and bread, and sat watching my guests eat with gusto.

Lucy cleaned her plate first. "Absolutely delicious, Vivien," she said as she got up for another pass at the buffet. I watched uneasily as she plopped rice on her plate and then got to the beef container. She stirred the spoon around a couple of times, then said to Viv: "This is absolutely the most delicious sauce I've ever eaten." Then she drowned the rice in tomato sauce and returned to clean her plate with enthusiasm.

When the last guest left I, with great tact, said to Viv: "I'm hungry. Could I have a hot dog?" Her eyes told me that she thought it a cruel joke.

"I'm sorry, sweetie," I said. "It was a beautiful party. Everybody got to know everybody better, and important professional friendships were made here tonight. Thank you." I kissed her, then said, "But I've never heard anything funnier in my life than Lucy Steven, stirring that empty pot and telling you that you make the best sauce she ever tasted."

A look of acute embarrassment filled Viv's eyes, then her cheeks puckered into a smile, then we both laughed wildly. These many years later I am still saying "four pounds," and she is saying "two pounds," and we are still laughing.

Many things transcend race — love, sex, yearnings for financial success, the desire to survive on a battlefield. I learned beyond doubt that people who have drunk, eaten, joked, argued, with each other have also sized up intellects, levels of integrity, human worth. No aspiring journalist, black or otherwise, can ignore this rule of life.

Every now and then I poke Viv in the tummy and say, "Have you ever thought about how far I might have gone if you'd bought *four* pounds of filet?"

CHAPTER EIGHT

I Am Honored

NOTHING SUCCEEDS like success. Them as has, gets; them as has not, begets. Success feeds on itself. Winners just know how to win.

Clichés, yes, but I learned in the wake of my 1951 trip across the South that they also are truisms of life in every place and time. The success of my articles "How Far From Slavery?" set in motion a string of events that would affect my life forever.

First of all, it meant that my publisher and editors would never again hesitate to give me any assignment. They knew that cub reporters rarely got written up in *Time* magazine after their first major assignment and that renowned publishers didn't often fly to distant cities to offer book contracts to rookie newsmen. The top brass at the *Tribune* celebrated with me when the Minneapolis Junior Chamber of Commerce (the Jaycees) cited me for "service to humanity" for writing the articles — and when Minnesota Supreme Court Justice Leroy E. Matson wrote that I had "performed an outstanding piece of public service for which we can all be grateful."

"Things can't get any better," I said to Viv, but they did. The Sidney Hillman Foundation gave me its award for "the best newspaper reporting in the nation in 1951" — plus a check for five hundred dollars, which equaled six weeks of my salary! The curators of Lincoln University, in Jefferson City, Missouri, cited me for "high purpose, high achievement, and exemplary practice in the field of journalism." And then the almost totally white Minneapolis Junior Chamber of Commerce named me Minneapolis's Outstanding Young Man of 1951!

Viv must have sensed my head swelling with each honor, because just prior to the Jaycees' awards banquet she volunteered some advice. First, she said, "That old green monster, jealousy, lurks in every newsroom. Start acting like a celebrity and other reporters, and more editors than you think, will be out to cut you off at the legs." Second, she said, "Take seriously that sign in the *Tribune* morgue that says NOTHING WILTS FASTER THAN LAURELS THAT HAVE BEEN RESTED UPON."

I got her message, and at the Jaycees' awards dinner gave emotional but honest praise to John Cowles and the editors who had believed in me enough to send me across the South and print my articles.

Rest on laurels? I was awaiting the publication of my book *South of Freedom* with almost the same nervous passion that I had felt awaiting the birth of our first son, Carl Jr. A lot of nice things happened before publication, including the Book Find Club's selection of my volume as its book of the month.

But my agent had told me that the book review section of the Sunday *New York Times* was what mattered above all else. Being reviewed there said "healthy baby," and not being reviewed meant "stillborn."

The *New York Times* of August 3, 1952, was a bitter disappointment for me when I saw the name of my reviewer, Hodding Carter, a white Mississippi editor and publisher whom I had criticized severely in the book. And already searing my mind was the headline THE BITTER SEARCH FOR FIRST-CLASS CITIZENSHIP, a warning that either Carter, or whites at the *New York Times*, were slapping the "bitter black man" label on me, which they so often did to a Negro who didn't tap-dance and say, "Yassuh, boss."

Depression set in immediately when Carter objected to the title of my book:

Because of his or his publisher's provocative choice of title I approached with some hostility this angry account of a native's return to his Southern homeland. I was not hostile when I had finished it, only depressed by a vivid reminder that changes which a white Southerner thinks are swift seem snail-like and indecisive to a Southerner who is not white and who suffers from color barriers.

Hodding Carter had read in my book that I considered him and other white gradualists to be almost as much the enemy as Senator James Eastland of Mississippi and the other avowed racists. The *New York Times* could not understand that Carter could not write an unbiased review of my book; and I, till a generation later, could not understand that the *Times* and Carter had done damn well by me and my book, considering the mean climate in America.

The fact that the *Times* ran a notable painting of an aspiring black couple with that review did not ease the outrage of a young black author who read Carter's comment that

> The average white Southerner, and most white observers from the outside, believe that racially, things are moving very fast in the South, indeed. The average Southern Negro of middle age and older would likely agree. But Carl Rowan is no longer Southern, save that he grew to young manhood in Tennessee, nor middle-aged, nor white, nor average. He resents second-class citizenship and his protest is moving and sincere.

Had I been older, or more mature, I might have read those words as indication that a proud, relatively old white man in Mississippi was caught in a war between his heart and mind and the realities of publishing a paper in one of the most benighted states in the Union. But I was not old, or truly mature, so I went to bed that Sunday night in August of '52 thinking how Hodding Carter's last description of my book was that it was a "bitter report of a loyal and perhaps unquietly desperate American, who will not find in his lifetime full acceptance as a first-class citizen everywhere in his country."

"Like hell, I won't," I said to myself. Then I tossed and turned, and finally fell asleep.

Soon I sensed that some laurels might be wilting around the edges. So I surveyed the American scene, looking for issues and areas where my reporting might make a difference. One of the most emotional issues in the land was the segregation of schools from Texas and Kansas to the nation's capital, Maryland, and Delaware. The NAACP was on a roll in forcing universities to admit Negroes to law schools, and it was filing suits in many more places to attack public school segregation — part of a larger plan to overturn the 1896 Supreme Court decision (*Plessy* v. *Ferguson*) that declared "separate but equal" permissible under the Constitution.

"This is going to be the story of the decade," I told Bill Steven, "but most Americans don't know a damn thing about the lawsuits, the issues, the constitutional questions. We have an obligation to enlighten people."

Steven smiled at my brashness, and said, "Well, goddammit, let's enlighten them."

So off I went to Topeka, Kansas, to Prince Edward County, Virginia, to Wilmington, Delaware, to Clarendon County, South Carolina, and to Washington, D.C., the five areas lumped together in a Supreme Court challenge the world now knows as *Brown* v. *Board of Education*.

In 1953, however, the South was an immensely more dangerous place than when I took that 1951 journey. You cannot possibly understand what I was riding into unless you understand the depth of the fealty to white supremacy that undergirded Jim Crow in so many areas of life. Racial separatism in schools, as in buses, churches, theaters, housing, had little to do with education, and almost everything to do with the determination of the white power structure to maintain supremacy. Above all, it was an emotional maneuver to ensure that social equality never came about in this country.

I headed south again, knowing that even black civil rights leaders had long been in a quandary over the issue of social equality, especially because any discussion of it always deteriorated into an argument about intermarriage and racial purity. *Mongrelization* was the feared word in the Deep South. *Miscegenation* was the polite word in the North and West. Whatever you called it, at the time I left on that 1953 assignment, almost two-thirds of the states had laws forbidding cohabitation, sexual intercourse, or marriage between whites and Negroes, and in some states between whites and Native Americans, Chinese, Japanese, Malaysians, Mongolians, and any other person of color.

Even California, Colorado, Michigan, and eleven other northern and western states had miscegenation statutes — laws that their citizens moved to abolish during the atmosphere of wartime unity.

But in seventeen southern states nothing was adhered to more passionately than laws designed to "maintain the purity of the white race and the Negro race."

My home state, Tennessee, had a constitution forbidding "the intermarriage of white persons with negroes, mulattos, or persons of mixed blood, descended from a negro to the third generation," and the Tennessee legislature had set a penalty of imprisonment in the penitentiary of "not less than one (1) nor more than five (5) years" for anyone knowingly violating the antimiscegenation law.

Kentucky had a "broader" law that said: "Marriage is prohibited and void: 1. With an idiot or lunatic; 2. Between a white person and a Negro or mulatto. . . ."

Georgia law prohibited white persons from marrying anyone except other white persons, defined as "persons of the white or caucasian race, who have no ascertainable trace of either Negro, African, West Indian, Asiatic Indian, Mongolian, Japanese or Chinese blood in their veins."

Louisiana declared that "children of a negress by a white man cannot be legitimated by marriage" and said that "Whomever [*sic*] commits the crime of miscegenation shall be imprisoned with or without hard labor, for not more than five years."

Every lynching reminded every black man that sexual intercourse with a white woman was not the threshold of peril, for even a smile, a whistle, a suggestive word, could produce a mob of white men bent on killing.

Evidence abounded that even in the most "liberal" white circles of the North, glands ruled brains on this issue. So as a matter of strategy, many black leaders and white supporters of black equality tried to downplay the issue of interracial social contact, sexual activity, and marriage.

But the fundamental issues were a long way short of marriage. Wags referring to the school issue would say of two five-year-olds: "He doesn't want to sleep with her — just sit in the same class."

Then there was the question of housing, of blacks trying to move into white neighborhoods. Didn't most guys want to marry the girl next door?

It bothered me that the American media were not dealing with any of these issues in an honest, sophisticated way. An article or two would appear about the alleged number of blacks who were passing as whites. Regularly there was a spate of articles about some so-called authority who claimed that he could prove the intellectual inferiority of blacks. Some newsroom psychologist would pen a piece about how the children of a mixed marriage were rejected by both the black and the white communities. Hollywood dared to touch the subject in only the most sensational, venal, and often cowardly way. In 1912, Pathé produced a film called *The Debt*, about the tragedy of interracial love. The next year Kalem released *The Octoroon*, about the tragedy of whites with Negro blood. In 1915 D. W. Griffith starred Lillian Gish, Wallace Reid, Mae Marsh, and other early Hollywood celebrities in a movie that was to have a profound effect on American race relations over the generations. His *Birth of a Nation* portrayed black men of the Reconstruction years after the Civil War as brutal and corrupt defilers of white women.

When I was ten years old, in 1935, every black in McMinnville was caught up in the sensation of *Imitation of Life*, a Universal movie starring Claudette Colbert, Warren William, Louise Beavers, and Fredi Washington, in which a fair-skinned Negro girl made a desperate effort to pass for white. Still, eleven years later Memphis would ban *Brewster's Millions* because a Negro in this movie "acted too snappy and socialized too much with whites."

I had changed a lot since my days in McMinnville. But one thing of profound importance had not changed in the white South: the tendency to say glibly that "Niggers ain't ready for equality" and to try to justify it by asserting that "niggers" would never be ready because they were a subhuman species.

I thought about the slave trade that had dragged 2.7 million Africans to the Caribbean and the American colonies in the seventeenth century, 7 million in the eighteenth century, and 4 million in the nineteenth, and it occurred to me that while other immigrants had faced discrimination in America, none had faced the brutality and dehumanization that blacks had endured. No other group of Americans became the focus of debate over whether they should be treated differently because they were different from, and inferior to, white people.

In 1848 Ralph Waldo Emerson and Thomas Carlyle battled over

this issue, with Carlyle carrying public opinion with his assertion that "God has put into every white man's hand a whip to flog the black man." Americans had no trouble accepting Carlyle's description of the Negro as a "merry-hearted, grinning, dancing, singing, affectionate kind of creature."

A decade later, with a civil war looming, Stephen A. Douglas said in one of his celebrated debates with Abraham Lincoln: "I do not believe that the Almighty ever intended the Negro to be the equal of the white man. I am opposed to Negro citizenship in any and every form. . . ."

Douglas goaded Lincoln into saying that blacks and whites probably never would live together in "perfect equality; and inasmuch as it becomes a necessity that there must be a difference, I am in favor of the race to which I belong having the superior position."

Lincoln obviously anguished over the issue of race. He had said in Peoria, Illinois, in 1854 that "No man is good enough to govern another man without that other's consent." And in 1858 he said, "As I would not be a *slave*, so I would not be a *master.*"

Lincoln was most eloquent, most prescient, I think, when he wrote Joshua F. Speed in 1855 to say:

> I am not a Know-Nothing; that is certain. How could I be? How can anyone who abhors the oppression of Negroes be in favor of degrading classes of white people? Our progress in degeneracy appears to me to be pretty rapid. As a nation we begin by declaring that "all men are created equal." We now practically read it "all men are created equal except Negroes." When the Know-Nothings get control, it will read "all men are created equal, except Negroes and foreigners and Catholics."

Perhaps Lincoln was at his best in September 1858 when he debated Douglas at Edwardsville, Illinois, and said:

> When . . . you have succeeded in dehumanizing the Negro; when you have put him down and made it impossible for him to be but as the beasts of the field; when you have extinguished his soul in this world and placed him where the ray of hope is blown out as in the darkness of the damned, are you quite sure that the demon you have roused will not turn and rend you?

When I set out in 1953 to inform people about the issues involved in, the facts lying behind, the historic and moral importance of the *Brown* v. *Board of Education* case before the Supreme Court, I was under no illusions that my sudden celebrity really had changed my status as a black American. Some of the best — and worst — restaurants in Minneapolis and St. Paul had flagrant or surreptitious policies of ensuring that neither I nor any other black person could get a table. The real estate, savings and loan, and banking industries were in a conspiracy to restrict black families to ghettos that everyone understood to be "the colored areas" of south Minneapolis, and north Minneapolis around Olson Highway. It was beyond thought that a black might move into a house in Edina, Minnetonka, or even the suburbs populated by lower-than-middle-class whites. It was, in fact, something of a sensation when the Marquette National Bank loaned me $11,500 to buy the house at 3100 Forty-sixth Street, a neighborhood made up almost exclusively of white Lutherans. I had been accosted by Minneapolis cops when my wife — light skinned — and I left a barbecue place called The Plantation, because the cops peered into the night and figured they had a "darky" dating a white woman.

I went back South knowing that I wasn't a full-fledged American, even in the northernmost state in the Union. During that journey I saw examples of personal courage by vulnerable blacks that can never be erased from my mind.

I have wondered many times what ever happened to the short, black Methodist minister who leaned against the counter of his grocery store in Clarendon County, South Carolina, on a bright November day in 1953 and said to me: "We ain't asking for nothing that belongs to these white folks. I just mean to get for that little black boy of mine everything that every other South Carolina boy gets, and I don't care if the other boy's as white as the drippings of snow."

This brave grocer was at social war with the white dealer in livestock, feed, and fertilizer who only an hour earlier had said to me: "This fight on segregation is wrong, and it's gonna work to the detriment of these Nigras. We got a good bunch of Nigras here, and we got along fine till these outside influences came in here and started propagandizing. Segregation is our way of life. Both races want it. And if that [Supreme] Court rules we got to mix 'em, we're gonna make every effort to avoid it."

I sensed that behind those remarks lay deep and bitter turmoil for all the South. I so believed in my heart that the Earl Warren Court would outlaw racially segregated schools that Steven and I decided to call this series of articles "Jim Crow's Last Stand."

I felt that we were wise in our choice of a title when I stopped at a little Summerton, South Carolina, store and asked a quick-tongued, grandmotherish proprietor if the Court ought to say that the Constitution forbids Jim Crow schools.

"Mister, we live in hope," she said, lifting a can of salmon off the shelf for a customer. "That Court has got to cut this segregation out, 'cause I'm telling you, we Negroes have caught hell long enough."

I told her that I had interviewed twelve-term mayor H. C. Carrigan, and that he had said to me: "Negroes want segregation. I've got several farms and they all have Negroes on them. I sharecrop with them and they are all as happy as can be. You couldn't run them off. . . ."

The black woman in the little store interrupted me: "To hell with the mayor. I ain't scared of Carrigan, 'cause he ain't nothing but a meat man. He ain't no iron man."

I then knew that there was a "new Negro" in the South, even in pitifully depressed places like Summerton.

I harbored an optimism that even to me seems naïve — call it stupid — thirty-seven years later. I heard the talk of bloodshed, mayhem, murder, to protect white supremacy, but I couldn't take it seriously. I had walked the streets of Summerton with a Negro farmer, B. E. Hardy, who was outraged when I told him that some blacks were selling out to get home mortgages and loans for their farms.

Hardy stuck his face close to mine and said: "We got too damn many Negroes around here who ain't nothing but a white man's tool. They ought to've been dead before they were born.

"You just let 'em know that we Negroes down here are like Gideon's army. A few went down like dogs and lapped the water. The rest were fit to fight."

As I continued that 1953 journey my optimism increased, especially when I got to Washington, D.C., which the great diplomat Ralph

Bunche had found too steeped in Jim Crow to move there and take a key job in his country's government. But now William Rogers, the deputy attorney general in the early Eisenhower administration, had submitted a brief to the Supreme Court saying that segregated schools in the nation's capital were an embarrassment to the United States in the eyes of a rapidly changing world.

Still, I reported accurately and faithfully the cries of southern senators, congressmen, and others that ending segregation in the schools of the District of Columbia would be a social calamity.

Whereas "How Far From Slavery?" was carried in only a few brave newspapers, "Jim Crow's Last Stand" was printed in many. The fallout shocked — and pleased — me beyond anything I could have imagined. My peers in the journalism fraternity, Sigma Delta Chi, voted to give me the prized medallion for the best general reporting in the nation in 1953.

But before I could accept plaudits for "Jim Crow's Last Stand" I had another honor to accept. On January 2, 1954, the United States Junior Chamber of Commerce announced that I was one of America's Ten Outstanding Young Men of 1953.

People in McMinnville, Nashville, around Fort Schuyler, in Topeka, my old Navy buddies, all mailed me clippings of the stories and pictures of the chosen ten. My mother proudly baked me a batch of date bars, one of my favorite desserts. One sister thought this meant I could now send her more money. And there I, age twenty-eight, was, among "Douglas R. Stringfellow, 31, Ogden, Utah, U.S. representative, for espionage and sabotage activities during World War II which resulted in the capture of German scientist Otto Hahn and the unbalancing of the Reich's timetable in perfecting the atom bomb"; and "Billy Sol Estes, 28, Pecos, Tex., farmer and real estate owner, for unusual business accomplishments in agriculture and real estate"; and Frank Goad Clement, the thirty-three-year-old governor of Tennessee.

In accepting the award I said:

> Naturally, I'm quite pleased. I don't think any young man who, little more than a decade ago, left a small town in Tennessee with seventy-seven cents in his pocket and today finds himself honored on the same platform with the governor of that grand state could be anything but pleased.

I think I should be greatly troubled, however, if I had to accept this plaque as solely mine. With all due respect to the judges and to these other nine men, I must say that I believe it impossible to say that *these* ten young men are the outstanding in the nation for this year, or any year. I choose to think that, in my case, what the judges said is this:

> This man has written and talked about a thing called personal dignity. He has talked about that dream of an America where there are no second-class citizens. This man has written and talked about that much-cherished society where an individual is measured by the outpouring of his good deeds — whatever he contributes to his church, his community, his nation, and the world.

And I choose to believe that the judges then said:

> These things represent one of the ten top *causes* of this nation in 1953.

> Believing this, I share this honor, quite willingly, with the editors of my newspaper, the *Minneapolis Tribune*, for it was their courage that made it possible for me to write the articles and book for which I am being honored tonight.

My wife, Vivien, and I are deeply grateful to all of you.

As that audience applauded I told myself that I had said the right thing the right way. Then, with tears creeping from the corners of my eyes, I told myself that American public opinion had changed. And maybe I had helped to change it.

"I can't believe it," I said to Viv.

"Believe it," she said. "But remember that laurels wilt."

I remembered. The reality was that I had no time to rest on any laurels. Just one month and four days after that Sigma Delta Chi awards dinner, the United States Supreme Court, in the historic *Brown* v. *Board of Education* decision, declared unanimously that state-imposed racial segregation in the nation's public schools was unconstitutional.

The country was electrified, and I was almost in a daze, even though I had predicted such a decree, but not by a unanimous Court. I read:

Segregation of white and colored children in public schools has a detrimental effect upon the colored children. The impact is greater when it has the sanction of law. . . .

We conclude that in the field of public education the doctrine of "separate but equal" has no place. Separate educational facilities are inherently unequal.

Naturally, the *Tribune's* editors wanted me to write, often and at length, about what the decision meant. In my jubilation I wrote some foolish things about how Jim Crow was "a dead bird." I ridiculed people like Herman Talmadge of Georgia (son of the obdurate racist Eugene), who declared that the Court had "reduced our Constitution to a mere scrap of paper" and vowed that there would be no "mixing of the races" in the schools of Georgia as long as he was governor, because if necessary he would call out the militia to maintain segregation.

Like millions of Americans, black and white, I believed what I wanted to believe, so I chose to accept the prediction of Jonathan Daniels, editor of the *Raleigh* (North Carolina) *News & Observer*, that the Court's decision "will be met in the South with the good sense and the good will of the people of both races in a manner which will serve the children and honor America."

But as the threats of bloodshed and the cries of defiance erupted, I was unable to give them proper attention because a letter had arrived that would alter forever my career as a journalist and my thinking as a human being.

I had received a letter from a State Department official named Harold Howland congratulating me on being named one of America's Ten Outstanding Young Men. He asked whether I might be interested in participating in State's Leader-Grantee program, under which prominent citizens in labor, business, education, and other fields were sent abroad to lecture about the issues of the day. He said I was "under consideration" for a grant to go to India to lecture for three months on the roles of a free press in a free society. My eyes got bigger than doughnuts when I read that, if selected, I would be paid expenses plus $723 per month.

"Good Lord," I said to Viv, "that's more than double my *Tribune* salary!"

"Under consideration, hell," I thought as I decided to seize the initiative. I wrote Howland a letter saying, "I accept," sending copies of Howland's and my letters to Senator Hubert Humphrey. That produced a fait accompli. In short order I had a letter from the State Department asking if I could leave for India in early July.

Suddenly I faced the reality of what I had jumped into. Viv and I now had three children, including boys only fifteen months apart, the youngest being just past his first birthday.

"I leaped without thinking," I said to Viv. "There's no way in the world I could leave you guys for three or four months."

"Honey," she said, "you have the chance of a lifetime. And you don't have to worry about the kids and me. We'll be fine. Furthermore, we need the money — badly."

Her talk of needing the money emboldened me to make a proposal to Bill Steven and John Cowles, Sr.: "You continue to pay half my salary while I'm in India, and at the end of that experience I'll write a series of articles for you." They said yes so fast that I knew I was a lousy negotiator.

"Damn right," I told myself, "them as has gits!"

CHAPTER NINE

Immersed in India

I T WAS LATE AFTERNOON, July 9, 1954, when I arrived in New Delhi, and I knew immediately that I was not on a $723-a-month boondoggle. Riding from the airport to my hotel in the first great rain of the monsoon season, watching vultures hovering around dirty children whose ribs poked through disease-marked skin, seeing a magnitude of poverty that I had never witnessed, made me acutely aware that, physically, my assignment would not be a Far East frolic.

Then I gave my first speech to newsmen and ran into a barrage of criticism, and I wrote Viv a letter reeking of the racial generalizations that I had deplored all my adult life: "These Indians are the most argumentative, abrasive, know-it-all fucking people that I have ever met in my life."

Welcome, Carl Rowan, to a country fresh out of British colonialism, people's minds conditioned by Colonel Blimp superiority, national leaders trying to balance the lures of the United States and the Soviet Union. Welcome, Rowan, to a role in the cold war that you don't really understand, no matter what you've read about Senator Joseph McCarthy, and to a situation in which you just might get tarred as a black apologist for Talmadge of Georgia and all the other American racists spewing venom against the Supreme Court. Welcome, Rowan, to a lecture assignment where you'll face hundreds of questions over the weeks about white people in America murdering a black fourteen-year-old named Emmett Till because he allegedly whistled at a white woman.

In the eyes of India's ardent left-wingers, I was an enemy. So as I traveled thousands of miles, from rain-deluged Gauhāti in Assam State, to what then was a Communist enclave of Travancore-Cochin State, from Calcutta to Bombay, I was a choice target of America's foes. I recall my first speech in Calcutta, in the U.S. Information Service (USIS) library, to a group of college students. (USIS facilities are the foreign elements of the U.S. Information Agency, USIA.)

After the lecture, I invited questions and got one about college life in America. A young woman wanted me to explain panty raids. Then someone got up and asked if I had "the guts to call for the recognition of Red China." Others wanted to know what I thought of Senator Joseph McCarthy, of "the rape of the so-called spies, the Rosenbergs," and of the declaration that very day by the Louisiana legislature that the Supreme Court could go to hell, and would go to hell, before there would be any race mixing in the public schools of that state.

I was still naïvely optimistic about the willingness of the South to accept the end of Jim Crow. It had not dawned on me that even Boston and Pontiac, Michigan, would become embroiled in violence as white parents sought to keep their children from going to school with black youngsters. I was not a State Department lackey. I assailed racism and racists whose names were known to the Indians in my audiences. I simply went from Darjeeling to Patna to Cuttack to Madras, saying good things about my country because I believed that the society that had given me a break was in the process of taking great strides toward racial justice.

The low point came in September in Bombay. God, how the rains came, day and night, in waves and torrents. My bedding in the Taj Mahal Hotel was so dank and damp that I spent most nights turning, trying to find a dry spot. I lost seventeen pounds, thanks to a couple of bouts with dysentery after eating meats whose age had been masked by heavy doses of curry or chili powder and peppers.

But at least I had stopped lumping all Indians into one ugly, combative class. Educators had learned that I had the education newsbeat in Minneapolis, and they wanted straight talk about higher education in America. Word was out that I was a member of the American Newspaper Guild, and people wanted to know how this benefited me or how I could be a union member without the union telling me what to write.

Then came a speech at the Bombay YMCA, where, through maneuvers I don't understand till this day, a guy named R. K. Karanjia, the editor of a Communist propaganda sheet called *Blitz*, was selected to preside over the meeting.

I had read enough in *Blitz* about the horrors of America that I was not remotely surprised when Karanjia introduced me as

> an orator of unexcelled caliber . . . an excellent propagandist for the United States. . . . We are very eager to hear what he has to say about "a free press in a free society," for we know that the press cannot be free where it is dominated by imperialistic, capitalistic publishers and greedy, warmongering advertisers. We know a society cannot be free when it is overwhelmed by fear of McCarthyism and dominated by General Motors and the United Fruit Company. We are all interested in how a man with a black skin, who has been unable to know freedom because of it, can talk to us so learnedly about a free society.

My blood pressure went up, but I outwardly kept my cool. No need to bore readers more than thirty-six years later by repeating what I said. All you need to know is that someone in the U.S. consulate sent the State Department a detailed report on my donnybrook with Karanjia. And in the ways of Washington, someone in State leaked that report to the late journalist Peter Lisagor, who wrote that in my case "Uncle Sam finally gets his money's worth." And that provoked John Foster Dulles to send me a message imploring me to stay at least three more months and deliver the same lectures in Southeast Asia — meaning more lonely nights away from my family.

"The secretary thinks it's very important to our country," Ambassador George V. Allen told me of Dulles's request.

I had always been a sucker for the patriotic line, so that night I spent four hours going through the nerve-wracking process of getting a telephone call through to Minneapolis. The radio transmitter in Poona kept breaking up. Finally, Viv understood that I had said, "I'll lecture in Southeast Asia if you and the kids will get on a plane and come join me."

"We'll get on a plane," she said, and I felt joyous relief.

They had a terrible journey, but it produced what surely ranks as one of the grandest reunions any family ever had. I had prepared by renting an apartment in the Bharat Bank Building in Old Delhi, deep in the heart of Indian poverty.

I told the State Department that before going into Southeast Asia, I needed a month to write a series about India and Pakistan for the *Minneapolis Tribune*. I left Viv and the kids in that apartment while I went to Pakistan, only to learn later that they had been terrorized by a mongoose that thought it had proprietary rights.

As we set out across Southeast Asia, my journalistic hormones were raging. Colonialism was in its death throes in Burma, Malaya, Singapore. The French had resisted, and the United States had become the gendarme of the status quo, in Indochina. Dark clouds hovered over that area.

No one in our family will forget the night in Rangoon that daughter Barbara left her hotel room window open and the light on when we went to dinner. We returned to find that room, and the boys' room, infested with countless insects. We pulled twin beds together in the one "uncontaminated" room, and five of us slept there, Viv swearing till this day that she got the spot where two uneven beds met.

But there were memorable times, such as arriving in Bangkok, Thailand, and discovering that we could get reasonable facsimiles of hot dogs and hamburgers and Pepsi and 7-Up! And spending days in Penang, Malaya, learning the British custom of eating curries on Sunday, supposedly the day for making love, and swimming in waters that we did not know were full of poisonous snakes.

What Viv and I remember best, or most painfully, about that journey was our stop in Saigon, where, along Rue Catinat outside our Majestic Hotel, there was still a little bit of Paris. French soldiers and civilians sipped cognac or beer and made passes at Vietnamese girls of questionable calling. Sitting at the little outdoor restaurants, one could be oblivious to the reality that Vietnam already had suffered eight years of war.

But a walk across the street to the shores of the Mekong River put us face-to-face with the ravages of civil war. Some five thousand Vietnamese peasants were lying, squatting, crouching, even crawling on the decks of the *General R. R. Howze*, a refugee ship for people fleeing "the tyranny of communism" in North Vietnam. Cardinal Spellman was there to bless this mass of desperate old women, men suffering from TB, children caked in mud. It was painful to see how much a sack of rice, two bars of soap, and a candy bar meant to the women, or how precious two packs of cigarettes were to the men.

While Cardinal Spellman did the blessings, President Ngo Dinh Diem of South Vietnam did the promising. He was going to save Vietnam from communism.

I asked an American who had been trying to teach agricultural methods to the Vietnamese if he was coming back after home leave.

"No, I'm not coming back here," he said. "I've given it all I've got. But there are just too many damned things working against us. This place is lost."

"Why do you say that?" I asked.

"There is a party I'm going to tonight. Come with me and you'll find out," he said.

I found out by making only one statement to a cluster of Vietnamese: "I understand we can still stop communism in this country if we can make Diem as popular as Ho Chi Minh before the elections take place."

These pro-American, anti-Communist Vietnamese broke into laughter.

"How the devil are you going to do that?" asked one Vietnamese. "Diem cannot be as popular as Ho, who stayed in the jungles for years, who led the resistance against the Japanese, who led the movement to oust the French, who won the battle of Dien Bien Phu. Where was Diem all this time? Stashed away in some monastery, or in the United States taking it easy. You can sink a billion dollars in here but you aren't going to win until there is true representation of the people. And no matter how you figure it, Diem does not represent the people."

I knew that I would have to write some things about Vietnam that Americans were not reading, and probably did not want to read.

We returned to the United States in February 1955 on a day when the temperature in Minneapolis fell to twenty below zero. I went out to the detached, unheated garage and turned the key in my 1954 Chrysler. It started.

"That's a great omen," I said to Viv.

If it was an omen, it was of a development that I sure didn't expect. I was pounding the typewriter on a series of articles, "Asia: Terror and Turmoil," when I got a telephone call from John Cowles, Sr.

Wasting no time on formalities, he said, "Carl, you know there's going to be a mighty important conference of Asians and Africans in Indonesia in April."

"Yes," I said, "I was in Bogor, Indonesia, in December with Nehru, Sukarno, and others as they planned the Bandung Conference."

"I know you just got home, but what would you think of going back to cover that conference?"

"What?"

"Dulles called me to say it would be a service to the nation if you were there. Allen says you have access to the key people who will be there well beyond the access available to anyone in the foreign service. Think about whether you want to go."

"Mr. Cowles, I don't have to think about it," I said rapidly. "I could never pass up a chance to cover a meeting as important as this one will be."

"Great, Carl," he said, and hung up.

I went into the kitchen and said to Viv, "That was John Cowles. I'm going back to Indonesia in April to cover the Bandung Conference."

"What?" she shouted.

"Dulles told Cowles that it would be good for the country if I covered the conference," I explained. Then it hit me. Cowles had used the name "Allen."

"Christ, I think the Dulles who called Cowles was Allen, the head of the CIA, not John Foster, the secretary of state. Damned if I want anybody thinking I'm working for the CIA!"

I got so preoccupied in the rush to finish my series on Southeast Asia that I forgot my intentions to follow up discreetly and determine just which Dulles wanted me at Bandung. All of a sudden, it seemed, it was mid-April, and I was on a big Boeing Stratocruiser, crossing the vast Pacific for Sydney and Darwin, Australia, and then on to Jakarta, Indonesia. Ah, yes, whichever Dulles telephoned Cowles knew damned well that while the advantages of being a black journalist were not universally great, they could be of real importance at an Asian-African conference.

I was able to obtain access to key people, and some of it did come from the bold use of my color. The Indonesian government, fearing attacks by the Darul Islam terrorist groups, was protecting the conference site with 2,140 policemen and Amboinese soldiers toting submachine guns. I had to penetrate these guys to get inside the conference hall so I could talk to Premier Chou En-lai of Communist China. The great story, after all, was that Nehru and Sukarno had decided that the Peking government was no world pariah and must play a leading role in any gathering to discuss the future of the colored peoples of the world.

So one day, when delegates were walking in, I put on a look of the haughtiest, most important official, strolled past the Amboinese soldiers, and walked up to Chou's interpreter, Pu Shou-chang, a former Harvard student.

"Has His Excellency any comments about the attack on communism made yesterday by the gentleman from Iraq?" I asked Pu.

Chou overheard me and turned to reply himself, but in Chinese.

"He says he has come to Bandung not to quarrel but to help everybody. He does not want to quarrel," said Pu.

Chou invited me to a private meeting at which he talked frankly about many things and then gave me a set of prints of some marvelous Chinese cave paintings, which have adorned the walls of my offices and homes till this day.

The day after my session with Chou an official from the American consulate in Bandung brought me a cable from my managing editor, Paul Swensson. It said: EIGHT DISPATCHES RECEIVED PROMPTLY CONTENTS EXCELLENT SIGMA DELTA CHI PICKS INDIA ARTICLES FOR TOP AWARD.

"Holy Toledo!" I exclaimed to the consulate officer. "I just won the medallion for the best foreign correspondence of 1954. Let me buy you a drink!"

I pretended to be a delegate one more time, having bolstered my nerve by drinking a few martinis with the late, great reporter Philip Potter of the *Baltimore Sun*. We just had to get to Sir John Kotelawala, the prime minister of Ceylon (now Sri Lanka), who was about to make (I had a tip!) an explosive argument about Formosa (Taiwan) and fears that Peking was on the verge of using military force to reunite it with the China mainland.

Again, I just walked through the guards and their submachine guns and went up to kneel beside Sir John, who welcomed me warmly although he had met me only briefly on two occasions.

"Formosa for the Formosans," he bellowed. "Communist China must not attack. . . ." As Kotelawala talked on with incredible frankness, I felt what turned out to be a knee against my butt. It belonged to Potter, my pale-faced *Baltimore Sun* drinking buddy. In one of the greatest displays of nerve in the history of journalism, he had stayed on my rear and walked past the guards.

As we left Kotelawala and ran to type furiously a story that would scoop the rest of our colleagues, Potter blew his martini breath in my face and said, "I'm a fucking delegate, too."

Bandung was the most exciting assignment of my life, up till then. I slept ninety-five minutes my first night there. I never imagined that I could go so many days with so little sleep. But excitement and some bourbon, with a dash of youthfulness, can defy the laws of bodily need for a long time.

I crashed in happy satisfaction on that ride back across the Pacific, believing — again naïvely — that the nations represented at Bandung had seized a meaningful measure of power away from the Europeans who had ruled the world for so long.

Back in Minneapolis, I realized that I was no longer just a general-assignment reporter who had written hundreds of obits and interviews with down-and-out ex-celebrities looking for resuscitation in Minneapolis. I was no longer just the guy with the very desirable education beat. Suddenly, I was the *Tribune*'s expert on foreign affairs — the guy who got to interview Arnold Toynbee when he came to town.

But nothing mattered more than the judgment of my peers, almost all white, deciding who got the coveted Sigma Delta Chi prize for foreign correspondence. I went to the Waldorf-Astoria, noting that it was May 17, the first anniversary of the *Brown* v. *Board of Education* decision outlawing Jim Crow, to hear Bernard Kilgore of the *Wall Street Journal* say:

Carl T. Rowan's series ["This Is India"] combines masterful investigative reporting with pungent writing and objectivity in the best journalistic tradition. Here are fact finding, initiative, clarity, and organization in proportions no newspaper reader, however indifferent, can ignore and no journalist, however high his standards, can fail to recognize as a model of inspired craftsmanship.

Modesty had not been one of the personal qualities that had brought me to that point, and I made no pretense of abundant humility that magnificent night in New York. Still, I couldn't believe that Kilgore was talking about me.

A year later, on May 15, 1956, I was at the Sheraton Hotel in Chicago being cited for "the best foreign correspondence of 1955" for my articles on Southeast Asia and my coverage of the Bandung Conference. I had now won a coveted Sigma Delta Chi medallion three years in succession, something no other journalist ever had done. I left Chicago that night hoping fervently that the stories of my success would cause publishers, editors, station managers, and news directors to conclude that *they needed* some of the talent that was going to waste in black America.

CHAPTER TEN

Covering a Bus Boycott — and History

WHEN I CAME BACK from the Bandung Conference, Bill Steven didn't waste much time commending me on my new awards. "At my Minnetonka Club, and most every place else," he said, "they're still referring to Africa as 'The Dark Continent.' The goddam darkness is in the creases of their narrow minds. You ought to go to Africa, delve deep into the independence movement, and tell our readers something about the people and the countries that are going to affect our lives." So I went, and met and wrote about Jomo Kenyatta of Kenya, Kenneth Kaunda of Zambia, Julius Nyerere of Tanzania, and the leaders of Liberia, Nigeria, the Congo, and more.

It was Steven who said to me, after we'd both had about five scotches, "*Of course* Americans don't know much about India or Indonesia or Africa. Shit, they don't know anything about Canada." So he asked me to travel from one end of Canada to the other and write more than twenty articles about "Our Unknown Neighbors."

Till this day I tell him that only a sadist would have asked his so-called star reporter to spend weeks in Canada in January and February.

Steven remembered a conversation we had shortly after I came home from Bandung. I said, "I've been away too damned long. An orgy of racism is building up in America over the Supreme Court decision outlawing Jim Crow schools. This isn't just a southern story, because there will be violence in the North. But Senator Eastland, Governor Talmadge, editor Frederick Sullens of the *Jackson*

[Mississippi] *Daily News*, and others have turned the South into a time bomb. And our readers don't know a damn thing about it."

"Well, goddammit, let's tell 'em about it," Steven said. "When are you going back south?"

"I don't want to go alone and let our readers conclude that this is just a colored guy's new dose of propaganda," I said, "so let's add a white reporter to this assignment."

I was delighted when Steven picked my good friend and marvelous reporter Richard Kleeman to join me in taking a look at "Dixie Divided."

Kleeman and I were wading, unarmed, into the second civil war in 1956. In Halifax County, Virginia, we would hear Congressman William M. Tuck, a former governor, tell a rally of the Defenders of State Sovereignty and Individual Liberty: "I intend to resist with all the might I have this effort to distort the minds, to pollute the education, and to defile and make putrid the pure Anglo-Saxon blood that courses through the innocent veins of our helpless children. . . . If I have to believe in the mixing of the races in our churches to be a Christian, then I do not have that kind of religion."

The politicians and the press of the South had targeted their guns on the Supreme Court and the NAACP. The self-styled commander of the white-supremacy army was Senator Eastland, a Mississippi Democrat who had used his congressional committee post and a committee staff to conduct "anti-Communist" investigations that led him to declare that the Supreme Court was subversive and Communist influenced.

Moving across the South, Eastland exhorted white men and women to defy the Supreme Court:

> Before God, I now make the people of Mississippi this solemn promise. I will carry [our fight] in the North as well as in the South. The choice is between victory and defeat. Defeat means death, the death of southern culture and our aspirations as Anglo-Saxon people. . . . Generations of southerners yet unborn will cherish our memory because we preserved for them their untainted racial heritage, their culture and the institutions of the Anglo-Saxon race.

Incredibly, much of the southern press was more inflammatory than Eastland. In Richmond, Virginia, editorial page editor James

Jackson Kilpatrick was making the *Richmond News Leader* a fiery advocate of "massive resistance" in which the state would "interpose" itself between white Virginians and the Supreme Court and thwart all attempts at integration. Kilpatrick, to my disbelief, was honored by Sigma Delta Chi at the same ceremonies at which I was saluted for writing about the emergence of Asia and Africa.

Jackson, Mississippi, editor Sullens told the American Society of Newspaper Editors: "Mississippi will not obey the decision. If an effort is made to send Negroes to school with white children, there will be bloodshed. The stains of that bloodshed will be on the Supreme Court steps."

Perhaps no one worked harder than Sullens to make that a self-fulfilling prophecy. When the Vicksburg, Mississippi, NAACP petitioned the local school board to admit Negroes to white schools, Sullens ran a front-page editorial addressed "To All White Men and Women in Jackson":

> The NAACP, the radical Negro organization dominated by Communist-front leaders, threw down the gage of battle at Vicksburg. . . .
>
> Thurgood Marshall, mulatto chief counsel for the NAACP, threatens to sue not only county by county, but school by school, to drive the entering wedge in every community in the land. The NAACP is dedicated to widening this wedge, which was handed them by a subversive supreme court. . . .
>
> A mandate has been hurled at the white people of Mississippi to organize immediately.

Eastland had joined others in proposing "a resolution of nullification" — that is, having the state legislature declare the Supreme Court decision null and void and of no effect in Mississippi. But that state had a new governor, J. P. Coleman, its first in anyone's memory with any sense of racial sanity, who called the Eastland proposal "foolish" and "legal poppycock." All such a resolution would do, Coleman said, would be to "invite the President to send federal troops into Mississippi — and some of them would be Negroes — and certainly Mississippi can't whip the whole United States."

In North Carolina, segregationists were demanding abolition of the public school system; Jonathan Daniels, editor of the *Raleigh News & Observer*, was saying: "The most tragic proposal ever made in a presumably intelligent land is that the South solve the great public problem by putting an end to public education. What [those who propose this] urge is secession from civilization. Ignorance is no defense against integration or anything else."

Angry words were only part of a bitterly divided South. Blacks who tried to vote were being fired by white employers, beaten up, and even murdered. In the Mississippi Delta, a black man, the Reverend George W. Lee, tried to vote and persisted in getting other blacks to register to vote, even in the face of some brutal threats. On the night of May 7, 1955, as he was driving home to Belzoni, Mr. Lee was killed by two shotgun blasts fired from a passing car. The sheriff expressed doubt that Mr. Lee had been shot. He said the lead pellets in the Negro minister's neck and jaw "could have been fillings from his teeth."

The Ku Klux Klan was on the rise again. Across the South, White Citizens Councils of businessmen, bankers, police officials, and even judges were being formed to defend segregation — councils that one editor dubbed "uptown Ku Klux Klans." A band of Louisiana racists preferred to call themselves the Southern Gentlemen of Louisiana.

Kleeman and I were doing our pretrip research, making airline and train reservations, calling key blacks and whites in various southern cities and towns, when a fateful event occurred on December 1, 1955. In Montgomery, Alabama, the "Cradle of the Confederacy," a Negro seamstress named Rosa Parks refused to give up her seat on a city bus so a white passenger could have it. This woman defied the bus driver even though she knew that under the segregation laws of Montgomery and Alabama, bus drivers had police powers. Mrs. Parks was arrested. On December 5 Mrs. Parks was convicted and fined fourteen dollars, provoking some five thousand Negroes to gather at a Baptist church to begin what they called "a moral and spiritual movement of passive resistance." "*Stay off the buses*" was their cry, and that of the pamphlets with which they flooded black schools, churches, and neighborhoods.

Kleeman and I made a beeline for Montgomery. That first

evening there I was at the home of Mrs. JoAnn Robinson (an English instructor at all-black Alabama State College), where a boycott strategy session was taking place. I knew that the *Minneapolis Tribune* had an advantage that all the resources of the Associated Press, United Press, the *New York Times*, or any other news organization could never buy. I was the only reporter at this meeting that would eventually change the South and alter the nation's attitudes about race.

At Mrs. Robinson's house I was greeted warmly. I walked over to where the twenty-seven-year-old Reverend Martin Luther King, Jr., was pouring himself a tumbler full of Jack Daniel's. Then the Reverend Ralph Abernathy filled his own glass with the bourbon.

"Man, these are some modern preachers," I said as we were introduced. My milieu was still, in part, Warren County, Tennessee, where Baptist preachers pretended to be abstemious about most of the good things of life.

I cherish my notes from that evening, which I wrote on now-fading, cheap copy paper from the *Tribune*. Notes showing that King said to me, prophetically: "The Negro church will play a great role in the coming of integration. As soon as we can inspire the ordinary Negro minister to take a stand for integration, that will inspire Negro churchgoers to act."

King scoffed at editorials in the city newspaper, the *Montgomery Advertiser*, comparing the bus boycott with the White Citizens Councils' reprisals against anyone, white or black, who supported racial integration.

"Ours is an open and aboveboard protest for the birth of justice," he said. "The White Citizens Council's is a surreptitious movement for the perpetration of injustice, to preserve what is illegal, to maintain a deadening status quo."

I sensed immediately the most important of King's powers. He was a great communicator who spoke the white man's language magnificently. He knew the propaganda tricks of segregationists, and how to beat them at their game. He knew how to use words, symbols, rhetoric, to provoke guilt among Americans who liked to think of themselves as religious, decent, unbigoted.

I knew that I had discerned over one glass of Jack Daniel's what Grover C. Hall, Jr., editor of the *Advertiser*, would never comprehend. Hall wrote an editorial for the December 13 *Advertiser* saying that:

> The bus boycott here is a painful economic injury to the company.
>   But as a matter of the facts of life, Negro leaders should reckon with two realities:
> - The white man's economic artillery is far superior, better emplaced, and commanded by more experienced gunners.
> - Second, the white man holds all the offices of government machinery. There will be white rule as far as the eye can see.

Hall had no black reporter on his staff, no black social friend, who might have at least hinted that Hall was wrong and making a national fool of himself. But Hall had no way of understanding what one woman in that strategy session, Mrs. R. T. Adair, was saying: "If only the whites could realize that we are working to help Montgomery. As long as they keep Negroes bottlenecked, intimidated, and ignorant, they keep themselves ignorant.

"The white man in this town just does not want to believe that this is a people's movement. In that fact lies the real tragedy of the South: because of segregation, there is no communication between whites and Negroes."

I learned that night that it was indeed a people's movement. The Reverend Abernathy told me of a seventy-year-old black woman who had limped to his church one morning looking for a carpool ride to work. All the cars were out.

"You're old and crippled, and it's cold, lady," a young church volunteer said to the woman. "You take the bus to work. We'll understand."

Abernathy recalled the woman replying: "Children, I ain't got many days left. So I ain't walking for myself. I'm walking for my grandson. I want him to be able to pay his money and take his seat at the front of the bus." The old woman hobbled off toward her job.

Mrs. Robinson told me of a woman who quit her twelve-dollar-a-week job as a domestic when the white woman for whom she worked refused to drive her home. The black woman figured that if she took a taxi to work and back, her take-home pay would be only four dollars a week.

"I'd rather be rested and proud, with no money, than tired and humiliated with four dollars — so!" the black woman said, and walked away.

Fred D. Gray, a twenty-five-year-old black lawyer at that meeting, cited evidence of widespread white support for the Negro position regarding bus segregation and the boycott. He told of another black female domestic who had ignored the boycott and taken the bus to her job. Her white employer learned how she had traveled to work and fired her with this lecture: "If you have no race pride — if your own people cannot trust you — then I can't trust you in my house."

That strategy session at Mrs. Robinson's home remains one of my great memories as a journalist. Yet I knew that I was not the mouthpiece for this movement or for blacks in general. I had to get the other side of the story from whites like Hall and Police Commissioner Clyde Sellers of Montgomery.

So the next day I went with Kleeman to talk to Hall. He greeted us with the snide remark that "So many Negroes are leaving here for the East that pretty soon you fellows can stay home and cover the story."

Then he launched into the Sellers line that the boycott would end in a minute if black goons were not patrolling bus stops, intimidating would-be passengers, and riding the buses to mug and maim any Negro who did not honor the boycott.

I mentioned that I wanted to attend a White Citizens Council rally that was scheduled for that evening.

Hall replied: "I know that crowd — it's pretty rough. Now, if you want a good editor's tip, why don't you ride a bus and tell what they do to a Negro? That's how you find out about the labor union–type goons."

I could understand that Hall, Sellers, and whites of similar mentality could not believe that poor, "dumb" blacks could unite in behalf of such a boycott. But here they were, with blacks, who made up 75 percent of the city's bus traffic, staging a 98 percent–effective bus boycott and forcing Montgomery City Lines to raise fares 50 percent and still lose $3,200 a day.

When Hall repeated his suggestion that I ride a bus, I just looked him in the eye and thanked him for his time.

The following day I got a surprise, but a valuable lesson regarding the influence of a newspaper editor in enlightening or poisoning a community. The moment Kleeman and I had left his office, Hall sat down and wrote an editorial:

> A Negro reporter for one of the midwestern news and magazine empires showed up in the shop yesterday. He was as courteous and poised as any visitor the editor has had, he was smart and well-groomed. He had flown to Montgomery to report on the bus boycott in connection with a southern race relations piece.
>
> The last one he wrote in 1951 ["How Far From Slavery?"] was a bust. It was superficial without the slightest grasp of the durability of tradition and folk attitudes.
>
> Anyhow, he was a foreign correspondent duly credited by a foreign power so far waging only cold war upon the Confederacy. . . . The Negro wanted to know if Negro goons were . . . threatening and bully-ragging to keep indifferent Negroes from resuming bus riding. . . . [I told him]: "If you want to know the exact truth of what happens when a Negro boards a bus, why don't you yourself ride a bus?"
>
> He was deaf. Instead, he kept coming back to the prospect of attending the meeting of the Citizens Council.

A few days later, under the heading ERRATA, the *Montgomery Advertiser* reported that I had indeed ridden the bus. What Hall did not have the integrity to say was that I had also asked my white colleague, Kleeman, to ride a bus, and that neither of us had seen any goons. We had seen a black rider, here or there, and none was harassed in any way.

It was almost a fortnight later when Kleeman's and my series of articles on "Dixie Divided" began in a Sunday edition of the *Minneapolis Tribune* — preceded by an eerie Saturday-night-before incident.

Just before the first edition was about to hit the streets (about 7:00 P.M.), a *Tribune* editor telephoned my home to say, "The Montgomery bus boycott is over. Should we kill your first article, or can you alter it so it can still run?"

"What do you mean, the boycott's over?" I demanded.

"The wire services are carrying a Montgomery City Commission report that three Negro ministers have accepted a proposal to end the forty-nine-day boycott."

"Who are these Negro ministers?"

"All they say is that they are a Presbyterian minister, a Holiness bishop, and a Baptist minister."

"That sounds phony to me," I said. "Let the article run. I'm going to try to reach Reverend King or Fred Gray or someone."

It was close to 9:00 P.M. when I reached Dr. King. He was startled to hear of the phony announcement of a boycott settlement. He came to the same conclusion that I did: the whites had bought, cajoled, or threatened three blacks into acting as though they had authority to end the boycott, the assumption being that if the mass of blacks could be tricked into going back aboard the buses, it would be almost impossible to get the boycott going again.

King and his colleagues began to telephone frantically for volunteers, who went into the streets shouting, "The boycott is not over. No matter what you hear or read, the boycott is not over. Please do not go back onto the buses."

The word spread around Montgomery like wildfire, and the boycott held.

King would write at length in his book *Stride Toward Freedom* about how I "saved the bus boycott."

In truth, I did not. The Constitution and the United States Supreme Court saved the boycott — and the legal and social principles for which some sixty thousand black people, young and old, walked, and walked, and walked for well over a year, ending only after the Supreme Court upheld a lower-court decision that Alabama's state and local bus segregation laws were unconstitutional — on December 13, 1956.

That Montgomery bus boycott became an American legend. Rosa Parks is a folk hero. King is a martyr, the only black man and one of only a few men of any race to have a national holiday declared in his honor. But those days in Montgomery were not necessarily the most memorable of that journey to the South.

I remember with poignancy and pain going to Jackson, Mississippi, to see Gus Courts, the black storekeeper and NAACP official who was recuperating from being shot in the arm and stomach when he persisted in trying to vote in Humphreys County.

Courts settled carefully into a chair, so as not to aggravate his wounds, and said to me: "I just wanted to be able to say that I voted once before I died."

Every time I read of a new increase in the number of black mayors in America, of black elected officials in the South, of black participation in national political conventions, of presidential hopefuls courting "the black vote," I think of Gus Courts, who contributed as much to the rise of black political power as any man who ever lived.

While Kleeman journeyed to other parts of the South, I went to New Orleans, where history, of a sort, would be made on New Year's Day. A black player would participate for the first time in a Sugar Bowl game. Robert Grier, a fullback for the University of Pittsburgh, was to play against Georgia Tech, even though Georgia's governor, Marvin Griffin, had twice tried to stop Tech from playing if Grier was used or if fans were seated on a nonsegregated basis.

No hotel would allow Grier to stay with his teammates, so the entire Pitt team stayed in a Tulane University dormitory — the first time a Negro had stayed at Tulane. I would have been rejected by every major hotel, too, so I stayed at the home of my wife's brother's in-laws.

I chose not to ask for press-box credentials, wanting to see if I and other blacks could sit unsegregated in the stands. On New Year's Day I saw that while most Negroes were clustered in a Jim Crow area of the end zone, a few blacks from Pittsburgh and I had no problem taking our seats in white areas of the stadium.

The black fullback was cheered lustily when he ran for twenty-five yards, the longest run of the game. But he wound up as the goat, because a penalty on Grier gave Georgia Tech the ball on Pitt's one-yard line, from which Tech scored the only points of the game and won, 7 to 0.

After the game the Pitt players checked into the St. Charles Hotel, where the traditional postgame dinner and dance would take place. Grier checked into the all-Negro Gladstone Hotel. Grier ate at the dinner, but did not stay for the dance.

Meanwhile, I was having my own problems. I had been surprised to find that Negro air travelers could drink unsegregated at the airport bar but that I could not ride a limousine into the city because whites would be in the limo.

After the game, it took me more than an hour to get away from the stadium because of a city ordinance that forbade white taxis to transport Negroes and Negro taxis to carry whites. A Negro taxi was hard to find.

I got back to the home of my in-laws (once or twice removed) and found them all waiting to launch into a gigantic New Year's Day feast at which I was supposed to tell them all about Operation Integration at the Sugar Bowl. The dinner-table talk soon became a contest as to who could tell the best story about the absurdities and contradictions of racism in New Orleans.

The best tale was told by a member of this proud old family who was passing for white — who was, in fact, married to a prominent white New Orleans businessman. She had come to the dinner alone, apparently in secrecy, on a "night out." Her black family knew and approved. She told me of the day she was walking in her all-white neighborhood when a little dog rushed through a cracked gate, leaped at her angrily, tore her stockings, but did no meaningful physical damage before an elegant woman rushed out to grab the animal.

"I apologize, ma'am," the dog's owner said. "I'm so sorry. I'll pay for new stockings. I just don't understand what got into Bitsy. She never attacks anyone but niggers!"

Before he left, Kleeman and I filed a report from New Orleans that was important beyond our understanding and that of our editors (we made it article sixteen in the series, and they published it on page six). It was about an interview with a businessman named John U. Barr, who headed the executive committee of a group called the Federation for Constitutional Government. This group operated on the assumption that the races could not be kept separate just by railing against the Supreme Court decision, because most Americans didn't want to be labeled as racist. The FCG believed that the way to reverse the Warren Court was to build an alliance of conservatives in every part of the country — Minnesotans who opposed the United Nations; New Yorkers who favored the constitutional amendment proposed by Senator John Bricker of Ohio to limit the power of the president to make treaties with foreign nations; people who opposed organized labor, socialized medicine, high taxes, and economic aid programs.

I wanted to talk to this man who believed that by courting a mélange of conservative passions and prejudices his organization could stymie the Supreme Court and stop the civil rights movement in its tracks. I thought it a farfetched notion, yet I noted that some people of power and prestige were involved. Senator Eastland was a leader of the FCG, and he had expressed the formula for success very well:

> We are about to embark upon a great crusade, a crusade to restore Americanism and return the control of our government to the people. In addition, our organization will carry on its banner the slogan of free enterprise and we will fight those organizations that attempt with much success to socialize industry and the great medical profession of this country. This will give us recruits and add to our support in the north and west.

I telephoned Barr, who said, "I know who you are. I know you're a Negro. But I'll be glad to see you. I want you to know that I don't hate Negroes. I've been around them all my life. We love our Negroes."

Late one evening, in an austere office in a downtown New Orleans bank building, Kleeman and I met a mild, graying, grandfatherly looking man who sat surrounded by papers and pamphlets of the FCG.

He told us why he and his colleagues thought the Republic was in danger: "The Supreme Court decision [outlawing school segregation] is a usurpation of the power that belongs to the legislative branch of government. If allowed to stand and not successfully challenged, the integration decision means that the Supreme Court is the legislative body — not the judicial body."

How much would his group stress the race question?

"Well, in some sections of the South, our fight may become clouded in the segregation issue. On the other hand, the racial situation in some northern cities may be a predominant means for gaining support for our cause."

Barr said the goal was to elect enough conservative congressmen in the North and West to enable the Congress to overrule the Supreme Court decision by legislation.

"You're gonna find out that white northerners don't want their children going to school with Negroes either," he said.

"Is the fear of racial intermarriage at the bottom of FCG's efforts?" Kleeman asked.

"Certainly, the purity of both the white and Negro races is part of the thing that motivates our group. It's a pretty well-accepted fact that intermarriage is the goal of the NAACP," Barr replied.

As we started to leave, Barr said to me: "I like your voice. On the telephone. I like your approach." Then he told me about being in a restaurant near Baton Rouge where two white women "were drunk and dirty and smelly, and then this Negro, well groomed like you, came up to this little square hole cut in the wall and bought a beer and went away to drink it. I said to my industrialist friend that I'd much prefer having that well-groomed Negro in the restaurant drinking his beer than those dirty drunk white women."

I said, "Well, Mr. Barr, do you think you could get your friends in the Federation for Constitutional Government to go along with a law that says clean people sit on one side of a restaurant while the dirty, smelly ones must sit on the other side?"

"No. No, I'm sure they wouldn't," he said. "They'd be afraid some of the lower element would creep in."

"Would the FCG consider it unjust that if Ralph Bunche arrived in New Orleans tonight, he would not be able to get a room in a major downtown hotel?"

"I'd rather not comment on Mr. Ralph Bunche, if you please," Barr said.

I walked out of that bank building feeling smug. I could not imagine that he, Eastland, Talmadge, and others would one day find so many allies in the schools of Boston, on the school board in Pontiac, Michigan, in the police department of Philadelphia, the fire department of Detroit, the city council of Chicago. I was so politically unsophisticated that I could not conceive of a day when the Republican party platform would be almost a carbon copy of Barr's agenda, and a shrewd politician named Ronald Reagan would ride it to power.

Dick Kleeman and I returned to Minneapolis physically and emotionally exhausted.

I just wanted to lie down for a month or more. But we had sixteen articles to prepare on "Dixie Divided." Furthermore, my book on India, Southeast Asia, and the Bandung Conference was being published. No way I could get any sleep or rest awaiting the reviews of *The Pitiful and the Proud.* They were very good, and I rejoiced when the American Library Association selected my book as one of the best of the year, an honor it also had bestowed upon *South of Freedom.*

I was working on a book to be called *Go South to Sorrow,* lashing out at President Eisenhower, Hodding Carter, and other gradualists who, in my view, were compromising away the freedom of America's black people, when Bill Steven called me at home.

A great human tragedy was erupting in Hungary in 1956. Almost simultaneously a complex bit of Egyptian arrogance, followed by British-French-Israeli conspiracy, would shatter the fragile peace of the Middle East.

Steven said half-jokingly, "Rowan, don't you think you'd better rush to the United Nations and help them prevent World War Three?"

"Go to the United Nations?" I asked wearily. "Hell, I barely got home."

"Go to the UN," Steven said emphatically, "because the way I read the wires, the story there is war or peace."

It took me probably twenty-four hours to realize that Steven was sending me to report on the greatest crisis of the Eisenhower years, although neither of us foresaw that I would be writing about two simultaneous crises. I rushed to UN headquarters knowing that the world was at a very dangerous juncture and that I was on a journalistic assignment of great importance.

God knows that through the months of suffering "Delhi belly," badgering by Communists, dodging vipers, and enduring other perils of the Near East and the Far East, I had made the contacts crucial to covering what may yet be the most dramatic period for the United Nations. Bandung had been a blessing in this respect, because key officials of Egypt, Pakistan, Thailand, Burma, Ceylon, the Philippines, and more had decided that I was someone they dared talk to in confidence. Throughout my assignments at the UN, there never was a time when I telephoned Dr. Ralph Bunche, the brilliant, gentle black American who was the under secretary general, that he did not answer the telephone personally and say "come up for a chat" at such-and-such a time.

The U.S. ambassador, Henry Cabot Lodge, knew this, as did the people in the U.S. Mission to the UN who really were working for Allen Dulles and the CIA. They talked to me in search of a quid pro quo, hoping that I knew something they needed to know.

All this made for four of the most incredible weeks that any journalist ever spent anywhere.

The Middle East crisis had erupted in September 1956 when the British and French governments asked the UN to consider acting against Nasser's ending "the system of international operation of the Suez Canal," which included banning Israeli vessels. Egypt asked the UN Security Council to assail nations, especially Britain and France, that were taking actions that "constitute danger to international peace and security."

I look at my notes, reaching back to the Bandung Conference, and to my first visit to South Vietnam, and see that the French had one selfish goal in 1956. They wanted to ensure that other colonies, Algeria especially, would never become independent, and they hated Egyptian leader Nasser for his economic, military, and other support for the Algerian "terrorists."

The British Empire had crumbled, but not every British ego, and some yearned to get the rock out of their craws, put there by Egypt's Nasser when he nationalized the Suez Canal.

David Ben-Gurion and other Israeli leaders had said privately, and in top secret cables to Washington, that Nasser had led Arab moves to build a "ring of steel" around the beleaguered Jewish state.

A key source told me that Eisenhower and Foster Dulles regarded Nasser as a menace, but repeatedly warned the British that the consequences of taking military or other overt actions to overthrow him would be grave, indeed costlier than the Western alliance could bear. Allen and Foster Dulles both were warning Ike that war was possible, and Eisenhower was again warning Prime Minister Anthony Eden of Britain that all the Middle East, Asia, and Africa would be inflamed if the West acted militarily against Nasser. But Israel had been secretly armed by the French with Mystère jets and other weapons.

Then, in mid-October, the doubleheader of crisis began. In Poland, students, textile workers, and others paraded through the streets demanding the withdrawal of Soviet troops. The unrest in Warsaw, Wroclaw, Lodz, and other Polish cities only reminded millions of Hungarians of how much they hated the Kremlin's occupation troops, the KGB's security police, the Soviet assaults on the Catholic church, including the abuse of Cardinal Mindszenty. A mass rebellion for freedom was sweeping Hungary. But Nikita Khrushchev, first secretary of the Central Committee of Russia's Communist party, Premier Nikolay Bulganin, and their Polish stooges were having none of it. Soviet troops and tanks poured in.

On October 25 Eisenhower issued a statement saying that "The United States deplores the intervention of Soviet military forces . . . to continue an occupation of Hungary by the forces of an alien government for its own purposes."

The Russians didn't give a damn what Eisenhower said. They used some two hundred thousand troops and four thousand tanks in a November 4 assault that left fifty thousand Hungarians dead and wounded in the streets of Budapest alone.

Why didn't the Eisenhower administration do anything? Ike would later write what U.S. officials at the UN told me:

> In Europe we were aligned with Britain and France in our opposition to the brutal Soviet invasion of Hungary; in the Middle East we were against the entry of British-French armed forces in Egypt. . . .
>
> Sending United States troops alone into Hungary through hostile or neutral territory would have involved us in general war. . . . It was obvious that no mandate for military action could or would be forthcoming.

I was at the United Nations that Sunday afternoon when the General Assembly voted 50 to 8 for a U.S. resolution demanding that the Soviet Union withdraw its troops from Hungary. There was no surprise that all the Soviet-bloc delegates, including the Pole, opposed the resolution. What was a harbinger, as well as a sign of fear of the Soviets and the oncoming end of U.S. domination of the General Assembly, was the fifteen abstentions, mostly from newly independent nations of Asia and Africa.

By this time the General Assembly was involved in double emergency sessions — one regarding Hungary, the other on the Suez. I was working at least eighteen hours a day.

I had told Steven that I wanted an exemption from filing expense accounts because I had no time to keep track. We negotiated a deal that will seem unbelievable today. I would get thirty dollars a day for which I did not have to account. I stayed in the Roosevelt Hotel, took a couple of taxis a day, bought an occasional delegate a drink in the chief delegates' lounge, and still wound up with a profit of a few bucks a day! That was because I didn't have time to eat, except for an occasional midevening dash into the UN cafeteria, where the food was cheap but good.

On October 29 the Israelis attacked Egypt on several fronts, moving near the canal, for the avowed purpose of unblocking Egypt's obstruction to Israeli shipping through the Gulf of Aqaba. The next day the United States put before the UN Security Council a resolution asking all UN members not to use force in the Middle East. Ironically, the Soviet Union supported the resolution, while both Britain and France vetoed it.

The United States no longer needed intelligence about Mystère jets and intercepted evidence of a gross increase in cable traffic between the British, French, and Israeli governments to know that the three nations were involved in a daring and dangerous conspiracy.

This was near the end of the presidential campaign, and the Democratic candidate, Adlai Stevenson, was grasping for any excuse to attack Eisenhower. Mrs. Eleanor Roosevelt, who backed Stevenson, said Israel was justified in invading Egypt, a stance some thought might throw enough Zionists to Stevenson to give him the election. But a distinguished New York Jew, Senator Jacob Javits, whose Senate seat was at stake, refused to condone Israel's action and backed Eisenhower's handling of the problem.

I sat bleary-eyed in the UN General Assembly in the wee hours of November 2 when that body approved a resolution calling for a cease-fire in the Middle East. The vote was 64 to 5, with only Britain, France, Australia, New Zealand, and Israel opposing it. Here was international high drama the likes of which I had never dreamed of reporting.

I think the moment of truth for many delegates had come the night before when, in Philadelphia in a campaign speech,

Eisenhower laid it on the line as to why he had broken with Israel, Britain, and France and told all three to get the hell out of Egypt. I wrote about, and would for many months quote, portions of that brave speech:

> We cannot — in the world, any more than in our own nation — subscribe to one law for the weak, another law for the strong. . . .
>
> There can be only one law — or there will be no peace. . . .
>
> We value — deeply and lastingly — the bonds with those great nations [Britain and France] . . . with whom we now so plainly disagree. . . .
>
> But this we know above all: there are some firm principles that cannot bend — they can only break. And we shall not break ours.

Under Eisenhower's pressure, the fighting in Egypt was ending, but the situation in Hungary had become even more explosive. I said to Prince Wan of Thailand, "My president had the guts to tangle with the British, French, and Israelis. Will any Asians or Africans dare to criticize the Russians for what they are doing in Hungary?"

This mildest mannered of all the men I knew grinned embarrassedly and said, "We both may be surprised."

Reporters and most everyone else at the UN got a surprise on November 5, the day after Soviet troops crushed the Hungarian uprising. We got word that some six hundred British paratroopers had landed on Gamil Airfield to the west of Port Said, by the Suez Canal, and almost an equal number of French troops had parachuted to a point south of Port Said. The Russians said publicly that they had forces on the way to help Egypt, and Premier Bulganin warned Washington that if the British and French did not get out it would be the beginning of World War III.

You may be able to imagine the consternation of a single reporter from a Midwest newspaper at the United Nations trying to cover both a military conflagration in the Middle East and a grotesque Soviet act of oppression in Hungary. I make no pretense that I did that very well or came anywhere close to the competent coverage by our great newspapers or the wire services. I do say that I focused on what seemed to me the central issue. Would these nations represented at Bandung, crying for relief from the assaults of Western colonialism, have the guts, the integrity, to sound off against the rape of Hungary?

"Someone will," I told myself. "It won't be the Indian. It ought not be the Filipino, who will be dismissed as an American stooge. If it is someone from Central or South America, it won't make much difference, because the common conception is that the United States rules the hemisphere, and Latinos vote the way the Great Gringo says they should."

Over a resolution formally condemning the Soviet Union for what its troops had done to the people of Hungary, the great test came in a way that I never anticipated.

That incredible fall of 1956, I listened to the UN rhetoric that had shifted from the Middle East to Hungary, and I took notes saying that the speeches were routine. That is, until an obscure delegate from Burma, U Pe Kin, spoke on November 4. His words became the voice of free men everywhere.

"We, the people of Burma, look at the ravaged people of Hungary and say, 'There, but for the grace of God, go we.'"

The United Nations General Assembly voted, astoundingly, 50 to 8, with 15 abstentions, to formally condemn the Soviet Union and demand the withdrawal of troops from Hungary.

The question arose then, as now, as to how much this bothered the Kremlin. Did praise or denunciation by any part of the UN matter to the powerful nations who felt that their military, economic, political, or other interests came first? Could the UN keep the peace in the Middle East or anyplace else? I went back to Minneapolis saying "*No!*" But I knew that I would be back at the United Nations again and again.

CHAPTER ELEVEN

Fighting Racism and "the Diplomats"

WHEN THE EMERGENCY SESSIONS of the UN General Assembly were over, I dragged myself onto a Stratocruiser for the flight back to Minneapolis, certain that, in my weariness, I would fall into a virtual coma. I never slept a wink.

I sipped a drink and thought about how sanctimoniously outraged my countrymen were over what the Soviet Union was doing to impose communism on Hungary, and yet how tolerant they were of what the Klansmen, the White Citizens Councils, bankers and police chiefs, governors and university presidents, were doing to preserve Jim Crow in America.

In the mentalities of our White House, our Congress, our media, there were no "troublemakers on both sides" in Hungary. The villains were the brutal Soviet rapers of innocent Hungarians who had dared to reach out for freedom. But in America the air was filled with cries, even by Eisenhower and Stevenson, for a "moderate" approach to ending segregation and a national rejection of "the extremists on both sides."

I felt disbelief that any white American could dump Gus Courts, who merely wanted to vote, into the same box with the knifers, gunmen, and economic hit men who wanted to deny him the franchise, and then dismiss them all as "the extremists on both sides."

I admitted to myself that the Louisiana conservative, John U. Barr, might be right. The racists and reactionaries were waging a propaganda blitzkrieg that had the power to overwhelm America.

Their most damaging salvos were that blacks were inferior and deserved to be kept "in their place."

I had received at least ten thousand favorable letters about my articles in the *Minneapolis Tribune*, other newspapers, and *Look* magazine about the plight of Negroes in the South. But when the glow wore off, I realized that in 1956 the dialogue was the same as when Emerson debated Carlyle in 1848 or Lincoln fought with Douglas in the 1850s. The Americans shouting loudest about Soviet atrocities in Hungary were among those working hardest to dehumanize black Americans, to portray them as little more than beasts and demons.

With bitterness and laughter, in 1956 I read J. C. Furnas's book *Goodbye to Uncle Tom*, in which he documented an opinion that during the Revolution the Negro slave, "inured to fatigue and hardened and disciplined by slavery, made a better soldier than his master. No observer even went on record that the blacks broke in panic any quicker than whites." Jefferson thought blacks to be "at least as brave" as whites but attributed it to a mental shortcoming — "which prevents their seeing a danger till it be present."

In every war that followed, including the one in which I had just served, the cries went up that blacks were less developed mentally, could not absorb training, needed twice as many white officers to command and guide them, and would turn tail and run at the snap of a twig.

White fear of blacks who could read and write became so pervasive in America that in 1833 a white liberal was arrested in Connecticut for running an academy for Negro girls. A year later South Carolina passed a law making it a crime to teach either free or slave Negro children. Until the start of the twentieth century, most southern states prohibited or effectively discouraged efforts to educate blacks.

I sipped a manhattan remembering that white America had been bombarded with relentless loads of nonsense about racial differences, with not all the nonsense coming from people with dark racist motives. During slavery days, abolitionist C. G. Parsons argued that mulattoes were "the best specimens of manhood. . . . The African mothers have given them a good physical system, and the Anglo-Saxon fathers a strong mental constitution."

Harriet Beecher Stowe, whose *Uncle Tom's Cabin* is credited with bringing on civil war, was no believer in racial equality. She wrote that "when the white race shall regard their superiority over the colored one only as a talent entrusted for the advantage of their weaker brother, *then* will the prejudice of caste melt away in the light of Christianity." Stowe believed that black people were inferior wretches that a Christian God commanded white people to look after.

Years later, George Bernard Shaw would eschew racism (he thought) by contending that "The future of mankind belongs to its mongrels and not to its handsome but brainless Borzois."

Black Americans' dreams of equal opportunity and status in an unsegregated society were being beaten to death in the propaganda arena.

I talked to Whitney Young, Thurgood Marshall, Roy Wilkins, Martin Luther King, and other black leaders, saying that the primary black struggle was no longer in the courts or the Congress but in campaigns to win over white minds to the concept of integration, whether in schools, buses, restaurants, or American workplaces. I said that blacks could not just sit and seethe over the propaganda bilge being put out by racists — that we had to have a strategy to use the media to make our causes look honorable and just.

Every black leader understood what was happening, but not one of them, not one black organization, had the manpower, money, or other resources with which to counter effectively the efforts of Barr, Eastland, George Wallace of Alabama, and others of their mind-set, North and South.

Things hopeful and ominous were happening on a hundred fronts regarding black voting rights and efforts to desegregate Dixie's schools. The Congress was bitterly embroiled in warfare over the proposed Civil Rights Act of 1957, which would do many of the things the previous president, Harry Truman, had had the guts to ask for: creation of the six-member Civil Rights Commission; setting up the Civil Rights Division of the Justice Department; extending the authority of U.S. district courts to deal with any act of Congress involving civil rights, including the right to vote.

In the face of incredible opposition, two Texans, Lyndon B.

Johnson and Sam Rayburn, forged a compromise that made this bill acceptable to the Congress and the nation. Strom Thurmond of South Carolina filibustered against this bill for 24 hours and 18 minutes, breaking the 1953 record for the length of time a senator held the floor. But on the evening of August 24 Thurmond collapsed, and on August 29 the Senate passed the civil rights bill, 60 to 15. The House had approved it, 279 to 97.

"If Congress reflects the will of the people," I told myself, "maybe the racists aren't doing as well as I feared."

Four days later my optimism was shattered. Governor Orval Faubus of Arkansas ordered units of the National Guard to surround Central High School in Little Rock and prevent the entry of Negro students. Faubus's professed concern was that the entry of nine black children into huge Central High "might lead to violence."

The Little Rock school board petitioned the federal court to rein in Faubus, and Judge Ronald N. Davies ordered that no one interfere with "the opening of the integrated high school ... on September 3."

Faubus did interfere, ordering guardsmen to turn back the Negro youngsters. Eisenhower told Faubus that he would "uphold the Constitution by every legal means at my command." Thus began a drama that put a governor and the president on a collision course, precipitating a crisis that would last for years.

I rushed off to Little Rock, which I would visit several times during this first of the great school integration crises. I was never quite welcome in that city. I once went to the state capitol ground to observe a meeting of segregationists, only to have someone shout, "Hey, that's that nigger reporter." Several goons started after me, causing me to run faster than I ever did in the four-hundred-yard dash at Washburn U.

The hotels of Little Rock wouldn't rent me a room, so I stayed at the home of the NAACP president, Daisy Bates, and her newspaper-publisher husband, L. C. Bates. This was a pleasure, and a great journalistic advantage — until the racists began shooting through the Bateses' window and dropping an occasional homemade bomb. During my late-in-the-crisis visits we would put lights around the house and sit up all night playing poker, utterly afraid to go to sleep.

On many days in Little Rock I was a walking zombie, but I learned something about human courage there. From Daisy Bates, from the black children who were the social guinea pigs, and from many white people who refused to walk away from a commitment to justice.

I had become a member of a group called the National Citizens Council for Better Schools. At one of its meetings I met Hugh Patterson, publisher of the *Arkansas Gazette*, and we quickly became good friends. When I went to Little Rock I could always count on being welcome at the *Gazette*.

On one visit, around noon, I went into Patterson's office and he said, "Let's have a scotch."

"Hell, yes," I replied. "The sun's been over the yardarm for an hour."

As he lifted his glass toward me, Patterson said: "Carl, through all these months of crisis and violence, I have been saying to Louise [his wife] what a damned shame it is that you are not free to stay in the best hotel and eat in the best restaurant. The other night we were talking about it, and a painful and embarrassing reality hit me. It occurred to me that I, your friend, ought to be taking you to my club for lunch, or to our best restaurant for dinner. But they won't let me. And that means that Hugh Patterson, white publisher, white civic leader, is not free. The racist mob has enslaved me."

It was one of my most moving moments in Little Rock.

Afterward, I watched with pride — and some amazement — the vigor of the *Gazette*'s support for school integration, of its criticisms of Faubus. The mob roared, advertisers withdrew support, old friends walked away from Hugh and Louise Patterson, but they did not waver in their efforts to bring their city into compliance with the law of the land and basic concepts of justice.

As the crisis subsided, I accepted a speaking engagement in a town near Little Rock. Patterson telephoned to say that he would pick me up at the airport and drive me to my speech — "and then you'll spend the night at our house."

After the speech we came back to what the newspapers call "an exclusive neighborhood," where blacks were seen only by day in their jobs as cooks, maids, and yardmen. Hugh, Louise, and I sat up most of the night, telling each other stories about the ordeals of the previous years. As Hugh and I walked out for the ride to the airport the next morning, I noticed a few stares from white neighbors.

Patterson gave a guttural chuckle and said: "I feel a little freer."

By 1957, the American journalism scene had changed to the point that there was no need for a Ray Sprigle to blacken himself with walnut husks and pose as a Negro to find out what was happening to black people in the South — or North. Several newspapers were hiring black writers, and most every magazine in America wanted a black reporter to tell readers about racial conflict.

My byline was appearing regularly in the *Saturday Evening Post*, *Redbook*, *Look*, *Reader's Digest*, and black-owned *Ebony* magazine on subjects as diverse as how Viv and I taught our children about race to what Negroes really wanted and whether they were ready for equality. I threw the *Saturday Evening Post* a curveball by sending the editors an article entitled "Are White People Ready for Equality?" After considerable editorial consternation, they decided not to publish it.

This was in part fun and games, because I knew that my previous reporting from Asia, the United Nations, and Canada had made it clear that I could report well on anything. I had reached a level that the media call prestige, and I soon found out that carrying prestige meant accepting new levels of risk.

I was resting on a few new laurels when I got a telephone call from the late Era Bell Thompson, a managing editor of *Ebony*. "Mr. Johnson [publisher John H.] says Paul Robeson is getting a raw deal in the media and everyplace else. Nobody will tell his side of the story. He says you're the only journalist in America who can write the truth and not get destroyed by the McCarthyites. Will you consider it?"

This was the time when the McCarthyites had spread the notion that all Jews were potential spies, à la the Rosenbergs, all State Department and U.S. Information Agency (USIA) officials were Communist sympathizers or even traitors, and all blacks were ready to turn against the United States. Robeson, the former all-American football player at Rutgers and actor who sang "Ol' Man River" so robustly and played Othello so magnificently, was the furthest thing from a black quisling. He was angry to the point that he had once exiled himself to the Soviet Union, where he raged in defense of black manhood. Millions of Americans hated him for that.

"Era Bell," I said, "I know Johnson asked you to call and hang this sword over my head, because he knows that you and I are old friends. He knows how dangerous it is in this time to say anything half-decent about Robeson. But tell Johnny that I don't have to think about it. I'll be in Oakland talking to Robeson next week."

In the October 1957 issue, under the provocative title "Has Paul Robeson Betrayed the Negro?", *Ebony* carried my article with this explanation: "The Robeson story has never been fully told. We believe that any American, no matter to what degree the public has prejudged the case against him, ought to be able to get his story before the public. This is why we are publishing this story and why Carl Rowan was willing to write it."

Perhaps you can understand the virility of anti-Russian sentiment, the wide and destructive swath of anti-intellectualism and cowardice that McCarthy and his sidekick Roy Cohn had cut, if you read just one paragraph from that *Ebony* article:

Paul Robeson's voice is silent today. The great concert impresarios pretend he no longer exists. City officials padlock public halls at the mere rumor that he is coming. Hollywood wouldn't touch him with a long-armed Geiger counter. Ambitious Negroes shrink guiltily at the mention of his name. Autograph seekers who once trailed his every step have dropped by the wayside to make room for FBI agents. The Rutgers "old grads" who once fell over each other to offer social invitations when he performed in their town now curse his name and demand that it be stripped from the university's hall of fame. Newspapers that once carried rave notices of his magnificent talents now run an occasional item such as the following: "Danish dairy farmers have discovered American jazz increases the output of their cows as much as 30 per cent. But they say that the cows refused to give as much milk when Soviet anthems sung by Paul Robeson were played for them."

I reread that article on Robeson just before completing this book, and I felt proud that I had given the marvelous man a fair hearing, a decent break. And I remembered that journalistic peril does not lie merely in covering Saigon or Beirut; it lurks among the character assassins inside America who want to destroy those whose political and social views they detest.

Meanwhile, at the *Minneapolis Tribune* I was enjoying extremely controversial assignments. Bill Steven, who had this seemingly inexhaustible supply of ideas that would get *me* in trouble, called me in one day to say that a "rot" seemed to be setting in in scores of small towns in the Upper Midwest (Minnesota, western Wisconsin, and North and South Dakota). The towns that weren't growing seemed to be dying, he said, and I ought to go out and write about who and what was killing small-town America.

I gave Steven my look of suspicion and self-protection and said: "You want *me* to go to Worthington, Sauk Centre, or wherever and write about a lot of Babbitts who are messing up the Upper Midwest countryside?"

"Something bad is going on," Steven said. "Just tell our readers the truth."

I did intensive research. Then I bought a wire recorder on which I would tape my sessions with farmers, bankers, farm wives, farm-implement dealers, country doctors, newspaper editors, little-town businessmen. I saw farmers and businessmen going bankrupt because they were in the merciless grip of local bankers. I saw doctors drinking themselves to death because their accounts receivable were so overwhelming they couldn't pay their bills. I saw towns where a single family had ruled the roost almost forever and would not tolerate the infusion of new businesses.

I wrote all this and got assailed unmercifully, especially by the bankers who got to some people on the *Minneapolis Tribune* editorial page and in the advertising department. But when the chairman of the powerful Northwest Bancorporation, John Moorhead, called Steven to rant and rage, Bill's response was: "John, I'll make you a fair deal. Get yourself a recorder, go out into as many small towns and onto as many farms as Rowan did, tape-record as many interviews with bankers, implement dealers, and farmers as Rowan has, and then you write a series of articles. We might print it."

Moorhead would later tell me, at a Federal Reserve Board party, what Steven had said to him and that it had raised his level of respect for the *Tribune*.

This Steven was relentless. I was still slapping Band-Aids over the wounds from critics of my stories on those troubled communities when he told me that former-president Truman was going to be seventy-five years old on May 8, 1959.

"Yeah?" I said.

"If you were any kind of reporter," Steven said, "you'd get an interview with him."

"Sure," I said with sarcasm and left for the new home that Viv and I had built in the Minneapolis suburb of Golden Valley — over the protests of whites who relented only after they learned that they could not gain the support of Golden Valley officials and could not intimidate my family. I was by this time working almost exclusively out of my home, because magazine and book commitments took more of my time than did the *Tribune*. I hadn't answered Steven because I wasn't sure that I wanted to glorify Truman.

But Steven called me again. Never willing to make a few hundred bucks if I could earn thousands, I telephoned Herb Nipson, the editor of *Ebony*, to ask if he'd pay for an article on Truman. "Hell, yes," he said.

I did what all successful journalists do: call on old friends who are door openers. For me that meant Hubert Humphrey and Mrs. Eleanor Roosevelt. Within an hour after I called them, I got a call from Independence, Missouri, inviting me to Mr. Truman's home.

My secretary, Irene Rockstroh, and I began intensive research, and the more I researched, the more I admired this man of humble background, this so-called hack of the Kansas City Pendergast political machine, because I learned that long before Truman ever dreamed of becoming a U.S. senator or vice president of the United States, he was campaigning in the most racist areas of Missouri, preaching equality and never running away from a verbal battle with the omnipresent members of the Ku Klux Klan.

I began to realize that I was not going to visit just any old tired ex-president. Truman was the man who had saved Greece and Turkey from communism, who had approved the Marshall Plan, which made possible the economic revival of Western Europe. Truman had ensured the creation of the state of Israel and made the historic decision to drop an atomic bomb on Hiroshima and Nagasaki in Japan. These things, and the record of his response to the North

Korean invasion of South Korea, told me that I was about to interview a man who meant it when he said, "The buck stops here."

I got to Independence on the eve of Truman's birthday and
checked into the Muehlbach Hotel, where I and many other blacks
had once been denied lodging. Truman personally had insisted
that this distinguished old hotel abandon Jim Crow.

The next morning I took a taxi to Mr. Truman's home, arriving
early. After the formalities, he shooed everyone else out.

"Didn't want to do any interviews," he grumbled, "but you have
some damned persistent friends."

"They're nice people," I said.

"Hell, I know. Now what can I do for you?"

"I just want you to reminisce a bit about the most important
moments in your life." I rattled off my litany about Korea, Israel,
the Marshall Plan. . . .

Almost rudely, Truman waved his hand as if to say that I was
boring him with unnecessary flattery.

"None of that foreign stuff is what I remember most," he said. "I
am proudest of what I did for the ordinary people. Only a president
of high principles will look out for the common man. And never
forget that it's the little guy who needs someone in the White House
to look out for him."

Perhaps I was gauche, but I tried again to get him to say whether
he was proudest of his stand on Korea, Greece and Turkey, . . . or
what? His grumpiness I took as a signal that he thought me a bit
obtuse.

"None of 'em," he barked. Then the old history buff began a soliloquy about the Salem witch-hunts, the alien and sedition laws, the era
of the anti-Catholic Know-Nothings, the Ku Klux Klan outrages of
the 1860s and 1920s, and the 1928 campaign of endless bigotry
against Catholic Al Smith, the Democratic presidential candidate.

I thought, in 1959, that I was one hell of a student of, and fighter
for, racial justice, religious freedom, civil liberties, and human
rights. I was president of the Minneapolis Urban League and a
major force in the Minneapolis NAACP. I was on the Committee of
100, citizens across America raising money for the NAACP's Legal
Defense Fund. My dispatches from trouble spots at home and
abroad had informed Americans about everything from the Un-

touchables in India to the unbearable inequities in my own society. I was on a first-name basis with Martin Luther King, Jr., Daisy Bates, Whitney Young, Ralph Bunche. I was running to Birmingham, Nashville, Washington, St. Louis, and dozens of other cities every year, giving speeches that I hoped would help knock down the barriers of Jim Crow. But here I sat in Harry Truman's home, feeling humble, listening to this old pol try to teach me about the long trail of racial meannesses, political oppressions, religious intolerance, and class lunacies that had afflicted America.

When he paused for air, I jumped in, playing the simpleton: "Why would someone from Jim Crow Missouri become so concerned about civil rights?"

"I fought for civil rights laws because it was right. At the same time I realized that it was vitally important to our world leadership to make sure that everybody got the same treatment."

I remembered the grim prediction of 1948 that the pro–civil rights bloc was destroying the old Democratic coalition. This seemed to become a truth at the 1956 convention when the party was badly split on the issue of what it could promise fifteen million black citizens without alienating white voters.

The rift was so wide, the emotions so high, that during the late hours in that 1956 enclave, smoky, sweaty, weary delegates were almost clutching each other's throats. Texas's Sam Rayburn and other party leaders ordered that a microphone be set up in the public gallery. In a few minutes a short, jaunty man with steel-gray hair was delivering an unprecedented lecture to the convention.

"I say that this is a good civil rights plank," then seventy-two-year-old Truman said, "and I'm the greatest civil rights president the country ever had."

I reminded Truman of that convention and told him that after the delegates approved his compromise plank, a black delegate had said to me: "Well, even old Harry sold us out. It was worse than finding out that there really is no Santa Claus."

"That was a damned good plank in 'fifty-six," he shouted. "I know because I wrote it."

"Many delegates, black and white, felt that you wrote a compromise just to preserve party harmony."

With little bulldoggish barks he said, leaning toward my face: "I

... have ... *never* ... believed ... that ... the ... Democratic party ... should ... desert ... its ... principles ... to ... achieve ... harmony!"

He then reached into a little bookcase behind him in which there were well-used, even tattered volumes, books that I assumed must have special meaning for him. He pulled out a small book, waved it at me, and said, "This is where I stand. It's all in here. This is where I stand."

He was holding a copy of "To Secure These Rights," the report of the civil rights committee that he had appointed. It was this group that had shocked the nation with its documentation of lynchings, of the denial of voting rights, of inequality of educational opportunities, of discrimination in our armed forces. It was this committee's report, perhaps, as much as any other single thing in the 1940s and 1950s that drew people's attention to the special problems of the Negro in America and to the need for government to do something.

"How much credit for that report and its ultimate impact should go to Harry Truman?" I wondered. What had prodded him to appoint that committee? What was his real relationship to, his private opinion of, the American Negro? Was Truman just a shrewd Missouri ward politician who had been out to corral Negro votes in the crucial states of the North and West, or was he really the nation's greatest civil rights president till that time?

A look at the record shows this: No president in the nation's history stuck his neck out farther, or risked more in terms of his own political future or of the nation's well-being, in order to espouse the first-class citizenship of the Negro. Lyndon Johnson would *achieve* more, but at far less risk than Truman, who did it, according to his own testimony and to the best evidence that I can assemble, because he thought that to do so was of ultimate good to the nation and because in his early childhood he was imbued with a respect for individual liberty and the common people.

But why did he appoint the special civil rights committee? Truman related that during his early years in the presidency he was disturbed by repeated violence against Negroes, assaults on black servicemen returning to the South, and other violations, even by law enforcement officials. Out of a desire to get the facts behind these incidents, he said, he appointed the committee on December 5, 1946.

In January 1947, the fifteen noted citizens gathered at the White House and were instructed by Truman: "I want our Bill of Rights implemented in fact. We have been trying to do this for 150 years. We're making progress, but we're not making progress fast enough. This country could very easily be faced with a situation similar to the one with which it was faced in 1922" — an obvious reference to the period when the Ku Klux Klan spread terror across the country with its program of racial and religious persecution.

Ten months later the committee released its report, which was front-page news across the nation. But the committee did more than cite the nation's ailments in the field of human relations; it laid down a legislative program designed to cure those ills. What the nation wanted to know now was whether the farm boy from Lamar, Missouri, had either the inclination or the courage to accept the challenge of that report. Almost to a man, his aides said that to endorse or embrace that report would be political suicide.

On February 2, 1948, Truman made perhaps the most daring civil rights speech, took one of the biggest political gambles, of any president in history. In a special message to Congress, he called for a ten-point program to secure the civil rights of all the nation's citizens.

Before an audience that was in part bitterly hostile, he went virtually down the line with his committee, asking for:

1. A permanent commission on civil rights, a joint congressional committee on civil rights, and a civil rights division of the Department of Justice
2. The strengthening of existing civil rights statutes
3. Federal protection against lynching
4. More adequate protection of the right to vote
5. A federal fair employment practices commission
6. A ban on discrimination in interstate transportation
7. Home rule for the District of Columbia
8. Statehood for Hawaii and Alaska and more self-government for other U.S. territories
9. Equalizing opportunities for foreign residents of the United States to become naturalized citizens
10. Settlement of the claims of Japanese-Americans who had been put in concentration camps.

Angry southern congressmen threatened to sabotage the European Recovery Program (the Marshall Plan) and desert the president in his fight against a $6.5 billion tax cut being pushed by the Republicans. Truman now was faced with the traditional southern threat: "If you persist in your civil rights efforts, we will wreck the rest of your program. You cannot afford to have us do that." According to Mrs. Roosevelt, similar threats often had forced FDR to back away from strong civil rights proposals, primarily because Roosevelt was convinced that some southerners actually would sabotage his legislative program and risk the country's losing World War II before they would permit the Negro to emerge from peonage. Roosevelt dared not gamble.

These threats also came at a crucial period for President Truman. Europe was in economic chaos, and there was fear that communism would overrun the Continent unless Congress voted the aid necessary to produce economic recovery. But Truman refused to back down. He gambled that he could defy Deep South congressmen and still get the laws and funds that he needed to save Europe. Truman won that gamble.

Negroes and others began to acclaim Truman for his guts. The Interdenominational Ministerial Alliance of Greater New York awarded him the annual Franklin D. Roosevelt Award for "the greatest contribution to the cause of human rights." In 1949 the Negro Newspaper Publishers Association gave him the John B. Russwurm Award for "his courageous leadership and uncompromising stand in the fight for civil rights." That same year the Anti-Defamation League of B'nai B'rith bestowed upon him its American Democracy Legacy Medal.

Truman was hailed, not without justification, as a better friend of the Negro than Roosevelt — or even Lincoln. Time had mellowed Lincoln's contributions, had draped them in a sort of halo, obscuring the fact that Lincoln really did only what the terrible pressures of his time decreed he must do. The freeing of the slaves was as much a gift of fate, or of history, as of any belief Lincoln had in racial equality. As for Roosevelt, his gifts to the Negro were largely by-products of what he gave the entire nation. In pulling the country from a dreadful depression, FDR more than doubled the earnings of the average white man, and at the same time more than tripled the pitiful earnings of the average Negro. The New Deal started the black man toward economic security to the extent that he could stop thinking about his stomach and begin agitating for the basic rights that gave other Americans a sense of dignity and pride.

In urging laws to secure these fundamental rights, in throwing the weight of the presidency against segregation in the armed forces, in transportation, in schools, Harry Truman was waging an infinitely less popular battle than either Lincoln or Roosevelt dared wage. If all you asked was that Negroes not be held in slavery, or that they not be left to starve to death, millions of Americans North and South would go along, but when you demanded the end of racial separation, the ranks of supporters got thin. Truman found this out.

After Humphrey's dramatic speech at the Democratic convention in Philadelphia in 1948 that forced Strom Thurmond, governor of South Carolina, to lead a Dixiecrat bolt from the convention, a reporter said: "Why are you walking out? All Truman is doing is following the Roosevelt platform."

"I know. But that sonofabitch Truman really means it," Thurmond replied.

Still, in one of the great political coups of all time, Truman won a smashing victory in the presidential election.

But even in 1960 there were a couple of unwritten rules of journalism. The first was that while daily newspapers might hire a black, they did not assign him or her to the prestigious Washington bureau. The second was that editors in places like Minneapolis dared not send a local reporter into Washington to write about things that clearly were within the province of its Washington correspondents.

Cowles and Steven knew the rules. Furthermore, in the Washington bureau, which served the *Minneapolis Tribune*, the *Des Moines Register* and *Tribune*, and *Look* magazine, they had three of the best-known correspondents in the land: Richard Wilson, Fletcher Knebel, and Clark Mollenhoff. But someone decided "rules be damned!" And at another of those social occasions that became a business affair, Steven said to me: "We want you to go to Washington and do a series of articles on Jack Kennedy and Richard Nixon."

"How soon?" I asked.

"Yesterday," Steven said, laughing.

I didn't ask why he wanted *me* to interview the two presidential candidates. I suspect till this day that Bill was having fun helping me to break new ground. I didn't ask which direction the series would take, mainly because I always wanted that left up to me. I assumed that I was given this assignment because of a belief by Steven that I could gain access to both candidates and that I would be especially successful in drawing out each man's views on race and social policy, the issues on which the election would turn.

The following morning I was on the phone early with Mrs. Roosevelt, Senator Humphrey, and Eisenhower's attorney general, Herbert Brownell. They steered me to key people, and by noon I had appointments with both Nixon and Kennedy.

Then I rushed into the hard research that must precede such interviews. I studied in detail everything each man had said about important issues, including some dubious talk about an alleged U.S. "window of vulnerability" to a Soviet nuclear attack. I knew the worries of Kennedy that he might not get enough of either black votes in the North or white votes in the South to defeat Nixon. I was tipped off that Ike really didn't regard Nixon as qualified to be president and had said he would give less than tepid support if Nixon pushed the "white backlash" the way some of his advisers recommended. I talked to people I thought I could trust in both campaigns, fishing for subjects that the candidates were eager to discuss and for issues they probably hoped I wouldn't bring up.

I had no doubt that both would want to tell me how supportive they were of Negroes, because in the last close presidential election — 1948 — the black vote had been crucial. Black votes for Truman had exceeded several times over his 17,865-vote victory in California, his 33,612-vote margin in Illinois, and his triumph in Ohio by 7,107 ballots. This Nixon-Kennedy race was thought to be as close as that of '48.

I interviewed Nixon first. He was formal, in fact cold, in our introduction. He talked first of the "phenomenal shifts of Negro voters," referring to the surprising number of blacks who had chosen Eisenhower over Stevenson, and expressed confidence that Negroes would help give him the presidency.

I felt that his body language revealed that he wasn't confident or comfortable. He kept crossing and uncrossing his legs. He almost never looked me in the eye, acting as though he were reading answers to my questions off the wall or ceiling.

Nixon knew that in addition to the series for the *Minneapolis Tribune* I was writing an article for *Ebony* magazine. With a sort of imperiousness, he mentioned that he had word that both those publications would endorse him. He exuded an air of certainty that he was the inheritor of the Eisenhower throne.

At the end of the lengthy interview, I had the feeling that Nixon had seen me because he did not want to lose any black votes. He had given the interview because someone had told him that it was strategic courtesy.

Kennedy had real reasons for wanting to see me, because he was in deep trouble with black voters, most of whom wanted Humphrey in the Oval Office. So as the Massachusetts senator burst into the room where I was waiting, he seemed more nervous than I had been after that boyhood liaison with the girl on the swinging bridge. He was half an hour late and surely figured that was no way to influence a reporter.

Kennedy had been assailed in a Boston speech by Roy Wilkins as "a compromiser with evil." Wilkins was furious over Kennedy's joining James Eastland and the Senate southern bloc to attach what blacks regarded as a crippling jury trial amendment to the civil rights bill of 1957. Kennedy had been warmly endorsed by Governor John Patterson of Alabama, an arch-segregationist, who said: "I think he's a friend of the South." Those words were anathema to most black Americans. Worse yet, there had been widespread publicity about Kennedy's having breakfast at his Georgetown residence with Patterson and Sam Englehardt, a powerful and well-known Alabama racist. This led baseball hero Jackie Robinson to label Kennedy "the fair-haired boy of the Southern segregationists." Robinson, whose life story, *Wait Till Next Year*, I had written a couple of years earlier, had endorsed Nixon and declared in a newspaper column that "as long as he continues to play politics at the expense of 18 million Negro Americans, . . . Sen. Kennedy is not fit to be President of the United States."

After some preliminary polite exchanges, I got right to business with Kennedy. I said, "Senator, I think you are aware that one of your major handicaps is the fact that many Negroes have been led to believe that you have substantial support from segregationists and that you must have made some kind of behind-the-scenes commitment in order to get the support of these southerners."

Kennedy's face revealed irritation as he waved his hands in a gesture of despair.

"I don't know why people keep saddling me with that burden. Where is all this southern support they keep talking about? I didn't have fifteen southern delegates for me at the national convention.

"It seems to me that people would look at the platform. Everybody agrees that it's the strongest in the party's history. My people were architects of that platform. Many of the sentences in that platform are taken almost verbatim from speeches I had delivered earlier."

"I am sure, Senator," I said, "that one of the reasons this question continues to arise is that people vitally interested in civil rights have been led to believe that some kind of hanky-panky took place in the breakfast you had with Governor John Patterson of Alabama."

Now the senator's irritation was obvious. His face flushed redder.

"Yes, yes, that is my biggest burden, and for the life of me I don't know why people keep trying to discredit me with that when I am as innocent as any man ever could be."

He went on to explain that an Alabama acquaintance said that he was bringing Patterson and some other Alabama officials to Washington and that they would like to meet him. One of the officials in the party was Alabama state senator Sam Englehardt, a leader in the White Citizens Council and generally regarded as the man responsible for the gerrymandering that cut most of the Negro citizens of Tuskegee, Alabama, off the voting rolls.

"I had to see Governor Patterson, just as I would have to see any other governor who asked to meet me," Kennedy said. "If Ross Barnett of Mississippi called today and said 'I'll be in Washington tomorrow, I'd like to see you,' I'd have to see him. But he'd know where I stand.

"Now Governor Patterson went away and endorsed me without my knowledge and without my knowing why. But I don't know who'll endorse me. I can't control that.

"A lot more southerners probably will endorse the Democratic ticket, but not because they assume any kinship with my views on civil rights. Many will do it because they assume that's the only way to keep their seniority and the privileges accruing to them under the party system.

"My plea is that people look at *my* views, look at *my* record, look at *my* stand."

Kennedy spoke pleadingly for understanding that while Patterson was "the biggest cross I have to bear," no presidential candidate in a tight race wanted to publicly reject southern votes in advance if it wasn't absolutely necessary. Why couldn't Negroes ignore silly little things like that meeting, he wondered, and trust in him to prove as president that he was all for equality?

"But people remembered your votes on the same side as Eastland on the voting issue," I said.

A very defensive Kennedy said: "If you think I've sold out to the southerners, go back to 1957 around the time of the Little Rock school crisis and see what I said in Jackson, Mississippi." I had information in my research files that upon arrival in Jackson Kennedy was challenged by the Republican state chairman to declare himself on the school desegregation issue.

"I have no hesitancy in telling the Republican chairman the same thing I said in my own city of Boston," Kennedy had told his audience. "That I accept the Supreme Court decision as the supreme law of the land. I know that we do not all agree on that issue, but I think most of us do agree on the necessity to uphold law and order in every part of the land."

"Would Kennedy *really* uphold law and order during the turbulent years that lay ahead?" I wondered as I left that interview.

Then I read a campaign speech in Merced, California, in which he said: "In the election of 1860, Abraham Lincoln said, 'There is a God and He hates injustice. I see a storm coming, but if He has a place and a part for me, I am ready.' There is a God today and He hates injustice, and we see the storm coming. But I think He has a place and a part for all of us, and I think we are ready."

What was important to me was that Kennedy had pledged to throw the power and prestige of the presidency behind efforts to make America's Negroes first-class citizens. I, like thousands of other Negroes, had agonized over the fact that even though Eisenhower sent troops to Little Rock, he would not state categorically that he believed racial segregation to be not only legally but morally wrong. I felt then, as I now know, that the moral force of the president's office is more potent than his powers as commander in chief of the military. So I was pleased anew by Kennedy's campaign speech in Los Angeles, where he said:

> As a moral leader, the next president must play his role in interpreting the great moral issues which are involved in our crusade for human rights. He must exert the great moral and educational force of his office to . . . support the right of every American to stand up for his rights. . . . For only the president . . . can create the understanding and tolerance necessary.

There were those who said — and some still say — that the Kennedy who made those speeches was playing politics with civil rights. It is a silly argument, of course, because for a president of the United States, political considerations pervade every issue, every action.

Kennedy managed through well-written speeches and personal appeal to wipe out the early hostility of Wilkins, Robinson, and other blacks. Millions of black voters simply saw Kennedy as a friend and Nixon as someone not to trust. And that won Kennedy the presidency. In Illinois he won by 9,000 votes, thanks to 260,000 black supporters. He carried crucial Michigan by 67,000 ballots, thanks to the 250,000 votes he got from blacks.

After the election I watched Kennedy begin to draw key blacks around him — Frank Reeves, who would join the White House staff; Andrew Hatcher, who would become deputy White House press secretary; Robert Weaver, who would head the Housing and Home Finance Agency.

But I watched these things only out of intellectual and journalistic curiosity. I was not and never would be a politician.

I *was* an avid football fan. And that summer and fall I had developed a side career of writing about the football games of the University of Minnesota's Golden Gophers. Minnesota teams had been on hard times for years — ever since whispers raced around the country that the celebrated former coach, Bernie Bierman, refused to play any black in a thinking position, such as quarterback, center, or even running back. So the black high school gridiron stars avoided Minnesota the way a hummingbird would avoid a blizzard. Until, that is, the Gophers' new head coach, Mississippian Murray Warmath, came to me and said: "I just want to win ball games. And I can't do it without some of the good black players from Pennsylvania, Ohio, the South. I'll play any kid at any position where he beats out another kid. Would you help me to convince some great black prospects of that?"

"Yes," I said, "with this understanding. Any kid I help you recruit has got to study — hold up his grades. And some of the old alums who are giving players cars and money under the table will give these kids one thing: a promise that once they graduate the old alums will guarantee them a chance to get a decent job." We shook on that deal.

A few days later Warmath's backfield coach, Jim Camp, came to tell me that Minnesota's success depended on outrecruiting coach Woody Hayes of Ohio State, who allegedly had a great knack for endearing himself to the mothers of tough black kids in the coal-mining areas of Pennsylvania, with Mama talking son into going to school in Columbus.

Camp later brought to my house a potentially great black quarterback from Uniontown, Sandy Stephens, and two highly touted black running backs from Clairton, Pennsylvania — Judge Dickson and Bill Munsey. Black college quarterbacks were all but unheard of at the time. I said to Camp: "Tell Warmath to give me an assurance that if I talk Stephens into coming here, he'll play him at quarterback."

"We put our honor on that," Camp said.

The pros talk of franchise players — superstars who can turn a so-so team into a championship contender. These black guys transformed Minnesota from a perennial Big Ten also-ran into an exciting team. So exciting that I talked Steven into a deal by which I would become a weekend sportswriter, penning a page-one story in which I told my mythical grandma how the Golden Gophers fared. The Gophers did so well in 1960, as did my sportswriter gambit, that they won the championship and went to the Rose Bowl, and I went along to write my usual report to Grandma about the great gridiron war of January 1, 1961.

I was snoozing solidly in my hotel in Pasadena when the phone rang.

"Who the hell can this be?" I grumbled.

"Hey, Carl, Louis Martin here." One of the best and most honorable of all blacks to serve as confidant to a president was speaking. "President Kennedy wants you to join his administration."

"Hell, Louis, I'm half-asleep. What does the president want?"

"He wants you in the State Department."

"Doing what?"

"I think he wants you to replace Linc White, the State Department spokesman."

"Can I call you back?"

"The Man wants an early answer."

"Monday, Louis. Monday."

I went to the Rose Bowl game in as big a daze as did my Golden Gophers, who tarnished before 100 million Americans, losing to the Washington Huskies, 17 to 7. It hardly mattered, because my mind was on that call from Martin. After the game, I talked to Viv, and we agreed there was a hard decision to make. By this time I was getting five hundred dollars a speech, and the requests for lectures grew monthly. It seemed that all I had to do was suggest an article to the *Saturday Evening Post*, and the next mail would bring an expense check. To take a State Department job would mean cutting the family's income in half — just when we'd gotten a bit beyond struggling to make ends meet.

I couldn't wait for Monday, when I could discuss my situation with Hubert Humphrey.

"What are they offering you?" he asked when I got him on the phone.

"Louis Martin says they want me to replace Linc White."

"Hell," Humphrey said emphatically, "you don't want Linc White's job. You want to be his boss. Ask for the job of assistant secretary of state for public affairs."

"Martin tipped me off that they've picked Roger Tubby for that job. You know he campaigned heavily for Kennedy and I didn't do a damn thing."

"Well, take nothing less than deputy assistant secretary. Get yourself a green book and look up these jobs so you'll know what's hot and what's not. But let me tell you, my friend, that if they offer a job of deputy assistant secretary, take it. There's never been a black at that level in State. Those stuffy sonsabitches haven't recognized that black Americans exist. If you aren't willing to come in and help change things, nothing is ever going to change."

Before taking the long ride back to Minneapolis, I called Viv again and said: "Humphrey just told me that I'd be a fink not to take the State Department job. He says I owe it to Negroes and the country to try to open some doors."

"Honey," she said, "where you go, I go. At whatever loss of money."

I telephoned Martin to say that I would consider only the job of Tubby's number-one deputy. He called back within the hour to say, "President Kennedy says the job is yours if you want it."

I agonized for days, then on the night of February 1 wrote my official letter of resignation from the *Tribune*.

Humphrey had warned me about "stodgy State," but I had no real idea of what I was walking into — at least not until my appointment was announced and the front-page headlines popped up all over America.

In the context of white America, my job was no big deal. It didn't even require Senate confirmation. It was news only because "No Negro has ever held so high a job in the State Department."

I was determined that no one would say, with good reason, that Kennedy had given me the job as a token payment to black voters. Nobody in State was going to view me as just the window dressing "spook who sits by the door" (as one novelist had described token blacks) of the diplomatic entrance. Long before I was to go on the payroll, I was in the State Department reading briefing papers, studying the details of my responsibilities, meeting the key people who would be working under me, hobnobbing with the great and sometimes arrogant newsmen who would rely on me to give them information.

I learned quickly that the State Department was a virtual plantation. There were many blacks in State, but they were the messengers, the janitors, the low-paid secretaries and clerk-stenographers, the mail clerks and clerk-typists. The whites were in jobs paying $18,050 (Linc White), $17,000, $15,000, $12,000, but the blacks were, with rare exceptions, in jobs paying $4,000 to $5,000.

One day Frances Criss, the woman who would be my secretary for four and one-half years, said to me: "I've been protecting you from all the people who want to congratulate you. But there's a bureau employee that I think you'll want to talk to."

She brought in a lean man named John A. Skehan, who had a job as administrative assistant on the executive staff of the Public Affairs Bureau. He was the highest-paid black person in the bureau, earning $6,765 a year.

"Mr. Rowan," he said, "I thought you'd like to know what dramatic impact your appointment already has had on this bureau. I've been up for promotion several times, and always it was vetoed by the executive director of the executive staff, Lenore Reece, a dyed-in-the-wool southerner [she was earning $12,470 a year].

"The day the *Washington Post* and the *Star* carried front-page stories indicating that you would be her new boss, she called me in and said: 'John, I've got good news for you. You're getting a double promotion!' "

I knew immediately that there *was* one "trickle-down" theory that was genuine — that when a black person got a job at a supervisory level, the fruits of fairness fell on people below who had suffered through years of discrimination.

But I learned quickly never to underestimate the gall of the whites on the State Department plantation. Orlando A. Simmes, director of the administrative staff, salary $14,705 a year, came to me to say that no GS-18s, the top supergrade job status that I expected, were available. All he could get was a GS-15, paying $15,255, he said.

"Let me tell you something," I replied as calmly as the circumstances permitted. "I will accept no GS-15, no GS-16, and no GS-17. I came expecting $18,500 a year [Tubby was getting $20,000] and that is what you have to deliver, and I know that in this bureaucracy you have ways to do it."

Simmes gave me a look that my special antennae interpreted as saying, "This nigger is serious." He paused momentarily as though considering challenging me. Then, saying "I'll try again, sir," he left my office.

On February 10, just a few days later, Simmes sent a letter to my Minneapolis home, saying, "I have succeeded in getting you a temporary appointment as a Foreign Service Reserve Officer, Class 1, pending the time the Department receives authorization for additional supergrade positions.

"The salary you will receive is $18,450 per annum, which is as close as we can get to the GS-18, which is $18,500 per annum."

I wrote Simmes that the $50 shortfall wouldn't cause any crisis. Meanwhile, I had learned something important about the personnel policies of the federal government in general and the State Department in particular. The civil service and foreign service regulations didn't mean a damn thing when someone in power really wanted something done. Blacks, Hispanics, Asian-Americans could get good jobs only if someone with authority would go to bat for them.

But I was not yet in authority in the ways I wanted to be. I had to prove to a lot of people that I was not just a wet-behind-the-ears black reporter, thrown out of his league by a "liberal" president. I wanted to show early that I was not a tame black who would bend meekly to the white establishment. Fortunately, I got an early chance to disabuse State of this notion.

Both Louis Martin and Humphrey had assured me that the government would pay for moving my household effects to Washington. But when I submitted receipts and asked for reimbursement for $1,038.41, Simmes informed me that the office of the assistant secretary for administration had ruled adversely. The argument was that I was "different" from other foreign service appointments in that I was not slotted to go overseas.

I fired off a memo to Simmes demanding that he go at it again. He failed. Then I fired off a memo to William Crockett, the assistant secretary for administration. I'm sure I shocked him by telling him that a white guy named Edgar Comee had just come onto *my* staff with a foreign service reserve appointment — and with his moving expenses paid. I deplored the double standard and demanded to be reimbursed forthwith.

The next day an aide to Crockett walked into my office with a satchel full of discretionary cash and peeled off $1,039 for me.

I had already asserted myself in areas more important to the national interest than my bank account. On my very first visit to Washington, before being sworn in, I informed Tubby that I was appalled that the Public Affairs Bureau's public opinion studies staff was purporting to tell Secretary Dean Rusk and the president what Americans were thinking when neither the director, Foster H. Schuyler, nor anyone else in the office ever read a black publication. Tubby, a marvelously sensitive man, ordered that the bureau subscribe to the *Pittsburgh Courier*, the *Baltimore Afro-American*, the *Chicago Defender* newspapers, and to *Jet* and *Ebony* magazines.

Despite little concessions like these, I knew that I had walked into a hostile environment, into a State Department that was not properly educated to deal with the new world that was still emerging out of the carnage of the worst war man had ever known. The foreign service had many good men in it, but too many were southern elitists who in 1961 still carried the mental baggage of the Civil War era. Many had dismissed the Asian-African conference in Bandung as a mere aberration, believing that their own military power and economic wealth would always prevail. They did not believe that Russia or China could wield enough influence or give enough arms to Third World countries to make a difference.

President Kennedy was immersed in crises even in his first weeks in office. A CIA scheme to invade Cuba at the Bay of Pigs and inspire Cubans to rise up against Fidel Castro had blown up in the new young president's face, and he had to watch a Communist regime take roots some ninety miles from Florida. Khrushchev was making almost daily threats of warfare over Berlin. There was fear that the Soviets would establish "a beachhead in the heart of Africa," if the United States did not stand up against a plot by Congo official Moise Tshombe and Union Minière, a Belgian-controlled mining company, to have mineral-rich Katanga secede from the rest of the country. Laos was on its way to becoming a perennial basket case. And U.S. military involvement in Vietnam was secretly becoming greater day by day.

Part of my job was to tell America, through press briefings, conferences for editors and publishers, public speeches, and every way I could imagine, what the Kennedy administration's policies were regarding each of these crises and why those policies were in the best interest of American citizens — and mankind.

Another of my jobs was to attend the morning briefings of Secretary of State Dean Rusk when Tubby was unable to go. I sensed two things immediately: First, Rusk was an enigma who almost never said what he thought the United States ought to do in these crises. If he told Kennedy, he never shared it with his underlings, thus he would never be embarrassed when his assistants saw that Kennedy was following a different course, probably recommended by Secretary of Defense Robert McNamara or his national security adviser, McGeorge Bundy. Second, the State Department mentality was that the Public Affairs Bureau was not to sound off trying to make policy but simply to listen to what the "career experts" said and authorized Public Affairs to make public. Neither Tubby nor I would accept that. So many mornings I responded to a Rusk comment about what the White House or Defense Department wanted with the comment, "Mr. Secretary, that would be a serious mistake. There is no way we can sell that to either the American people or the rest of the world."

I would see the career guys whispering to one another, casting looks at me that seemed to say, "What does this blooming black guy think he's doing?"

President Kennedy was close to a public relations genius. He decided that he would have televised press conferences in the State Department auditorium, a forum in which he could display his sharp mind, wit, and telegenic charm. One of my jobs was to help prepare the briefing book of foreign policy questions he could expect and the replies recommended by the State Department. In the hours between Rusk's delivery of the briefing book and a press conference, all sorts of news developments would break out around the world. I got the job of meeting President Kennedy in the State Department garage before every press conference to bring him up to date. The public never knew that the Kennedy I met in the basement was far different from the one who stepped before the press and the TV cameras.

"United Press reported a half hour ago that U.S. 'military advisers' are actually leading South Vietnamese assaults near the North Vietnam border," I might say.

"What's wrong with these motherfuckers at UP?" Kennedy would almost shout. "Don't they have any goddam patriotism?"

"Sir," I would reply, "these newsmen think reporting the truth is patriotism. You're due on in five minutes, and this is what the secretary thinks you ought to say if you're asked about this. And trust me, you will be asked."

Before another press conference, Kennedy unloaded his frustrations as he read what the State Department hierarchy, through its labyrinthian system of clearances, suggested he say at a press conference. For example, a suggested statement about the Congo had to be approved by the African Bureau, the European Bureau (the metropole was Belgium), the United Nations Bureau, the Public Affairs Bureau, the under secretary for political affairs, and Rusk.

There were times after that when I cheated on the clearance system, because time restraints made it impossible to listen to a babble of mostly timid recommendation, and said to the president what made good sense to me. I was not his confidant or adviser, never had been, and never would have a day-to-day relationship, but I noticed that when he got into his press conference he used verbatim some of the off-the-cuff phrases that I had given him.

Those State Department garage conversations were brief at best, but on one occasion when he was angry upon arrival he said that the CIA was out of control (the Bay of Pigs fiasco obviously still rankled him), the military attachés were loose cannons, and he was going to send Under Secretary of State Chester Bowles to conferences where everyone representing the United States abroad would know that the U.S. ambassador was "king," and no one in any mission was to do anything without the ambassador's knowledge and approval. He said he hoped I'd go help Bowles spread the word.

I thought he was just blowing off steam until I saw that, on May 1, 1961, Kennedy sent personal letters to all U.S. chiefs of mission informing them that they were his alter egos and the absolute superior officials in the countries where they were posted. I went with Bowles to conferences in Europe, Africa, the Far East, and Latin America, and my mere presence in an important role changed the mind-set of many ambassadors. (Till then, the unwritten rule was that American Negroes could serve in Liberia, the Canary Islands, and few places else. A black career officer, Clifton

Wharton, had broken new ground by being named minister to Romania and then ambassador to Norway.)

At these meetings I won the acceptance and respect of a lot of ambassadors and foreign service people who had thought of me as a Kennedy payoff to black voters. When I talked policy substance on the basis of my months in India and Southeast Asia, my coverage at Bandung, my weeks at the United Nations, my travels in Africa and Canada, I sensed that our envoys realized that I was no political hack.

But, as is so often the case in life, I made friends in these meetings by stumbling upon something that made them laugh. Bill Attwood, an old friend and the former *Look* magazine editor who was then ambassador to Guinea, asked at the Lagos, Nigeria, conference if I would brief the ambassadors and their wives on the rising racial violence in America.

"Hell, no," I said.

His face reddened in embarrassment as he asked, "Why not?"

"Because I got sandbagged the last time I talked about race," I said cryptically. "I'll explain at the damned briefing."

I told this diplomatic group that I was reluctant to talk because of what had happened the first Saturday Kennedy gave me the day off. I had gone out to mow my lawn at Sixteenth and Hemlock streets, where apparently no blacks had lived before, and I had barely started my mower when a beautiful blonde rolled up in a chauffeur-driven limousine. I recounted the drama.

"Boy!" she called.

I figured she wasn't talking to me, a State Department honcho. "*Boy!*" she shouted.

I flicked the motor off and said, "I beg your pardon, ma'am?"

"Tell me, how much do you get for mowing lawns?"

"Well, the lady at *this* house lets me sleep with her."

The ambassadors and their wives laughed wildly.

"But wait," I said, "I haven't explained how I got sandbagged. My wife and I gave a dinner at which some Africans were present, and one kept haranguing me about how there was no racial justice in America. I tried to silence him by telling the lawn-mowing story. In dumb and dogged persistence he asked, 'Just when did this terrible incident occur?'

"I said that it was an apocryphal story. He asked what 'apocryphal' meant. I said it means it's not really true. Whereupon, from the other end of the table, Viv shouted: 'It sure as hell isn't.' "

That story went around the world in a lot less than eighty days. I was on a moving walkway in the San Francisco airport when a woman going in the opposite direction leaned over and asked, "Mr. Rowan — mowed any good lawns lately?" I was getting on a plane with Rusk to go to the United Nations when Rusk said, "Carl, I sure as hell hope that lawn-mowing story is true."

"Why?"

"Because I just heard President Kennedy tell it to Sir Harold Macmillan on the transatlantic telephone."

I had begun to think that the barrier that Humphrey had led me across wasn't all that bad.

That is, until Rusk told me that the president wanted me to accompany Vice President Lyndon Baines Johnson on a trip around the world.

Rowan and sister Jewel,
circa 1930.

Rowan and cousin Lou
Lillian Higginbotham
at 1942 high school
graduation.

Rowan at eighteen as
Navy V-12 officer
trainee.

Rowan at nineteen as
one of the first twenty
black Navy officers in
American history.

Rowan with postwar
classmates at Oberlin
College, 1946.

The Rowan family (Carl
holding Carl Jr., Vivien
holding Jeff, and
daughter, Barbara)
rejoices on return from
Asia, 1955.

Rowan working with Adlai Stevenson at the United Nations during the 1962 Cuban missile crisis.

President Kennedy discusses Rowan's assignment as ambassador to Finland.

Opposite: Rowan with Eleanor Roosevelt at Hyde Park, where he went for a picnic in 1957 and stayed thirteen days.

Kennedy discusses
Finland's key role in the
cold war era.

Minnesota Finns honor
Rowan with a sauna.

Vivien Rowan about to attend the National Day dinner in Finland.

Sons Jeff and Carl Jr. join in a proud moment.

Johnson tells why he chose Rowan to replace Edward R. Murrow as Director of the U.S. Information Agency.

Johnson and Sen. Hubert H. Humphrey wish Rowan well in his USIA job.

Ambassador Rowan welcomes President and Mrs. Johnson to Helsinki in 1963.

Rowan is welcomed during one of many visits to South Vietnam.

The late Larry Fanning, left, and the late Will Munnecke announce that Rowan has broken another barrier and become a nationally syndicated columnist for the *Chicago Daily News* and the *Chicago Sun-Times*.

USIA chief Rowan and wife, Vivien, chat at the Berlin Wall, 1964.

Rowan returns to
McMinnville, Tennes-
see, in 1971 and is
greeted warmly by an
old family friend.

Rowan with his beloved teacher "Miss Bessie," Mrs. Bessie Taylor Gwynn.

Photo by Maurice Sorrell, courtesy of Johnson Publications

Rowan at his boyhood home—still an impoverished place but now with electricity.

Photo by Maurice Sorrell, courtesy of Johnson Publications

Rowan shoots the bull with boyhood buddies, McMinnville, Tennessee, 1971.

Rowan as Gridiron Club thespian, with old friend Charles Bailey.

To Carl Rowan,
Best Wishes —

Jimmy Carter
Rosalynn Carter

Rowan at the White House interviewing President and Mrs. Carter.

The Rowans welcome Vice President and Mrs. Bush to the 1987 Gridiron Dinner.

The Reagans came to the Gridiron Dinner when Rowan was president.

Rowan interviews Supreme Court Justice Thurgood Marshall for two prize-winning television specials.

CHAPTER TWELVE

Travels with Lyndon

HAD NEVER MET Johnson. But I got hints that he was someone to watch closely, to rein in when his political exuberances got out of control.

Johnson had scared the hell out of the intellectuals around Kennedy with his little soliloquies about how he could tell what was in a man's heart by looking into his eyes and how if anybody ever gave him a chance to sit down with the leaders of the Soviet Union and look into *their* eyes he would see what's in their hearts and would have a basis for solving most of the problems of the world. It unnerved me to think that I had the job of going on a trip during which I would be telling the vice president of the United States what he could and could not say.

As if that did not create a perilous enough position, I knew that one of Johnson's assignments was to figure out whether or not the United States could save Indochina by supporting the Saigon dictator Ngo Dinh Diem or whether it had to get rid of him. But I was also aware that the United States really didn't have a Vietnam policy at that time. All anyone knew was that President Kennedy wanted to prevent a Communist takeover of South Vietnam and that Diem was a pain in the derriere to Washington. As for the more sophisticated elements of U.S. policy, about all that the White House was sure of was that the North Vietnamese had made a conscious decision to take South Vietnam, and orders had gone out from Hanoi to the North Vietnamese cadres in the South and to the Vietcong to step up their attacks.

Kennedy was now pumping military advisers into Vietnam by the score and trying to keep the magnitude of his commitments from the American public. Uneasy about the mess, Kennedy was not of a mind to throw any countries to Moscow or Peking by default, and he was certainly not of a mood to have the Republican opposition accuse him of being soft on communism. Some of us thought that he had asked Johnson to go to Southeast Asia so that he could have someone else to point the finger at once he committed American troops to that war.

A few days after I learned that I was to accompany Johnson, a story was leaked about his impending trip. I went to the first meeting of State Department, Defense Department, CIA, and other officials with Johnson and discovered that we had a vice president who was paranoid about the press and especially about leaks. He walked into the meeting and said, apropos of nothing, "I want you State Department folks to know that I think you're a bunch of little puppy dogs, leaking on every hydrant." He began to rail against whoever it was who had leaked the story, then set forth his theory about how you discover who a government leaker is.

"I tell you, you just write down the name of the reporter who wrote that goddam story, and you wait a few weeks and you're gonna see that reporter write something nice about the leaker because the reporter's got to pay that guy off, and I can tell you I'm waiting to see if there's a nice profile about old Chester Bowles, 'cause I think he's the one who leaked the story about my trip."

I sat there in astonishment, absolutely certain that the leak came not from Chester Bowles but from the president of the United States.

We all learned during that trip that there is nothing anyone could say about Lyndon Johnson that was so good or so bad that it was not true at one time or another, and generally all in the same day.

Johnson was drinking a lot of Cutty Sark in those days, and the more he drank the meaner he got. He abused his staff verbally in ways that I could not believe. Yet, when sober or in one of his better moods, he spoke with greater eloquence and understanding about the economic and social needs of the poor nations, and about injustice in the United States, than any individual I ever knew in my life.

That 1961 trip was wild beyond anything I could ever have imagined, and totally because of the frustrations, the insecurities, the foibles, the meanness, of this man. There were two constant sources of blowups throughout the trip: what Johnson considered to be administrative slipups, and the activities of the press.

For example, he frequently complained about the beds. In Nicosia, he called Assistant Secretary of State William Crockett in and motioned him over to the bed. "Look at this," he said as he pressed down on the bed. "This is no goddam mattress. They got me sleeping on a bunch of springs wrapped up in a tow sack."

In Tehran he complained bitterly that the mattress was not stiff enough. Someone found a board and put it under the mattress. The bed still was not stiff enough, he said. I suggested putting the board on top of the mattress, a suggestion that was not viewed as funny by Johnson.

Also while in Iran, the journalists traveling with him decided not to accompany him on a visit to a village. The newsmen, who had been with him all morning, had to get back to Tehran to file their stories for the Sunday papers.

Later, he called me in to ask: "What kind of bunch of goddam pansies have I brought sixteen thousand miles only to have them sit around in air-conditioned rooms drinking whiskey while I am out meeting the people? No wonder we are not getting anything in the newspapers back home. There is not a thing in the *New York Times*. I think that reporter must have found himself a girl or two. He must be doing something with somebody, because he sure as hell ain't doing no newspapering."

A few days later, in Ankara, he and I came in from a trip through a teeming bazaar, and he was in a rage about the newspapermen.

"Carl," he said, "I went out this morning to try to meet the people and it was a total flop. I kept sticking my hand out in friendship and the only thing I ever could reach was a goddam bunch of newspapermen. I had about thirty photographers in front of me knocking each other down and a bunch of reporters behind me hanging on to my goddam coattail and Secret Service to my left and my right pushing down women and children. What can we do, Carl? Jesus, I guess we have just got to live with these goddam newspapermen."

Johnson wanted badly to be respected, even loved, by the press and couldn't understand that his personality was suited perfectly to rubbing the media the wrong way.

In reaching Bangkok, the U.S. Information Service officer had put in Johnson's room a summary of U.S. press articles about his trip. The Associated Press was reporting that he had "$40 million in his pocket for Ngo Dinh Diem." Johnson read the articles in my presence, grunted a few times, but said nothing. A couple of hours later he walked up to me and asked in a voice drooling with sarcasm: "Mr. Roe-ann, do I look like I'm wearing any goddammed glass pants?"

"Not to me," I replied.

"Then how come that reporter for the goddammed AP can see forty million dollars in my pocket for Diem?" Then he went into a tirade about "all the damned thumb-suckers and think pieces and other horseshit speculation about what I'm doing when the ones doing the writing don't know a damned thing."

"Mr. Vice President," I said, "I am not your press secretary, but since you have come to me I am going to speak in that role. There are a lot of reporters traveling with you. Their publications have paid a lot of money to send them. These reporters are going to file stories every day. If you give them some facts, something specific, they'll write about that. If you give them nothing they'll write thumb-suckers and think pieces."

"You suggesting I oughta meet with that bunch of bastards?"

"I am."

Johnson stalked off.

That night, to my surprise, a couple of newsmen told me they were going to the Johnson press conference, which no one in the official party had mentioned to me. I went to the meeting.

Johnson opened by saying, "I want y'all to know that I don't want to meet with you. But Mr. Roe-ann says I have to. You know, he doesn't work for me. If he did I'd fire him for bad advice. But he works for the State Department."

After the first really probing question, Johnson turned to me and said: "And you're the dummy who told me to submit myself to this?"

The press corps grew silent, with every member looking at me.

"Mr. Vice President," I said, "who the dummy is will be determined by how the questions are answered."

You could have cut the tension in that room with a quill. Johnson took another question and abruptly broke up the press conference.

As the last newsman walked out, I walked up to Johnson and said: "Mr. Vice President, I think we had better get a few things straight early on. I have seen that you have a habit of insulting members of your staff in public. I want you to know that I don't play that game. If you insult me in front of these newsmen, I will insult you. I didn't ask to come on this trip; I didn't ask for the State Department job; President Kennedy asked me. If we can't work on a basis of mutual respect, I will take the first flight back to Washington."

Johnson was stunned. But I knew that I held the trump ace. Johnson had revealed to me that he wanted more than all else to have Kennedy and Rusk think that he had done a good job. He was intelligent enough to know that if I left there would be headlines all over America saying BLACK OFFICIAL LEAVES PARTY OVER VP INSULT. Johnson surely didn't want that.

"You stay here," he said. "I won't be insulting you in front of any reporters, 'cause I'm not seeing 'em anymore."

But at dinner on the rooftop of Saigon's Caravelle Hotel, Elizabeth Carpenter, Mrs. Johnson's press secretary, came to my table to say, "The vice president's eating over there. He wants to know where the photographers are."

"I assume they're somewhere doing what we are doing — having dinner," I said.

"The vice president wants you to go get them so they can take his picture."

"I won't do that."

"You want me to tell the vice president that you won't go get the photographers?"

"Correct. You tell him that it would hurt him and me to ask them to leave dinner to take his picture."

I don't know what she told Johnson. I figured that he couldn't get any angrier at me than he already was.

The next day, to my astonishment, Johnson telephoned me in the middle of the lunch hour and said, "If you still think I ought to talk to the reporters, I will."

"I do," I replied. "When will you receive them?"

"Hell, right now!" he said.

"A lot of them are at lunch now, but we'll have them here soon," I said, hiding my exasperation.

Another State Department officer, David Waters, and I jumped into two cars and went to the popular restaurants to spread the word. Having rounded up a respectable contingent of reporters, we went back to the vice president's quarters. I went in first to find Johnson sitting on his bed with just his drawers on.

"The press people are here," I said.

"Hell, bring 'em on in," he said gruffly.

There followed the only press conference that, to my knowledge, a senior American official held in his skivvies.

Later that day, on orders from the White House and the State Department, I was to join his aide Horace Busby in writing one of the most important speeches Johnson would ever give — an address to the Vietnamese National Assembly on the morning of May 12, 1961.

There was a state dinner on May 11 that lasted till almost midnight, so we were a bit on the weary side when we holed up in a room in Gia Long Palace to write Johnson's speech, based partly on what Johnson wanted to say and more on what cables from Washington said he should say.

At about 2:00 A.M. there was a rap on the door. I opened it to see Johnson standing there in brown-and-white striped pajamas.

"Hi, Carl. Hi, Buz. Y'all got any beer?"

"No, sir."

"Well, let's drink some damned beer, because I can't sleep; I want to talk and I need some advice."

I awakened a servant sleeping nearby and browbeat him into going to get some beer.

As we sipped beer that we did not need, considering the importance of the speech that we were writing, Johnson began to tell stories . . . on and on and on.

Busby slipped me a note saying, "I've heard all this. If you leave the room he'll go back to bed and we can finish this fucking speech."

I crumpled the note and stuck it in my pocket, then listened to a few more stories. Then I said, "Mr. Vice President, we are writing the speech that you are supposed to give at ten A.M. My secretary is sitting in the foyer typing your speech as we send pieces of it down. I must go tell her not to go to sleep, because there is more to come."

"Humph," Johnson growled as he took a swig from his third beer.

After what I thought was a proper interval, I went back to the workroom and put my ear against the door. Not a sound. I opened the door and took a step in and was assailed by the Texas drawl I knew too well.

"Mr. Roe-ann," Johnson said, "this is why our country is going to hell. The vice president of the United States is sitting here at three o'clock in the morning, needing some crucial advice from you, and you're down there diddling your secretary."

I kept my composure and asked, "What advice do you want?"

"I want you to tell me whether I should buy Perle Mesta's house."

"Buy the house of Washington's celebrated hostess with the mostest?" I asked myself, then replied:

"Well, I think —"

"Now wait a minute, dammit, till you know why I need your advice."

Then Johnson told me how he had let "a so-called liberal, Stu Symington [Democratic senator from Missouri], talk me into joining the Chevy Chase Club." He said that when Lady Bird tried to give a party for Lynda Bird, "they asked for the guest list, saying they wanted to be sure there were not too many Jews or any Negroes invited.

"And I said, Lady Bird, I'm gonna buy you a goddammed house where, if you wanna give a party, you won't have to give any sumbitch your guest list.

"Now my question, Mr. Roe-ann, is whether you think I ought to buy Perle Mesta's house."

"Buy it," I said and took a big swig of beer.

A few minutes later the telephone rang. Johnson's real estate agent was calling and got instructions to buy The Elms immediately.

Johnson got up to go back to bed. At the door he turned to me and said, "If I ever get to be president, I'm gonna get a law that says even you or any Negro could buy Perle Mesta's house."

Busby and I sighed in relief and went about putting some brave platitudes into Johnson's speech.

Later that morning Johnson told the National Assembly of his meeting with President Diem: "I informed your president that the United States stands ready to assist in meeting the grave situation which confronts you. I have gone into detail with your president. There are many things the United States is willing to do."

I should not have been surprised, but I was, when I saw the *New York Times* headline saying JOHNSON ASSURES SAIGON OF AID IN ARMY BUILD-UP . . . MILITARY AND OTHER BACKING AGAINST REDS PLEDGED IN SPEECH TO SOUTH VIETNAM ASSEMBLY — HE SEES NGO DINH DIEM.

I began to sense the immensity of the quagmire into which we were wading. I made my usual morning visit to talk to Johnson about press coverage only to find that he was on the toilet stool. I tried to keep a proper distance only to hear LBJ shout, "If that's you, Carl, come on in. I need somebody to talk to."

I squinched up my nose and went in. He wanted to talk about his remarks at the Saigon reception he and Mrs. Johnson had given.

"I saw communism's allies today," Johnson had told a distinguished gathering of Vietnamese. "They are the sickness, illness, poverty, misery, hopelessness, that I saw when I walked this morning among ragged Vietnamese children."

"Did I say the right thing?" he asked me.

"Of course you did," I said, laughing to myself since I had written those lines.

"I don't know about this fellow, Diem," Johnson said. "He was tickled as hell when I promised him forty million dollars and talked about military aid, but he turned deaf and dumb every time I talked about him speeding up and beefing up some health and welfare projects. I spent two hours and forty-five minutes with him; tried to get knee-to-knee and belly-to-belly so he wouldn't misunderstand me, but I don't know if I got to him."

On May 20 Johnson was thrown into a blue funk by this *New York Times* editorial:

> On the Asian tour in which he is engaged, Vice President Johnson has conducted himself with a flamboyance that must, at times, have been bewildering to the people and leaders he has visited.
>
> He has plunged into crowds to pump hands and talk with bystanders. He has boarded buses and wandered into roadside hamlets in pursuit of contact with the Asian common man. In India he hauled a bucket up from a forty-foot village well while telling a grizzled farmer that he grew up as a poor boy who "had to draw water for horses and mules."

Other visiting Western officials before him, including Mr. Nixon and Mr. Khrushchev, have used popularity techniques in Asia similar to those Mr. Johnson has been employing. No matter how much they may represent genuine good-will, these techniques are in questionable taste. Some Asians are extroverts and may even enjoy the folksy manners of a Western election-campaigner. Others are not and prefer dignity and reserve in public personalities. We seriously doubt that Mr. Johnson has helped the cause of the United States very much by behavior which at times seemed more reminiscent of election campaigns in Texas or more designed to make news than to achieve serious diplomatic objectives.

Johnson's outrage spilled over on everyone, especially *New York Times* correspondent Robert Trumbull.

By the time we reached New Delhi, Johnson had me on his premier "out" list and had told his top aide, Walter Jenkins, that he no longer was required to clear speeches, or the proposed joint communiqué with Prime Minister Jawaharlal Nehru, with me.

"Great," I said. "I have lots of friends in Delhi, so I'll party tonight." I did, returning to the hotel at well past 2:00 A.M. Jenkins was waiting, as was my secretary, Fran Criss.

"The vice president changed his mind and wants you to clear the proposed joint communiqué before he goes for breakfast with Nehru," Jenkins said.

"What is this crap?" I asked as I read a passage about how the United States regarded India as a "good bet" and was willing to gamble a little money on her nose. "India is no racehorse," I said. "Nehru will find this condescending. This section must be taken out."

"But the whole thing has been mimeographed," Jenkins said.

"Then why the hell am I reading it?"

"Do you want your secretary to do a new version, only to find out that the vice president and Ambassador [John Kenneth] Galbraith prefer the one that's already done?"

"No. I'll settle for your putting a note under each man's door telling them that I object to this passage."

That was done. I held a press briefing the next morning and had just finished when Johnson arrived from the breakfast meeting with Nehru.

"Carl," he hollered, "goddammit, you were right again."

"What?"

"About that communiqué. You were right. Now, don't you tell Galbraith I told you this, but I wanted to take your advice, and Galbraith didn't. So when Nehru gets to the part you found offensive, he scratches it out. He throws the piece of paper up in the air. So we ain't got any damned communiqué."

"I'm sorry to hear that. I truly am."

"Listen," Johnson said as he poked a finger into my chest. "You just go on standing up for what you believe in, and never be afraid to get knocked down for what you believe in."

"Thank you, sir," I said as I started to walk away. I had taken perhaps twenty paces when I heard that familiar voice shout, "Hey, Carl!" I turned around to see a solemn Lyndon Johnson stare at me for a moment, and then he said: "But you'd know that, wouldn't you? 'Cause you been getting knocked down all your life."

Johnson had misjudged the honesty and integrity of Galbraith, who said to me hours later that he had made a mistake in insisting that the communiqué be given to Nehru as first written.

But that little episode sealed a friendship between Johnson and me that was based on mutual respect. That friendship would run upon some hard times, but it lasted until Johnson's death. I simply accepted the fact that there were three or four Lyndon Johnsons.

I saw two Johnsons on the day we visited Agra and the Taj Mahal. LBJ had been told emphatically that there was to be no kissing or loud behavior at the Taj Mahal. At one point we were stunned to see Johnson planting passionate smooches on Lady Bird. Then he let go a Texas yodel that shook the roof.

An offended American newsman said to me: "God help us if that man ever becomes president."

I just laughed, because that irreverent side of Johnson didn't bother me.

I encouraged Johnson to continue his unconventional brand of diplomacy (regardless of the *New York Times*). But I never dreamed he would carry it as far as he did. When we arrived in Pakistan, Johnson plowed into a pocket of impoverished people and got carried away with southern hospitality. He invited Bashir the Camel Driver to visit the United States and stay in the Waldorf-Astoria Hotel. This became a sensation in the Pakistani press.

After we returned to the States I got a call from Johnson one day. "I've got a problem that you caused, and you've got to help me solve it," he said.

"A problem I caused?"

"Yeah. You were the one who told me to invite that camel driver."

"I wh . . . wh . . . wh . . ." I stuttered.

"Now I've got to bring him here or look like a phony. But the sumbitch has disappeared. What do I do now?"

"I'll bet the Pakistani government has kidnapped Bashir," I replied. "Either because they don't want an illiterate camel driver coming here to represent the country, or they think they're taking you off the hook. You've got to get word to President Ayub Khan that you are serious about Bashir coming here."

Johnson got to Khan, the camel driver surfaced — came to the Waldorf-Astoria — and turned out to be a charming representative of Pakistan.

Too bad Johnson had not always been as charming as Bashir. I remember the night in Ankara when I was just preparing to go out to dinner and the phone rang. The vice president wanted me to join him for a drink. I got to his room to find several other members of his staff, Ambassador Raymond Hare and his wife, and the Turkish chief of protocol and his wife, sitting around listening to the vice president chat. He ordered a drink for me and seemed to note just the moment when I sat back cozily.

Then he said: "Carl, my friend, have you seen those eighty-three photographs that USIA wants to send to every post we have got in the world?"

"No, sir, I have not," I replied.

"Well, you have missed seeing the goddamnedest collection of so-called photographs ever put together. They have got me cross-eyed, pop-eyed, bug-eyed; they have got me looking like walking death. Don't you reckon USIA's got no business sending any damn photographs out without your seeing them?"

I explained that USIA was an independent agency and that normally I wouldn't pass review on photographs they send out, but if he wanted me to assume that responsibility on this trip, I would.

"Marie," he said, "go get that damn bunch of photographs if you can stand to hold them in your hand long enough to get them here."

He got the photographs and thumbed through them, passing them to me one by one as he made assorted uncomplimentary remarks about photographs, the photographer, USIA, and the press in general.

"Why, there is not a picture in the whole damn bunch that is worth throwing at a howling tomcat."

"Mr. Vice President, I disagree," I said. "There are some photographs that are worth sending to all of our posts."

"You what?"

"I disagree. There are some usable photographs here."

"All right, dammit, you pick out three and then everybody here can know how bad your judgment is."

I selected what I thought were the three best photographs and handed them to him. He studied them one at a time and conceded that I was right.

"But you would agree that three out of eighty-three is a pretty damn poor average, wouldn't you?"

"Yes, I would."

"Imagine that. Wanting to send that damn bunch of photographs around the world. Why, that would be just like sending out eighty cases of the smallpox and three virgins.

"If I were a dictator the first thing I would do is abolish USIA. It's never been worth a damn. I would send Ed Murrow back to CBS and I would send this damn photographer back up to Madison, Wisconsin, where he could run a tractor. That is about the skill he has got.

"And Rowan, my friend, find [press secretary] George Reedy and tell him that I am deeply appreciative of the fact that he concurs with [USIS public affairs officer Robert] Lincoln in the decision to ship these eighty-three pictures around the world. You get him on the phone and tell him they can ship out the three you picked, but I want them to burn the other eighty if they can concur on how to strike a match."

A few days later as he stepped off the plane in Athens, Johnson motioned vigorously to his military aide, Colonel William Jackson. He said to Jackson: "You have done it again. You and that goddam advance party have done it again. You have got the photographers over here taking pictures from my right side. Bill, I don't know how long it is going to take you to learn that you no more have a picture taken from your right side than you sleep with your daughter."

At the end of this journey, the utterly fatigued Johnson party stopped in Bermuda to rest for a day and a half and to give the vice president a chance to formulate his report to President Kennedy. I had two bourbons and went to bed for a long sleep.

But my dreams of rest were punctured by the telephone and a Texas voice that said, "We need to talk. I'm going to hold a press conference. What are these bastards gonna ask me?"

"Well, they're certain to ask you how serious you think the Communist threat is in Vietnam and the rest of Asia."

"What should I tell 'em?"

"Just tell the truth about your impressions, about what you feel. They probably will ask for specifics about your talks with leaders, what they wanted and what you promised, but they don't expect you to tell them."

Johnson actually told them a bigger truth than he could possibly have imagined. He said that "the struggle to preserve freedom in Southeast Asia will be long, costly, and in many instances dangerous." He said that the outcome of the struggle against Communist insurrection, subversion, and terrorism "will depend on not only the determination and resolve of the free peoples of Asia, but upon the steps we take to help them preserve their liberty."

That news conference went so well that I decided to hell with resting and got ready for the big home-going party. Liz Carpenter and Bess Abell had asked me to write special lyrics to a song everyone knew, so I penned something entitled "Around the World with LBJ." That night we all sang with gusto:

> *Around the world with LBJ,*
> *We sweated hard, we lost some lard*
> *Way out in old Taipei.*
> *Around the world with Lyndon B.,*
> *He filled us full of Bob Trumbull*
> *And that goddammed AP.*
> *It must have been in old Saigon*
> *He met the press, and what a mess,*
> *With just his drawers on.*
> *No longer can we go to distant climes —*
> *He has irked the* New York Times.

We all guffawed, but noticed that Johnson did not crack a smile.

The following day, as we journeyed to Washington, where he would report to President Kennedy, Johnson surprised me by uttering a sentence of approval of the press.

"Some pretty good stories today," he said.

I never knew what Johnson told President Kennedy, but my gut feeling was that he described Diem as a hard man with whom to deal and a burdensome partner in any fight for freedom.

Upon returning from the Bermuda "rest stop," I slept almost twenty-four hours, something I had never done before, even in my teen days, and have not come close to doing since. When I came out of the fog of weariness, I said to Viv: "I'm worried by what's going on."

I reminded her that both Kennedy and Johnson had badgered the Eisenhower-Nixon administration, demanding that they tell Americans the truth about Ike's policy regarding Vietnam.

Eisenhower had said in 1952, "I would never send troops [to Vietnam]." In February 1954, he said: "I can conceive of no greater tragedy than for the United States to become involved in all-out war in Indochina." Nixon had said on April 16, 1954: "It is hoped that the United States will not have to send troops there, but if this government cannot avoid it, the Administration must face up to the situation and dispatch forces."

"Viv," I said, "Ike was putting military men in there when he issued his public warning against it. Kennedy and Johnson knew it, and so did Bill Knowland, the Senate majority leader. Ike was playing the same secrecy game that Kennedy and Johnson want to play."

In fact, on May 16, 1954, Knowland had warned Eisenhower that "using U.S. ground forces in the Indochina jungle would be like trying to cover an elephant with a handkerchief — you just can't do it."

"Johnson just took a handkerchief to Southeast Asia to try to cover a big, mean elephant," I said, "and he and Kennedy don't want the public to know it."

Kennedy was sending in a wave of military advisers — sixteen thousand of them. These "advisers" were engaged in combat, just as the Soviet Union and China would soon send their warriors into secret warfare in Vietnam.

I told Viv that the slope was getting slipperier, and the war toboggan was moving at a seemingly unstoppable speed, propelled by the promises to Diem that Washington had ordered me to put in Johnson's speech to the National Assembly. Yet I was no inside-government protester of what the United States was doing. I believed fervently that Ho Chi Minh and the Vietcong were the aggressors, and that the United States could help the South Vietnamese to repulse them at an acceptable price. But I didn't think we could do it in secrecy or without the solid support of the American people. I was arguing in State Department meetings and saying in public speeches that "In this society, no foreign policy can succeed if it does not have the understanding and backing of a majority of Americans."

There was no honest effort in the Kennedy administration, or in the office of Lyndon Johnson, to tell Americans the truth so as to obtain their support. But the secrecy wasn't fooling astute members of the media.

James B. "Scotty" Reston wrote in the *New York Times* that "the United States is now involved in an undeclared war in South Vietnam. This is well known to the Russians, the Chinese Communists, and everybody else concerned except the American people."

Lyndon Baines Johnson was the most eloquent advocate I'd ever heard of the idea that the United States could be the greatest society ever built if it would only utilize the presence of the most incredible melting pot man had known. Educate fairly the blacks, Hispanics, Asians, and others, he said, and no other country in the world would be able to compete with America. Let blacks, Hispanics, Asians, and others wallow in the discriminations of racism and penny-pinching, he said, and America would become a second- or third-rate power.

But something always seemed to get in the way of Johnson's intellect, his marvelous humanity, his vision for this nation. His fears of the Kennedys, especially Bobby, warped his judgment. Johnson knew that combat involvement in Indochina was a losing proposition, but he could never say it or write it to President Kennedy, because that would turn a Texan who always wanted to be ten feet tall into a wimp.

*   *   *

I repeat that there is nothing so bad or so good that you could say or write about Lyndon Johnson that it was not true, often in the same day. This is because Johnson was a combination snake-oil salesman, browbeater, humanitarian, and clever political leader. He was the bravest of the arm-twisters ever to serve as Senate majority leader. No one has ever matched him in his ability to get legislation through the Congress, legislation that the nation desperately needed, like the social programs of his Great Society, and even congressional action the nation would have been better off without, like the Gulf of Tonkin resolution.

Even while appearing to be a strongman, Johnson had one of the greatest inferiority complexes I ever saw in a high-level public official. He talked over and over about the fact that he had not been born rich like the Kennedys, that he had not gone to Harvard but "a little crappy Texas college," so some people looked down upon him.

Johnson was sensitive about anything he could construe to be a personal slight. I remember that in 1962 our plane arrived in Rome a bit early, and through a communications foul-up, top Italian officials were just a few minutes late. Johnson never forgot it. Whenever we had a chance to have a drink, he would remind me that in the embassy there was a foreign service officer named Outerbridge Horsey who he thought was responsible for the foul-up. He told me in forty-three different ways that "any son of a bitch named Outerbridge Horsey has got to be a foreign service cookie-pusher, and you can't expect him to do a goddam thing right."

In truth, Johnson wasn't blaming Outerbridge Horsey. He was blaming the Italians, and I was not surprised that on the day of our departure Johnson stayed on at a school until we could never make the airport in time for the departure ceremony. Finally, although it was not my responsibility, I whispered in his ear, "Mr. Vice President, we must leave for the airport; the Italian officials will be waiting." Johnson jerked his shoulder at me in anger and said, "Let the sons of bitches wait. You and me got to go back to the hotel."

"Back to the hotel?" I said. "There is no way in the name of heaven we can go back to the hotel without being at least an hour late at the airport."

"Listen, my friend, you and me are going back to the hotel 'cause I got a guy waiting for me there with my shirts and my silk suits. Ain't no way I'm gonna leave this damn city without my shirts and my suits and knowing that they fit," Johnson said.

So while most of the others went to the airport, Johnson and I rode back to the Excelsior Hotel. We went to his suite where, indeed, a shirtmaker and a suitmaker were waiting. Johnson tried on the shirts and decided they were beautiful. He tried on the suits and said they were acceptable. He looked at me once and said, "I'm buying these fuckers, but none of 'em looks as good as that silk suit you've been wearin' which I reckon you got at J. C. Penney's."

I said, "Hurry, Mr. Vice President, the Italian officials are waiting."

"Ugh," he grunted as his valet gathered up the shirts and suits, and then he said, "Goddam, has anybody made any arrangements to pay these guys?"

The valet shrugged his shoulders.

I said, "Mr. Vice President, I am sure that Bill Crockett and Outerbridge Horsey will find a way to ensure that these gentlemen are paid."

At the mention of Outerbridge Horsey, Johnson gave me an evil glare and then said, "Hurry, we got to get to the airport."

I had stepped out the door and Johnson was moving in that direction when I heard him shout, "Mr. Roe-ann, get the hell back in here." The Secret Service guys looked as though something dreadful had happened to him. I walked back in to find him pointing at the ledge of the window where a half-full bottle of Cutty Sark was peeking around the draperies.

"I told that goddam Walter Jenkins a thousand times that I wasn't going to go around the world leaving a trail of half-empty whiskey bottles. Mr. Rowan, you and me got some serious drinking to do."

To my astonishment and that of the Secret Service fellows, Lyndon Johnson and I sat down and polished off that half bottle of scotch. Then we went to the airport, where the waiting Italian officials were livid. The ceremony was brief, our plane took off, and as I was about to go to my seat and leave the Vice President and Mrs. Johnson alone for a while, he reached over and poked me in the back with his finger and with a little grin said, "We let the sons of bitches wait."

I wondered anew where this man of such volatile personality might take America.

CHAPTER THIRTEEN

Rowan the Troublemaker

I SUPPOSE it is natural that anyone who travels with and advises a vice president would develop some sense of esteem, some belief that he has shattered all barriers of bigotry. I took on a sense of self-importance that had nothing to do with reality. I forgot that inside government, and especially in America at large, I was "just another nigger." And, I soon learned, a troublemaking nigger at that.

I got into a lot of controversies that fixed upon me the "troublemaker" label, first because I inserted myself into the business of trying to influence policy through a public speech, second because I unwittingly became a sucker for do-gooders inside government, and third because I clung to the view that "I'm not going to take any shit off anybody."

My idealistic, or arrogant, attempt to influence policy got me into a nightmarish national and international controversy only months after I took the State Department post. The situation in the newly independent Congo (present-day Zaire) was deteriorating rapidly, and I was put on the Congo task force that was to develop policies for the nation.

The situation, as described in a State Department document, was this:

> The Congo was turned over to African leaders (on June 30, 1960, after more than a year of rioting) who had no governmental or administrative experience. There had been no self-government in the Congo at the national, provincial, or territorial levels. The top

9,000 administrative positions had been and still were filled by Belgians. Only in 1957 had the Belgians started taking Congolese into the lower levels of civil administration. No Congolese had advanced to executive positions in private enterprise, which was dominated by a very few large Belgian holding companies. In the whole country there were perhaps 16–20 college graduates, almost none of whom were political leaders.

I had been to the Congo as a journalist, so I knew that the situation was worse than State's assessment. I knew that the Belgian king's granting independence was a cynical public gesture. King Baudouin and Belgium's political leaders felt that as black chaos proliferated, the white colonial rulers would continue to run everything and especially exploit the mineral wealth of the Katanga.

Ironically, two men whom the Belgians had arrested and been forced to release, Patrice Lumumba and Joseph Kasavubu, became prime minister and president, respectively, of the new nation.

The chaos the Belgians hoped for developed quickly. Tshombe, premier of Katanga, declared secession. When Belgium sent in troops ostensibly to restore order, Kasavubu and Lumumba declared that a state of war existed between the Congo and Belgium and asked for United Nations intervention to prevent the secession of Katanga. Kasavubu fired Lumumba. Lumumba fired Kasavubu. A new character, Joseph Mobutu, arrested Lumumba, whose ties to the Soviets so bothered U.S. officials that CIA agents tried to poison his toothpaste. The Congo became a comic but tragic and murderous opera.

Kennedy and his top advisers had decided that it would be a foreign policy tragedy if Tshombe were allowed to pull Katanga away from the rest of the country, whose people would, in anger, surely invite Soviet forces in. The problem was that most of the Kennedy administration was intimidated by the many ex-McCarthyites who were still in Congress and on editorial boards across America. They still thought they could save colonialism. They viewed Tshombe as a stalwart anti-Communist, thanks in part to a man named Michel Struelens, who was in the United States waging a clever pro-secession campaign with money provided by Tshombe and his mining-interest cronies.

The Kennedy administration was getting the hell beat out of it because of its Congo policy. So a tendency toward caution in the White House, a sort of post–Bay of Pigs syndrome, was encouraged by rampant cowardice in the State Department. On the Congo task force there were people who joined me in wanting to put on a major public assault against those supporting secession, as did G. Mennen Williams, the assistant secretary of state for Africa. But the clearances just weren't there for such a forthright stand.

So I walked in where the hankie wringers dared not tread with feelings of self-declared bravery. In a speech on December 27, 1961, before the forty-seventh anniversary conclave of Phi Beta Sigma fraternity in Philadelphia, with many black envoys present, I lashed out at Tshombe and his "big-money campaign" to convince Americans that they ought to support Katanga's secession. I deplored colonialism and its stifling of black intellectual growth and assailed Belgium and Union Minière for their economic rape of the Congo. I accused them of opening a way for a Soviet triumph in black Africa — a triumph that could be prevented only by support of Kennedy's policies.

Even before I gave that speech a ton of criticism had been dumped upon me. After the speech I was attacked in editorials in hundreds of newspapers across the land. On the train back to Washington, the Pullman-car porter said, "Mr. Rowan, looks like you've got your ass in a sling. But I'm with you."

"Thanks a lot," I thought as I read that members of Congress and the press were asking Kennedy and Rusk if they would disavow my remarks.

When I got back to State there was a message to go to see George McGhee, the under secretary for political affairs. He opened by saying, "Now, Carl, you understand why foreign service people go out to give speeches and never say anything. It's safer that way."

To go out and never say anything was foreign to my makeup. I wanted to launch an angry tirade against yellow bellies, but I liked George McGhee, even when I saw him squirming on "Face the Nation" as Roger Mudd pressured him to renounce my speech and one given by Assistant Secretary Williams.

McGhee wouldn't do that, because he had seen a cable from the United Nations Secretariat calling our speeches "very helpful," one from Ed Gullion, the U.S. ambassador to the Congo, applauding our speeches as "forceful, useable," and one from Ambassador Joseph Palmer in Nigeria saying that our speeches would "create new opportunities for quiet cooperation between the U.S. and the Government of Nigeria on Congo matters."

I saw the deviousness and duplicity of the ways in which the State Department worked, and other agencies still work. George Ball, State's number-two man, sent McGhee, the number-three man, a "confidential" memo saying: "One of the consequences of our attacking Union Minière would be to give our own position a taint of association with that of the Afro-Asians who I suspect reflect strong anti-capitalist tendencies."

But Rusk, a classy guy, had a circular sent to dozens of embassies and all posts in Africa, surely with Kennedy's approval, saying:

> Rowan's speech is center of controversy, but posts should emphasize that every policy consideration in speech is, *repeat is* in complete accord with Department's policy; Rowan's discussion of Union Minière and its alleged role in Katanga's secessionist efforts represent no question of policy, but were Mr. Rowan's personal analysis of the situation. FYI Important that posts understand that Department has not, *repeat has not* denied validity of Rowan analysis.

That was little comfort when I saw that *Business Week* was virtually calling me a whore who was out turning tricks without Madam Rusk knowing about it. Or when Milburn P. Akers of the *Chicago Sun-Times* called me a State Department "hatchet man" who had "hit a new low of some kind."

When I was deep in the dumps, telling myself that I had no one to blame for this controversy other than myself, I got a hand-delivered note from Vice President Johnson.

"Carl," the note said, "down in Texas we say that under an attack like this you just act like a jackass in a hailstorm. You hunker down."

I hunkered down through months of assaults. I'd asked for them, and I got them. But I look back in satisfaction, noting that the Tshombe–Union Minière–Katanga secession never took place. The Russians never got their beachhead in Africa, and I survived for many other days of troublemaking.

*   *   *

The do-gooder instinct had gotten to me earlier, during my first days at State, when the noted broadcaster Raymond Gram Swing and the man I was replacing at State, Edwin Kretzmann, came to me to say that our country was being damaged grievously by stories about racial bigotry at the Metropolitan and other clubs in the District of Columbia. They said they belonged to the Cosmos Club, a club of intellectuals, authors, scientists, which surely would admit me and put the lie to the notion that all Americans were social racists.

"What's the fee?" I asked.

"Fifteen hundred dollars," Kretzmann said.

My eyes sort of closed in shock. That was a fortune, especially considering the cut in pay and the fact that I couldn't accept a nickel for giving a speech.

Viv opposed allowing our names to be submitted for membership at first. But I convinced her that it was in the national interest, so we borrowed fifteen hundred dollars to join a club we didn't need or want.

I had completely forgotten the application for membership until mid-August 1961, when I opened a copy of *U.S. News & World Report* and saw my photograph bracketed with that of President Kennedy in the "People of the Week" section. There were also photographs of Angier Biddle Duke, chief of protocol, and George L. P. Weaver, assistant secretary of labor. Adjoining President Kennedy's and my photographs was one of the Cosmos Club with a caption stating, "Mr. Kennedy and Mr. Rowan are candidates."

I noted that Duke had resigned from the Metropolitan Club after nearly twenty years' membership because the city's oldest and supposedly most exclusive club refused to admit new Negro ambassadors to membership. With some forty Caucasian envoys holding honorary memberships, it was patently clear that the ambassadors of the new states of Africa were being barred solely on the basis of race. Had there been any doubt, the Metropolitan Club had erased it when it reprimanded George Cabot Lodge, son of Henry Cabot Lodge, the vice presidential candidate, for taking Weaver, a Negro, to lunch at the club. Young Lodge had resigned, as had Attorney General Robert Kennedy.

Still, it was not until I read the *U.S. News* article that I realized what a burning issue the clubs had become in Washington — or that the president of the United States and I might become jointly involved at the center of a racial storm.

At the same time I became aware that President Kennedy had an application pending, I also took cognizance of the procedure by which the Cosmos Club elected new members: the names were put at the bottom of a list and applications were considered in order. Only when an applicant's name reached the top of the list would he be considered. As fate had it, my name had gone on the list prior to that of the president's, so the membership committee would have to rule on my application first.

A week or so after the *U.S. News & World Report* article appeared, I got a call from Swing asking if he could see me at the earliest possible moment. We agreed to meet for lunch — at the Cosmos Club. I had barely slapped the first pat of butter on one of the club's delicious popovers when Swing advised me that my application had become a source of feverish controversy within the club.

"But, Ray, when you and Ed begged me to permit the entry of my name you assured me that acceptance would be routine," I said.

"We honestly believed that, Carl," Swing replied. "Yet I must confess that even at that time I had reason to believe that one member of the admissions committee was an out-and-out racist. However, I knew that it took two negative votes to blackball an application. My honest view was that the racist member was a moral coward and would not dare to have his racism revealed in the face of eleven members who clearly felt the Cosmos Club, being the intellectual club that it is, ought not adopt a nonintellectual, bigoted stance. But I just had an experience, Carl," Swing went on, "that bothers me very much."

"What's that?" I asked.

"I had a member of the admissions committee call on me. I don't want to reveal his name, because I am still hopeful that this thing will not become a public ruckus with a lot of people embarrassed. However, this man said to me: 'Ray, you know that I'm not a bigot. I count Negroes among some of my best friends' — honestly, that's what he said. But he said that some of his closest friends in the club had told him that they become physically ill in the presence of Negroes. He told me that he probably would have to vote against your application in deference to these friends.'"

I laughed heartily, but Swing sat unmoved, his face mirroring a grim seriousness and an embarrassment that he could not hide.

"I hate to say that we're in a bit of trouble," he said.

"No, Ray, I guess it's the Cosmos Club that's in a little bit of trouble."

"I assume that we've got to mount a campaign to change one vote on the committee," Swing said, "because I'm sure that you agree that there is no such thing as withdrawing our nomination of you."

"You read me with absolute correctness, Ray. I won't say I've never run away from a fight, but I've never run away from this kind of fight."

Back in my office, alone, I sat reflecting on the luncheon revelations. "Mount a campaign. . . ." I had no way to mount any campaign. If I knew 10 of the 2,250 members of the Cosmos Club, I was not aware of who they were. But Ray Swing more than made up for my lack of knowledge about who wielded influence in the Cosmos Club, and he set about waging the kind of campaign he thought was necessary to prevent his club from dropping into racial disgrace.

My first knowledge of what Swing was up to came on November 1, when I received a copy of a letter that an old friend, David J. Winton of Minneapolis, had written to the admissions committee, telling them that I had "made a singular contribution to a better relationship between our country and India" and urging my admission.

Eight days later, I received a copy of a letter that John Kenneth Galbraith, the U.S. ambassador to India, had written to the Cosmos Club. He wrote:

> I have just learned that my much-admired friend, Mr. Carl T. Rowan, Deputy Assistant Secretary of State, has been proposed for Cosmos Club membership. I am writing in much more than routine fashion to endorse and applaud this nomination. At a time when the Cosmos Club is adding exceptionally illustrious names to its rolls, it is particularly pleasant to contemplate Mr. Rowan's membership. . . .
>
> As one of the older members of the Cosmos Club, at least in years of membership, I can think of few things more rewarding than to have Mr. Rowan on our rolls.

I am afraid it was a case of naïveté that I did not realize that Galbraith was the Cosmos Club member who had nominated John Fitzgerald Kennedy for membership. Since there was so little I could do, I never really became personally involved in the behind-the-scenes finagling, lobbying, propagandizing. In my view, here was a case where the white people would have to sort out their own consciences. Yet I would be lying to say that I held a *detached* view of what was taking place. No one relishes being blackballed from any organization. And even though I had been a Negro for a long time — thirty-six years, in fact — I still could not say that I had become calloused, immune to the slights and humiliations that had caused flashes of hate to surge through the bellies of millions of blacks in the three hundred or so years that they had been in America. I was concerned. But my concern was tempered by the realization that whatever occurred would, in the long run, have more bearing on the well-being of white Americans than on me or other black Americans, for it still was the white man who had so very much to lose and the Negro so pitifully little at risk.

Late on the night of January 8, 1962, my telephone rang, and Swing, in a voice breaking with anger, informed me that the admissions committee had met and, as he had feared, my nomination had been rejected.

The story became front-page news in the *New York Times*, the *Washington Star*, the *Washington Post*, and hundreds of other newspapers across the country. It had become big news only in part because this club of Washington's intellectuals had rejected the top-ranking Negro in the United States State Department. It was front-page news because Galbraith had promptly resigned, taking out with him (with John F. Kennedy's blessings) the application of the president of the United States.

The press corps descended upon me for a comment about my rejection. It was clear from the way some of them phrased their questions that they hoped I would assail the Cosmos Club as a bastion of bigotry. I said, "It is my understanding that this is Washington's club of intellectuals. If it is the intellectual judgment of the membership committee that I do not merit membership, I can do no more than note this judgment and wish the club well."

That night President Kennedy telephoned me, dialing himself and without the use of a secretary.

"Your statement was perfect, Carl," he said. "You couldn't have hurt the bastards more with a cannon."

One of the most fascinating aspects of the whole episode was to watch prominent white Americans grapple with their consciences as they tried to determine how to respond to their club's action. Swing resigned immediately, of course. Joining John Kenneth Galbraith in resigning were such distinguished Americans as Bruce Catton, the historian; Howard K. Smith, the television commentator; Edward R. Murrow, director of the U.S. Information Agency, who asked that his nomination be withdrawn; Harlan Cleveland, assistant secretary of state for international organization affairs; Jerome B. Wiesner, President Kennedy's top science adviser; Larry L. Winship, editor of the *Boston Globe*; and the Right Reverend William G. Ryan, president of Seton Hill College.

Many prominent Americans chose not to resign. Among them were Nelson Rockefeller, the governor of New York, who said that he intended to stay in the club and fight to change the policy; Ernest K. Lindley, former *Newsweek* columnist and then special assistant to the secretary of state; Senators Ernest Gruening of Alaska and John Sherman Cooper of Kentucky, who stated publicly that the club should not have racial bars and that they intended to fight to see that they were removed.

My first inclination was to laugh scornfully at those who talked of staying to fight from the inside. On reflection, however, I decided that enough Americans with enough prestige had resigned to make dramatically the point that the Cosmos admissions committee was out of step with the times, and very possibly out of step with the club's membership.

That Cosmos Club episode gave me notoriety. It also made me wonder if Hodding Carter had been right when he wrote, in that 1952 book review, that I would not find equality in America in my lifetime. I was finding out the hardest possible way that while I could break barriers in the press, in government, in Washington neighborhoods, there were emotional walls out there in white America that I was not supposed to try to climb.

In November 1961, the presidents of all America's land-grant colleges had asked me to speak to them in Kansas City. After the address, a few of them invited me to join them in listening to music at a nightclub called the 88 Keys. I walked unknowingly into a situation in which the group was told, "We don't serve Negroes."

Those college presidents were embarrassed, but I was damned angry. I could have said, meekly, "OK, let's go somewhere else." But no barriers get broken with that kind of cop-out.

"Where's the manager?" I asked.

"At home."

"Get him on the phone."

"He won't talk to *you.*"

Now I was fuming, giving no thought to the costs of adding to the troublemaker image. I telephoned the *Kansas City Star* and told an editor what was going on. When the newspaper got through telling the 88 Keys owner who was in the party and about what damage the stink would do to Kansas City, he decided that his little cabaret did indeed serve Negroes.

"Did you ever notice that most bigots are cowards?" I asked my hosts.

On January 19, 1962, I gave a speech in Little Rock where prominent blacks and whites celebrated their triumph over the Jim Crow ideas of Orval Faubus. A white businessman offered his corporate plane to fly me to Memphis after dinner, so I could catch the wee-hours American Airlines flight to Washington. The flight was a bit late, so the pilot and a friend asked me to join them for coffee.

"I don't drink coffee, but I'll chat with you."

As we sat down, a waitress rushed over to say, "I can't serve you."

"What's the problem?" the pilot asked.

"We don't serve colored."

"Well," I said, "I hadn't planned to order anything, but under these circumstances I'll have to."

She stalked off and came back to me with a cop. The two white men from Little Rock intercepted the policeman and surely told him that I was a State Department official. I heard the cop say, "It's gonna take somebody higher than me to handle this one."

While everyone awaited the arrival of a high-ranking policeman, the flight came in and I flew off to Washington. I was awakened early the next morning by reporters wanting to know about "the Memphis incident." A Memphis city official called to apologize.

The now-defunct *Washington Daily News* sent reporters into the streets to ask "Is Carl Rowan incident prone?" and found a couple of black government officials who allegedly said they avoided such incidents "by never going where I know I'm not wanted."

That made my blood boil, but Viv and I mostly laughed at these revelations of the breadth and depth of Jim Crow. We knew that being "incident prone" did not bother our friends, and surely not President Kennedy, who was trying to take racism out of the social world that he controlled. I sensed this, which is why I went to the State Department before I formally took the job he had offered me. I wanted to be up to speed on my first day.

One January day in 1961, secretary-to-be Fran Criss said: "Good news, Mr. Rowan. You and Mrs. Rowan have been invited to President Kennedy's first state dinner — a white-tie-and-tails affair for President Bourguiba of Tunisia."

I groaned to myself. "My wife is still in Minneapolis. I'll probably be back in Minneapolis at the time of that dinner. I don't have any white tie and tails. Would you please regret?"

Fran was silent for a few seconds. Then she said, "Mr. Rowan, I hope that I'm not being presumptuous in saying that in your new job the only reason you can give for declining a White House invitation like this is that you have two broken legs."

She got my attention.

"Fran," I said, "I accept. Get my wife on the phone, and after that, tell me where I can buy white tie and tails."

As we reached the White House, we bumped into another black "New Frontiersman" who was sporting what obviously was a brand-new set of tails. He leaned over to me and half whispered, "Carl, goddam this integration is *expensive!*"

And so it was. But it was worth it. That night in the East Room of the White House blacks and whites danced together, reveling in the twist, waltzes, and the jitterbug.

From that party forward, even the most benighted hostesses knew that integration was in and Jim Crow was out. It became de rigueur to have one of Kennedy's top blacks at your party if you still wanted to qualify as the "hostess with the mostest." I have told the story — so many times that it cannot possibly be apocryphal — of answering the telephone one day and accepting a dinner invitation from a prominent woman. I still swear that upon my acceptance I heard her say to someone, "I just got *me* one!"

The entrenched old guard at State not only ceased to think that they could "get Rowan," but a lot of them said to me that they agreed with my demands for personnel changes that would make the foreign service reasonably reflect the population of America.

So Rusk, Bowles, Ball, Crockett, and others began "bold" moves to make the State Department and foreign service something better than a lily-white enclave of relatively privileged Americans. But nothing much changed, no matter the lip service, the meetings, the memos.

I thought the struggle was hopeless, and I was ready to get out of government in March 1962 when Tubby told me that he was out as State's top public affairs officer. Obviously, I felt that I ought to get the top public affairs job. But Kennedy had a top aide, Ralph Dungan, who had other ideas. He argued that no Negro could go before New York Democratic congressman John Rooney and a host of southern senators and come out with a decent public affairs budget. I was furious when I learned in April that Robert Manning was being brought in to replace Tubby, and that Manning was bringing in his own deputy, James Greenfield. No, Greenfield would not be the "ranking" deputy in a formal sense, but Dungan surely intended that in the reality of office power, Greenfield would step ahead of me.

I wondered who had bought the Dungan line about a black person being unable to convince Congress to appropriate a decent budget. Kennedy? Rusk? I was of no mind to resign over this insult. I simply vowed that neither Greenfield nor anyone else would step ahead of me without my becoming an aggressive articulator of foreign policy ideas. If I had been a pain in the ass to the foreign policy establishment, they had better hold on to their saddles for some new bumps.

But just when I might have succumbed to paranoia, I received a remarkable assignment. Till this day I have no idea how I was named to be a member of a supersecret committee charged with getting U-2 pilot Francis Gary Powers out of prison in the Soviet

Union. But it surely occurred to me that I was no longer just "a token Negro" when I was told that I would be one of a handful of officials who would try to get Powers exchanged for the Soviet master spy, Colonel Rudolf Abel.

Rudolf Ivanovich Abel had entered Canada in 1948 posing as Andrew Kayotis, who had died in Lithuania the year before. He then sneaked across the Canadian border and took up residence in Brooklyn under the name of Emil R. Goldfus, posing as an artist-photographer. He was in fact the Russian spy master in the United States. His studio had concealed transmitters through which he communicated with Moscow.

Abel operated effectively until 1957, when one of his agents, a boozing woman-chaser named Reino Hayhanen, was ordered back to the Soviet Union. En route, Hayhanen realized his likely fate back home and defected to the U.S. embassy in Paris, where he blew the cover of Colonel Abel of the KGB.

Abel was arrested and convicted of espionage. His court-appointed lawyer, a distinguished U.S. intelligence operative, James B. Donovan, asked the judge not to sentence Abel to death because the United States might be able to use him some year in a trade to rescue an American agent. The judge sentenced Abel to thirty years for espionage, plus fifteen years for two lesser charges, and the Russian agent was locked up in the federal penitentiary in Atlanta.

Ironically, it was Donovan who was the chief negotiator with the East Germans, including an East German woman called Helen, who pretended to be Abel's wife, on a possible swap for Powers.

My job, aside from giving input to our tight little group on what we could believe and who seemed deceitful, was to be sure that the Kennedy administration could explain satisfactorily to the American people whatever deal Donovan and others could make.

It would take another book for me to tell what Powers's U-2 flights over the Soviet Union meant to U.S. intelligence and to explain that we wanted Powers out urgently because, though some Americans doubted his patriotism, we knew that he had not told the Soviet interrogators several very important secrets. Let it suffice for me to say that for weeks we Americans played a lot of tricky games until a deal was made to trade Powers for Abel the morning of February 10, 1962, on the Glienicke Bridge between East and West Berlin.

This exchange, one of the best kept secrets of my years in government, was to take place at about 3:00 A.M. Washington time. Pierre Salinger, the White House press secretary, was informed of the imminent exchange only hours before, and he erupted in anger that he had been kept in the dark about the negotiations.

"You'll have to be here to brief the press," he said to me sharply, "because I don't have any of the goddammed details."

"I had planned to be here," I said.

After dinner at home, I tried to take a nap, but my mind was racing with thoughts of something going wrong, with concerns about how much I could tell the press about why we would give up a Soviet master spy to get back a pilot whom a lot of Americans considered a traitor.

At about 1:00 A.M. that dark Saturday morning, I got into my personal black Lincoln Continental and drove to the southwest gate at the White House. Two Secret Service men leaped up, shining flashlights on my windshield.

"You want that gate," one shouted, pointing to an entrance to the residence, where a Kennedy party was still in full swing.

"No, I want this entrance," I said.

One agent came to the open window on the driver's side and asked me, "For whom are you driving?"

I stuck my ID card out the window. Even in the darkness I could see his face redden as he said, "I'm sorry, Mr. Rowan."

The story was so sensational that it was not difficult to please the press. I did not have to tell them that I was late for the briefing because the deal damned near fell apart during wrangling on the Glienicke Bridge. I went home and tried to sleep but still couldn't because I was riding a high, totally intoxicated with thoughts of the incredible twists and turns of the negotiations. I could hardly believe that I had been so deeply involved in one of the great dramas of the world of intelligence and espionage.

Life at State would have been a lot simpler if I had lived by the old military axiom that you must never volunteer for anything.

On the morning of February 17, I sat in my office reading the cable traffic when a proposed message to Saigon caught my eye. Kennedy had erupted into such anger a few days before over an AP story from Vietnam by a reporter who had accompanied American advisers on a helicopter mission and reported growing American involvement in the war against the Vietcong. Now Salinger and Arthur Sylvester, the assistant secretary of defense, had drawn up an order that hereafter no newsmen were to be transported on U.S. helicopters or taken to battle areas where any U.S. involvement was ascertainable. In short, the instructions were to completely draw the curtain on the U.S. press.

Salinger and Sylvester were both senior to me, so the prudent thing would have been for me to keep quiet. But I couldn't, because the proposed press rules offended me both as a former newsman and as a citizen of a society in which an informed public means everything. I told my direct boss, Robert Manning, of my feelings, and he was equally disturbed.

"I'm going up to see Rusk," I said.

"Go, with my full support," Manning replied.

"The president hasn't been in any controversy compared with what he'll face when this gag order leaks. And it will leak," I said to Rusk.

"But the president thinks stories like that AP dispatch are harmful to everything he's trying to do in Southeast Asia," Rusk argued.

"The story was factual. Sure it makes the president's life and your life more difficult. But do you suppose the press is going to lie down and go to sleep once you ban them from helicopters and battle areas? These gag orders will only make them more zealous in their investigations of new levels of U.S. involvement."

"You've convinced me," Rusk said, "but you've got one angry man in the White House to convince."

"Do you object to my talking to the president?"

"No," Rusk said. "Call McGeorge Bundy and see if you can get an appointment."

I telephoned Bundy, Kennedy's national security adviser, who naturally wanted to know what I wanted to talk about. I gave him a condensed version of my objection to the Sylvester-Salinger press restrictions. Minutes later Bundy telephoned me to say that the president would see me immediately.

I walked into the Oval Office, nervous, with scant attention to civil niceties, saying: "Good morning, Mr. President. I just came to see if

I can convince you not to send press rules to Vietnam that will get you in a lot of trouble."

Kennedy was more sparing of niceties. "Now, Carl," he said, "isn't that a bunch of shit?"

"When this telegram leaks and your ass is in a sling, you won't think it's a bunch of shit."

I sensed that Kennedy was jarred that I came back at him with the same kind of language he had thrown at me.

"Sit down and let's discuss this," he said.

"The AP story was to be expected," I said. "You will never be able to wage a secret war in Vietnam. If you don't give maximum feasible cooperation to the press, the press will give maximum opposition to you. And you won't win."

The telephone rang. From the president's remarks I discerned that Salinger was calling from the West Coast. Sylvester had heard of my objections to their proposed secrecy rules and of my impending meeting with Kennedy and had called Salinger to ask him to weigh in against me.

I don't know what Salinger said, but I sensed that already Kennedy had doubts about the press restrictions that he had ordered out of anger. The phone call over, Kennedy asked me: "What do you think my policy ought to be?"

"Maximum feasible cooperation," I said.

"What the hell does that mean?" he asked. "Fly the sons of bitches out to where they can write that U.S. advisers are orchestrating the killing of women and children?"

"Mr. President, I can't draw up here today, or tomorrow, a perfect set of press guidelines. You and I know that that war situation changes by the hour. United States involvement is escalating. These newsmen are not dummies. They know it. All you can promise is maximum feasible cooperation. And I can't put on paper what the shit 'feasible' is going to mean tomorrow or next month. But maximum feasible cooperation is the least that you can afford to promise."

"OK," said Kennedy, "you rewrite the guidelines and get Pierre and the others to go along, and I'll approve."

I went back to State and reported to Manning and Rusk that the president had relented and that I was commissioned to revise the directive that we thought foolish. I went to Sterling J. Cottrell, director of the Vietnam task force, and informed him of my meeting and asked him to join me in writing a directive that could gain clearance by all the individuals and agencies involved.

Cottrell and I worked hours. Drafting did not mean simply using a pencil or typewriter. It meant telephoning Sylvester, Salinger, the USIA, and others to determine how much liberalization of press rules they would stand for. It meant deliberately making some language ambiguous to allow the ambassador in Saigon to make judgments on the basis of specific crises. Finally we produced a cable that was approved by Averell Harriman (assistant secretary of state for the Far East), Rusk, the Defense Department, USIA, and the White House.

As evidence that we meant business about cooperating with the press, I telephoned Tokyo (with USIA approval) and ordered Charles Davis, an experienced information man, to proceed to Saigon immediately. I told Davis that his sole responsibility was to meet the complaints of newsmen about obstacles thrown up by government to prevent them from really covering the war.

I trudged home to a very late Saturday night dinner.

"The kids are asleep," Viv said, not pointedly, but in a way that got my attention.

"Yeah, and I feel like a goddammed bum to come home so late. In this job it seems I never see them."

"Are you happy with today's work?"

"I'd say I'm a hero if I didn't have to tell you that I'm leaving for Honolulu tomorrow."

On February 18 I flew to Honolulu with Secretary of Defense Robert McNamara, Harriman, Sylvester, and others. A major item of business was to be sure that General Paul D. Harkins, commander of MACV (Military Assistance Command, Vietnam), understood that American newsmen could ride military helicopters and otherwise use military transportation in covering the war.

Everyone at the Honolulu Conference approved the new press guidelines. I came back to Washington feeling like a weary winner. I was surprised months later when Kennedy asked if I would serve on the U.S. delegation to the United Nations in the fall of 1962, a post I would hold simultaneously with my job as deputy assistant secretary.

I accepted, but without much enthusiasm, because it had become a political necessity to have one black face on our UN delegation, and I knew I would be it. With Adlai Stevenson, Sr., as the permanent U.S. representative with cabinet rank and his top deputies Francis T. P. Plimpton, the highly regarded foreign service officer Charles W. Yost, and Philip M. Klutznick of Chicago, how was I going to be anything but window dressing?

But Plimpton got the mumps, and I, to my amazement, was assigned to take over the issues of Hungary, the Koreas, and the Palestinian refugees. I was running my tail off from one contentious meeting to another. The Soviets soon learned this, so they would wait until I was in a meeting about the Palestinians in one committee, then move to get North Korea into the UN in another committee. A U.S. delegation staff member would run like hell to drag me out of meeting number one so I could give a speech opposing the Russians in meeting two.

Meeting two erupted into laughter one day when I rushed in, gave my speech, and saw the Russian voted down, only to have him say loudly in English: "Where do they keep that guy? In a telephone booth outside this room?"

This was my first substantive dealing with the Palestine issue, either as government official or journalist. Did I learn a few lessons! The first one was that I couldn't trust Arab or Israeli. Once, on instructions from Washington, I asked the Israeli representative not to introduce a resolution that I knew would torpedo all discussions and negotiations. After allegedly consulting with his government, he vowed that Israel would not introduce the resolution.

That evening, just before going to my hotel, I was in the chief delegates' lounge when the representative of the Central African Republic joined me for a drink. I bought him a second, and as he sipped the last bit, I stiffened at his gratuitous revelation: "I'm introducing an important resolution on the Palestine question tomorrow. I thought you'd be interested."

"Indeed I am! What is the substance of your resolution?"

He spelled it out, and in every detail it was the resolution that the Israelis had vowed not to introduce.

"Two more," I said to the bartender. As we sipped our third drink, I said to the African, "Level with me. Did the Israelis ask you to introduce this resolution?"

His red eyes fixed on me as though he were in pain, then he said just above a whisper, "Yes."

I talked him out of that course of action and made a point of saying to the Israeli the next day: "The Central African delegate isn't going to introduce that destructive resolution either, you'll be glad to know."

The Cuban missile crisis erupted during that session of the UN General Assembly. Tension among the delegates was unbelievable as the United States and the Soviet Union moved eyeball to eyeball, closer and closer to a nuclear confrontation. Delegates from the smaller countries were almost desperate for daily reports on the status of the conflict. So I was assigned to fly to Washington every morning, get briefed to the extent that officials thought wise, then fly back to New York to brief the ambassadors.

"No war, no war!" I would say as I rushed in, and they would cheer as though I were giving them the latest score of a Super Bowl game.

During that stint at the UN I learned why Stevenson failed twice to be elected president — and why the voters were right in rejecting him. Stevenson was one of the most indecisive men I have ever met in high office. He lacked balls.

With his rank, he had the right to sit in on meetings of the cabinet and the National Security Council. But even when momentous issues were being decided, when war or peace was at stake, he would stay in New York — then bitch to me and surely others about the decisions that were being made in Washington.

Once, when he was talking about my joining his staff permanently, I asked why he so rarely attended the meetings in Washington.

"I always feel like an outsider," he said, "and it really isn't worth the hassle."

I knew that he was talking to me about joining his staff for only one reason: the black media were assailing him for the almost lily-white makeup of the U.S. Mission. He wasted no time getting to the growing criticism of him.

"How dare they attack a man with my record?" he asked rhetorically.

To his surprise, I answered: "Which record?"

"My record as governor of Illinois, as presidential candidate, as an advocate of racial equality."

"Governor," I said, "we all come to realize from time to time that our view of our record does not jibe with the public's view of our record."

"You mean they don't know my record?"

"No, I mean they do understand your record — here at the UN. They think it is a white man's preserve, and the staffing gives justification for that."

Stevenson looked at me as though I had insulted him, but he chose not to make an issue of it.

"That's why I asked you to talk with me. You've done a fine job here. I'm hoping that instead of resuming your job in Washington you'll become a permanent member of my staff with the rank of ambassador."

"In what slot?"

"The Trusteeship Council."

"So I'd be fourth or fifth in the pecking order?"

Stevenson squirmed in obvious irritation. It seemed that he had expected me to leap joyously at the invitation to work with him with the title of ambassador, no matter what my ranking.

"You'd have important work to do," he replied.

"Now, there is the little matter of perks. You, Plimpton, and Yost all have chauffeur-driven Cadillacs. Would I have one?"

"Well, er . . . uh . . . we are under severe budget restraints."

"You mean I wouldn't have a car and driver?"

"Not under current budget circumstances."

"Do you think I would take a job where the three white ambassadors ride in chauffeur-driven cars and the black ambassador stands on the street hailing taxicabs? This would have a devastating impact upon the ambassadors here from Asia, Africa, Latin America — the very ones with whom I would have to deal."

Stevenson's discomfort seemed acute. "I might be able to arrange something in a new budget year," he said.

"I just don't think this is a smart move for me to make," I said as I got up to leave.

"Maybe we can talk again," Stevenson said in something short of a friendly voice.

Without my knowledge, Stevenson went to a Washington meeting that President Kennedy was having with Roy Wilkins, Whitney Young, and other civil rights leaders. Stevenson literally said, "Hello . . . Carl Rowan is joining the UN Mission with the rank of ambassador."

When Young called to congratulate me, I exploded. I telephoned President Kennedy to tell him that I was outraged that Stevenson would do this, but I didn't want the White House embarrassed by putting out any announcement, because I would not take a job at the UN. When he asked why, I said, "Let's look at one point that may seem trifling, but is very important in the world of diplomacy. Stevenson, Plimpton, and Yost would have chauffeured cars; Stevenson says I'd have to take taxis. That would defeat any purpose of adding a black person to the mission."

"Well, goddam," Kennedy said. "Is Adlai so dumb that he can't understand that?"

"Apparently," I said.

I was newly enraged later in the week when the black newspapers came out with headlines blaring, ROWAN TO BE UN AMBASSADOR.

I telephoned Wilkins, Young, and Bunche and key newsmen and explained why I would not work for Stevenson — ever. I resumed my spot as Manning's deputy.

I had been in the State Department almost two years. With the support of Rusk, George Ball, Chester Bowles, and Bill Crockett, I had brought some blacks into the foreign service. I was feeling good again about my service in government, except for the fact that my family and I were living from paycheck to paycheck. On a late-February day in 1963 when I was especially in the dumps about my finances, I got a telephone call from my longtime friend Larry Fanning, editor of the *Chicago Daily News.*

"Tell Kennedy good-bye and we'll drink a few scotches while you sign a fifty-thousand-dollar contract."

"A what?"

"We'll guarantee you at least fifty thousand dollars a year to do three columns a week."

"You're not shitting me?"

"Would your old buddy shit you?"

"Jesus Christ, Larry," I said. "I'm due on the seventh floor for a big reception I'm helping to host. Let me think about this."

I walked out of the reception to a telephone and asked the White House operator to get me President Kennedy, who I knew was in Florida. To my surprise, Kennedy came on immediately.

"Mr. President," I said, "you were nice enough to bring me into government. I've enjoyed being a part of your administration. And I thought I ought to tell you first that I'm going to resign and go back into journalism."

"Goddammit, Carl, you can't leave now. Is someone giving you a bad time?"

"No, no, no. It's just that my wife and I have used up all our savings, and the *Chicago Daily News* has offered me more money than I ever dreamed of making."

"I understand the money problem, but you've just got to stick with me a bit longer. Listen, I've got an ambassador in Finland that I'm dying to replace. Would you stay with me if I named you ambassador to Finland? You'd get free housing and food and other allowances, and that would ease your financial problems somewhat."

Ambassador to Finland? Kennedy made it sound so important. Fifty thousand dollars a year? That looked good too. I telephoned my office and asked Fran Criss to get me the country report on Finland.

Back in the reception, I asked Edward R. Murrow, the director of USIA and my ally in many a bureaucratic war, if I could have a word with him. We stepped aside, and as he puffed a cigarette that seemed to bring beads of sweat to his chin, I told him of my dilemma — and that I was leaning toward the *Daily News* offer.

"There is no way you can leave government," Murrow said.

"Why not?"

"Because if you leave, there won't be a wet eye in the State Department." While I laughed aloud, only a toothy, subdued grin wrinkled his face.

As I was driving home, Finland country report in hand, I said to myself: "Murrow is right. Not one of the bastards I've been fighting will weep at my departure."

Viv and I stayed up late that night, discussing the choices before us. The three children seemed oblivious to the possibility of my earning at least fifty thousand dollars a year. They wanted us to read aloud from the report on life in Finland. Viv and I went to bed knowing that there would be many more months of budget squeezes.

The next day I telephoned Kennedy to say that we would be happy to take the post in Finland.

CHAPTER FOURTEEN

Mr. Ambassador

AMERICANS who have watched incredible revolutions in Eastern Europe and the Soviet Union and have heard the cries for independence in Lithuania, Latvia, and Estonia in 1989 and 1990 may have some understanding of the importance of being ambassador to Finland in 1963 and 1964. But not many Americans, or Finns, understood what was at stake when I set off on what turned out to be both a tough and delightful assignment.

A number of Americans thought Finland was part of the Soviet Union. Others remembered Finland standing tall against Russian invaders in 1939. Still other Americans praised the Finns as "the only people who paid their war debts."

Few people, even in the media, saw Finland as an intelligence asset for the Western world, a dogged believer in capitalism, democracy, a free press — a tiny country trying to hold on to those things despite pressures from a humongous neighbor defined by the ideology of Lenin, Marx, Stalin, and other Communists.

The American diplomatic community was confused as to what America's posture should be toward Finland and its president, Urho Kekkonen. My job, Kennedy said, was to help the Finns to "keep the faith," to cling to independence and freedom, until that certain day came when the Kremlin would realize that it could not oppress its neighbors.

Most Finns gave no serious thought to what I would try to do. They were overwhelmed by the "oddity" of getting a black American ambassador. One newspaper felt compelled to tell Finns that the new envoy would be "an educated Negro." Other journals intensified the public preoccupation with my race by hyping the coverage of racial conflict in Birmingham and Selma, Alabama.

With the help of George Ingram, a foreign service officer who would be deputy chief of mission, I tried a ploy to get the Finns off race, and it worked marvelously for a while.

We sent our Italian greyhound, Gomez, ahead to Finland in care of George and his wife Ashton before we boarded the USS *United States* for the journey to Europe, where we caught a Finnair Caravelle for Helsinki. It was, by luck, one of the smartest things I ever did. When they opened the door of that plane and we stepped onto the mobile ramp into the bright sunshine of May 17, I spotted Gomez with Ashton. Gomez saw, smelled, or heard something, leaped from Ashton's arms, and dashed across the tarmac as though a fat rabbit were his prey. The dog bounded up the ramp and made a majestic leap into the arms of Carl Jr. The camera flashes made it look like a Fourth of July display.

On May 18 our little Italian greyhound became the most famous dog in Finland. This canine, not the new ambassador, was on page one of virtually every newspaper in the country, with head-lines welcoming "Comez," "Comet," "Gomet," and in rare cases "Gomez."

But I was breaking ground that not even my dog could blur from Finnish minds. I soon found myself called, in a big magazine spread, "The Most Colorful Ambassador in Helsinki." Women's magazines fought to write articles about Viv's skin color, her quiet reserve, her wardrobe. The concentration on our race and color surely reached its apex on the evening when a prominent Finnish group gave a crayfish dinner in our honor.

After many a tail of the midget Finnish lobsters had been broken off, placed on buttered toast, sprinkled with dill, and then ingested and washed down with vodka followed by beer, one of my hosts reached the epitome of hospitality. He led the Finns in a rendition of the song "Old Black Joe."

I looked over and saw George and Ashton, from Mississippi, almost dying in their seats. Viv and I were shaking our heads and laughing. Ingram leaped up and went to talk to one of our hosts. A somewhat inebriated Finn came to my table to say, "Mr. Ambassador, we meant no offense. We got word weeks ago that you liked to sing, and Stephen Foster songs were your favorites."

Recountings of that dinner, even in the smallest of Finnish towns, liberated Viv and me from the silly fixations on race — much, I was told, to the comfort of Kekkonen and other government leaders.

The international milieu of 1963, which surrounded my being ambassador to Finland, included recurring crises over Berlin. The war in Vietnam was escalating, with greater involvement every day of the United States, the Soviet Union, and China. The arms race was on at a fever pace, with testing of nuclear weapons in the atmosphere killing sheep, contaminating children's milk, and condemning innocent Americans, Russians, and thousands of others to die in a generation of cancers.

Kennedy, and especially Humphrey, were pushing hard for a nuclear test ban agreement, and it was made clear to me that I was to make Kekkonen *our* agent of influence. We needed desperately to have the Finns endorse the test ban so as to inspire other nations to pressure the Kremlin to go along. The Finns joined us, and the world got the first great nuclear weapons scale-down, a treaty that told kids the world over that they no longer had to worry about strontium 90 popping up in their milk shakes.

The Eastern bloc ambassadors in Helsinki were not untouchables, but the Washington hierarchy was clearly hostile to the idea of a U.S. ambassador getting friendly with the "puppets" from Hungary, Czechoslovakia, Romania, or even Poland. It was almost as bad as the long-running and foolish prohibition against American diplomats talking to representatives of the Palestine Liberation Organization. It seemed to me that not talking to people of other nations, even those perceived as enemies, only prolonged the grievances and misunderstandings that led to stupid wars.

Kennedy, Rusk, and others knew this, I was sure, but the political situation in America tied their hands. No Democratic president at that time could dare to open a dialogue or establish diplomatic relations with China without being run out of Washington.

But I was thousands of miles away, with no president, no Congress, breathing down my neck — something that made an ambassadorship in a nice place like Helsinki one of the best government jobs in 1963. So I determined to ignore instructions based on political fear in what ways I could.

I began with Olga Connolly, who as a Czech citizen named Olga Fikotova had been the Olympic discus-throw champion in 1956. She had married an American track and field competitor, Harold Connolly, and the Czech government was punishing her by making her parents virtual prisoners. She and Connolly were in Finland on teaching grants.

"I've tried everything," said Olga. "I've prayed. I've begged. I've thrown myself on my knees in front of Czech officials. All I get is cold and ruthless rejection. Some of my friends tell me that you might get my parents out."

"My God, I don't know why anyone would tell you that. I have no contacts with the Czechs, don't know the ambassador, or anything. But give me some papers, some documentation, and when I make my courtesy call on the Czech ambassador I'll explore the possibilities."

I was eager for anything that might make forty-eight courtesy calls something other than the boring wastes of time that they usually were. When I greeted the Czech ambassador, Frantisek Malik, I said: "Mr. Ambassador, we could spend a half hour engaging in the inane banter that usually is part of these courtesy calls. Or we could turn provocative and rush into the polemics of the cold war. I don't like either choice. Could I break with protocol and talk with you as one human being to another?"

He looked flummoxed but, as I expected, said, "Of course!"

"We both have parents, we both have children, all of whom we love deeply. A marvelous young woman named Olga Connolly — you know her as Olga Fikotova — has parents in your country whom she loves very much. She wants them to be with her."

He looked stricken. "Er, uh . . . er, uh . . ." he stammered, finally adding: "Mr. Ambassador, er . . . uh . . . that's a very interesting demarche —"

"No, no, no," I interjected. "It is not a demarche. It is not a diplomatic initiative. No one in Washington, or my embassy, knows that I am talking to you as just one human being to another. You know and I know that governments and diplomacy often get in the way of common sense and simple human decency.

"I'm just asking you to make a little human gesture, knowing that one day you will have a right to ask me to reciprocate."

The courtesy call suddenly was over. I shook hands with a very flustered ambassador, wondering what the result would be.

When a few weeks had passed and I had not heard anything, I telephoned him.

He answered my call: "Oh, Ambassador Rowan, how are you?"

"Fine. Have you heard anything about Olga Fikotova's parents?"

"Prague knows," he said in a subdued voice.

"What?"

"Prague knows," he said in almost a whisper. I surmised that this was nothing he wanted to discuss at length on the telephone.

"Bless you," I said.

Several weeks later the Czech government gave exit visas to Olga Connolly's parents. I told her of this by telephone, and she came to the embassy crying, "Thank you, thank you, thank you!"

I was getting a solid idea of what kind of ambassador I wanted to be. I learned early to despise the protocol affairs, the ceremonial stuff, the white-tie national-day party — all were barely tolerable, and I felt they were not what I was in Finland for. Yet I understood that this is what occupies so much of the time of every ambassador in every land. The diplomatic community lives in a spirit of unflinching masochism.

I wanted to get to some real Finns to try to find out why they were different from the Latvians, Estonians, and Lithuanians who had succumbed to political and economic domination by the Soviet Union. Kekkonen and the diplomats aside, I wanted to know what the ordinary people of Finland thought.

I got early and startling clues when I saw the statistics on which foreign language was being studied by Finnish students. Some 70 percent were studying English, about 28 percent were studying German, but only 0.1 percent were studying Russian. It was an incredible insult that so few Finns even bothered to study the language of their next-door neighbor.

My judgment was that I could tap into this trust for America, this distrust for Moscow, this love for most of the things the United States stood for, with speeches that went beyond what previous ambassadors dared to say. So I talked publicly about "the anguish of the enslaved, whether in South Africa or Siberia." One Finnish journalist called this "a little jolting, but welcome."

I asked my staff to arrange early visits to key cities. The first was to the city of Hämeenlinna, which was not far from Helsinki. The townspeople put on a splendid luncheon (at which I learned that in coming months I would eat an awful lot of reindeer meat), and I was just dying to show off how much Finnish I could speak — which was *a lot* by the standards of most any other ambassador to Finland from any country. The devil gave me my chance during the luncheon when I was approached by two lovely young women carrying pots, one of which I assumed held coffee, the other tea.

The blonde who was in the lead said, "*Mita te haluatte, suurlahettilas?*" — or "What would you like, Mr. Ambassador?"

I had learned in the previous few days that if I said, "*Haluan teeta,*" it meant "I want some tea." But if I said, "*Haluan teita,*" it meant "I want you." The devil already had me, so I said with emphasis: "*HALUAN TE-I-TA!*"

Both young women broke into grins, and the one closest to me said in flawless English: "Hot or cold, Mr. Ambassador?"

The table erupted in laughter. Next day a local newspaper said that "The new ambassador speaks fluent Finnish," which was one great joke of a compliment.

"You are, I repeat, the freshest thing I ever met," Viv said at the end of that luncheon.

"I know," I said, being smart enough to laugh.

There is another side of being an ambassador that involves no glamour and certainly not much fun. It is the job of receiving, listening to, tending to, the needs of Americans who are traveling in your country. Especially Americans with political connections to the president who named you ambassador.

I thought I was in a safe haven in Finland for a while, because Americans liked to go to Paris and London in the summer. If they came to Scandinavia, they thought Stockholm was the end of paradise, and they would fly from there to the Soviet Union to see what life was like behind the iron curtain. I wasn't besieged with visitors, which meant that my modest representation budget was still in good shape. But some favorable *New York Times* articles about me put Finland high on the tourist map, and suddenly my embassy staff was pouring gin and vodka that I never imagined I'd have to pay for.

I gave an old-fashioned American Fourth of July party with hot dogs and hamburgers, sack races, ice-cream cones, egg rolling, dancing to Chubby Checker, Glenn Miller, Duke Ellington, and when I read the press I thought I was really getting to the Finns. Then I got a cable telling me that my priority was to take care of some Americans. Robert Kennedy informed me that Arnold Sagalyn, a prominent Washington lawyer, and Joseph Tydings, of the noted Maryland political family, were coming to Helsinki. Bobby asked if I would extend "appropriate courtesies."

I was naïve enough to think I could escape just by having a car and an embassy person pick them up at the airport. My savvy economic counselor, Les Edmond, said, "Sir, I read that telegram as a request that you do something special for them, like give a luncheon." So I did.

The first thing Tydings said when he and Sagalyn arrived at the residence was that he was going to run for the Senate. After lunch he asked if I would have a picture taken with him in the garden. "Of course," I said, and as we walked out he asked, "Which way to the Soviet Union?" I pointed east and he positioned himself for a photo gazing in that direction. Weeks later I saw one of Tydings's campaign ads, with me in the picture, boasting that he had "met with the American ambassador in Finland" to discuss developments in the Soviet Union.

Tydings won a seat in the Senate.

But the most important visitor of that summer of '63 was Lyndon Johnson. When the State Department informed me that his visit was imminent, the embassy went into shock. Nothing tears up an embassy more than a visit by a U.S. president or vice president. The details of preparation — of coordinating with the local government, of meeting Secret Service requirements, of seeing that all in the visiting party have hotel rooms, of ensuring that the host president gives the proper dinner and that the ambassador gives a dinner to which exactly the right local officials and citizens are invited — become a monumental chore. Especially when the ambassador decides to lay on a Texas flavor by having huge pits dug in a nearby park where flown-in Texas beef can be barbecued and served to the Finns.

The arrival of the Johnsons created a sensation among the Finns, who had not known the excitement of a visit by an American vice president or president — ever.

The Johnsons were a beautiful family, and the Finns found Lynda Bird especially fetching, beautiful black hair being so rare in this land of blonds. The dinners and the barbecue were successes that I was proud of. The serious meetings with President Kekkonen went precisely as we hoped they would. But then came Johnson's visit to the Finnish equivalent of the Tomb of the Unknown Soldier. We had sent instructions to Washington, I had told Johnson personally, and the embassy had given him written instructions, with copies to his military aide, Colonel Jackson, that there was to be no speech at the cemetery. The Finns would regard it as a sacrilege.

When we got to this hallowed ground, Finns surrounded it in vast numbers to see the vice president of the United States. Johnson surveyed them and, to my astonishment, reached into his pocket and pulled out speech notes. I half hollered to Colonel Jackson, "Go remind him — *no speech!*"

LBJ gave Jackson a Doberman-like snarl and began to give a speech. The Finns were at first disbelieving, and then I could see outrage on their faces.

At the end of the ceremony I asked Jackson to come with me. At the sight of Jackson, Johnson's face flushed red, and he said, "Colonel, one of these days you are going to understand that anytime I see a crowd that big, I'm gonna give a speech, even if I don't have a goddam speech."

"Colonel Jackson is right, Mr. Vice President," I said. "In cables, briefing papers, and today's embassy instructions, you were told — *no speech.*"

"That's right, honey, no speech," interjected Lady Bird.

Johnson snarled at her and said, "Not a one of you seems to know when to give a goddammed speech."

The vice president stalked away, angry at me, his wife, Jackson, and the Finns.

"This," I told Viv that night, "is one of several Lyndon Johnsons that millions of people pray will never become president."

While Johnson was in Finland there was an earthquake in Iran, and he wanted to go there to demonstrate American caring. The White House said no. In one of his soliloquies, Johnson gave a late-night version of his view that he could look into the eyes of Soviet leaders and see what was in their hearts. I got a secret back-channel message saying, "Do what you must, under any circumstances, to prevent Johnson from going to the Soviet Union."

As the Johnson plane lifted off the runway in Helsinki, I said to Viv: "What a pity. A man so great in so many ways, and so mean and petty in others."

I'd had an outraged member of the Secret Service tell me that *he* had thought of killing Johnson. I'd had members of the press tell me that it would be a national disaster if Johnson ever became president. He was a towering man one day and a damned fool the next. I couldn't read him. I just had to hope that he never became president.

My duties as ambassador had been complicated in awful ways by the war in Vietnam. One weekend, when we visited a country home, the delicacy of a fresh salmon cooked on an outdoor fire was tarnished with questions about why the United States was engaging in "an imperialistic venture."

The less-than-wished-for main course of reindeer tongue was not made more palatable by questions about why the United States backed "a bunch of crooked dictators in Saigon" instead of "a genuine patriot, Ho Chi Minh."

Vietnam was all the Finns wanted to talk about, except the police dogs, water hoses, and mean cops in Birmingham, Selma, and other bastions of Jim Crow. I could belie, almost by just showing up, the notion that my country was hopelessly racist. But I could not wipe out the belief of most Finns that the United States was fighting an unjust and losing war in Southeast Asia. This bothered me, not because I personally had come to oppose my country's policy regarding Vietnam, but because the obsession with Vietnam in both Washington and Helsinki made it difficult for me to deal with other serious problems.

One was intelligence. I knew that the air attaché's plane — or, when I asked for it, the ambassador's plane — was engaged in an activity not spoken of in those days: ELINT, or electronic intelligence. The Finns and the Soviets knew, too, that this was a spy plane.

I knew also that in one of my buildings there were young U.S. military men monitoring aircraft takeoffs from Leningrad and other Soviet airfields and that they could tell you in a second what kind of aircraft had left the runway. Ours was a sophisticated and important listening post.

I also knew that the Soviets knew what was going on. They occupied a building across from our building, where they monitored what we were monitoring.

I remembered the Kennedy-Rusk-Bowles proclamation that the ambassador was in charge and that no one in the mission, CIA, FBI, National Security Agency (NSA), or even the Commerce Department was to do anything without the approval of the ambassador.

The Powers–U-2 drama was fresh in my mind, and I wanted to make sure that if Viv and I were riding the embassy plane on an official visit to Oulu or another city, some CIA or NSA crewman was not engaging in a form of electronic espionage that could get us shot down. I didn't want to get into a mess where I'd have to tell a destructive lie of the sort Eisenhower told when Powers's U-2 was shot down.

There were other things, not as dramatic, not part of the cold war, that I wanted my government at least to consider. But I quickly learned one thing about the bureaucracy of the U.S. government — the State Department, the White House, but also every niche of an incestuous group of people wanted to do things their way and ignored anybody who had a new idea. I sent cable after cable to State, but nothing changed — nothing, whether relating to intelligence or anything else. I decided that I would have to talk to President Kennedy personally. So I cabled the State Department that I was coming back on consultation.

The passions of racial conflict were inflaming America. The war in Vietnam had become a political plague. Kennedy, so admired for a brilliant inaugural address, was being pilloried, vilified, in most of the conservative precincts of the land.

I flew back to Washington and got the last appointment that John F. Kennedy had before he flew to Dallas to give a speech.

The Kennedy to whom I talked that November night had learned the painful way that even words of wisdom, vision, nobility, and bravery are not self-fulfilling. On the domestic scene, governors like George Wallace of Alabama and Ross Barnett of Mississippi kept walking on his words about civil rights and racial justice. Conservative editors were assailing him. Ted Dealey of the *Dallas Morning News* had stood up in a gathering of publishers to tell the president face-to-face that the nation needed a knight on a white horse, and he, JFK, was not it. Kennedy had said the right things, but he lacked the allies in Congress, the knowledge of which arms to twist, which closet skeletons to rattle, to get his social programs through Congress.

We talked seriously about Finland for a while, then Kennedy said to me, almost apropos of nothing, "Carl, a lot has happened in the months you have been out of Washington. Hatred is spreading across this country like a cancer. The bigots, the Birchites, are like a plague. They get bolder every day. I suppose you have read about the disgraceful things that they did to Adlai Stevenson down in Texas. [They spat on him.] This trend is dangerous for the country. It endangers you, me, and human rights and all that this administration stands for. I have made up my mind that a president is obligated to use the prestige of his office to try to halt this goddam madness. I have concluded that I am partly to blame because I haven't gotten out among the people enough. I'm going to Texas tomorrow partly because I believe it is something I am obliged to do."

As Kennedy paused in his discussion of the plague of hatred sweeping across America, I got a chance to ask him something I had wondered about for more than two years: "Mr. President, I hadn't campaigned for you, as I never have campaigned for anyone, and I've always wondered why you offered me a job in your administration."

Kennedy gave what seemed to me a little laugh of embarrassment and said, "Do you remember coming to Washington prior to the election to do a series of articles on Nixon and me? Well, I had been told by my brother and others that your publisher, John Cowles, was going to endorse Nixon. And you were going to do an article for *Ebony* magazine, and I was told that Johnny Johnson at *Ebony* was going to endorse Nixon. And you had just written the biography of Jackie Robinson, who was supporting Nixon and kicking my ass wherever he could. And I figured you had come down to do a hatchet job on me. Oh, I eventually saw your articles, and I said to myself, 'Goddam, these are eminently fair,' and I never forgot your name."

Two days later I was having lunch in the Jockey Club when the State Department sent a messenger to tell me that President Kennedy had been shot in Dallas.

Some have written that Mr. Kennedy was in Texas, dragged there unwillingly, to try to patch up a petty political feud that neither Lyndon Johnson nor Governor John Connally could solve. But my conversation with the president indicated that he was going on a mission to restore the sanity, the sense of decency, of the American people.

Millions of Americans remember precisely where they were and what they were doing when they learned that Kennedy had been assassinated. Most of them wept, but I sat tearless that fateful night, thinking about the craziness and brutality of the men who ruled, or wanted to rule, the world. Kennedy had approved the coup in which Diem was assassinated. Kennedy had approved efforts to kill Cuba's Fidel Castro. Now someone had killed Kennedy. Washington was full of whispers that the Soviets had hired Lee Harvey Oswald to kill our president; that Castro had wreaked the ultimate revenge; that the Mafia had put JFK on its hit list because Attorney General Robert F. Kennedy had pulled a double cross by trying to imprison the people who had helped his brother win the election; that LBJ somehow was behind the assassination because that was the only way he would ever become president.

As the rumors and innuendos flew, I remained certain of only one thing: there would be no end to assassinations and attempted murders of public officials in America, because the country was full of ideological crazies in powerful positions and had an abundance of run-of-the-mill lunatics. Still, I found it hard to accept the horror that the president with whom I had just conferred, who had talked to me so bravely about his duty to fight American racism, was dead.

I have hated attending funerals since I went to one of a beloved relative when I was six or seven years old. Funerals seemed, and still seem, to be such morbid exercises in masochism. But I knew that for very personal reasons of appreciation and respect I had to go to the Kennedy funeral.

At the end of services, Johnson walked up to me and said: "Come to see me, my friend. I need to talk to you right away."

There was no way that the new president of a grieving nation, a new president watched by a thousand newsmen, could talk to anyone without arousing rumors and speculations.

I went to see President Johnson the next day. I found him still harboring the notion that the Soviet Union was behind the murder of Kennedy and might be targeting him, hoping to kill off the American political leadership. He wanted to know if I had any contacts in Finland who might shed light on Soviet involvement in the assassination or on Soviet intentions for the future.

"You just call me privately if you learn anything that I need to know," he said.

Then, abruptly, Johnson turned to a discussion of civil rights and the growing racial violence.

"I told you before," he said, "that I'm a goddam sight more liberal — and genuine — than the liberals you been courting. I've got to do something to heal America, and I wanna do it right. And I need you to help me to do it right."

"I'm at your service, sir."

"I need more than your damned service," Johnson said. "I need you to tell me which Negroes I should listen to, which ones I can trust, and which ones are gonna get me in a lot of trouble."

I wasn't about to become the black kitchen cabineteer who stood in the shadows, whispering to Johnson that this black was acceptable and that one was not. So I ducked his reference to individuals and said, "You'll make a great nation greater, sir, if you can get legislation to end segregation in restaurants and theaters and other public places, and most of all grant Negroes the right to vote."

"Well, goddam," Johnson said, "I thought at least you'd been around me long enough to know that I'm gonna do that!"

"You've got a lot of people waiting, Mr. President," I said. "Thank you for talking to me, and remember that the White House telephone operator knows where I am."

Johnson scrunched his face up into a hundred wrinkles, and his eyes seemed a bit teary as he gave me an *abrazo* hug in which, with three slaps, he almost collapsed one of my lungs.

Shortly after I got back to Finland, I read a gossip item in *Time* magazine: "Within hours of President Kennedy's death, Lyndon Johnson called in Ambassador to Finland, Carl Rowan, 38, for a chat. Since Johnson's problems of the moment hardly included the diplomatic climate in Helsinki, it seems certain Rowan was getting a job offer."

Johnson and I had not spoken a word about any new job, but press stories escalated about what job I was going to get. Knowing how much Johnson detested leaks, I sent him a message saying that I had nothing to do with the press mess.

It turned out, however, that the dope sheets and the newsletters knew more than I did, for Lyndon Johnson did have plans for me in his administration.

In early January of 1964 I returned to the embassy residence from a dinner at the Danish embassy and fell asleep while trying to read briefing papers. The telephone awakened me, and I picked up the receiver to find that Johnson was saying: "Come home, Carl, I need you."

There was no mention whatsoever of why I should return to Washington. But I knew what to do. I awakened my administrative officer and ordered him to get me a reservation on the first plane out of Helsinki to Washington.

Meeting me at the airport in Washington was Bill Moyers, a good friend, a close adviser to the president, who said: "Carl, if you let the president know that I've told you this, I'll kill you, because he will fire me. You know how he is about leaks. But he's going to appoint you as director of the U.S. Information Agency. But he doesn't have all his ducks in line with regard to the senators from the South. He wants you to stay incognito at the Madison Hotel, where we've booked a room for you, until he has talked to Senators [John] McClellan [of Arkansas], Allen Ellender [of Louisiana], and others. He knows that he can't afford a situation where you are not confirmed."

I would later learn that Moyers was going beyond the bounds of friendship, because he had wanted the job of director of the U.S. Information Agency above any other possible post, but he dared not ask Johnson for it. And now that Johnson had chosen me, he was giving me not only his support, but some advance information that was particularly valuable.

So, on instructions, I holed up in the Madison, knowing what few other people did: that on December 19, 1963, Edward R. Murrow, USIA director, had written President Johnson, saying:

> As you know, I was separated from a cancerous lung in early October. The doctors assure me the operation was successful, and that recovery to date has been normal. However, it will be several months before I can resume full-time duty. Were I to continue as director of this agency during that period it would mean that I could not direct its affairs as I would wish, as I have tried to do, or as you are entitled to expect it to be directed.
>
> Shortly before he died, I spoke to President Kennedy and told him I might feel obliged to resign. After his tragic death, it had been my hope to continue to serve my country under your leadership. My inability to do so is deeply disappointing.
>
> I would be grateful if you could arrange to relieve me of my duties by mid-January.

So I was invisible by day, the press having no idea that I was in Washington. At night I saw my closest friends, but I was greatly relieved when, on January 21, Johnson decided that he had all his "ducks in line." He announced that Murrow had resigned and that

> after the most careful study, I have concluded that the man most eminently qualified to supervise this vital program of telling America's story abroad is Carl T. Rowan, our present ambassador to Finland.
>
> Mr. Rowan — like our country — is young and dynamic, and he has had a breadth of private and governmental experiences that are especially valuable qualifications for this job. . . .
>
> He is superbly qualified by training and experience to carry on the work of Ed Murrow. . . . I have recalled him immediately [from Finland] for the post of director of the USIA.

CHAPTER FIFTEEN

LBJ and the
Civil Rights Revolution

I F I H AV E not made it clear earlier, let me say it now: Lyndon
Baines Johnson was egocentric, domineering, imperious, mean,
insecure, cornpone, unfaithful, crude. He was also generous,
brave, a fighter for the little guy, loyal to friends and causes — and
damned effective. It all depended on which LBJ you encountered,
with how much Cutty Sark in him, or how many woes and worries
were beating down upon him.

Because Johnson was all these bad things, and all these good
things in abundance, more journalists and bureaucrats in Washington practiced psychiatry without a license on this flamboyant
Texan than on any other president in American history.

Knowing all this, I questioned my own sanity when I agreed un-
hesitatingly to leave the tranquility of an ambassadorship to return
to Washington where I would be close to this utterly unpredictable
president.

I knew why. Because the job as director of the United States
Information Agency was far-reaching and challenging. I would
have control of the Voice of America, beaming America's story to
many millions of people in the Soviet Union, China, Poland, Cuba,
Hungary, and scores of other countries — people who literally
risked their lives to listen to VOA on their little transistor radios. I
would be in command of a worldwide news service similar to AP
and UP — the wireless file that all U.S. ambassadors and embassy
personnel relied on (many saw no meaningful daily newspaper) to
keep them abreast of world events, including public statements by

U.S. officials. I would supervise a worldwide staff responsible for briefing the press in foreign countries, handling Fulbright grantees and cultural exchange programs and exhibits — and running a large chain of libraries in which people still dreaming of freedom could read about Thomas Jefferson, Abe Lincoln, FDR, and JFK. I would become the "publisher" of scores of magazines and books tailored to make people enslaved under communism believe that the American way was the better way.

And Johnson had made the job more desirable by asserting that I would attend meetings of his cabinet and of the National Security Council. I accepted the USIA post with alacrity — and great excitement.

The White House press release of January 21, 1964, about Murrow's resignation and Johnson's appointment of me could not have been more full of my praises if I had written it in my most immodest moments. I knew that friends Bill Moyers and Johnson aide Jack Valenti had overseen the wording, but I had no doubt that Johnson personally had approved every sentence. He wanted the nation to understand that my appointment was no sop to blacks, not even an affirmative action gesture, because he really believed that I was "the man most eminently qualified to supervise this vital program of telling America's story abroad."

On that very January day of the press announcement I learned anew that when Johnson believed in what he was doing, he left nothing to chance. He looked for ways to emphasize his goodness and decency.

Marguerite Higgins, the great *New York Herald-Tribune* war correspondent, and Peter Lisagor of the *Chicago Daily News*, one of the finest Washington correspondents ever (they were having a not-very-secret affair), invited me to lunch at Marguerite's home on Twenty-fourth Street. I had been there several times when I was in the State Department to enjoy Maggie's special dish, beef ragout, and sometimes to do a little choice leaking on instructions from officials as high as President Kennedy.

As I rode in the State Department car to lunch, I thought about the paucity of blacks who practiced journalism in the power centers of Washington. I wondered when my black colleagues who worked at the edges would discover how Higgins and Lisagor gained and retained a preeminent status. They had the guts to regard press secretaries, presidential aides, and presidents as equals whom they invited to break bread.

The thought was provoked by Maggie's telephone call telling me that Moyers would join us at lunch to "informally discuss politics and policies." Then she told me that Moyers had called to ask if Valenti could join us.

At 1:15 I arrived in this cozy neighborhood and saw a couple of men casing the area.

"Hell, those are Secret Service guys," I said to the driver. "I can smell one a mile away."

But my suspicions did not reach the reality of what soon occurred. The White House limousine, carrying Johnson as well as his huge security entourage, rolled into Twenty-fourth Street, causing great excitement among the neighbors.

It was an absolutely delightful luncheon. Johnson told several anecdotes at my expense: "I tried to fire him in Bangkok, dump him in Saigon, leave him in India and Pakistan," he said. "But he kept coming up with some sumbitch camel driver or something that told me I ought to keep him."

I told a couple at his expense: "Marguerite, nothing in your war correspondence days would have prepared you for what Nancy Hanschman [Dickerson] had to face when Johnson became the only vice president in history to hold a press conference in his drawers."

My recollection was that Nancy never got away from lunch to see the great Johnson bedroom performance, but it made for a great luncheon story that even set Johnson's face into long, red ripples.

Then Johnson turned serious, as he always did after a couple of scotches and some wine.

"I got a lotta problems," he said. "I've got a brazen Communist attempt to conquer Asia on my hands. I've got Negroes revolting in America — and I know Mr. Roe-ann sides with that revolution. I got troubles in Central America that the people don't even know about. I gotta figure out how to pay for these fucking wars and keep my commitment to feed, educate, and care for the people of this country. Now, I can't do it if Maggie Higgins and Pete Lisagor abandon me and echo the know-nothings on social policy and the goddam liberals like Mary McGrory on foreign policy."

Johnson always had a winner going, hands down, until he went into his hard-sell soliloquies. But on the whole the luncheon made me feel really good about my appointment, even though I had anguished a bit in my knowledge that I was coming home from Finland in the best years and the worst years for both Johnson and my country.

Those were the best years because we were in a half decade in which breaking barriers was a great and glorious preoccupation of federal officials from the Oval Office to the Justice Department to the State Department to thousands of lower offices. Knocking down old doors and letting justice enter was a challenge accepted in a million pulpits, on the floor of Congress, and in myriad schoolhouses, restaurants, theaters, and polling places.

I knew, from Johnson's behavior at the Higgins-Lisagor luncheon, that he felt he had set up Georgia Democrat Richard Russell, Ellender, McClellan, and the rest of his old Senate colleagues from the South in a way that made it impossible for any of them to go against me without being called a bigot.

I was a lot more concerned than Johnson was, knowing that my insistence on distributing Murrow's film *The March* would make me some powerful enemies, because this "I have a dream" film featured Dr. King. Ellender, I had been warned, hated USIA and liked me even less. The day after that luncheon I read Tom Wicker's story about my appointment on page one of the *New York Times* and almost croaked. He described me as a "tough-talking and controversial former journalist." (In 1964, black men were not supposed to be "tough-talking" or "controversial.")

The *Washington Star* said, "We are not at all sure that Mr. Rowan, despite his many talents, is qualified for the job." The *Star* cited my "brash speech" in Philadelphia opposing the attempted Tshombe steal of the mineral resources of the Congo. I was dumbfounded to read an editorial in the *Chicago Daily News*, whose editor had tried to hire me at $50,000 a year, describing me as a "bull in a china shop."

I knew that Johnson would read every word of these attacks.

I was told by a White House secretary that Johnson guffawed when he read Fletcher Knebel's comment in his column, "Potomac

Fever," that "Negro Carl Rowan is named head of the U.S. Information Agency. Nobody can win at this job. When the white man transfers his burden, he sure picks a heavy load."

And Johnson's secretary told me that Johnson said, "I could almost cry," when he read two items: an editorial in the *Washington Daily News* saying "by the standards of any race, color, or creed, Carl T. Rowan is admirably equipped for the assignment just given him by President Johnson." And a column in which Maggie Higgins said: "President Johnson has now surely given the final blow to the stubbornly prevailing myth that in racial matters he 'talks liberal but really doesn't mean it.' "

Nice, temporarily consoling stuff. But no one rests easily when he or she is up for Senate confirmation to a very important and controversial post — especially no black person who is under attack in powerful parts of the media.

Back in Finland, awaiting confirmation, I saw anew the truth of the old saying that a lie is halfway round the world before the truth gets its boots on. Ed Savage, my press man, brought me the USIA wireless file in which I read, with my gut wrenching, that newspapers across the country had resurrected a phony story that I had tried to censor the media in Vietnam when in fact I had talked Kennedy out of muzzling the media.

Through this trauma, I learned a couple of things: Most members of Congress are fair and decent, but too many get led into meanness and venality by overweeningly powerful committee staff members who want to harpoon someone. And some newspaper editors, reporters, editorial writers, are lazy, relying on old clippings, never calling the person they are about to attack or ridicule — but on the whole, the American press is pretty damn good about figuring out who is or is not a villain.

Back in Washington, I had an appointment before the Senate Foreign Relations Committee, hoping it would confirm me as the highest-ranking black person in the whole United States government. No matter what Johnson had said about me privately to southern senators, or in press releases, these guys would want to make their own judgment as to whether I was just a black incompetent chosen to further Johnson's ambitions to be elected to his own term as president.

Furthermore, word had been relayed to me that some northern senators, like George Aiken of Vermont and Bourke Hickenlooper of Iowa, had expressed doubt that any black person could speak for America. I decided I ought to talk to the senators about what this country is and what it strives to be.

On February 25, 1964, I went before the Senate Foreign Relations Committee determined to disarm my foes with my opening statement. I said:

> Surely there are those who would ask: "Just what *is* this country, Carl Rowan, and what *does* it strive to be?" I must answer in many ways. America is capitalism with a conscience — a country in which laborers own homes, automobiles, new refrigerators, but, more important, where ordinary men have an extraordinary voice in the affairs of their government.
>
> America is a rocket pinpointed on the moon and Polaris missile submarines cruising as sentinels of the deep — military might never surpassed in history, but harnessed by a sense of responsibility for man's destiny and by a national desire for peace within freedom.
>
> And this nation is a social ferment — a society caught up in a concern for its aged and its ill, full of compassion for its impoverished . . . a people struggling as no society *ever* struggled to achieve a unity that transcends the incidental boundaries of religion, race, national origin. America is leadership — a nation whose destiny it has become to man the far-flung ramparts of freedom, marching with the fearful and the weak, the hungry and the harassed, toward the goal of a peaceful world community of free and independent states.
>
> Mr. Chairman, brevity forbids my saying all that this nation is. But I think that I have said enough to justify my fundamental belief that all we need wish the world to know about us is the truth. Through face-to-face contacts, through television, films, and radio, and through the printed word, we shall spread the truth, and I am confident that the truth will keep us free.

Senator William Fulbright said, "Thank you, Mr. Rowan. That is a very excellent statement."

Next up was Hickenlooper, and I waited for the harpoon as he spoke of me as "a newspaperman and a public official of great ability and experience and accomplishment."

Then he asserted that I had "advocated certain strong opinions that could be considered quite emotional" about issues "close to your heart." I knew he was talking about racism in America. I couldn't believe that Fulbright of Arkansas was giving me a gentlemanly ride to confirmation while this Iowan was trying to block my way.

Hickenlooper then went into a tirade about Murrow's film about the 1963 March on Washington, about how it suggested that the Negro "had no freedom in this country, had no liberties."

Hickenlooper seemed stuck for a moment when I told him that one of our ambassadors could use this massive protest to say to a president of another country: "This illustrates the right of peaceful protest, the obvious economic well-being of those who participated, the fact that millions of white Americans are concerned and are showing a feeling of conscience about this subject."

Hickenlooper switched to the phony allegations about my trying to muzzle the press in Vietnam, then he went on about my speech on Tshombe, Michel Struelens, the Congo, the Katanga lobby, and then back to the film concerning the March on Washington.

At some point, I sensed that Hickenlooper was talking for the record. I didn't believe that he would vote against me and felt that if he did, while Fulbright voted for me, he would look like the lightweight that he was.

If I had any worries, they vanished when Hubert Humphrey took over the questioning, scalpeling his way to the heart of the issue:

"Had this film about the March on Washington been screened by the secretary of state and the president?"

My answer: "Yes."

"Had either objected to showing it abroad?"

Answer: "No."

"Had Murrow or anyone else consulted with you before the film was made?"

Answer: "No."

"Was the footage in this documentary from newsreels and programs that were easily available to Tass and other television networks around the world?"

Answer: "Yes, but when the Soviet Union found out that it was to be a peaceful march, supported by the Johnson administration, it canceled plans to take the *Telstar* feed and broadcast it in the Soviet Union."

I sat in immense admiration of Humphrey and the skill with which he demolished Hickenlooper without ever mentioning his name.

"Mr. Rowan," Humphrey said almost sarcastically, "are you aware of the fact that you have been politically lambasted and tarred and feathered by the Havana radio on your appointment? . . . You are described as an apologist for the racist and imperialist system. [Havana radio says] 'Rowan is the same Negro who was denied restaurant facilities at an airport in his native state. What brazen hypocrisy — a northern American whose third-rate citizenship bars him from the right to use a public facility in parts of his native land. . . .' "

Humphrey told how he had gotten a transcript of the Radio Havana broadcast and said, "This broadcast indicates, Mr. Rowan, that your appointment was merely a cover-up for race prejudice in the United States and that you are lending yourself to an evil plot. Would you like to make any comments?"

What a magnificent setup from a friend, a great public servant! I made a few comments, after which, as was his style, Humphrey made *a lot* of comments in which he praised me beyond anything even my wife or children could take seriously.

When Humphrey finished, the hearing was over. I had won unanimous confirmation in the committee, as I would in the Senate.

But while I celebrated my victory, a warning pulse kept reminding me about "the worst of times," that gruesome, rapidly escalating war. I first had to accept the reality that in my job as director of the U.S. Information Agency I would be involved only tangentially in the great civil rights struggle, but I would become inescapably entrapped in the deepening quagmire of the war that engulfed Indochina — in fact, all of Asia and much of the rest of the world.

But no warning light about Indochina, no concerns about Johnson's personality, could squelch my excitement over a chance to be back in Washington and in the midst of events that were so profoundly important.

*　　　*　　　*

The remembrances of the Vietnam War are still so painful that I do not want to deal with that conflagration now, or with the LBJ who found it infinitely more painful than I did. Allow me, please, to reminisce about the LBJ who turned out, plain and simple, to be the greatest human rights and civil rights president America has ever known.

Many civil rights leaders, black and white, still held serious doubts about the strength of Johnson's commitment, but I did not, because I had already seen him under intense pressure. Johnson not only had made his civil rights commitment, but he was proud of it.

He said, "We got some real fighting to do to get a civil rights bill. You're gonna find out sooner or later that I'm a damn sight better on this issue than those Kennedys."

That would take a lot of doing by Johnson. President Kennedy had federalized the Mississippi National Guard and put U.S. Army troops on standby in Memphis in order to force the admission of James Meredith, a twenty-nine-year-old Air Force veteran, as a student at the all-white University of Mississippi. Two people had died and many more were injured in that 1962 confrontation. In 1963, Police Commissioner Bull Connor of Birmingham had used police dogs and fire hoses to thwart a civil rights march led by the Reverend Martin Luther King, Jr., and other ministers; bomb blasts had ripped the home of King's brother, A.D., and the black-owned A. G. Gaston Motel; then, on the Sunday morning of September 15, a bomb exploded in the Sixteenth Street Baptist Church during a children's Bible class. Four girls aged eleven to fourteen were killed and scores were injured. That same year, on June 13, Medgar Evers, the thirty-seven-year-old NAACP leader in Mississippi, had been gunned down in the doorway of his Jackson home.

An outraged Martin Luther King, inspired in part by Kennedy, spoke on August 28, 1963, when more than two hundred thousand Americans of all races met at the Lincoln Memorial in what will forever be known as the great civil rights March on Washington, about which USIA had done its inspiring movie.

I sensed in 1964 that Johnson was motivated by profound emotion over these events, but also by a burning desire to get through Congress civil rights legislation that the late President Kennedy had said was "politically impossible."

Johnson proposed an incredible, sweeping piece of legislation. It assured voting rights by prohibiting registrars from applying different standards for black and white voter applicants (Title I); made it a federal crime to discriminate in the use of public accommodations (Title II) and public facilities (Title III); and authorized the federal government to provide assistance to all school districts involved in desegregation (Title IV). The tenure of the Civil Rights Commission was extended (Title V); the Census Bureau was made to compile voting statistics by race in areas designated by the Civil Rights Commission (Title VIII); and a Community Relations Service in the Department of Commerce was established for investigating and resolving racial disputes at the local level (Title X). The act also prohibited discrimination on the basis of race in any program receiving federal financial aid (Title VI) and gave federal agencies power to deny funds to agencies practicing discrimination. Employment discrimination was outlawed, and a commission was established to investigate charges of discrimination in employment and, where necessary, to mediate in such charges (Title VII). Higher federal courts could prevent lower federal courts from sending a civil rights case back to a state or local court when such a step might compromise the case of an appellant (Title IX), and criminal contempt cases that arose from any part of the act (save Title I) were given the right of jury trial (Title XI).

I was barely back in Washington when, on February 10, 1964, the House passed Johnson's bill, 290 to 130. The word was all over Washington, however, that Senator Everett Dirksen, the minority leader from Illinois, was opposed to the portions of the bill that would force restaurants, hotels, and theaters to admit blacks and to Title VII, which would create a fair employment practices commission.

"Without those sections there's no damn civil rights bill worth a fart in a hailstorm," Johnson said to me. "I'm gonna get the whole bill, if I can get some help from you and them fast-talking, do-nothing liberals out there."

"What motivates this man Johnson?" I asked myself, remembering that he had defended racial segregation when he was a congressman from Texas. I knew that he wanted to prove that he was a bigger man than his beginnings and his background suggested. Over beer that long, speech-writing night in Saigon, he had made revealing comments.

"I don't like to admit it," he had said, "but a man has to vote for a lot of things if he wants the votes of Texans that he doesn't have to support if he wants votes from the whole country."

And then: "Bobby Kennedy thinks I'm an ignorant Texas hayseed. But I know more about what the little people of America need than he does. When did that sumbitch last miss a meal?"

Sometimes politicians do great things for small reasons. I was glad that, if it was in fact the case, Johnson was motivated by a desire to prove that while he couldn't articulate his views and goals in a Harvard accent, he was as modern a leader as JFK.

John F. Kennedy had, actually, disappointed a lot of Americans in his handling of James Meredith's attempt to become the first black student at the University of Mississippi. Sure, Kennedy finally issued Executive Order 11053, authorizing the use of federal troops to ensure Meredith's admittance, but there was disturbing evidence that he had chickened out in conversations with Mississippi's governor, Ross Barnett. There were ugly rumors that Bobby Kennedy had told his brother not to go overboard in antagonizing the South, or he would not be reelected in 1964.

Now Johnson faced not just one racial crisis but hundreds. Blacks were rising up against segregation in restaurants, movie houses, public parks, and more; they were staging sit-ins and being arrested in huge numbers. Martin Luther King, Jr., prisoner 7089, had written a "Letter from a Birmingham Jail" that had aroused much of the nation, including Johnson.

My entire journalistic career had embraced a personal war against the gradualists, the whites of power who asked black Americans to "wait." I was surprised, but immensely pleased, when the president told me that he had read that letter from the Birmingham jail in which King explained in these words why blacks would not wait:

I guess it is easy for those who have never felt the stinging darts of segregation to say "wait."
But when you have seen vicious mobs lynch your mothers and

fathers at will and drown your sisters and brothers at whim; when you have seen hate-filled policemen curse, kick, brutalize and even kill your black brothers and sisters; when you suddenly find your tongue twisted and your speech stammering as you seek to explain to your six-year-old daughter why she can't go to the public amusement park that has just been advertised on television, and see tears welling up in her little eyes when she is told that "Funtown" is closed to colored children, and see the depressing clouds of inferiority begin to form in her mental sky, and see her begin to distort her little personality by unconsciously developing a bitterness toward white people . . . then you will understand why we find it difficult to wait.

It was a year after King wrote that letter that Johnson expressed fear to me that he might not get his civil rights bill through the Senate. Southern senators skilled in parliamentary maneuvers had stalled progress on the bill after debate began in late March. After a National Security Council meeting one day, Johnson gave me a "come here" waggle of his index finger, indicating that he wanted a private chat.

He said: "Old Dick Russell is against me, and he's the one I worry about. I told your friend Hubert [Humphrey] that if you damned liberals don't get off your asses and do something, Russell is gonna wind up with your peckers in his pocket."

This was vintage Johnson. I had learned in 1961 that when he really wanted something, no language was too coarse, no tactic too tricky, for him to use in the pursuit of success.

A few days later I got a call asking me to come to a meeting that turned out to be just a discussion among Johnson, Humphrey, and myself.

"Hubert," Johnson said, "the country can't go on like this. Little girls are getting their heads busted open 'cause they wanta drink a Coca-Cola at the soda fountain at Rich's Department Store in Atlanta."

"I know, Mr. President," Humphrey said. "We have got to stop it."

"But, goddammit, I can't stop it," Johnson said, "if they filibuster my civil rights bill to death in the Senate. I can't pass the bill if I can't break the filibuster, and that means getting Ev Dirksen and a couple of Republican senators from the mountain states to vote for cloture."

"I know," Humphrey said.

"I suppose you know that Dirksen is pissed off at Negroes? Do you know that, Carl?" Johnson asked. "He thinks blacks in Illinois shit all over him during his reelection campaign. Hubert, you have got to soothe some ruffled feathers."

For a moment I wondered why I was there, because I had not had a chance to utter a word. Then it occurred to me that Johnson was talking for the historical record. He wanted a black man to see that it was he who directed the greatest of civil rights senators to get his bill passed by the Senate.

"Remember, Hubert," Johnson continued, "Ev is a proud man. So don't pull any damned protocol. *You* go see *him.*"

"I'm on my way to the Hill right now," Humphrey said.

As the senator neared the door, Johnson almost shouted: "And Hubert, don't forget that Dirksen loves to bend his elbow. I want you to drink with him till he agrees to vote for cloture and deliver me two Republicans from the mountain states."

Humphrey would later joke with me that he drank himself "damned near blind," but he "got to" Dirksen.

For just over three months the battle in the Senate raged furiously, with amendment after amendment proposed, and more than one hundred roll-call votes. In the end it was Dirksen who gave Johnson a triumph. He supported Johnson in a 71 to 29 vote for cloture. Dirksen's "revision," which was Johnson's original bill, was approved by the Senate and signed by Johnson on July 2.

Millions of Americans breathed sighs of relief at the passage of the Civil Rights Act of 1964. Some whites extolled a president who had exhorted them to be better than they imagined they could be. Yet deep bitterness lingered in the South. Only eleven days before that Senate vote, civil rights workers Michael Schwerner, Andrew Goodman, and James E. Chaney, two Jewish and one black, were reported missing in Mississippi. On August 4 their bodies would be found, buried by a bulldozer, near Philadelphia, Mississippi.

Black Americans wanted more than the right to sit next to whites in a theater or to stay in a white hotel. They wanted full citizenship, which meant the untrammeled right to vote. So they demonstrated. In the early days of February 1965, more than three thousand black people were arrested in Selma, Alabama, for protesting discrimination in voter registration. On February 4, a federal judge ordered the end to the use of an extremely difficult literacy test on blacks trying to register to vote. But white authorities were unbending.

On March 9, President Johnson asserted that "all Americans" joined "in deploring the brutality with which a number of Negro citizens of Alabama were treated when they sought to dramatize their deep and sincere interest in attaining the precious right to vote."

When I saw Johnson a few days later, he said cryptically: "I gotta go back to Congress."

Johnson knew that to secure passage of the Voting Rights Act he had to raise the matter to the level of a national imperative. And there was no better way to do that than to have a president from Jim Crow Texas go before a joint session of the Congress and exhort the nation to heed his cry for political justice.

I saw in a single day, March 15, 1965, all of God's permutations of Lyndon Johnson as he tried to ensure that his historic appeal to the Congress would not be rejected.

I saw the crafty LBJ, telling Lady Bird to ask me to escort her to the president's box so that my black face would guarantee that it wouldn't look like the Mississippi legislature. The shrewd Johnson displaying some white southern backing by asking former Florida governor LeRoy Collins to sit with Lady Bird and me.

When I got to the White House a couple of hours before the Capitol Hill speech, I saw the mean, neurotic Johnson. His speech was not yet written, mainly because he kept prancing and adding ideas or bellowing and throwing out passages. He greeted me with the declaration that "every goddam body around here thinks he's smarter than I am. I told them what I wanted to say, but this shit has no resemblance to what I want to say."

Valenti whispered to the president that there could be no more changes, because there wouldn't be time to get them on the Tele-PrompTers.

"If you can't get it on the TelePrompTers, then I can't speak," Johnson said, as if he believed he could stand up a nation. "Jack, goddammit, this has got to stop. What's wrong with the girl who's typing it? She must have fourteen goddam wooden fingers, because she has had it all afternoon." Then, with hardly a pause, Johnson said, "I want her to retype this section about blacks lying down in the highway in Selma."

Later that night I saw the Lyndon Johnson of compassion, of fervor for justice, as he told that joint session why he thought the Voting Rights Act was morally right and a national imperative:

> There is no constitutional issue here. The command of the Constitution is plain. There is no moral issue. It is wrong — to deny any of your fellow Americans the right to vote. . . .
>
> There is no issue of states' rights, or national rights. There is only the struggle for human rights. . . .
>
> It is the effort of American Negroes to secure for themselves the full blessings of American life.
>
> Their cause must be our cause too. Because it's not just Negroes, but really it's all of us, who must overcome the crippling legacy of bigotry and injustice. *And we shall overcome!*

The Congress roared its response to this speech, which was the essence of the Lyndon Johnson who cared about ordinary Americans and would put his political life on the line.

A couple of hours later I saw the insecure Johnson. He asked me to come to the White House and have a drink.

Up in his living quarters, he asked for scotch and demanded that someone turn on the TV and find some commentary on his speech. Then he asked the White House telephone operator about the calls his speech had provoked. She made the mistake of ignoring the favorable calls and simply telling Johnson that there had been "seventy-five to one hundred protests." That brought up the Johnson who could badger and ridicule innocent people, such as this woman who had done nothing but answer the telephone.

"How many, honey?" I listened to Johnson ask her. "Seventy-five or a hundred? What did they say — that I'm letting the Negroes take over the country? Well, tell me, honey, do you think I oughta resign tonight?"

I looked at Lady Bird, expecting some facial expression of embarrassment, even disgust. She was the perfect Buddha. I remembered that during two trips around the world I had never seen that woman lose her cool.

A day later I saw LBJ, master politician, in action. He was strumming on Dirksen's ego as though it were a harp. He got Dirksen to join Senate majority leader Mike Mansfield in shutting off a filibuster, and on May 26 the Senate passed the Voting Rights Act, 77 to 19. The House passed this bill on August 3, and Johnson signed it into law on August 6, after announcing that on the following day the attorney general would, on the president's orders, file a lawsuit challenging the constitutionality of the poll tax in Mississippi.

The actions of these several Lyndon Johnsons is why there are now close to eight thousand black elected officials in the United States.

No matter where I go now to give a speech, someone asks if Johnson really believed in racial equality. Did he feel bound by the lofty views of John F. Kennedy? Was LBJ just feathering his political nest, locking up a black vote that helped him to a landslide in the 1964 election?

I obviously don't know. I think he took pride in his personal realization that emotionally and intellectually he had grown far above his early years as a Texas congressman, or even as the Texas senator accused of stealing an election.

Whatever Johnson was, and whatever motivated his many changes of personality, one thing I know: no president ever gave a more powerful, truthful, lead-a-nation speech on race relations than Johnson did in his commencement address at Howard University on June 4, 1965.

In a speech that may some year be declared the equal of Lincoln's Emancipation Proclamation, Johnson took a stand in favor of affirmative action that I think defies assault, even contradiction. He was eloquent, and probably a half century ahead of his country, when he said:

> This voting rights bill will be the latest and among the most important in a long series of victories. But this victory . . . is not the end; it is not even the beginning of the end. . . .
>
> Freedom is the right to share fully and equally in American society, to vote, to hold a job, to enter a public place, to go to school. . . .
>
> But freedom is not enough. You do not wipe away the scars of centuries by saying now you're free to go where you want and do as

you desire and choose the leaders you please. You do not take a
person who for years has been hobbled by chains and liberate him,
bring him up to the starting line of a race and then say, you're free to
compete with all the others.

Negroes are trapped, as many whites are trapped, in inherited,
gateless poverty. They lack training and skills. They are shut in slums
without decent medical care.... We are trying to attack these
evils....

Much of the Negro community is buried under a blanket of
history and circumstance. It is not a lasting solution to lift just one
corner of that blanket.

If "blanket lifter" Lyndon Johnson could have had his presidency
judged on that speech alone, or on his civil rights record alone, he
would today be ranked with Lincoln and FDR as one of the nation's
greatest leaders.

Given the luxury of social tunnel vision, not many white Americans would remember that fewer than 750 blacks were in college in
this country at the turn of the century and only 274,000 when
Johnson pushed through the Federal Aid to Higher Education Act
of 1965 — *but* 1,133,000 young blacks were going to college in
1981, when Ronald Reagan cut them off at the campus gate.

Americans would know that Johnson opened the gates to higher
education to many more whites than he did blacks. And that he
backed a consumer protection movement that ensures that little
girls now sleep in nightgowns that won't go up in flames at the tiniest
spark. LBJ fought for automobile safety, wanted to protect our
environment from pollution, and even wanted the government to
safeguard citizens against improperly made artificial eyes and de-
fective screws used to hook up hips.

In these times of rampant drug abuse, crime, family breakups,
failures of education, school dropouts, and more, I remember Johnson, and especially that speech at Howard. And I know that, whatever his foibles and idiosyncrasies, Lyndon Baines Johnson was the
best president that the poor, "at risk" people of America ever had.

CHAPTER SIXTEEN

A War, Dr. King, and the FBI

A T THE TIME of that speech at Howard, LBJ had problems that one might think transcended any concern about black voting rights. He had a terrible war escalating in Vietnam.

From the first day I took on the leadership of USIA in February 1964, I knew that when Johnson got heartburn, I got colic almost endlessly, and whenever there was a crisis — Berlin this month, the Congo the next, Cuba one week, and then Laos or Vietnam — it brought angst and loss of sleep to the director of USIA. But I couldn't concentrate simply on world crises. I had the before-everything-else task of securing from Congress a budget that would allow me to maintain a staff of more than thirteen thousand people, carry out an unprecedented information-psychological-propaganda campaign regarding the Vietnam War, and still have the resources to speak coherently to the rest of the world about a variety of issues.

I had not forgotten that one of the excuses for not making me assistant secretary of state when Roger Tubby left was that Ralph Dungan convinced President Kennedy that Congress wouldn't give a Negro an ample budget for the Public Affairs Bureau. That State Department budget for public affairs was pennies compared with what I would have to request for USIA.

I had to see Congressman John Rooney of Brooklyn, who was a virtual dictator in the House Appropriations Committee's decisions as to the level of funding of the State Department, the Commerce

Department, the FBI, and USIA. My budget advisers told me that Rooney was one of the meanest bastards of all time — that he slashed funds for proposals that didn't mesh with his private notions of what constituted a good information program and that almost alone he was responsible for ambassadorships going to fat cats, to big political contributors, because Rooney wouldn't approve decent representation allowances for poor and middle-class ambassadors.

There was a little sweat on the backs of my hands as I approached Rooney's office.

He greeted me with warmth, saying, "I liked what you said about what this country is."

"Thank you, sir."

"Are you expecting trouble with your budget?"

"God, I hope not!"

"I want you to be a success, so I'm going to level with you as I have with only a few people coming up here looking for big money. I'm going to fight for you to get every damned dollar that you can make even a reasonable case for. But you'd better come up here prepared to defend what you are, or are not. And I want you to be prepared for a special problem."

"What's that?"

"Martin Luther King."

Rooney went on to show me that he was no nineteenth-century Scrooge passing judgment on twentieth-century budgets. He was a man violating secrecy regulations to ensure that I did not get blindsided by lawmakers who despised King.

He told me that his committee had already held budget hearings for the FBI, and J. Edgar Hoover had asked for millions more dollars because the FBI had to hire more agents and use more resources to keep check on a "Negro revolution" that had become a threat to U.S. security. Hoover had told the committee that King was "the most dangerous man in America" and "a moral degenerate."

"Then," Rooney related, "Hoover said he had brought tapes and documents to illustrate how the FBI was on top of the threat represented by King, black revolutionaries, and their foreign allies."

Rooney told me that a lot of congressmen had been inflamed by an alleged FBI tape recording of what Hoover called "an orgy" in King's suite at the Willard Hotel in Washington, D.C. Hoover said that the FBI had "at least fifteen reels of tape" about sexual "entertainment" and conversations between King and Abernathy that might lead to the conclusion that there was a homosexual relationship between the two ministers. Rooney said Hoover played portions of one tape for him that was designed to create deeper revulsion toward King.

"What's on the tapes that is disturbing everybody?" I asked Rooney.

He looked at me as if doubting whether he should answer. He looked at his notes, which someone already had typed out for him. Then he replied: "Hoover played us a tape with sounds indicating that someone was having intercourse in one room of the King suite. But it clearly wasn't King, because we hear him saying to a man Hoover identified as Abernathy, 'Come on over here, you big black motherfucker, and let me suck your dick.' "

"God," I thought, "an FBI director who is suspected of being a homosexual has gone to Congress to try to destroy our greatest civil rights leader by portraying him as a homosexual!"

"Mr. Rooney," I said, "I can't talk against a tape I've never heard. But I can tell you that wherever black men gather in a party, the language, the back and forth, may have no relationship to reality. Blacks, and others, I am sure, down a few drinks and lie about their sexual prowess. They throw the word 'motherfucker' around like 'buddy' or 'pal.' They talk about sucking dicks or cocks, which meant a vagina in Tennessee, the way they talk about eating a slice of watermelon. And it may not have a damned thing to do with any behavior they intend to carry out."

After I thanked Rooney for leveling with me, we shook hands, and I walked out in a semidaze.

I was not totally surprised, because I had been reading intelligence reports indicating that someone was following King everywhere, reporting in detail on what Abernathy would recall years later as King's "weakness for women" and his lurches away from sobriety.

I learned immediately that there are many levels of top secret clearance, including some regarding electronic intelligence, spies in the skies, and other matters that I had never heard about. My job and my participation in cabinet and National Security Council meetings gave me a broad "need to know" about things that had never been entrusted to any black official — and only to a very few white ones.

Each morning I got a special supersecret intelligence briefing, a document hand delivered by a special agent who sat while I read it and took it back, this procedure to ensure that none of my secretaries or aides would ever see the contents. I read weighty stuff about troop movements and weapons tests in the Soviet Union; Israel's, India's, and China's progress toward building nuclear weapons; coups that seemed in the making — but also some titillating gossip about the health and the mistresses of world figures.

I noticed in March of 1964 that these briefings contained an extraordinary number of references to Dr. King and his private activities. It was clear that the FBI had agents shadowing him wherever he went, providing items for the intelligence briefing such as: "Confidential informant saw King return to Las Vegas hotel, staggering drunk, hanging on to the shoulders of redheaded white woman." Or, "Confidential informant says King held secret meeting with white man believed to be agent, or agent of influence, of Soviet Union."

I read these things and asked myself, "What the hell is going on here?" Then I would remember a half-dozen episodes of the past that seemed of trifling import but, put in the context of what the FBI was saying, became very important.

There was the time in 1961, during the trip around the world, when Johnson told me that Hoover hated Bobby Kennedy with a passion, but still did Kennedy "the favor of bugging my summer cottage and other places. The little sumbitch [Kennedy] is trying to get something on me so he can get President Kennedy to dump me in 'sixty-four." And the time in Rome, in 1962, when, after we'd polished off a half bottle of Cutty Sark, Johnson said, apropos of nothing: "You'd better tell your colored buddy to beware."

"My colored buddy?" I asked.

"Goddammit, Martin Luther King," LBJ whispered so loudly that I was sure the Secret Service detail heard him. Johnson leaned toward me, pooching his lips to give emphasis, and said, "They're after him more than they're after me."

Yet I was stunned by the Rooney revelations of the extent to which Hoover had gone to destroy King's reputation. Especially when Rooney said, "You can be sure that all this is being circulated to the president, newspaper editors and columnists, college presidents. . . ."

I knew that Hoover's hatred of this most articulate, most inspiring of all the civil rights leaders, and King's apparent vulnerability to Hoover's assaults, jeopardized not just my USIA budget but the whole campaign for civil rights and black equality. I could not mount defenses against all these things, but I had to protect my budget against assaults by people who believed that in distributing a movie that made King the hero of the March on Washington, I was glorifying what Hoover was calling a "sex pervert."

Now I understood better my earlier courtesy call on Senator Ellender, who showed unmitigated hostility to USIA. Ellender, then sixty-seven, had been featured unflatteringly in *Time* magazine in an article about his taking two girlfriends on an Asian junket and his demands for special privilege. Ellender wasted no time in telling me that he thought USIA personnel had spread the salacious stories about him and his friends.

"It's a sissy outfit," he said bluntly. "I know it was your guys [at that time I hadn't even taken control of USIA] leaking those stories to *Time*. You've got a bunch of funny birds who can't stand the notion of a real man getting a piece of tail."

"Good Lord," I said to myself, "this is one of the guys who is going to harpoon me because I won't kill a movie about Martin Luther King."

I wondered what effect the Hoover tapes and briefings were having on President Johnson. My gut feeling told me that he didn't give a damn if King were involved in an orgy in the Willard Hotel. Johnson had some rather "liberal" views about men and their weaknesses for women.

Johnson did not get really concerned until King began to rail publicly against his Vietnam policies. Johnson figured that he was doing so much to lift blacks out of modern bondage that it was traitorous for any influential black to attack him on the war issue. And then Hoover began to barrage Johnson and others with stories that King's speeches were being written by white agents of communism.

Several days after my visit to Rooney, I read a story about King's deploring the war. I was not surprised when, in midmorning, the flamethrower, my direct line to Johnson, rang. Johnson didn't even say hello or identify himself. He said: "My friend, I've put my ass on the line, just like you asked me to do in Saigon and Delhi and the Taj Mahal, and every damn place you could lobby me about the rights of Negroes. [I didn't remember lobbying him at any of these places because I never imagined his becoming president.]

"And your friend King is now sabotaging my efforts," Johnson went on. "He's making me look like a fool. He's got a goddam nest of spies around him. And he's starting to oppose his own country on Vietnam. Whata you think I oughta do?"

"You oughta talk to him," I said, trying to bring a little sanity to the discussion.

"Shit, *you* oughta talk to him," Johnson said. "And tell him about all these reports, and how he's making it goddam hard for me to get some justice for Negroes. And I'm gonna talk to Ralph Bunche and Roy Wilkins and Whitney Young and find out why they haven't talked to King."

When Johnson hung up my first emotion was of irritation, but it quickly dissolved into sorrow for King. By this time I was seeing undocumented FBI reports that "an influential adviser of King" — a reference to Stanley Levison, the New York businessman and King aide whom the FBI had so successfully portrayed as a "Communist" and "Soviet courier" that President Kennedy himself asked King to stay away from him — was traveling to Mexico to meet a top official of the Soviet KGB. I asked if the FBI or CIA had photographs of such a meeting and was told that no one ever had been able to get a picture of the King adviser and the KGB man together. The FBI produced reports as to which of King's speeches had been written, or heavily influenced, by his "Communist" advisers. From time to time the documents brought to me mentioned the possibility of Dr. King "being killed by one of the husbands he has cuckolded."

I considered this ominous and a possible setting up of a motive for someone to kill King. So, against my judgment at the time Johnson telephoned me, I called King in Atlanta. I leveled with him completely about the documents and the charges that were crossing my desk. I told him how the president was being bombarded with slanderous materials and how Johnson felt that King was becoming a liability to his social and civil rights endeavors.

I learned during this conversation that Johnson had indeed talked to Bunche, Wilkins, and Young, and each of them had talked to King — although none could tell him in ugly detail, as I did, what Hoover was saying about him. "As an old friend," I said, "I get an eerie feeling when I see documents suggesting that some jealous husband, or the KGB, may want to kill you. Please be prudent."

King told me that he had already promised Bunche, Wilkins, and Young that he would break off his relationship with Levison and that he would conduct himself in such a way as to make it impossible for Hoover to portray him as a pro-Communist traitor. I called Young, who confirmed that King had made such a commitment to him, Wilkins, and Bunche.

I was sick at heart a few weeks later to see in the morning intelligence report an FBI claim that informants had seen King meeting clandestinely with "the communist whose influence he is under." When the courier left my office, I wrote a note for myself saying that "surveillance of King obviously intensified. Problem worse, dangers grow. Think what you can do."

I talked again to my very close friend Whitney Young and neither of us had any idea of what we could do. The two of us just shook our heads when the feud between Hoover and King burst more and more into the public arena. On November 18, 1964, Hoover told a group of women reporters in Washington, D.C., that King was "the most notorious liar in the country." Days later, Hoover went to Loyola University to give a speech in which he railed against "sexual degenerates in pressure groups."

King was so skilled a speaker-propagandist that he never believed a doddering old FBI director could destroy him. The FBI's record, its venal practices under Hoover, King felt, were so shameful that there was no way aging Hoover could splatter him in a pissing match.

King did not take into account the number of virile young men and sexy young women who were willing to do Hoover's bidding. King never imagined that in order to "neutralize" him, the FBI would try to break up his marriage and provoke his suicide by sending a portion of one of the tapes made at the Willard Hotel to his wife, Coretta.

This FBI caper, masterminded by Bill Sullivan, I later learned, got to King in ways that neither I nor the top civil rights leaders had been able to do. On November 21 the FBI had mailed a tape recording of some of King's private "entertainment" to his home in Atlanta, hoping that Coretta would listen to it and confront King. A letter accompanying the tape said, "King, there is only one thing left for you to do. You know what it is. . . . There is but one way out for you. You better take it before your filthy fraudulent self is bared to the nation."

This tape shook King up and made him consider a truce with Hoover, which led to an infamous meeting on December 1, 1964. Intelligence reports that I saw said that Hoover started the meeting by telling King how much dirt he had on him. Hoover wrote a memo claiming that he had "taken the ball away from King at the beginning" and that King had apologized for earlier criticisms of the FBI.

I was appalled by that meeting. I wanted King to show prudence, to protect himself, but not to capitulate to J. Edgar Hoover! Tapes the FBI made even of Martin and Coretta's pillow talk caused me to speculate that she had indeed confronted him about his personal behavior and that this provoked him to ask for the meeting with Hoover. (Much later, I asked King if his wife had listened to the "suicide" tape. He claimed that he walked in just as she was putting it on the machine and that he engaged her in conversation on other issues, and she never heard what was on the tape. I was sure Martin was lying to me.)

King and his aides surely could not have imagined that any December 1 "truce" would hold. That meeting was nine days before King was to receive the Nobel Prize, something that drove Hoover nuts. Even as King was in the truce meeting, the FBI was distributing a thirteen-page monograph on King's alleged private life to officials in the United States and Western Europe, trying to prevent King from receiving the Nobel Prize, getting an audience with the pope, or being honored in Atlanta upon his return from the Nobel ceremonies.

Just thirteen days after that truce meeting, Sullivan wrote a superior: "Realism makes it mandatory that we take every prudent step that we can take to emerge completely victorious in this conflict" with King. So the FBI accelerated its program of character assassination against King, distributing allegations of immorality to Francis Cardinal Spellman, the pastor of the American church in Paris, the American ambassador in Tokyo, assorted newspaper editors and columnists — and the Internal Revenue Service, which had invited King to speak to its workers on equal employment opportunities.

The uglier Hoover's campaign became, the harder it was for any other black leader to have a sensible conversation with King. He thought Young, Wilkins, Bunche, and others were jealous of his leadership. The great American issue was less and less civil rights and more and more opposition to the war in Vietnam. Like almost all great public figures, King was shifting to the issue that made the headlines. And he was making more and more enemies.

As much as Johnson was angered by King's attacks upon his policies, the president showed how much bigger a man he was than Hoover. The FBI director had turned his powerful agency into a ruthless foe of blacks and the civil rights movement because Hoover hated the idea of black equality and because King had dared to criticize him. Johnson refused to blame all blacks, or abandon the civil rights movement, because of his irritation with King. Or so I thought.

I remember poignantly Johnson telling me of the time when, as vice president, he was asked to go to San Antonio to give a campaign speech in behalf of Congressman Henry B. Gonzales.

> I got to this shopping center, in the midst of a helluva crowd, and was told that some black guy would introduce me. Then I saw them push this decrepit old man up into a pickup truck, and I heard the black guy say: "Ladies and gentlemen, I was born about a hundred yards from where this truck sits, in poverty and unremitting bigotry. I thought America was committed to racial cruelty forever. I never dreamed that I would live long enough to see the day when a Negro man would be asked to get up here to introduce a white Texan vice president of the United States, who is gonna ask y'all to vote for a Mexican."
>
> Tears were flooding out of my eyes, and I had trouble climbing into the pickup truck. But don't you ever forget, Carl, that a man ain't worth a good goddam if he can't cry at the right time.

While I had had no predisposition to psychoanalyze my president, I could not escape the observation that Johnson realized deep in heart and mind that there really was no light at the end of the tunnel in his dark nightmare of U.S. military intervention in Vietnam. In one conversation about what he should include in a speech to the American people, Johnson said to me prophetically: "I have a feeling that I should trust this intelligence data about as much as I'd trust a Fort Worth whore."

As USIA director, I had a solemn mandate to help my country prevail in the worst war situation in its history. I was supposed to win the world to our side. In my enthusiasm to do so, I left myself and my agency open to criticism and ultimate failure.

In 1964, Johnson asked me to accompany Rusk and McNamara to Saigon to reassess the state of the war and make recommendations as to the next course of U.S. action.

I sat in the Saigon briefings of MACV (Military Assistance Command, Vietnam) and felt little knots of doubt in my stomach as I heard the Pentagon version of what was going on. I got on helicopters to visit a few places in the countryside, flying over areas controlled by the Vietcong. On my return to Washington, I wrote President Johnson the following memorandum on April 21, 1964:

> During the recent trip to Saigon with Secretary Rusk, I came to the conclusion that *the weakest part of the war operation, both on our part and that of the Government of South Vietnam, is in the field of information and psychological warfare.* According to a report by the Military Advisory Commission as well as information gathered by USIS, this is true on both a nationwide basis and a province-by-province basis.
>
> It is my judgment that *the Vietnamese people will never give sufficient support to the war effort until certain glaring gaps are closed* in the information-psychological campaign.
>
> In view of the importance of public opinion in Vietnam, in this country and in the world at large, I believe that *top priority should be given to a large scale United States program to improve the GVN* [Government of Vietnam] *ability to win the support of the people and to tell its story abroad.*

I had erred. I had believed that we could mount some propaganda campaign that would impel Vietnamese, North and South, to denounce political slavery, slaughter, tyranny, but I underestimated the factors of anticolonialism, nationalism, hatred of racism, anger over economic exploitation for generations.

Still, I wrote President Johnson that memo suggesting that we could do through a propaganda campaign what our troops could not do on the ground and our diplomats could not do in a hundred world capitals where there was a lack of support, even wild condemnation, of what the United States was doing in Vietnam.

In hindsight, I know that my memo was a mistake. Given the mandarin arrogance of Ngo Dinh Diem and the shameless crookedness of Vietnamese leaders who followed him, the colonial arrogance of Frenchmen who preceded him, and the venality and incompetence of those who at the time held power in Vietnam, how could any propaganda campaign succeed?

I erred especially because my memorandum gave substance to the excuses given Johnson by CIA Director John McCone that we were failing because we weren't broadcasting enough to the people of Vietnam. At Johnson's behest, I ordered that USIA transmitters in the Philippines and elsewhere be cranked up on an almost around-the-clock basis, trying to assure even the lowliest peasant in Indochina that the Vietcong, the Communists, were their real enemies.

But when Johnson got a dose of bull from McCone and others, he would cry for more broadcasting, more leaflets dropped on Vietnamese villages, more of whatever it was that USIA was supposed to do.

Then some Madison Avenue patriots got into the act. They got to Johnson with a message that we would win if we just used good old American advertising techniques to sell American policy to Asia and the rest of the world.

One day the flamethrower rang with what seemed horrendous urgency. I heard this slower-than-usual drawl begin with "My friend . . ." and I knew I was about to get some bad news.

"Some people on Madison Avenue tell me that we're losing the minds of the people in Vietnam because USIA isn't selling my policies the way they sell soap and cornflakes. Now, I told 'em that you're the damnedest salesman of an idea I ever met, and that I have total confidence in you, but I thought you ought to know that the advertising experts think they have a better way."

A whole lot of curse words popped into my mind, but I restrained myself. "Mr. President," I said, "the next time one of these hucksters calls you, please tell him that people need and want soap and cornflakes, so they are easy to sell. It's just a matter of which brand they buy. But nobody wants war, or napalm bombs, or having their villages wiped out, or seeing thousands of GIs fucking their women. I'm trying to sell what people wouldn't buy at a fire sale."

Johnson must have sensed that I was seething. "My friend," he said, "I just wanted you to know what they're saying."

That summer of 1964 I saw desperation growing in almost everything Johnson did regarding the war. It seemed as though the gods were conspiring to lure him deeper and deeper into a terrible morass in Vietnam. All my waking hours, like those of Rusk, McNamara, McGeorge Bundy, and, most of all, Johnson, were consumed by the war. I did not want to attend every meeting related to this conflict, but I did not want USIA and its Voice of America and other departments to operate on even momentary ignorance. I was getting the support that I had asked for in my memorandum regarding the informational-psychological warfare program, but I was becoming increasingly uneasy. Every time I went to a meeting of the cabinet or the National Security Council, I could see that there had already been a little rump session ahead of it. Johnson, Rusk, McNamara, and Bundy would come in with a proposal to the council asking approval of something that they had already decided to do.

"What the hell?" I said to myself. "The president doesn't actually need a Security Council vote to do a damn thing. If he wants to order war, he can order it."

As the weeks rolled by, the conflict worsened, and Johnson continued to say, "We want no wider war." But I had the feeling that he wanted an excuse to lay on North Vietnam the kind of blow he really believed would stop Ho from trying to take control of South Vietnam.

My suspicions reached a serious level on August 2, 1964, when telegrams started flowing into the Pentagon and the Security Council about an alleged attack on a U.S. destroyer by North Vietnamese PT boats. The Pentagon announced that while on

> routine patrol in international waters, the U.S. destroyer Maddox underwent an unprovoked attack by three PT-type boats . . . in the Tonkin Gulf.
>
> The attacking boats launched three torpedoes and used 37-millimeter gunfire. The Maddox answered with five-inch gunfire. Shortly thereafter four F-8 aircraft joined in the defense of Maddox, using Zuni rockets and 20-millimeter strafing attacks. The PT boats were driven off, with one seeming to be badly damaged and not moving, and the other two damaged and retreating slowly.
>
> No casualties or damage were sustained by Maddox or the [U.S.] aircraft.

I read with more than passing interest the transcript of a Radio Hanoi broadcast charging that the United States had sent warships into the Gulf of Tonkin to shell islands in the territorial waters of North Vietnam and that U.S. fighter bombers had attacked a North Vietnamese border post and village on August 1. The United States denied the charge, but I did not totally believe the denial. A sixth sense told me that the United States was doing some things about which even statutory members of the National Security Council had not been informed.

Johnson called in the press and told them that he had asked the USS Turner Joy to join the Maddox, that the patrols in the Gulf of Tonkin would continue, and that the two destroyers were to attack any force which attacked them in international waters.

Then, on August 4, reports flashed in that both the Maddox and the Turner Joy were "under continuous torpedo attack." I knew that Johnson had talked for weeks about how to get a resolution out of Congress that would make it clear that he had the power to wage war as he saw fit in Vietnam. The so-called raids on the USS Maddox and the USS Turner Joy gave him the opportunity he wanted. He called in the leaders of Congress and played them like a violin. He whipped up anger and resentment and even suckered Senator Fulbright into helping to push through the Tonkin Gulf resolution, which said:

Whereas naval units of the Communist regime in Vietnam, in violation of the Charter of the United Nations and of international law, have deliberately and repeatedly attacked U.S. naval vessels lawfully present in international waters, and have thereby created a serious threat to international peace;

Whereas these attacks are part of a deliberate and systematic campaign of aggression that the Communist regime in North Vietnam has been waging against its neighbors and the nations joined with them in the collective defense of their freedom;

Whereas the United States is assisting the peoples of Southeast Asia to protect their freedom and has no territorial, military or political ambitions in that area but desires only that they should be left in peace to work out their own destinies in their own way: Now, therefore, be it

Resolved by the Senate and House of Representatives of the United States of America in Congress assembled, that the Congress approves and supports the determination of the President, as Commander-in-Chief, to take all necessary measures to repel any armed attack against the forces of the United States and to prevent further aggression.

A lot later I was talking to Johnson about that episode in the Gulf of Tonkin. I said, "There was always something strange about it. I never could believe in my heart that those vessels ever were attacked."

"You ain't the only one who has had some doubts," Johnson said. "This goddam military, I just don't know when I can trust 'em and when I can't. The only ones who make my belly rumble more with doubt is the intelligence bunch. You don't know what they know for sure, or what they are pulling out of the fog and handing to you. It's hell to have to make decisions on the basis of information you aren't sure you can trust."

I left that session feeling a bit better, thinking that Johnson was leveling with me. But as the weeks went by I noticed that more things were happening, and decisions were made outside the cabinet room and outside the confines of the National Security Council. Meanwhile, I was devoting more of the resources and manpower of USIA to the war. I had come aboard determined to make assignments in the agency fair, so I had broken up the old European gang.

I sent one senior officer who had spent most of his tenure in France to be public affairs officer in the Congo. He moaned and wailed and even told me that distress over having to go to the Congo had rendered him impotent. I was so outraged by this crybaby that I told him, "In that case you won't have to worry about getting into trouble with any of those girls in the Congo." But now I was sending numbers of officers into Vietnam, which was becoming more and more dangerous. The officers didn't like it, their wives detested it, but almost all the officers went like good soldiers, believing that it was in the interest of the nation.

I finally got fed up with trying to support policies about which I had had no voice, so on December 2, 1964, I wrote the following memorandum, personal and confidential, to President Johnson:

> My decision to write is prompted by the lack of a USIA role in the current consideration of our policy in Vietnam. Despite frequent statements to me at all levels of the White House and State and Defense Departments about the magnitude of USIA's responsibility in Vietnam, not one USIA official has been involved in *any* of the talks dealing with our future policy and actions in that country. And I have been denied access to materials relating to these discussions with the explanation that the denial is based on White House orders.
>
> I complain most vigorously — and not as a matter of personal pride or curiosity. It is a hard, practical fact that if USIA is to play a role of constructive consequence in Vietnam, or elsewhere, it cannot operate in a vacuum of detached ignorance. As the director of an agency whose single most crucial operation is in Vietnam, I have the greatest need to know not only what the major thrust of policy is, but also those vitally important nuances that can be gained only through firsthand participation in policy deliberations.

Johnson responded by making sure that I was in on a lot more sessions — ostensibly all of them where decisions were made, even regarding clandestine actions. It was almost seven years later that I realized the true extent to which Johnson had deceived me.

The president and a handful of intimates were misusing the National Security Council as an approval cover for clandestine war operations that were never discussed in Security Council meetings.

On Saturday, February 7, 1965, I was in bed with the flu. The

White House operator called. There would be an emergency meeting of the National Security Council in an hour. Then I got a call informing me that the Vietcong had raided a base at Pleiku, killing eight American servicemen and wounding sixty-two.

"Honey, you can't go to any meeting," Viv said. "You can't even make it from the bed to the bathroom."

But it is amazing how the body pumps adrenaline in an emergency. I drove myself to the White House and forgot how sick I was as I listened to the story of the terrible Vietcong deeds at Pleiku. Johnson, Rusk, McNamara, and Bundy already had a plan of action, including maps of places in the southern part of North Vietnam that U.S. planes were to bomb in "retaliatory raids."

We were told that no bombs would be dropped anywhere near Hanoi, because Soviet prime minister Aleksey Kosygin was there on an official visit.

When the Security Council approved the bombings, my supply of adrenaline began to wane. It was obvious to me that Johnson was less than comfortable with this decision to bomb North Vietnam for the first time, and he motioned me to stay for a few minutes.

"Remember my key line, my friend," he said. "We want no wider war."

Then he elaborated: "Just between you and me, all I want to do is bloody their noses a little bit and maybe they'll leave their neighbors alone."

CHAPTER SEVENTEEN

The Slow Death of a President

WHEN JOHNSON SAID to me that the USIA had to convince the world that he wanted "no wider war," Johnson was revealing his greatest fear: that a conflict he already was losing to Ho Chi Minh would be expanded into a military dustup with the Soviet Union and what the press referred to as "hordes of Chinese forces."

I did not know whether Johnson was aware that just as Kennedy and he had put American combat troops into Vietnam in phony roles as advisers, so had the Soviet Union and the People's Republic of China.

I left the meeting with Johnson, went home, and telephoned my deputy Don Wilson to tell him what was going on: that the Voice of America should report the news truthfully, but that no editorial or commentary should make this crisis appear to be a confrontation between Johnson and Kosygin, or the United States and the Soviet Union.

I was in a deep sleep when the phone rang. It was another call from the White House telling me that there would be another meeting of the National Security Council in an hour.

I returned to the White House and listened to McNamara talk about how "surgical" our bombings had been, looked at photographs purporting to show which "military" targets our bombs had hit, and just knew in my heart that this briefing was designed to con Security Council members, but most of all the commander in chief.

At the meeting's end Johnson waggled a finger at me and again said, "I want no wider war. I don't want Kosygin to feel humiliated."

To Wilson's and my amazement, one of the Voice of America commentators decided that this was a perfect time to attack Kosygin and the Soviet Union. Minutes before this commentary was to be aired, my deputies Wilson and Burnett Anderson killed it.

I was outraged. Never had I asked anyone to monitor or tell me how the Voice of America conducted its news programs. Or how it structured its documentaries. But I believed that when VOA editorials were involved, the president of the United States, in or out of crisis, had a right to say, "We must not threaten Kosygin. We must not insult Peking. We must make it clear that I want no wider war."

Yet some egomaniac in the Voice of America had taken it upon himself to challenge the Russians and Chinese to fight it out with the U.S. in the rice paddies of Indochina!

A few people at the Voice of America had been chafing for years to get out from under control of Ed Murrow, previous directors, and now me. The current director of VOA, Henry Loomis, was especially ambitious, and I think figured that with a young, black boss he could pull off a coup.

I summoned Loomis to my office, lashed him as utterly irresponsible, and said: "If you can't understand that the president and I determine the editorial content of what goes out on the Voice of America, your ass is gone."

Black men hadn't talked to white men like that in almost three centuries in America, but I did what I knew I had to do. Then I joined Rusk, McNamara, and others on one more trip to Vietnam to see if the light at the end of the tunnel was a mirage.

I was deep in the bowels of Vietnam when I was passed a cable from Don Wilson that Mary McGrory of the *Washington Star* had written an interpretive report claiming VOICE CHIEFS CHAFE AT CURBS.

McGrory had swallowed whole the Loomis propaganda that VOA suddenly was being censored, and, to my utter shock, Scotty Reston of the *New York Times* echoed McGrory in a bit of knee-jerk journalism in which neither contacted me or any member of my staff to establish the veracity of Loomis.

Back from Vietnam, I called Loomis into my office and told him that out of ill-founded pride he had lied to McGrory and his VOA associates just to get a few cheap headlines.

"You want independence?" I continued. "I'm giving it to you. You're out at VOA. The Johnson people have a job for you in the Commerce Department — I think."

Johnson was by this time too worried about the war to give a damn about censorship of VOA — unless it widened the war. What was important was Johnson's motivation for approving one action or another.

Johnson told me that he had to bomb North Vietnam "because that damn cigar-smoking [General] Curtis LeMay is pushing me, and I gotta let him know that I'm as tough as he is."

The need to show Texas toughness grew, and in almost every meeting of the cabinet and Security Council Johnson gave some version of this soliloquy:

When I was a boy in Texas, my grandpappy used to tell me, "Boy, don't let that bully chase you off the school ground, 'cause if you let him chase you off the school ground, he's gonna chase you down the street. And if you let him chase you down the street he's gonna chase you right into your yard. You let that bully chase you into your yard and he's gonna chase you right on up onto your front porch. And the next thing you know that bully's gonna be back in your bedroom raping your little sister." We're doing what we're doing in Vietnam 'cause we can't let the bully chase us off the school yard.

In June 1965 Johnson said, "The United States seeks no wider war," but all the time he was widening U.S. involvement. And he was getting messages from Saigon suggesting that the whole mess would be wiped up if only our people out there had a few more troops to bloody the noses of the people in Hanoi and of the soldiers they were sending into South Vietnam. Johnson asked top aides to approve retaliatory bombing raids on North Vietnam even while keeping it secret from those aides that the United States was *provoking* the Communists into the acts against which we were retaliating. Only intuition, suspicion, and a piecing together of vague references in certain top secret and "no distribution" telegrams enabled some of us who sat on the council to conclude that there was a Plan 34A.

Defense Secretary McNamara, Secretary of State Rusk, CIA Director McCone, Presidential Adviser Bundy, and General Maxwell Taylor, sometime presidential adviser and sometime ambassador to Saigon, were the key men calling the signals that Johnson asked the Security Council to endorse, willy-nilly.

The Tonkin Gulf episode, five months before the Pleiku raid, was a blatant case of misuse of the National Security Council. The full Security Council never was told that the United States had carried out two destructive 34A raids against North Vietnam only hours before North Vietnamese torpedo boats allegedly attacked the destroyers *Maddox* and *Turner Joy*. Nor was the Congress told this before it voted, 88 to 2 in the Senate and 416 to 0 in the House, for a Gulf of Tonkin resolution that broadened the president's war-making powers.

By this time Johnson wasn't just lying to me. I knew that the president who had done so much for me was walking into calamity.

One day in 1965 I was at the West German embassy for lunch. The ambassador told me that "Mr. President wants to talk to you." I went to a phone to hear Johnson say, "John McCone has been talking to me. He says we could win this goddam war by winning over the people of Asia if we could just get a place to put a million-watt medium-wave transmitter in that region."

I knew that we were on an unsecure line, but since the president had spoken so openly, I replied, "Sir, they've tried for five years to find a place for that transmitter. India, Thailand, everybody has turned the U.S. down because they think this is a war of rich, powerful white people against poor Asians. Did McCone tell you how to change this fact of life?"

Johnson leaned on me as though I were the nation's last hope. He said that "McCone and Rusk and Bundy and the other white boys" could never "talk turkey" to the Asians. But I, "being colored," might be able to persuade them.

"My friend," Johnson said, "America needs that radio station and your friend needs you."

"Mr. President, I'll do my damnedest," I said.

I went back to the luncheon table, where I could hardly eat or carry on a decent conversation. I was pissed over McCone's ploy to blame the sad state of the war on the lack of one radio station. I kept thinking about how I already had too much of USIA's manpower and resources devoted to a dreadful war. I thought about how I was relaying "surveys," "reports," and "analyses" to Johnson, suggesting that the people of South Vietnam were supporting the United States and whichever scoundrel happened to be in power in Saigon at the time, even when I felt queasy about those analyses.

I knew that almost no other country in the Western world shared the CIA and Pentagon views that victory was just around the corner. And that, too, affected Johnson's psyche. I became concerned when he would go into one of his monologues lashing out at Japan, India, Thailand, France, West Germany, and others for "running from a fight."

Just when there was concern that Johnson might be going over the deep end emotionally, he would speak lucidly about his refusal to go into a land war with "Chinese hordes" or a war that might drag in the Soviet Union.

But as the summer of 1965 came on, I noticed that Johnson became more needy of support and more secretive and distant. He was coming to believe that he had only a military solution. Except that he didn't want to tell the American public that he was resorting to a solution that involved increasing the U.S. military force in Vietnam to 550,000.

I had kept the promise that I had made to Johnson at that German embassy luncheon. McCone and others had tried for five years to make Project Teak, the radio station scheme, a success, but they still didn't have a site for the powerful broadcast vehicle.

I had a relationship of mutual respect with many Asians. When I learned that Thailand's foreign minister, Thanat Khoman, was to come to the United Nations, I went to New York to talk to him. I knew that Thailand already had said no to the transmitter, but I wanted Thanat to know how much I wanted it in Thailand, because Johnson wanted it *somewhere*.

Thanat spoke with the candor I expected. He said that powerful Thai leaders, Pote Sarasin and others, viewed the Vietnam War as racist, not as a struggle for the freedoms of Asians, but that he still backed the war. He wanted to gamble that a million-watt medium-wave transmitter might make a difference. "But there is no chance my government will permit it on our soil if it is seen as submission to racism," the foreign minister said. "The only chance of approval is if you come to Bangkok to head the negotiating team. If you make the request, it will be impossible for Pote Sarasin and others to cry 'racism.' "

"You have my word," I replied. "You tell your government how important this transmitter is, and prepare for my coming. Give me twenty-four to forty-eight hours' notice, and I'll be in Bangkok."

I made that promise even though I had seen that Johnson was falling apart in the face of rising criticism in the press and Congress, and antiwar violence in the streets that made him almost a prisoner in the White House. He expressed ever greater concern that if I left town, or the country, for any reason, "some sumbitch in Congress will criticize USIA, and you won't be here to answer."

I noticed, however, that my presence wasn't as crucial to Johnson as it had been in 1964. More and more the war decisions were being made outside the cabinet and prior to any meetings of the National Security Council. Johnson, McNamara, Rusk, and Bundy were making the tragic commitments, and others in the cabinet and Security Council were called in to rubber-stamp the decisions.

My top aides at USIA knew where I was all of any working time, and that I was not in meetings where decisions were made to escalate the U.S. military presence or intensify U.S. bombings in Southeast Asia. I was embarrassed.

"To hell with him," I told myself, and stopped working past noon on Saturday so I could go to the Falls Road Golf Course to protect my four-handicap.

One day a strange bit of fate intervened. I went to another luncheon at the home of Marguerite Higgins. Over her ever-magnificent beef ragout, Marguerite said to me: "Carl, if a guy named Tom Dorsey from *Newsday* ever telephones you, talk to him. You might like what he has to offer."

After lunch I went to the office to prepare to go to Boston to dedicate the Edward R. Murrow Center at Tufts University. When I got to Boston I had a message from my office that "a Mr. Dorsey of *Newsday*" wanted to fly up and have dinner with me.

I had dinner with Dorsey and listened to him spell out details of an offer that only a fool could refuse. I would break the barrier against black syndicated columnists, with a contract guaranteeing that I could write anything I wished about anybody or anything. I would be given, up front, thousands of dollars for travel and research. And then Dorsey really impressed me. He knew I had sons thirteen and twelve years old. His syndicate would guarantee college tuition for them.

I telephoned Viv and gave her the headline details of the offer. "Honey," I said, "if I didn't have a commitment to the president I could tell you that my days in government are over."

"Whatever you decide, honey," Viv said in that special voice that let me know she wanted me to accept Dorsey's offer.

At USIA I had a telegram from the U.S. embassy in Bangkok saying that Foreign Minister Thanat wanted me in Bangkok urgently. Project Teak was going to be rejected again unless I showed up to sell it.

I called McGeorge Bundy at the White House and asked him to inform the president that I was leaving immediately for Thailand to salvage the radio station. Less than five minutes later Bundy called to say that the president didn't want me to leave the country because of what might happen in my absence.

"Uh-huh," I said to Bundy. Then I picked up the flamethrower and got Johnson.

"Mr. President," I said, "within the hour you will have my letter of resignation. You wanted a radio station in Southeast Asia. I put my honor on the line with Thailand's foreign minister. I cannot work for a man who forces me to dishonor my word."

Johnson went into a tirade about all of his top aides "who only want to go to Brazil and Paris and New Delhi to buy rugs," and he hung up. Less than five minutes later I got a call from Valenti, informing me that the president wanted me to know that if I felt it necessary to go to Bangkok, it was all right with him.

"No, Jack," I said. "It may be OK today, but five days from now I'll have to face the same shit. I resign."

"The president wants you to come over and talk to him," Valenti said.

I went to the White House, where Johnson urged me to stay.

"I can't do that," I said.

He put his arms around me and said, "I love you like a son."

I learned that before I got back to my car, Johnson had called Leonard Marks and asked him to replace "his son" as USIA director.

How to resign? What to tell the press? I had, in all my years in government, made it a point never to lie to my former colleagues. They knew that if I didn't tell them the truth, I would tell them nothing.

I wrote a resignation letter in which I told the truth. I let almost every grievance I had against Johnson flow into that letter. Then Viv and my top aide, Les Edmond, and his wife, Shom, counseled restraint. They reminded me that in America resignations, unlike divorces, were rarely grounded in ugly truths. They said, correctly, that sections of the media would go nuts if they knew about Thanat and the radio transmitter. Thanat and the Thai ambassador to Washington beseeched me to keep them out of the mess.

"Sleep on it," Viv said. "What good purpose will be served by your lashing him publicly? He was always fair and respectful to you until he got entrapped in this Vietnam mess. You know that he's just not himself. Sleep on it."

I stayed awake on it. I thought about the fact that Johnson was fast becoming persona non grata, sneaking like a thief in the night to public occasions where he might encounter war protesters.

I remembered his special anger over criticisms of his war policies by Martin Luther King, Jr., and his fury over reports that King's speeches regarding Vietnam were written by two men alleged by the FBI to be "part of the international Communist conspiracy."

I tossed and turned, remembering Johnson once saying to me, "You see the same goddammed top secret eyes-only reports I see. Secret fucking meetings in Mexico between KGB agents and a King confidant. Then King speeches calling me a murderer — me, the Texas motherfucker who went against every goddam white adviser I ever had to stand up and say black people in America must be equal."

I lay in bed, thinking about how Johnson had a thousand paranoias going. He suspected that the entire intelligence community was playing him for a fool; that his well-educated top advisers were treating him as a barnyard dummy, and the minorities to whom he had delivered his political clout, moral heart and soul, and historic legislative protections were about to drown him in a river of rubbish foisted on Martin Luther King, Jr., by some "KGB agents."

As I pondered my resignation letter I knew that there was more to Johnson's paranoia. He was getting reports — from the FBI, the CIA, or someone — that foreign governments were sneaking money into the United States to finance a black revolution that would go far beyond the civil rights march of 1963.

As the warnings went to Johnson, black activists Stokely Carmichael, Rap Brown, and others were supposedly paid by Russia, China, Libya, or someone to "Burn, Baby, Burn," rendering U.S. cities to ashes.

"Horseshit," I had told Johnson. "Some cities will burn because of black disillusionment and rage, but not by direction of the Kremlin."

So after "sleeping on it," I made a bleary-eyed decision that it was not in anyone's best interest to elaborate on my reasons for leaving.

With anger muted, I decided for the first time in my life to just plain lie to the press. On July 8, 1965, I wrote Johnson the following:

Dear Mr. President:

It is with genuine regret, and after considerable soul searching that I submit to you my resignation as Director of the United States Information Agency. I think you know how grateful I am of the confidence and trust that you have placed in me, and the kindnesses that you have shown me, over the four years of our association. Thus you can appreciate the difficulty with which I have come to my decision. After more than four years of public service, however, personal and family reasons dictate that I return to private life.

I expect to return to a career in journalism. I hope that through this medium I can still make a contribution to your and our country's efforts to protect and extend freedom at home and abroad.

I should like to make my resignation effective at the earliest reasonable date.

With warmest wishes to you for strength, wisdom and God's blessings, I am . . .

Two days later Johnson wrote:

Dear Carl:

I accept your resignation as the Director of the United States Information Agency with sincere regret. You have brought to the job professional confidence and unusual devotion to public service. Your experience and your own personal qualities have set precedents which will challenge your successors for years to come.

For four years you have given loyal service to the government and people of this nation. I understand the sacrifices which have been involved in that service and appreciate the reasons which led to your decision to return to private life. As you leave, I want to join with your many friends and colleagues in wishing you continued success.

I was a free man again.

Lillian Wiggins of the black Washington newspaper, the *Afro-American*, thought she smelled a rat. She figured that I had been fired because "no colored person voluntarily leaves a job paying thirty thousand dollars a year." Little did she know that on the day that my resignation was announced, the late Don McGannon of Westinghouse Broadcasting came to my office to offer me thirty thousand dollars a year to do three three-minute television commentaries a week. I was dumb enough to think I couldn't say anything in three minutes, only to learn that too much can be said in that time. Whatever, thirty thousand dollars a year for just shooting off my mouth seemed like a fortune in 1965.

Meanwhile my friend Larry Fanning of the *Chicago Daily News* and the *Chicago Sun-Times* reminded me, correctly, that I had promised that I would never take a job with any journalistic institution upon leaving government without giving the Chicago papers a chance to bid.

Fanning outbid everybody, including Dorsey and *Newsday*, the *Los Angeles Times*, and others.

It seems like nothing today, but on August 5, 1965, the Washington press corps was caught up in the story of a black guy breaking the barrier against newspaper syndication. I held a press conference in which I revealed that in addition to the Westinghouse agreement I had an exclusive contract to write for *Reader's Digest*, and would soon be going round the world for that magazine, and that I would do three columns a week "on any subject of choice" for the *Chicago Daily News* and Publishers Newspaper Syndicate.

I confess that I enjoyed the thought of freeing my family from financial stress, but money was just a blip on my mind. I kept thinking of a president who wanted a powerful radio station in

Thailand and let his personal quirks and insecurities block achievement of a five-year goal. I never stopped thinking about my president wallowing in paranoia, seeing spies and traitors on U.S. campuses and in street demonstrations.

I knew that my resignation represented no rush for a pot of gold. I was simply escaping a sinking ship.

CHAPTER EIGHTEEN

Did the FBI Help
Kill Dr. King?

I HAD LEARNED a lot during four and one-half years in government. The top members of the federal bureaucracy were a lot more dedicated and hardworking than I had been led to believe. Members of the foreign service were far from striped-pants cookie-pushers. Most of them never saw a pair of striped pants and were working under circumstances where the climate and often the governments and peoples were hostile — where their health and lives were in danger.

I had also seen many dismaying things, such as dishonest efforts to frustrate White House foreign policy or to halt foreign aid or to discredit unfairly U.S. officials by a few members of the House and Senate who had the instincts of the great crucifier Senator Joe McCarthy. I was amazed to see how much government was run, policies put in place, through leaks — friendly leaks to puff up a pal or send up a trial balloon for a policy under consideration, and hostile leaks designed to subvert a policy or heap trouble upon a political or policy rival. This was a brutal game played by each president and most of the officials of consequence below him.

But my greatest disillusionment involved the FBI and Hoover.

Like most Americans born in the 1920s, I spent my young years in adulation of the FBI. With homemade slingshot or bow and arrow, or that rare cap gun brought by Santa Claus, I roamed the pastures of Tennessee in the mid-1930s, pretending that I was one of Hoover's vaunted G-men who were chasing down and killing John Dillinger, Baby Face Nelson, Pretty Boy Floyd, Machine Gun

Kelly, and the Barker-Karpis gang. I had never seen an FBI shield, but I knew that the FBI symbolized fidelity, bravery, integrity. Walter Winchell told me so when I listened to my neighbor's radio. Warner Brothers made the impression indelible when it starred James Cagney in *G-Men.*

For at least two generations, I was among that great mass of Americans who viewed the FBI as the essence of patriotism, honesty, efficiency — an organization that "always got its man," whether it was Bruno Hauptmann, kidnapper of Charles A. Lindbergh's baby; Klaus Fuchs, the British traitor; or Colonel Rudolf Abel, the master spy of the Soviet Union.

I was not in Washington or the State Department long, in 1961, before I learned that there was an FBI far different from the one Hoover had written about in pulp magazine articles, or the one extolled in comic strips, books, and movies. The FBI was coercing bank officials to reveal, illegally, the deposits in and withdrawals from bank accounts of people the bureau was watching.

I reveal here for the first time that I gave my notorious, troublemaking speech in Philadelphia in 1961, about the efforts of Moise Tshombe and Union Minière literally to steal the mineral deposits of Katanga by splitting it off from the Congo, because I knew precisely what their lobbyist, Michel Struelens, was doing. The FBI had coerced banks into providing lists of all the recipients of monies paid out by Struelens. There were transcripts of all Struelens's telexes and other communications with Tshombe and his associates. The State Department would not allow me to reveal why I could give that speech with such confidence, because top officials knew that much of the information on which I based that speech was gathered illegally by the FBI.

I knew, by this time, that the sleazy campaign against Dr. King was unique only in its intensity and brazenness. It was humorous to Johnson, in private moments, that Hoover's agents were surveilling Richard Nixon and his friend Bebe Rebozo, reporting to Hoover on anything Nixon did that looked like an indiscretion. While Johnson laughed about Nixon, he constantly was bitching about the FBI watching him too closely and perhaps bugging his places. He had reasons to be suspicious, because during the 1964 presidential campaign Johnson had used Hoover to get the FBI to spy on his opponent, Senator Barry Goldwater, and Goldwater's aides.

Hoover remained in power because when an agent or a wiretap revealed some apparent sexual or financial indiscretion — such as a 1966 report by the Hong Kong agent about Nixon's contacts with a woman named Marianna Liu — Hoover would go to that person and say, "I have this report about you. I'm sure it's not true. I just want you to know that I'll tuck it away and see that it doesn't get all around town."

Johnson had called Hoover in to tell him delicately that he was sick of public feuding between him and Martin Luther King and he sure wished Hoover would do something to clear things up, because the public attacks were hurting his presidency.

Still, Johnson dealt gently with Hoover, who, among the unknowing masses, was a sort of American icon.

Becoming a columnist was one of the great moments of my life — especially when Andy Anderson, president of my syndicate, and Larry Fanning told me that I was "starting in more than one hundred newspapers with circulation greater than any beginning column we ever heard of."

"That's goddam great," said Fanning, "considering that not a single newspaper in Georgia, Mississippi, Alabama, Louisiana, South Carolina, or even North and South Dakota, Montana, New Mexico, Arizona, will buy you. Even Ralph McGill says he doesn't dare put you in the *Atlanta Constitution* right now."

The syndicate had done a fantastic job of selling me, not as a black, but as someone with valuable information about the workings of government and the nuances of the foreign policy disputes that were wracking the nation. It also sold my "youth," sending to all daily newspapers a listing of the age brackets of twenty-four columnists. I note now, with sadness, that only four of those named — Robert Novak, Rowland Evans, William Buckley, and Carl Rowan — are still alive and writing columns.

Andy Anderson established a rule that in cities with more than one newspaper, the first one to ask for the column and offer a decent price would get it. I wanted to be in the *Nashville Tennessean*, but, to my amazement, the conservative *Nashville Banner* got there first. While the *Washington Post* dawdled, the *Washington Star* cut a handsome deal. Kay Graham of the *Post* telephoned me to ask that I use "author's rights" to take the column from the *Star* and give it to the *Post*. I said I would not dishonor the commitment to the *Star*, a decision that guaranteed that I would never find a real slot in the *Post*, even after the *Star* folded. (One of the saddest developments of my quarter century of writing a column is that so many great newspapers that carried it — the *Chicago Daily News*, the *Philadelphia Bulletin*, the *Miami News*, the *Los Angeles Herald-Examiner*, three New York newspapers, and more — have gone belly-up.)

Fanning said I had to write a column inviting myself into the homes of my readers. So I wrote:

> I am a stranger on your doorstep today. Good manners require that I explain my presence and my purpose.
>
> I have come to inform, to provoke, to prod, to inspire — to become a factor in that great process through which the people of a democracy make the decisions that spell life or death for nations, and even civilizations. . . .
>
> It is well that I answer at the outset a question that probably has arisen in many minds: is this a column on civil rights?
>
> The answer is NO. It is a column about Americans and the nation and world in which they live.
>
> But because race is such a vital factor in our American society . . . discussions of race and civil rights must find their way into this space from time to time.

It wasn't long before the editor of the *Memphis Commercial-Appeal* told a syndicate representative "in confidence" that if I wrote one more column dealing with racism he would cancel the column. I called Anderson and said, "Cancel the *Memphis Commercial-Appeal*," and he did.

All columnists of any consequence make enemies. The first one I made was Johnson, who seemed unable to believe that I would question any part of his Vietnam War policies. Johnson quickly put me on the "don't invite to the White House" list.

Bess Abell, the White House social secretary, told me: "Your and Viv's names have gone into the Oval Office on eight dinner guest lists, and eight times your names have been scratched out."

I watched Martin Luther King's comments about the war become strident beyond my belief. On March 5, 1967, he went to a meeting of civil rights leaders in Great Neck, Long Island, and devoted much of the session to trying to get other Negroes to join him in attacking U.S. policy toward Vietnam. He failed. So King lashed out on his own with a historic speech at the Riverside Church in New York on April 4.

In bitterly emotional, often poetic phrases, he delivered the most scathing denunciation of United States involvement in Vietnam ever made by so prominent an American.

He labeled the United States "the greatest purveyor of violence in the world today" and accused it of "cruel manipulation of the poor."

He said the people of Vietnam "languish under our bombs and consider us — not their fellow Vietnamese — the real enemy."

He said the women and children and the aged of Vietnam "watch as we poison their water, as we kill a million acres of their crops."

He said U.S. troops had wounded twenty South Vietnamese civilians for every member of the Vietcong wounded.

He said the United States "may have killed a million of them — mostly children."

He said U.S. policies had degraded the children of Vietnam to the point where "they beg for food" and are "selling their sisters to our soldiers, soliciting for their mothers."

He said American soldiers "test out our latest weapons" on the peasants of South Vietnam "just as the Germans tested out new medicine and new tortures in the concentration camps of Europe."

He accused President Johnson of lying about peace overtures from Hanoi, and American officials in general of hiding or ignoring the fact that membership of the National Liberation Front (NLF, the political arm of the Vietcong) "is less than twenty-five percent Communist."

Martin Luther King concluded by urging "Americans who find our course in Vietnam dishonorable and unjust to become conscientious objectors." And he asked our government to end all bombing of North and South Vietnam, unilaterally to stop other military actions, and to accept an NLF role in any future Vietnam government.

The reaction across the nation and the world was immediate and explosive.

Civil rights leaders wrung their hands and began to plan steps to take the already splintered movement out from under the onus of King's broadside. It was clear to many that the thirty-eight-year-old Atlanta minister had placed American Negroes in their greatest dilemma since the post–World War I era, when a resurgent, freewheeling Ku Klux Klan tried to restore America's colored citizens to involuntary servitude. In short time, Roy Wilkins, executive director of the NAACP; Whitney Young, executive director of the National Urban League; Ralph Bunche, Nobel Prize–winning United Nations under secretary; Senator Edward Brooke of Massachusetts; and other prominent Negroes would disagree publicly with King. They would accuse him of a grave tactical error, of jeopardizing the civil rights movement by linking it to the peace movement.

Pro–civil rights congressmen took the floor to denounce King, and a few to praise him. Radios Moscow and Peking, the Soviet news agency Tass, and the New China News Agency joined the American media in spreading King's words to distant capitals. The directors of Freedom House in New York, a national organization dedicated to strengthening democratic institutions and then chaired by Leo Cherne, said King had "emerged as the spear-carrier of a civil disobedience program that is demagogic and irresponsible." It said the Nobel Prize–winning preacher had lent his "mantle of respectability" to an anti–Vietnam War coalition "that includes well-known Communist allies and luminaries of the hate-America left."

King replied sharply that Freedom House had stooped to McCarthyite smear tactics.

Meanwhile, King plunged onward, compounding the anger and suspicion by leading a New York peace march at which New Left and Black Power advocates like David Dellinger of *Liberation* magazine and Stokely Carmichael, former leader of the Student Nonviolent Coordinating Committee (SNCC), titillated the crowd by deriding talk of a negotiated settlement in Vietnam. Both used these same words: "If you're being raped, you don't want to negotiate, you want immediate withdrawal!"

King then proceeded to arouse political passions by naming Senators Robert Kennedy of New York and Charles Percy of Illinois as the best presidential candidates in 1968 "from the standpoint of civil rights."

The *Washington Post*, long a loud supporter of both King and the civil rights movement, said of King's Vietnam declarations:

> Dr. King has done a grave injury to those who are his natural allies in the great struggle to remove ancient abuses from our public life; and he has done an even graver injury to himself. Many who have listened to him with respect will never again accord him the same confidence. He has diminished his usefulness to his cause, to his country and to his people. And that is a great tragedy.

Whitney Young called me after that speech — I was a columnist now — to ask if I had talked to Martin. "I've talked to him, and talked to him, and told him what the FBI is doing to him. But it seems to go in one ear and out the other," I said.

"What the hell is he doing," Young asked rhetorically, "trying to find a new way to commit suicide?"

I telephoned King again and said that he had compared the greatest civil rights president in history with Hitler and that millions of young blacks would suffer as a result.

"It is simply a matter of conscience," King replied. "I'm more than a civil rights leader; I'm a clergyman, charged with bringing Judeo-Christian ethics to bear on the sins of our time."

"Goddam, Martin," I said, "don't you have enough dangerous enemies without getting the Vietnam War zealots on your ass?"

"A good man never has enough enemies," he replied.

You must view this conversation in the context of the times, a period of the greatest civil rights gains black people had ever made in America — and have not made since. Johnson had used his incredible (and in some cases almost immoral) skills at arm-twisting on Capitol Hill to push through the Public Accommodations Act that said states and individuals could no longer force blacks to sit in the back of the bus, in "the crow's nest" of a theater, or to go to the back of a restaurant and buy a sandwich handed through a cubbyhole. In 1965 Johnson had railroaded through the Voting

Rights Act that fulfilled the dreams of people like Gus Courts who just wanted "to say that I voted once before I died." In that same year Johnson had secured passage of the Federal Aid to Higher Education Act, which financed an explosive increase in the number of black high school graduates who could enroll in college.

Whatever Johnson's faults, I felt that he did not deserve the gratuitous insults of being called a Hitler and a child killer.

That Riverside Church speech provoked several black leaders to distance themselves and their organizations from King. Whitney Young stepped forth first, on April 5 saying that the civil rights movement and the Vietnam War issue should be made separate.

Negro citizens "have as their first priority," he said, "the immediate problem of survival in this country. They are therefore concerned about the rat tonight and the job tomorrow.

"The limited resources and personnel available to civil rights agencies for work in their behalf should not be diverted into other channels."

On April 11 a top-of-page-one headline in the *New York Times* blared: N.A.A.C.P. DECRIES STAND OF DR. KING ON VIETNAM. The sixty-member board of this oldest civil rights organization said that King had made a "serious tactical mistake." On April 12, in a rare public statement of controversy, Dr. Ralph Bunche said that King should not try to lead both a civil rights campaign and a crusade against American involvement in Vietnam.

Baseball hero Jackie Robinson said: "Dr. King has always been my favorite civil rights leader, but I don't agree with him on this issue."

I had doubts that King, the man who had shown such a splendid sense of public relations and propaganda, had written that Riverside Church speech. I wrote a column in which I said that in the field of civil rights the moral imperatives were pretty clear — imposing Jim Crow, denying people the right to vote, were wrong.

"But Vietnam is a complex issue where the moral imperatives are cloudy and confused. It is plain foolhardy for American Negroes to burden the clear cut moral issue of racial equality with the bitterly complicated controversy over the war in Vietnam."

Roy Wilkins read that column and called me to say that he was deeply troubled and had been "needling Martin, telling him that he is saying a lot of things just to get his name in the newspapers and his face on TV."

"Yes, but the publicity is getting worse," I said. "And he won't listen to anybody. Perhaps I can get to him by writing a few things."

So I wrote an article critical of King for *Reader's Digest*. When it hit the stands on August 28, 1967, the *New York Times* ran an article headlined: ROWAN CALLS DR. KING'S OPPOSITION TO WAR PERIL TO RIGHTS GAINS. The *Times* article quoted former King aide Andrew Young, who would become notorious for putting his foot in his mouth and regurgitating it publicly, as saying that I was "almost the worst kind of sophisticated Uncle Tom."

King telephoned me to say that he disavowed Young's comment. "You think I made a mistake," he said. "I think I did the courageous thing. Let's be friends and leave it at that."

I soon got a call from Bill Sullivan at the FBI asking me to meet with him privately at headquarters. I was surprised when Sullivan told me that he was meeting with me without Hoover's knowledge. Having read those intelligence reports at USIA, and knowing how Hoover operated, I couldn't imagine that anyone under him would do anything that he wouldn't like. And it was the worst-kept secret in Washington that Sullivan hoped to succeed Hoover if he ever retired, so why would he risk Hoover's outrage by talking to me?

Sullivan laid out so many documents, so many details, about King's alleged Communist activities that I believed he honestly was sharing great secrets with me. But I got suckered.

In hindsight, I know that I had enough warnings about the FBI not to get flam-floozled. After all, in March 1964, in the briefings in my office at USIA, it had become obvious that some powerful people in the intelligence community were out to get King.

The next time I saw a CIA official who I knew trusted me, I asked, "What the hell is going on regarding Dr. King? Who's going to get him?"

"It ain't us," he said. The next day I got hand delivered in an eyes-only plain envelope a copy of an FBI memorandum written on May 22, 1961, by G. H. Scatterday to senior FBI official Alex Rosen, assistant FBI director for the General Investigative Division. The memo was the first I had seen of FBI efforts to link King and the entire civil rights movement to Communists.

I had not forgotten that in 1962 King had sounded off, rightly and bravely, about the FBI's apparent hostility to the civil rights movement and its seeming inability to find and arrest white southerners who had committed crimes against blacks. That year, a headline-grabbing racial fracas had broken out in Albany, Georgia. King, jailed during the Albany movement, angered by the federal government, lashed out at what he considered the contrived incompetence of an FBI that couldn't seem to find white violators of the law. Howard Zinn of the Southern Regional Council produced a highly critical study of the FBI's role in Albany in which he said that local FBI agents were "vaguely-interested observers of injustice." King came on stronger, describing FBI agents as "white southerners who have been influenced by the mores of the community. To maintain their status, they have to be friendly with the local police and people who are promoting segregation." That infuriated Hoover, who promptly sent Robert F. Kennedy a memorandum asserting that two of King's advisers were or had been members of the Communist party.

The truth is that I had swallowed whole the conventional line within the Washington press corps that Sullivan was the one good guy in the FBI, the civil libertarian, the man who was standing up against Hoover's excesses and abuses of power. It would not be until 1974, when FBI Director Clarence Kelley sought to convince me of his honesty and his determination to clean up the FBI by allowing me to read thousands of secret documents, that I would realize the role that Sullivan really was playing.

For the last days of 1962 and much of 1963, Sullivan had worked under the illusion that Hoover's attitude toward black Americans was that no group in America had rejected the blandishment of communism as forcefully as Negroes. It had not sunk into Sullivan's head that Hoover was almost crazed by Zinn's and King's criticisms of FBI agents at Albany. So in August 1963, Sullivan and his Domestic Intelligence Division produced a seventy-page analysis of the Communist party's influence on American Negroes. The ultimate sycophant, Sullivan highlighted the "failure of the Communist

Party in achieving any significant inroads into the Negro population."

Hoover wrote by hand a withering commentary:

This memo reminds me vividly of those I received when Castro took over Cuba. You contended then that Castro and his cohorts were not Communists and not influenced by Communists. Time alone proved you wrong. I for one can't ignore the memos as having only an infinitesimal effect on efforts to exploit the American Negro by Communists.

A week later, on August 30, 1963, the chastised Sullivan produced a memo to the FBI's third-ranking A. H. Belmont saying:

The Director is correct. We were completely wrong about believing the evidence was not sufficient to determine some years ago that Fidel Castro was not a communist or under communist influence. On investigating and writing about communism and the American Negro, we had better remember this and profit by the lesson it should teach us. . . .

Personally, I believe in the light of King's powerful demagogic speech yesterday [sic] he stands head and shoulders over all other Negro leaders put together when it comes to influencing great masses of Negroes. We must mark him now, if we have not done so before, as the most dangerous Negro of the future in this Nation from the standpoint of communism, the Negro and national security. . . .

This Nation is involved in a form of racial revolution and the time has never been so right for exploitation of the Negroes by communist propagandists. Nineteen million Negroes constitute the greatest single racial target of the Communist Party, USA. *This is a somber reality we must never lose sight of.* . . .

We regret greatly that the memorandum did not measure up to what the Director has a right to expect from our analysis.

Even Hoover knew sucking up when he saw it. He responded angrily to Sullivan, writing: "I can't understand how you can so agilely switch your thinking and evaluation."

In Hoover's FBI, everybody was agile in switching thinking and national security evaluations, according to what they perceived to be the whims, the personal animosities, the special prejudices, of Hoover.

Sullivan wrote Belmont another memo on September 25, 1963, in which he groveled in apology for his "failed" interpretation of Communist infiltration of the black civil rights movement. Sullivan asked for Hoover's forgiveness and an opportunity to do better and show that Communist infiltration of Negroes had not "reached the point of control or domination."

Hoover responded with the ominous comment that "certainly this is not true with respect to the King connection."

Martin Luther King had become an obsession, a primary security target of Hoover, and days after that groveling memo from Sullivan, the aging FBI director asked Attorney General Kennedy for permission to institute technical surveillance of Dr. King's residence and the Southern Christian Leadership Conference (SCLC) office in New York City. After Kennedy squirmed for a while, permission was granted.

Meanwhile, the FBI had come up with a new report on "Communism and the Negro Movement." Belmont sent a copy to Hoover's lifelong friend and companion, FBI Associate Director Clyde A. Tolson, accompanied by a Belmont letter saying:

> The attached analysis of Communism and the Negro movement is highly explosive. It can be regarded as a personal attack on Martin Luther King. There is no doubt it will have a heavy impact on the Attorney General [Kennedy] and anyone else to whom we disseminate it.

"We must do our duty," Hoover replied to the Belmont letter, adding that "I am glad that you recognize at last that there exists such [Communist] influence."

The FBI hierarchy, and Sullivan especially, simply caved in to the racism of Hoover.

I was at Case Western Reserve University in Ohio, sharing a lecture platform with Mayor Carl Stokes of Cleveland, on April 4, 1968, when someone walked to the podium and handed me a note, asking me to read it to the audience. Only as I read the shocking note aloud did I learn that Dr. King had been assassinated in Memphis, Tennessee.

"Jesus, they got him . . . !" I mumbled.

I used the word "they" without any sense of what I meant by it. We ended the speeches hurriedly, and I telephoned Washington to get the grisly details. At about 6:00 P.M. King was on the balcony of his room at the Lorraine Motel in Memphis when someone shot him with a high-powered rifle, the bullet tearing the major neck blood vessels and severing the spinal cord at the root of the neck. King had been rushed to St. Joseph's Hospital, where he was pronounced dead at 7:05 P.M.

I rushed back to Washington, where I made an appointment to see Sullivan immediately. I still trusted him, partly because, in private, he professed so much contempt for his boss, Hoover, and because I had not read the FBI files, later shown to me by Kelley.

"Do you have any good leads?" I asked.

Sullivan began to talk about "the large number of cuckolded husbands who had reason to kill him," remarks that triggered the first of what would become my many deep doubts about this FBI front man.

But we newspapermen, like presidents and secretaries of state, are often suckers for what is passed off as intelligence or offered as inside information that no other reporter is getting. So I listened seriously as Sullivan embellished his earlier stories about a King aide meeting secretly with a Soviet contact in Mexico City and his musings about whether King might have "given the Communists some reason to bump him off."

Then Sullivan laid out a series of scenarios that he said the FBI was pursuing. On May 3 I dispatched a column, based on sessions with Sullivan, in which he cited the possibilities:

1. That James Earl Ray, the alleged assassin, was the hired killer in a Cuba–Red China plot
2. That the assassin squad of the Soviet secret police was somehow involved in the plot
3. That Ray was hired indirectly by certain black nationalists who paid him with money made available by foreign sources

I emphasized that the dominant theory — and hope — among FBI agents directing this investigation was that the killer was a loner who murdered Dr. King out of his own crazy, racist views.

It is history that James Earl Ray, an alleged racist, robber, hopeless criminal, was apprehended in Europe and that he confessed to killing King, tried to recant on his confession, but nevertheless was sentenced to ninety-nine years in prison. Ray is still in prison, after one escape attempt.

But the record be damned! My gut told me in April 1968 that no lone man showed up in Memphis on his own to kill King. Deep in my heart I felt, based on all the intelligence data that I had seen while at USIA, that someone in the U.S. government had put out a contract to "neutralize" this black preacher — "neutralization" being almost synonymous with a death sentence in the argot of the intelligence community.

My suspicions intensified in the summer of 1969 when I read about boxer Muhammad Ali's attempt, in federal court in Houston, to overturn his five-year sentence for refusing to be drafted. That case forced the FBI to reveal that it had been engaged in massive eavesdropping on Ali, King, and other black Americans. Agent C. Barry Pickett of the FBI testified that for eight hours a day, five days a week, for four years, he had used a telephone tap and a microphone planted in the home of Elijah Muhammad to listen in on conversations of the late leader of the Black Muslims. This was 8,300 hours of eavesdropping by one FBI agent on a single black American. Common sense suggested that whereas Pickett worked eight hours a day, at least two other agents were eavesdropping for a minimum of 16,600 hours — with someone covering weekends.

Hoover at that time had been FBI director for more than forty-five years. I was fed up with his intimidating Nixon and Johnson to the point where they kept giving him exemptions from the mandatory retirement law. So I wrote a column that ran on June 14, 1969, in the *Chicago Daily News* under the headline WHY FBI'S HOOVER MUST GO, and in the *Washington Star* the following day under a similar headline. I said:

> A society is never in more peril than when the people lose the ability to identify a genuine threat to personal liberty.
>
> The kind of abuse of and contempt for the law manifest in the King and Muhammad Ali eavesdroppings becomes almost inevitable when a man is left in a key job as long as Hoover has been.
>
> Hoover ought to be replaced — immediately.

That column hit the FBI like a thunderclap and provoked feverish comment around the nation. On June 16 Clyde Tolson sent me the following letter:

Sir:
My attention has been called to the malicious article which you wrote in the Sunday *Star* . . . concerning Mr. J. Edgar Hoover. . . .
For your information, the wire tap on Martin Luther King, Jr., was specifically approved in advance in writing by the late Attorney General of the United States, Mr. Robert F. Kennedy. This device was strictly in the field of internal security and, therefore, was within the provisions laid down by the then President of the United States.
It is to be hoped that you will give the same publicity to this letter as was given to your scurrilous editorial.

I had FBI sources who had warned me that Hoover wanted to put the wiretap monkey on the back of Bobby Kennedy and his brother, both dead, so I tried to nail Tolson to the wall. I wrote him:

Sir:
I have your letter of June 16 and duly note the righteousness of your indignation.
I shall be happy to give publicity to the information contained in your letter. I am sure, though, that you will agree with me that the public ought to have more than one smattering of the truth. Would you be so good as to answer the following questions? Upon receipt of your reply, I shall be happy to make the answers public.
1. On what date did the late Robert F. Kennedy approve in writing the wire tap on Dr. Martin Luther King, Jr.?
2. Did the wire taps and buggings of Dr. King continue during the Attorney Generalships of Nicholas deB. Katzenbach and Ramsey Clark?
3. Did either Mr. Katzenbach or Mr. Clark specifically approve in writing the wire tap on Dr. King?
4. Was Attorney General Clark apprised of the fact that the FBI considered Dr. King a potential security risk?
5. Has the FBI ever used electronic surveillance on other civil rights leaders, namely Roy Wilkins? Whitney Young? Ralph Abernathy? James Farmer? Floyd McKissick?
6. When you say a device is "strictly in the field of internal

security," what criterion does the FBI use to determine when "internal security" is involved?

7. Has the FBI ever tapped the phones of any members of Congress as part of its process of guarding internal security?

Tolson replied without responding to any of my questions, asserting that "there is no need to continue this correspondence."

Two women reporters, Vera Glazer and Malvina Stephenson, interviewed Hoover and asked him, "Who started this wiretap controversy?"

"That racist columnist, Rowan," he said, and they wrote a column that provoked little headlines across the country about "Racist Rowan."

I was surprised that I had wound up in the middle of a great public feud with this "American institution," J. Edgar Hoover. But I confess that I liked it. I decided to stay on the offensive, so I wrote another column for June 25, which the *Washington Star* headlined REPEAT: TIME FOR HOOVER TO GO.

Sullivan telephoned for another meeting, at which he said: "The old monster is enraged." This meeting was a surprise, since I knew that the FBI had set out secretly to find a "Negro leader" to replace King, and that Bunche and I had been blackballed from getting FBI information on grounds we'd foil the plot.

"I suppose my phones are tapped and my office and bedrooms bugged?" I replied.

"No," said Sullivan, "he hates your guts, but he has never dared to tap or bug you."

I gave Sullivan a stony look, knowing that he was the guy in the FBI who was ordering or approving the wiretaps, buggings, and unlawful burglaries. I still didn't know the whole game he had been playing regarding King, but by now I was a wary listener.

I told Sullivan that I was deliberately prodding and attacking Hoover and the FBI, because I felt in my gut that there was something fishy about the March 10, 1969, plea of guilty by James Earl Ray in which he accepted a ninety-nine-year sentence in prison.

I asked Sullivan a few questions:

• When, according to reports I received while director of USIA and information I got from the White House after I returned to journalism, the FBI had people watching Dr. King every minute of every day, why were there no FBI agents at the Lorraine Motel to see what happened to the civil rights leader?

• Why, according to calls to me from Memphis, were two black firemen, Norvell E. Wallace and Floyd E. Newsum, suddenly assigned away from Fire Station No. 2, which overlooked the Lorraine Motel balcony on which King was shot? Was there a conspiracy to remove any possible black witnesses to the murder?

• Why would the murderer leave a blanket-wrapped bundle at the scene of the crime, containing a Remington Gamemaster rifle with his fingerprints on it, plus binoculars and a sales slip that made it easy to determine where they were purchased?

I got garbage answers.

I didn't ask Sullivan everything that was running through my mind then. There are so many doubts about the truth and justice of Ray's incarceration and about the FBI's possible involvement in, and investigation of, the King murder, that I am left after all these years with questions:

• I ask about the travel bag that was dropped along with the rifle near the motel where King was killed. There was underwear in that bag that Memphis police said belonged to Ray. But Birmingham lawyer Arthur Hanes, who was Ray's lawyer until the day before Ray's trial was to begin, established that the underwear in the travel bag was so small that "James Earl Ray couldn't have gotten his big toe into [it]."

• I ask how Ray could or would leave the good life of California to drive to a strange city, Memphis, and in two and one-half hours alone find Bessie Brewer's flophouse and rent precisely the room from which a sniper could kill King as he stood on the balcony of the Lorraine Motel.

• I ask why no one paid any attention to the expressed doubts of Judge W. Preston Battle, Jr., that despite Ray's plea of guilty, this confessor acted alone.

• I ask why Hanes was fired so peremptorily, with a new lawyer, Percy Foreman of Houston, coming in to convince Ray that if he did not plead guilty to first-degree murder and accept a plea bargaining of ninety-nine years in prison, he would die in the electric chair.

• I ask why Hanes would talk so adamantly about criminal elements in New Orleans, who allegedly lured Ray to Memphis, holding a deadly grip of fear over his ex-client. (How eerie that criminal elements in New Orleans have been cited as the possible assassins of John F. Kennedy.)

• I ask why, when minutes after the killing of King the FBI had a gun, binoculars, and other items bearing the alleged murderer's fingerprints, did the bureau stay on a wild goose chase for Eric Starvo Galt, only to discover after fifteen days that Galt was really James Earl Ray. Let me simply give you the explanation from the January 11, 1977, report of the Justice Department task force:

> The Bureau sought first to identify and locate the murderer using the obvious leads. They checked out aliases, tracked the traces left under the Galt alias, and used the known fingerprints from the murder weapon and the contents of the blue zipper bag left on South Main Street to eliminate suspects. This backtracking ended in Atlanta. At *this point* [emphasis added] the Bureau initiated a check of the crime site fingerprints against the white male "wanted fugitive" print file. This produced the almost "instant" discovery that the wanted man, Galt, was James Earl Ray, an escapee from Missouri State Prison. In fact the "instant" discovery was a tedious hand search in a file of some 20,000 prints.

The delay in initiating that "tedious" search for a white male allowed James Earl Ray to make some remarkable moves in the United States and into Europe.

Aside from Ray's claim that he was set up by New Orleans "criminal elements," and his postcourtroom claim that Foreman and the federal government manipulated him into pleading guilty, no one has answered these questions to any investigator's satisfaction.

Once it became clear that Eric Starvo Galt was really James Earl Ray, the FBI did an incredible job of tracing Ray's daily moves from April 23, 1967, when Ray escaped from the Missouri state prison, right up to April 5, 1968, when the fugitive picked up his laundry at the Piedmont Laundromat in Atlanta. The FBI could discover that Ray had paid $1,995 for a 1966 white Ford Mustang in Birmingham on August 30, 1967; paid $29 for dance lessons at a studio in Los Angeles on December 6, 1967; paid $105 to attend the International School of Bartending in Los Angeles on January

20, 1968; and spent $1.83 in the Rexall drugstore in Whitehaven, Tennessee, on April 3, 1968, the day before King was killed.

Almost a month elapsed before the FBI acknowledged having a clue to what had happened to Ray. During this period of investigation, according to the Justice Department task force of 1977, Hoover displayed striking arrogance. The task force cited Hoover's "reluctance to provide the Civil Rights Division and the Attorney General with timely reports on the course of the murder investigation." It noted that when Ramsey Clark suggested making a progress report to the nation, Hoover wrote: "We are not going to make any progress reports."

When Clark authorized prosecutive action against Eric Starvo Galt, the FBI, without consulting the attorney general or the Civil Rights Division, chose Birmingham as the venue in which to file a criminal complaint. Hoover chose Birmingham, records show, because he "could not rely on the U.S. Attorney at Memphis" and "would lose control of the situation."

The task force accused Hoover and his aides of "marked discourtesy" to Clark and Assistant Attorney General Fred Vinson. It said that when Vinson telephoned to complain about being "kept in the dark," a Hoover assistant hung up the phone.

The task force called these FBI actions "highly improper." I have always believed them to be highly suspicious.

While the FBI was agonizing over "a cold trail" and Hoover was ensuring that no one else took control of what was supposed to be one of the greatest manhunts in American history, Ray simply took a bus from Atlanta on April 5, after picking up his laundry, and arrived in Cincinnati about 1:30 A.M. on April 6. He took another bus to Detroit, where he crossed into Windsor, Canada, in a taxi and then took a train to Toronto.

No plausible explanation has yet been put forth as to where Ray got the money for these travels. Speculation exists that money was passed to Ray by one of his brothers or another member of his family. The Justice Department found that at one point Hoover ordered that Ray's relatives be put under surveillance, but for some reason the order was not obeyed.

Ray did earn $664 working as a dishwasher and cook's helper in Winnetka, Illinois, from May 7, 1967, through June 25, 1967. Theories were leaked that he committed robberies, burglaries, bank heists, and more, but no such holdups ever were corroborated. So nine years after King's murder the Justice Department would say that "the sources for Ray's funds still remain a mystery today."

The Justice Department task force added: "In light of the fact that a good deal of mystery still surrounds James Ray and the assassination, particularly the means by which he financed his life style and travels, we concluded that on the basis of the information which was uncovered, the Bureau should have pursued this line of the investigation more thoroughly."

Whatever the source of Ray's funds for bus and rail tickets, meals, and simple survival (he would be spending bigger sums), he began on April 8 to pull off a caper that, till this day, almost no one believes he achieved without some sophisticated, prearranged assistance. This man, who would later be described as stupid and sloppy by the FBI's Sullivan, is supposed to have gone to the Toronto public library and found newspapers listing the 1932 births of George Sneyd and Paul Edward Bridgman. Ray is supposed to have rented rooms under both names, had passport pictures made under each name, and filed for a Canadian passport under each name.

While waiting for a passport, Ray supposedly visited bars, in one of which he saw a TV show saying he was on the FBI's Ten Most Wanted list. Somehow the "greatest manhunt in history" did not reach into Toronto, so on April 24 Ramon George "Sneya" got a Canadian passport. Under that name, Ray bought a round-trip ticket to London, from which he quickly flew to Lisbon, allegedly looking for work as a mercenary in the Portuguese colony of Angola. That failing, he got his passport name corrected to "Sneyd" and flew back to London, where, as the legend goes, he tried and failed to get a job as a hired killer in any British ex-colony.

Meanwhile, the Royal Canadian Mounted Police had searched thousands of passport applications and found a photo indicating that Sneyd was James Earl Ray. On June 8, 1968, Ray sought to fly to Brussels looking for a job as a mercenary, but as he awaited his plane at London's Heathrow Airport, he was arrested by detectives on charges of using a fraudulent passport and carrying a loaded revolver.

Sullivan would later write that a mean-spirited Hoover delayed the announcement of Ray's capture until the time of Robert F. Kennedy's funeral, so as to diminish TV coverage of the slain former attorney general's burial.

On May 2, 1972, at the age of seventy-seven, J. Edgar Hoover died in office — after forty-eight years as head of the FBI.

I hoped that Hoover's death might induce some top FBI people to talk about a possible conspiracy to kill King. But Hoover had surrounded himself with people who, with rare exceptions, shared his mentality.

But thank God for our system of checks and balances. There are times when a good reporter can unearth things that no congressional committee even knows how to investigate. There are other times when a zealous congressional committee, with the power of subpoena, can put officials under oath and ferret out some amazing truths.

It became apparent to many members of Congress in the early 1970s that the CIA, the FBI, and other intelligence agencies were out of control. Especially worrisome were the circumstances surrounding the assassination of King and the evidence of U.S. involvement in the assassinations, or attempted assassinations, of Fidel Castro in Cuba, Patrice Lumumba in the Congo (now Zaire), Rafael Trujillo in the Dominican Republic, General Rene Schneider in Chile, and Ngo Dinh Diem in South Vietnam. So the Senate created a Select Committee on Intelligence, chaired by Frank Church of Idaho, with John G. Tower of Texas as vice chairman. Other members were Philip A. Hart of Michigan, Walter F. Mondale of Minnesota, Walter D. Huddleston of Kentucky, Robert Morgan of North Carolina, Gary Hart of Colorado, Howard H. Baker, Jr., of Tennessee, Barry Goldwater of Arizona, Charles McC. Mathias, Jr., of Maryland, and Richard Schweiker of Pennsylvania.

It elicited some of the most extraordinary testimony from leaders of the intelligence community that Americans had ever heard.

It was bannerline news across America on November 16, 1975, when James Adams, assistant deputy director of the FBI and the bureau's link to Congress, told the Senate Intelligence Committee that there was "no justification" for twenty-five separate efforts to harass and discredit King.

Adams stunned senators and the nation by revealing that shortly before King was to leave for Stockholm in 1964 to receive the Nobel Peace Prize, the FBI sent King the anonymous letter suggesting that the civil rights leader kill himself. The letter was accompanied by an FBI "composite" recording of what FBI bugs and wiretaps had picked up in at least sixteen hotels and other places where King had spent a night.

"King, there is only one thing left for you to do," the FBI letter said. "You have just 34 days [the number of days before Christmas] in which to do it. There is but one way out for you."

Some FBI "genius" had found that King allegedly had tried to commit suicide as a teenager, so the King haters in the FBI felt certain that their letter and tape would cause King to kill himself. But let me pick up here from the *Washington Star*'s report on Adams's testimony.

Reporter Norman Kempster wrote:

> King did not kill himself. But another FBI dirty trick may have indirectly contributed to his assassination. . . .
>
> The FBI files show that the Bureau leaked to a friendly reporter that King was staying in the white-owned Holiday Inn [in Memphis] during his participation in a sanitation workers strike that included a boycott of white-owned businesses. A Bureau memo said King should be called a hypocrite because he was not staying in the Lorraine, a black-owned and black-patronized motel.

Clearly, the FBI used the media to manipulate King into moving to the Lorraine, the site of an easy assassination.

There were moments of intense drama that November day of Adams's testimony, summoning all Americans to ask themselves what freedom from police-state tactics meant to them.

None of the revelations in the committee's report was more dismaying to me than Sullivan's testimony on November 1, 1975. Asked about the magnitude of the effort to destroy King, he said, "No holds were barred."

The five-year statute of limitations had run out, so no prosecution of Sullivan and others was possible except in the rare exception of proof of a conspiracy.

Asked why the FBI was so determined to destroy King, Sullivan blamed it on Hoover's bigotry.

Asked why he and other FBI officials would not stand up to Hoover, he said he and the others "had homes with mortgages to pay."

The Church committee findings not only reined in the CIA and FBI (even today the Bush administration is trying to loosen the restrictions) but it prompted a Department of Justice inquiry by a special task force that said on January 11, 1977:

> • The Bureau's . . . illicit dissemination of raw investigative data to discredit Dr. King [efforts were made to find dirt on Coretta King, too], the efforts to intimidate him, to break up his marriage, and the explicit and implicit efforts to blackmail him, were not fully known to the [Justice] Department, but were none-the-less ordered and directed by Director Hoover, Assistant to the Director [Cartha] DeLoach, Assistant Director Sullivan and the Section Chief under him.
>
> • The Bureau's illicit surveillance produced tapes and transcripts concerning King and many others. These may be sought by King's heirs and representatives. Worse still, they may be sought by members of the public at large under the Freedom of Information Act. We recommend that these tapes and transcripts be sealed and sent to the National Archives and that the Congress be asked to pass legislation denying any access to them whatever and authorizing and directing their total destruction along with the destruction of material in reports and memoranda derived from them.

It was probably a "coincidence" that less than three weeks after that task force recommendation became public, U.S. District Judge John Lewis Smith, Jr., ordered that the FBI should file with the National Archives all of the FBI tapes and documents growing out of the wiretaps, buggings, and other surveillances of King, and that the materials regarding King not be made public *for at least fifty years*, except by court order.

No matter what any statute says, when it comes to raw bilge about people whom the FBI doesn't like or the administration in power wants to neutralize, the FBI still leaks like a sewer in a hurricane.

Hoover had been dead for more than three years, which had something to do with the sudden boldness of those esteemed senators. Some would never have endorsed those denunciations of FBI procedures while Hoover was alive.

Blackmail aside, I knew that Hoover had survived for forty-eight years as the most fearsome figure in the American government because he knew how to fight. He had invisible battalions of loyalists who were silent until he signaled to them to go to war.

The new FBI director, Clarence M. Kelley, was a far different breed from Hoover, though publicly defensive of an FBI he was trying to change dramatically. He read my doubts and concerns in my articles and made it clear that he wanted Americans, especially black Americans, to get the truth. He also acceded to all my requests for conversations. One day I said to him, "If you want me to trust, give me access to your files on King." He blanched, fell silent, then asked me to let him think about it. A couple of hours later he telephoned my office to say, "We'll put thousands of documents at your disposal." I spent days at the FBI, poring over those documents, astounded by the ongoing fervor of those seeking to destroy King. Here are a few items that I noted:

> September 20, 1957 — FBI Director Hoover sends memorandum to special agent in charge of Atlanta office ordering special vigilance in watching "the racial situation."
> May 1962 — FBI includes King on secret list of persons to be rounded up in event of national emergency. King's name was to be "placed in Section A . . . and tabbed communist."
> December 23, 1963 — High-level nine-hour strategy session held in FBI headquarters on how to "neutralize" King. Idea of placing "good-looking female plant" in King's office is discussed. (Explaining this during 1975 secret testimony, Sullivan tells senators that "no holds were barred. . . . This is a rough, tough business.")
> December 29, 1963 — *Time* magazine chooses King as "Man of the Year." Hoover writes across memorandum informing him of this: "They had to dig deep in the garbage to come up with this one."
> January 8, 1964 — Sullivan memo labels King "a fraud, demagogue and scoundrel" and proposes that the FBI pick and promote a new black leader to replace King.
> April 14, 1964 — After receiving April 1 request from Hoover for ideas as to how to "completely discredit the effectiveness of Martin Luther King, Jr., as a Negro leader," the Atlanta office of FBI suggests: (1) fomenting a rift between King and Roy Wilkins of the NAACP; (2) feeding data to press to inspire critical stories about

King; (3) giving false information "to certain discontented SCLC employees"; (4) fabricating SCLC stationery in FBI laboratory and forging King's signature on letters advising SCLC donors that the IRS is checking the SCLC so as to halt flow of funds to King's organization; (5) arranging phony telephone calls to SCLC creditors to make them believe the organization is in financial distress and to incite them to initiate collection proceedings; (6) considering searching through the trash thrown away by the SCLC office in Atlanta; and (7) examining King's bank account and credit card records.

April 24, 1964 — Hoover expresses "the Bureau's gratitude" to the Atlanta agents for their "aggressive imagination."

If Clarence Kelley, Attorney General Ed Levi, or anyone at the White House thought allowing me to read thousands of documents would pacify me, they soon found out how wrong they were. Many of those documents had enraged me, especially that attempt by Sullivan to kiss an angry Hoover's ass by writing that King was "the most dangerous Negro . . . from the standpoint of communism."

I later wrote columns demanding new investigations of the assassination, which drove conservatives like William F. Buckley, Jr., up the wall. But in April 1976, Levi ordered the Office of Professional Responsibility to conduct an investigation. On January 11, 1977, the Justice Department task force came to these additional conclusions:

• One alleged Communist was a very influential advisor to Dr. King [but] he did not "sell" Dr. King any course of conduct or of advocacy. . . . Dr. King was no threat to domestic security.

• [The security investigation of Dr. King] should have been terminated on the basis of what was learned in 1963. That it was intensified . . . was unwarranted . . . and very probably . . . felonious.

• The Attorney General and the Division charged with responsibility for internal security matters failed badly in what should have been firm supervision of the FBI's internal security activities. . . .

• Almost no blacks were in the FBI special agent's corps in the 1960s and none in the Bureau's hierarchy. This undoubtedly had the effect of limiting not only the outlook and understanding of the problems of race relations, but also must have hindered the ability of investigators to communicate fully with blacks during the murder investigation.

• No evidence of a continuing conspiracy was found.

On the basis of my study of thousands of FBI documents, I could concur in everything in the task force report except the inability to find evidence of a conspiracy. The chronology that I compiled from those documents reeks of evidence of a conspiracy at the highest levels of the FBI — to neutralize King for sure, to hire a killer who would never know who paid him — possibly.

But even at the time of the task force report, the prosecution of bureau personnel was legally or politically impossible. Death had claimed Hoover and others. Sullivan would be killed in a hunting accident on November 9, 1977.

Neither death, the passage of time, nor anything else will ever end the suspicion, the speculation, about who really killed Dr. King. I shall go to *my* grave believing that Hoover, Sullivan, and others in the FBI had a role in silencing the black man they professed to fear, but surely hated.

Ralph Abernathy, King's closest friend, created a furor in October 1989 when he published memoirs in which he claimed that King had a weakness for women and that on the night before the civil rights leader was assassinated he had friendly liaisons (sexual by implication) with two women and then a hostile encounter with another woman whom King allegedly knocked across a bed.

Civil rights leaders with short memories, including Ben Hooks, Jesse Jackson, and others, leaped all over the aged and soon-to-die Abernathy, in an arrogant telegram raising less-than-kind assertions that King's "second banana" hadn't written such "gross inaccuracies and painful distortions" but that they were authored by "people with ulterior motives and large financial resources" — people taking advantage of "our friend Ralph" who has had "two massive strokes that resulted in major brain surgery."

I thought some of the people who signed that telegram had lost their minds. It was a case of twenty-eight blacks joining in a knee-jerk reaction because they had not done their homework. If they had read the 1977 official report of the special Justice Department task force, they would have seen that Mrs. Georgia M. Davis of Louisville, Kentucky, told authorities that she, Mrs. Lucie Ward, and King's brother, the Reverend A. D. Williams King, arrived in Memphis and checked into the Lorraine Motel at about 1:00 A.M. Mrs. Davis says that they stayed up awaiting King, who arrived in a taxicab with Abernathy and an aide, Bernard Lee, at about 4:30 A.M. This document continues Mrs. Davis's account:

> Dr. King was invited to room 207 where he visited with his brother, Mrs. Davis and Mrs. Ward until about 5:00 A.M. He then went to room 306 where he and Rev. Abernathy were registered. About a half hour later Dr. King went to room 201 where he visited with Mrs. Davis for approximately one hour. Afterwards he returned to room 306 for a strategy meeting scheduled for 8 A.M.

So some facts had long been around about the night before King's assassination.

Did Abernathy write about King's "weakness" because of a long-wounded ego, suffering from the fact that neither black nor white America ever recognized him as most effective with the masses, the ordinary people? Or, knowing precisely what was on the tapes made at the Willard Hotel in 1964, was Abernathy shielding himself against future revelations that the FBI had accused him of having a homosexual relationship with King?

It really doesn't matter, and I wish black leaders had understood that when Abernathy's book came out. Their ill-informed attacks on Abernathy raised to new levels of public attention the innuendos and assaults begun by Hoover, Tolson, Sullivan, and others.

All this stuff about King's sexual appetite is of trifling consequence compared with the still-chilling reality that under Hoover the nation's highest law enforcement agency tried unlawfully to destroy his reputation in hopes of thwarting the movement toward racial equality in America.

What is of vital importance is the telling of what Hoover and his sycophants did to make even presidents of these United States cower under the assumption that Hoover had in his "personal files" data that, if made public, could destroy them.

The compelling point is that Americans who have decreed that no person may serve more than eight years as president must never again permit either a tyrant or a saint to serve eight-plus, let alone forty-eight, years as the head of the FBI.

It is imperative that the burgeoning number of black mayors and other black elected officials (almost eight thousand in 1990) learn something from the tragedy and the aftermath of the King assassination. Blacks holding real power who don't keep their noses clean become prime targets of both law enforcement officials and political character assassins.

Martin Luther King, Jr., was one of the most brilliant men I ever knew. But he also was one of the least prudent men I ever knew. Imprudent in his personal behavior, even when he knew he was being watched and recorded, and defiantly reckless in his lack of concern about the violent enemies who gathered around him.

King was having a fatal encounter with his own belief that those enemies couldn't really touch him. They gave him the kiss of death. And no black American, however high in business and industry, should dare to forget that such ruthless enemies still abound.

But let us remember that the history books tell us that prominent men are not always discreet. If they were, we would know nothing about Thomas Jefferson's fathering the children of a black slave, Sally Hemings, or about Richard Nixon's abusing the IRS, FBI, CIA, or his ordering a third-rate burglary of Democratic headquarters at the Watergate. Perhaps it was not prudent for John F. Kennedy to go to Dallas and ride around in a convertible when he knew the level of hatred that existed there. Or for Abe Lincoln to go to the theater in a time of great passion over another war. Or for Ronald Reagan and Oliver North to try to trade arms to Iran for American hostages.

We overlook imprudence and myriad indiscretions in honoring the great people of this nation, and Martin Luther King, Jr., surely was one of them.

Who drives down New York's FDR Drive fuming over the fact that FDR had a long affair of the heart with Lucy Mercer? We honor some men because of their large and indelible contributions to the building of a society based on freedom, economic security, justice, and hope. When children celebrate Martin Luther King's Birthday, the emphasis must be on his courage, his oratorical skills, his uncanny leadership, his ultimate sacrifice in the struggle to widen the parameters of liberty in America, not just for black people, but for everyone. How marvelous it is to note that despite an unprecedented FBI campaign to vilify King, to destroy his reputation, the

American people chose to focus on his greatness, his vision that one day the American reality would match his dreams.

It says something good about America that we have a national King holiday, while virtually the only mention of Hoover now is from people clamoring to take his name off the FBI building.

CHAPTER NINETEEN

The Reagan Years

MY WORST POLITICAL FEARS began in 1980 when Ronald Wilson Reagan assumed the presidency. Here was a man with great acting skills with which to cover up his ignorance about vital issues; a man who was so lacking in meaningful contact with black or poor people, or women who had to work for a living, that no scheme to reward the rich and punish the poor provoked objections from his conscience.

But none of this was a great surprise in 1980. The antecedents were obvious in the 1960s and 1970s. During my first months in the State Department I began to have deep, uneasy feelings about an actor–turned–rabble-rouser named Reagan when I read a cable about Ronnie joining Dr. Fred Schwartz of the Christian Anti-Communist Crusade for one of that group's McCarthyite rallies. Then I read that Reagan had spoken at a fifty-dollar-a-plate fund-raiser for the reelection of Congressman John Rousselot, a national official of the extreme right-wing, antiblack, anti-Jew John Birch Society. Other news stories told me that Reagan was anti–Social Security, anti–corporate tax, anti–arms control, anti–public schools, and opposed to any effort to open any kind of peaceful relationship with the People's Republic of China.

Reagan had said in the autumn of 1965 that he favored the Civil Rights Act of 1964, but eight months later he declared that he would have voted against this "bad piece of legislation." He opposed the 1965 Voting Rights Act, arguing that it was "humiliating to the South." After California's legislature passed the Rumford Act, which prohibited owners from offering property for sale or rent and then withdrawing it for racial or religious reasons, Reagan wanted to repeal this law. He once said to blacks that the Rumford Act was "a form of fascism," asking the blacks: "You wouldn't want to sell your house to a redheaded Kiwanian if you didn't want to, would you?" In 1967 Reagan opposed the federal fair housing law that was passed in 1968.

I remember how, in 1966, Reagan used his radio program to fan the flames of white fear and hatred over black demonstrations and violence in the streets. In one of these programs he said: "Every day the jungle draws a little closer. . . . Our city streets are jungle paths after dark, with more crimes of violence."

Even in those days Reagan had a reputation for talking without facts.

In 1976 I began to understand what Reagan was and why he was so effective. While most politicians indulged in demagoguery, Reagan showed a ruthless instinct for zeroing in on the vulnerabilities of voters. In denouncing the food stamp program, Reagan painted a picture of some hardworking taxpayer at the checkout counter in a supermarket wondering how he could pay for his few pounds of hamburger. Then, as Reagan dramatized things, along came "a strapping young buck" with a pile of T-bone steaks and a fistful of food stamps.

In 1968 even Richard Nixon had not been conservative enough for him, so he tried to snatch away the nomination. In 1976 he moved to deny the Republican nomination to a sitting Republican president. When it became obvious that "good old Jerry Ford" was slicker at using the powers of the presidency than he had imagined, Reagan showed that he could abandon all kinds of adhesions to political ideology in the interest of winning. His speech to the 1976 convention was a spellbinder — and he almost stole the nomination, losing to Ford by 1,187 delegates to 1,070.

Then Reagan made sure that he would have a clear run at the Republican nomination in 1980 by refusing to give meaningful support to Ford. Jimmy Carter won the presidency, and Reagan spent four years as the great attacker.

We watched history repeat itself — a sort of replay of 1968 when Nixon exploited the white backlash to urban violence and ran as Mr.

Law 'n' Order, when white liberals rejected Hubert Humphrey because of his role in the Vietnam War, and when many black voters stayed home on the grounds that "all these honkies are the same."

The setting for the 1980 elections was more ominous than for those in 1968, despite the absence of antiwar hysteria. America was less supportive of programs of social and racial justice. The people were more caught up in the instincts of selfish survival.

Reagan knew what the mood of the nation was, which is why he refused to join President Carter, Congressman John Anderson, and Senator Edward Kennedy in speaking at the national convention of the NAACP in Miami Beach in July. Reagan figured that he could win without black votes.

Reagan's problems with black Americans grew deeper. There had been a lot of laughter in early 1980 when a New Hampshire snowstorm grounded Reagan, who hoped to be at a campaign fund-raiser in Chicago. An amplified telephone hookup made it possible for Reagan to communicate with his wife and some two hundred supporters in Chicago. Press members were aghast when they heard Nancy Reagan say to her husband: "I wish you could be here to see all these beautiful white people."

United Press reported that even Nancy was surprised at what she had said, and that she paled slightly and said, "Beautiful black and white people." Later she said, "I'm so sorry, I didn't mean it."

In August 1980, Reagan finally tried to meet his race problem head-on. He went before the convention of the National Urban League to argue that he was not "the caricatured conservative" who is "antipoor and antiblack." Reagan attacked those who spoke of black inferiority, saying that all blacks needed was "opportunity." Then he used a tactic that had served him well through the years: he quoted a well-liked Democrat. He used precisely the words Senator Edward M. Kennedy had used at this Urban League convention to spell out black America's three top priorities: "Jobs, jobs, jobs."

Reagan won applause from this middle-class black audience when he said he was going to make the economic pie bigger so blacks could have a bigger piece. But by September Reagan found himself in trouble again when Patricia Roberts Harris, the secretary of health and human services, quoted an editorial from the newspaper of the Invisible Empire, Knights of the Ku Klux Klan, asserting that Reagan was the Klan's preferred candidate and that "the Republican platform reads as if it were written by a Klansman."

At that time it must have been obvious to Reagan that he was not going to get a lot of support in black America. But he couldn't have cared less.

There are, as I think about it, three ways to change the policies of America, to "repeal" the legislation of another president, another era, without a single vote being cast in a single committee of the Congress. The first, which is long-range, is to alter the American mind-set. In his inaugural addresses and fireside chats FDR worked at this, exhorting Americans to "put their faith once more in the forgotten man at the bottom of the economic pyramid." Reagan used his television speeches to try to convince Americans that tax policies that favored the rich would enrich the poor.

A second way to change this society profoundly is to alter the makeup of the Supreme Court, which decides who can do what constitutionally. Roosevelt tried to pack the high tribunal, to his regret. Reagan packed the Supreme Court, to the certain future regret of a majority of Americans.

The third and fastest way to repeal the legislative past can be called executive sabotage. No president in my memory ever used this tactic as ruthlessly and successfully as Reagan. Nixon had shown the way by putting a right-wing fox named Howard Phillips in the chicken coop called the War on Poverty, previously headed with compassion and distinction by Sarge Shriver. Phillips did so well at dismantling the Office of Economic Opportunity that the gap between black and white family incomes, which had been closing dramatically, began to widen again to the tragic proportions of 1990.

Nixon was a timid user of executive sabotage compared with Reagan. Reagan brought in a South Carolina dentist, James B. Edwards, as secretary of the Department of Energy. While Edwards and others were in office, pollution and an indifference to safety got so bad that all the reactors capable of producing materials needed to recharge U.S. nuclear warheads had to be shut down. Admiral James Watkins, the secretary of energy, in 1989 began a thirty-year cleanup that nuclear experts say will cost "hundreds of billions of dollars."

A literal army of Reagan aides got into trouble, either because they were defiant of environmental and other laws passed by Congress or simply because they saw a governmental post of power as a passport to riches.

Remember Edwin Meese III, Reagan's attorney general; William Bradford Reynolds III, Reagan's head of the Civil Rights Division of the Justice Department; Clarence Pendleton, Jr., the late black head of the U.S. Commission on Civil Rights? These were people chosen to run the clocks back in terms of civil rights, racial equality, affirmative action, and just about everything else that had been achieved in three decades.

James Watt became a national joke as secretary of the interior, resigning and becoming the butt of other jokes when it was revealed that he had banked hundreds of thousands of dollars after a call to Samuel Pierce, the secretary of Housing and Urban Development (HUD).

Pierce seemed for years the most innocuous of the black appointees. He just sat voicelessly over the destruction of programs for low-income housing, watching the numbers of homeless Americans grow to dismaying proportions. Those who ridiculed him as "Silent Sam" had no idea that he also presided over a great scandal in which money intended to provide housing for poor and middle-class Americans was funneled into the bank accounts of hustling Republicans. A judge and jury eventually will decide what kind of Reagan cabinet member Pierce really was.

There were many ways in which I got a fair chance to decide what kind of president Reagan was. None was more important or revealing of Reagan than my observations as a member of Washington's Gridiron Club. This is a group of high-profile journalists who, since 1895, have had the audacity to ask the president, vice president, chief justice, and assorted public servants to come to a yearly white-tie dinner where they will be insulted in song and dance.

Ronald and Nancy Reagan never missed a Gridiron dinner. Reagan was at home no matter how biting the lyrics about him. I remember how heartily he laughed when we brought a member of the club onstage, posing as Budget Director David Stockman, to sing to our audience the following lyrics to the tune of "Carolina in the Morning":

Nothing eases tensions like reducing widows' pensions in the morning.
Nothing could be sweeter than to beat a welfare cheater as a warning.
For the hungry children knocking on my door,
I'll have a balanced diet ready by 'eighty-four.
Oh, what fun to swing the ax while easing up the income tax
For yo' folks.
Gather round the guillotine and watch me being really mean
To po' folks.
If I had Aladdin's lamp for only a day,
I'd make a wish and here's what I'd say:
Freeze my heart to zero so I'll be my Ronnie's hero
Every morning.

Reagan laughed heartily at each Gridiron dinner, but he was not amused when some of us kept reminding Americans that his vice president, George Bush, had accused him of engaging in "voodoo economics" when he promised that he would reduce taxes by more than two hundred billion dollars a year, increase spending on the military by over a trillion dollars over five years, and still balance the budget in 1983. Quite naturally, since I was one of the few columnists writing those things, I was not a candidate for an invitation to dinner at the White House.

If I am lucky enough to get old and sit around in a rocking chair telling my grandchildren and great-grandchildren about my career as a journalist, I shall tell them that I was never prouder than in those days of 1981 and 1982 when I kept sticking it to a riches-seeking president who was making already-miserable circumstances almost intolerable for America's poor people.

I know that my grandchildren will not remember, or even understand, that as the lines of hungry people grew longer in city after city, Reagan was moving to wipe out 340,000 public-service jobs, claiming that they were "dead-end jobs" and thus not worthy of the people who were desperate to feed and shelter their families within some reasonable parameters of self-esteem. They will have no way of recalling that Reagan was, in the first months of a terrible recession, forcing a million poor people off the food stamp rolls, reducing medical-care funds for the poor and for impoverished pregnant women and newborn babies, and trying to cut the federal contribution to the education of youngsters in public schools.

But I shall tell my grandchildren that I was one of the few journalists in the land to write bluntly that Reagan's agenda "is neither fair nor humane, but cruelty covered up by glib cliches."

As unemployment grew dramatically, so did the length of the lines at the soup kitchens. The steel mills were operating at less than 60 percent of capacity. Assembly lines of the great American auto factories were shutting down. Farmers were facing foreclosures. Americans were losing their homes. The housing industry was in acute distress. So by March of 1982 I would write:

> Almost everybody in America seems to know that the country is in an economic mess that borders on a great depression — except Reagan.
>
> The President dismisses as "sob sisters" those Americans of every political stripe who see calamity in his budget proposals which would add perhaps half a *trillion* dollars to the national debt in just four years. It is difficult to determine whether Mr. Reagan is absurdly stubborn, a slow learner who has landed a job that is above his level of competency, or just an ideologue imprisoned in a maze of right-wing cliches.

I was fuming when the president talked about how the newspapers were loaded with want ads for jobs for people who really wanted to work — a suggestion that anybody on unemployment rolls was just a lazy bum. I asked the White House to tell that to the 4,508 people who had lined up in Hempstead, New York, to apply for 296 jobs ranging from dishwasher to desk clerk at a new hotel. I asked him to tell that to the 11 million Americans who were jobless and were desperately eager to find work, or to the 700,000-plus families that had been thrown into poverty since Reagan took office.

But I was learning that there were perils to the business of criticizing a president of the United States who had been elected by a landslide.

I knew when the election returns were in that it would not be any fun being a columnist in America, except for those conservatives who suddenly had become the darlings of the nation's editors and publishers. Reagan had been in office less than four months when I realized that things might be more difficult than I had expected.

In one situation the editor was honest enough to tell his readers that he was canceling my column because of my criticism of Reagan. Richard Sept, the managing editor of the *Daily Tidings* in Ashland, Oregon, wrote Kenneth Reiley, the sales manager of Field Newspaper Syndicate, announcing that he was canceling my column and that of Erma Bombeck. Sept first cited the poor economy as the reason to cancel Bombeck. But in explaining the cancellation of my column, he wrote: "The economy played a minor role in this decision. Our primary reason for canceling is a sense that Rowan has recently lost touch with reality since Reagan's election."

Remember, now, that there can't be a handful of black people among the readers of the *Daily Tidings*. But the readers of that newspaper came to my defense. Every now and then, when the critical mail gets heavy because of something I've written, I pick up that file relating to Ashland, Oregon, and chuckle. For example:

> And so it was that on the very day that Reagan first entered the White House normally sharp-eyed and keen-witted Rowan suddenly became a columnist wearing blinders.
>   A remarkable transformation indeed.

And another subscriber:

> Perhaps we should lend an ear to Mr. Rowan, who speaks to and for all of us when he brings warning that hope is dying at the same time that drugs and weapons are proliferating among large segments of the U.S. population.

And another:

> Is Rowan upsetting because he does not go into the soft shoe yassuh boss routine? If he'd tone down his writing and "behave himself like a good nigger" would you reconsider?

The thing that came through to me from all those letters was that the American people want to read and hear differences of viewpoint, as expressed extremely well by a man named William Ashworth:

> You ask for comments on your decision to drop columnist Carl Rowan from the paper because of his strident anti-Reagan stance. Very well, here is a comment.

I think the decision is abominable. . . .

It is the duty of the journalistic community to present both sides of any issue — the seamy underside as well as the glittering surface. Rowan has been a remarkably consistent and efficient voice pointing out the seamy underside of Reaganomics. At times he has been the only voice. You should not punish him for his consistency and courage; you should not deprive us of a chance to agree or disagree with him, as is our wont.

Somebody once accused Mark Twain of "preaching." His response was, "I only do it because the rest of the clergy seems to be on vacation." Carl Rowan must not be deprived of his voice because the rest of the clergy is on vacation.

I am proud to say that in 1990 the *Daily Tidings* is still running the Rowan column.

This may strike you as terribly anti-intellectual, or a Rowan version of voodoo, but it is a reality that discerning black people can smell a racist a mile away. Those who have gone through decades of suffering the slings and barbs of bigotry have a sixth sense that tells them who in white America is a friend, and who a foe. Black people know that sometimes their greatest enemy is not an Orval Faubus who throws little black schoolchildren to an Arkansas mob, or a George Wallace who stands in the doorway of the University of Alabama, trying to keep blacks out, but white people of power who would never utter a racist sentence in public, yet who quietly and privately will do everything they can to keep black people as the slave class in this society.

Anger over moral issues is the mother and father of self-righteousness. I did not have to look far to find anger. Reagan and his Justice Department and other appointees found ways to keep me outraged. There was Reagan's reluctance to extend the Voting Rights Act of 1965, which guaranteed a measure of political power for millions of blacks. There was his attempt to give tax-exempt status to Bob Jones University and the Goldsboro Christian Schools, institutions that practiced racial discrimination. And then the restoring of tax-exempt status to the Prince Edward Academy in Farmville, Virginia — an academy that was created to educate white children after all public schools were closed to avoid desegregation. "How," I asked myself, "could any president ignore the fact that he was giving a tax subsidy to whites who had left black children bereft of education for years?" Then Reagan tried to wipe out Legal Services for the poor.

One of my most memorable periods of the Reagan years was the time of celebration of the two hundredth anniversary of the U.S. Constitution in 1987. The Gannett Corporation people at the flagship station, WUSA-TV, asked me to host and help produce a one-hour special that would help Americans to understand what the Constitution really means. With a marvelous producer, Jeanne Bowers, we developed a program called "Searching for Justice: Three American Stories." Stories about a woman in Ohio who had been on death row; about Norma McCorvey, the real-life Texas woman who had made the history books as "Jane Roe" in the landmark abortion case; and about the legal struggle to desegregate colleges in the South and Southwest.

The program became a sensation. On the night that it was to be broadcast it produced the two lead stories on "CBS Evening News with Dan Rather." First, there was the interview that I had done with Supreme Court Justice Thurgood Marshall in which he rated American presidents, calling Reagan "the worst." The White House, the Justice Department, some other justices, and a lot of editors were stunned, because no sitting justice had ever before spoken so frankly, publicly, about a sitting president. Second, there was the incredibly emotional scene in which McCorvey told me that contrary to the story spread wide over the years, she had not become pregnant as the result of being raped. "Jane Roe" had become pregnant in a liaison of passion, and she had said rape only because she thought that might work better to establish a woman's right to an abortion.

Reagan tried to dismiss Marshall's rating of him with humor. He suggested that Marshall was too old to know what he was saying.

I then did a one-hour TV documentary called "Thurgood Marshall: The Man," which won the Alfred I. duPont–Columbia University Silver Baton, one of the two most coveted awards in American television.

The impact of those two shows made 1987 one of the most glorious years a reporter could ever have.

*　　　*　　　*

It was Saturday noon, December 5, 1987, and I had just been elected president of the Gridiron Club, that once all-male, lily-white bastion of journalism.

My colleagues were having fun with the fact that the Gridiron Club was passing a racial milestone — its first black president in its 103 years. We exchanged many jokes, but no one was gauche enough to write about it.

I learned early in my membership, after getting about five hundred elbows in my ribs from more senior members rushing to the front of the chorus at the celebrated spring dinner, that it means something to journalists to be able to speak lines, sing songs, try to dance, make fools of themselves in any Thespian manner, when their editors and publishers are in the audience.

More important, perhaps, was the opportunity for journalists to solidify relationships with talk show hosts and sponsors, to "pay off" their sources of leaks, by inviting corporate leaders, movie stars, cabinet members, to the only dinner I know of where no amount of money can buy you a ticket. You have to be *invited* to the Gridiron dinner.

But the active journalists in the Gridiron Club know that the ultimate payoff is becoming president, showcasing your newspaper, sitting for hours beside the president of the United States, giving the traditional "Speech in the Dark" in which you can display your wit and your disdain for the buffoons who are wasting the public's money or violating the people's trust.

I, who had written at least a hundred columns excoriating Ronald Reagan, was going to have the "privilege" of sitting beside him during a long, long night.

"Dear God, what can I talk about with this man?" I asked myself as I was driving home after my election.

I recalled, that cold December Saturday, that Reagan had been to seven straight Gridiron dinners, making him one of the few national leaders who had not bugged out. Lyndon Johnson had concocted any number of excuses to avoid the satire, the sometimes cutting criticisms, that are in the songs, dialogue, and even dances of a Gridiron affair.

I had my previously expressed hostilities toward the Reagans, but I also had my responsibilities as Gridiron president. I knew that no matter what gripes I had, the spring dinner audience would want to give a warm good-bye to the Reagans, who promptly notified me that they would be delighted to attend.

I asked Mrs. Reagan to sing a farewell song, but after we Gridironers had sung a good-bye song loaded with political bite. This woman, who had once offended me with that remark about "all these beautiful white people," was warm and friendly as she met me and other Gridironers at the Capital Hilton for a rehearsal of what we all knew would be a showstopper. I watched her with rapidly vanishing uneasiness.

She rehearsed her number four times over for about forty-five minutes, kissed pianist Les Karr, and gave me a glowing good-bye.

On Saturday, March 26, 1988, the Reagans arrived at 7:04 P.M. in a driving rain. They got out of the White House limousine wrapless, he in the traditional white tie and tails, she wearing a trademark red gown.

As we walked up the steps and took the trek toward the head table, the president began to tell me a story of the Secret Service, and "shooting from the hip," but he got interrupted quickly.

Suddenly the orchestra was playing "Hail to the Chief," the guests were standing to give rousing applause, and Reagan was taking a place on my right while, across the lectern, Mrs. Reagan stood on Viv's left. Stood because, in more than a century of Gridiron tradition, no one had been able to sit down until a Gridiron quartet sang "There's music in the air," and the Gridiron president gave his "Speech in the Dark."

"You see, these FBI agents, cops, and others drop to their knees to fire at criminals," Reagan continued his story, "but the Secret Service guys stand up so their bodies can protect a president or other target of assassination. They shoot from their hips. . . ."

Many Gridiron presidents have had humorists, even writers for Johnny Carson and Bob Hope, conjure up funny lines. But I had written my own speech, choosing to ridicule the "first black in history" obsession of white journalists and to deal in light sarcasm with my serious concerns and outrages regarding the Reagan years.

I broke all the Gridiron traditions by letting Reagan and the other guests sit and listen to my "Speech in the Dark" in the light, a bow to one of my teacher's warnings that smart guys should be "seen as well as heard."

I told the Reagans and others that I was pleased to have them present "to help the Gridiron Club make history. For the first time in one hundred and three years, this club has a president who is . . . from McMinnville, Tennessee."

I turned to Reagan and told him that my Gridiron presidency was exactly like his. Every time I took a nap, some young whippersnapper tried to stage a coup.

"That, Mr. President," I said, "is why I'm going to double the support I've given you in my columns over the last seven years."

I noted that Reagan guffawed above the laughter of the audience.

Charlie McDowell of the *Richmond Times-Dispatch* had only told me that "Reagan is a talker." He didn't warn me that Reagan would talk to me during the other closely scheduled chores that I had to do.

"Mr. President!" boomed the voice of Emory.

I was supposed to stand and say, as Gridiron history decreed: "Mr. Alan S. Emory of the *Watertown* [New York] *Daily Times*, the music chairman of the Gridiron Club!" But as Emory was giving his cue, Reagan had me by the arm and was saying, "Now, about this business of me calling Ollie North and Admiral John Poindexter heroes. . . ."

As politely as I could, I silenced the president for the moments it took me to turn the audience over to Emory. When I sat down, Reagan was still in midsentence: ". . . I meant that they had been military heroes, but not necessarily heroes in their handling of this weapons-to-Iran matter."

"Well, that's quite a difference, Mr. President, and I'm not sure Americans understand it," I said.

"I want you to know that I never thought I was exchanging arms to Iran for American hostages," Reagan said, "and some people did some things without my authority."

"Isn't it true that Mrs. Reagan thinks North and Poindexter and perhaps Bill Casey [the late CIA director and the leader of the 1984 campaign in which Reagan won the presidency] co-opted, or took over, your presidency?"

"She's not happy with any of them," Reagan said.

I kept glancing at the table filled with my guests, Lee Iacocca from Chrysler Corporation, my editor Fredrica Friedman from Little, Brown and Company, my sons Carl and Jeff, and daughter Barbara, and I could see that they were wondering what Reagan and I were talking about. Then the tone of the conversation eased.

"Carl, I need to take a leak. Do I have to go to that toilet that's a mile away?"

"Mr. President," I said, "there's a bathroom just outside the door."

"Let's go," he said, and as we got up there was a shifting of security agents that I thought could only be noticed by someone who had been in government and spent years dealing with the Secret Service. Some thirty White House aides slithered toward that room.

Reagan and I walked into "my reception room" and I found that it had been transformed into a bastion of technology that could launch World War III in seconds.

"You all know Ambassador Rowan," Reagan said, revealing that he remembered parts of his briefing.

He went into the john, came out, and said: "It took me years to learn that you Gridironers call this 'the piss break.' "

We then returned to the dining room, and Reagan, sipping his wine, began telling me that "You never really understood me on this business of racism."

"Mr. President," I said, "I have never written a column criticizing you that was based on personal or political opposition. I have written every column out of a profound belief that you didn't understand America's racial problems, and that you rejected the black Americans who could help you in favor of the blacks who would become sellouts, quislings, traitors."

Reagan replied: "I tried hard to win friendship among blacks, but I couldn't do it. I talked to black leaders after my election in 1980, and they went out and criticized me in horrible ways."

"And that's why you went almost eight years refusing to talk to the acknowledged black leaders of America?" I asked.

"They attacked me at the outset, so I said to hell with 'em," Reagan replied.

"Sir," I said, "I've criticized you in my columns because I believe that any president of all the people must talk to all the people and their leaders."

"You know something?" Reagan said, with a long pause. "I should have talked to *you* seven years ago."

Reagan seemed to sip his wine a little faster and to talk less. As Mrs. Reagan left the head table to go onstage, he said, "She seems nervous as hell," and in the damnedest segue I can recall, said, "She wanted me to tell you that we are not the enemies of poor and black people."

I had been drinking my wine a little faster, too, and was emboldened to say what I really felt.

"Mr. President," I said, "I know that you and she want to believe that. But the people you have named to the Supreme Court, the appeals courts, the district courts, are not the friends of black people, or my children, or poor black pregnant women, or anyone who is needy in America. That is the rap against your presidency."

Reagan reddened, then he pointed to our left down the head table to where his then national security adviser Colin Powell was sitting.

"Now there," Reagan said, "is one of the smartest black men I ever knew."

I got the message. Reagan was saying that as the first president to put a black man in so critical a job, he didn't have to argue about his commitment to racial equality. I knew that, for this Gridiron dinner, Reagan was ready to end our serious discussions.

We Gridironers knew that we could use wicked song and dance to singe any president, but the Reagans, Kennedys, and others who had wit and style would always win any Gridiron dinner jousts. Still, we sang our farewell jabs at the Reagans:

> *Thanks for the memories*
> *Of Stockman and Jim Watt,*
> *That Iran-Contra plot,*
> *Of Ollie and Bill Casey,*
> *The diversions you forgot . . .*
> *Oh, thank you, so much.*
>
> *Thanks for the memories*
> *Of Nancy playing Rose*
> *In second-handed clothes,*

> *And banishing Al Haig*
> *And bloodying up*
> *Don Regan's nose . . .*
> *Oh, thank you, so much.*

Mrs. Reagan came onstage to great applause and gave a fetching response:

> *Thanks for the memories*
> *Of all the times we had,*
> *The happy and the sad.*
> *Looking back Don Regan*
> *Doesn't even seem so bad.*
> *Oh, thank you, so much.*
>
> *Thanks for the memories*
> *Of all the whole press corps.*
> *At times I cursed and swore.*
> *You sometimes were a headache*
> *But you never were a bore.*
> *I thank you. Bye-bye.*

As the dinner guests gave roaring applause, she stepped to the mike for this encore:

> *So, thanks for the memories.*
> *It's time to say good-bye.*
> *Oh, how the time does fly.*
> *Ronnie's loved these past eight years*
> *And so I confess have I.*
> *So thank you. Bye-bye!*

A few days after the dinner I reported a bit of my conversation with Reagan to Charlie McDowell and Allan Cromley of the *Daily Oklahoman.*

"It's not over," said Cromley. "You'll surely get a private invitation from Reagan."

A few weeks went by before I got a call from the White House asking if I would have lunch privately with the president on May 9.

It was an extraordinary occasion during which I saw the many facets, mind twists, and vulnerabilities of a president whose views and actions dominated American life in the 1980s. A president whose appointments and policies will affect the American mind-set, and legal posture, on issues like abortion and civil liberties well into the next century.

When I was taken to Reagan, he said: "I hear you and Howard Baker [brand-new White House chief of staff] were bunkmates in midshipman school in World War Two."

"Platoon mates, sir — two of the luckiest guys ever to come out of Tennessee."

"I don't have any press people watching over this luncheon, which is just between you and me, but I know Howard would like to join us."

"I can't think of anyone I'd rather have join us than my old Navy buddy," I replied.

Baker walked up with a big smile on his face, and we sat down to a bowl of corn soup, some raw carrots, and a few balls of melon.

"This Reagan sure knows how to get even," I thought, as I surveyed the victuals at hand.

Then, out of nowhere, he hit me with a punch that reminded me that presidents watched the television show "Agronsky and Company cum Inside Washington," which I had been on for nineteen years, but they never remembered who said what.

Reagan started to scold me gently for saying on TV that his wife had consulted an astrologer and decided that he would be sworn in as governor of California at precisely one minute after midnight.

"I was not the one who mentioned the midnight swearing in," I replied. "I didn't even know that you were sworn in at a minute past midnight. You've got me confused with someone else."

Reagan sniffled, blinked his eyes several times, and said: "Well, then, I'm sorry. I got it wrong."

Reagan was "bleeding" over "revelations" by his ousted chief of staff, Donald Regan, that Mrs. Reagan used an astrologer to decide the time of important presidential events and had kept him virtually inactive after his prostate surgery because the stars weren't in the proper alignment.

"Dammit," said Reagan, "most of these things are absolutely untrue. And, dammit, I'm not going to stand by and let anybody railroad my wife.

"She didn't fire Don Regan. He wasn't fired, as a matter of fact. He had said several months before that he just had to get back to private life. Then, when this Iran-Contra thing came on, he said, 'You know, I don't think I should jump ship now.'

"Regan set the date of his resignation, so I had to find someone to replace him. When the story leaked that Baker would replace him, he became incensed. He thought Nancy was the leaker. Wrong. I telephoned him to apologize for the leak, but he wouldn't take my call."

Reagan's outrage over Regan's remarks just rolled out, like mud from a gully washer. Asked about Regan's claim that Nancy pressured him to fire the late CIA director William Casey, Reagan scrunched up his nose, fought to get air up it, and replied: "Never happened." Knowing that Casey could never again function as the nation's top spy, Reagan said, "We went to him [in the hospital] with the proposal that he resign as CIA director, but with an assurance that when he was able to resume work there'd be a post for him here in the White House. Mrs. Casey was happy with that."

He sipped soup, talked about the benefits of eating raw carrots, then eased into the real reason for inviting me to lunch.

"Carl, I suggested this [meeting] when we were together [at the Gridiron dinner] because I had a feeling often that you didn't have the straight thing on me and racism and so forth. . . . Carl, I was on the side of civil rights years before anyone ever used the term 'civil rights.' "

I said I knew it couldn't be pleasing to have black leaders describe his administration as "eight years of disaster for the civil rights movement."

Reagan didn't eat another bite as he went through a long speech about how his administration had prosecuted successfully more job, housing, and other discrimination cases "than all the other administrations put together." This was so erroneous as to be laughable, but it was obvious that the president believed the figures put before him by Justice Department and other sycophants.

I listened to him tell me how, as governor of California, he had been the best friend minorities ever had. I heard about how his Catholic father was the victim of "extreme prejudice." I listened to his story of a hotel refusing to let a black member of his football team stay there, and how he took the black to spend the night at his home. I just sipped soup as he went on and on about how Meese and Reynolds and their Justice Department were powerful foes of racial discrimination.

My soup gone, I said: "Well, you know I told you at that [Gridiron] dinner that there was not one iota of personal malice in any column that I wrote. But . . . you went down to kick off your presidential campaign in Philadelphia, Mississippi, where the three civil rights workers had been killed [in 1964]. In the view of a lot of people . . . that was an affront."

"I don't even remember that I did that," Reagan replied.

As I left the White House I told myself that that single sentence exposed the essence of Ronald Wilson Reagan. He often didn't know what he was doing, and he rarely remembered what he had done.

But as Reagan's eight years wound to an end, I looked at the record and the legacy of this extraordinary man. I saw that:

• Under voodoo economics, "fiscal conservative" Reagan had tripled the national debt, saddling each American family with an obligation of $48,000 as of 1990, transforming the United States from a creditor to a debtor nation. The annual interest on that debt equaled $2,400 for every American child.

• Reagan had, from fiscal 1981 through fiscal 1988, increased the defense budget by 30.6 percent, while reducing funds for programs to help low-income Americans by 2.6 percent.

• While Reagan had failed in his efforts to abolish the Department of Education, he curtailed destructively the federal government's contribution to public education. Education's share of the federal budget fell from 2.5 to 1.7 percent, and the federal share of education spending fell from 10.8 percent in 1980 to 8.7 percent in 1988. Some congressmen fought off Reagan's attempts to virtually wipe out federal funds for education; still, with inflation factored in, Reagan cut federal funds for education by two billion dollars a year from 1981 to 1988.

• Reagan almost killed Lyndon Johnson's dream of higher education for all qualified blacks, Hispanics, and poor whites. The American Council on Education (ACE) reported that in 1988 only 23 percent of low-income black males were enrolled in college, compared with 37.2 percent thirteen years earlier. Reagan's policies wiped out much of what was a burgeoning middle class among blacks and Hispanics. An ACE report stated that "By 1988, the college participation rate of middle-income blacks had fallen to 36 per cent from 53 per cent in 1976, with black males hit most severely. Corresponding rates for Hispanics were 46 per cent in 1988 compared to 53 per cent in 1976."

• I looked at Census Bureau data, analyzed by the nonpartisan, nonprofit Center on Budget and Policy Priorities in the nation's capital, and learned that under Reagan, the rich got richer and the poor got poorer. In 1988 the wealthiest one-fifth of all U.S. families received 44 percent of the national family income, the largest share ever recorded since the Census Bureau began collecting such data in 1947. The poorest one-fifth of American families received 4.6 percent of the national family income, the *lowest* share since 1954.

• I saw that the poverty rate for black high school graduates had become four times as high as the poverty rate for white high school graduates, and the infant mortality rate for blacks in the United States was worse than that in Cuba, Bulgaria, and Czechoslovakia.

I knew that I could never absolve Reagan of personal blame for what had happened to my country. I also knew that my reasons went far beyond issues of race, economics, education. It was becoming clear that his most enduring legacy would be felt in the nation's judicial system.

During his eight years in office Reagan made 360 lifetime appointments to the federal bench, including the appointment of three Supreme Court justices (Sandra Day O'Connor, Antonin Scalia, and Anthony M. Kennedy), the elevation of William H. Rehnquist to chief justice, and the appointment of nearly half the full-time appeals court judges.

From their earliest days in Washington, the president and legal advisers like Ed Meese made clear that one of their major goals was to achieve a more conservative judiciary — one that was "strict constructionist," passive on civil rights, tough on crime, conservative on social issues like abortion, pornography, and school prayer.

The rightward shift in the courts started slowly, picked up steam as Reagan appointees filled the federal bench, and reached a high point after Reagan left office.

One of the most obvious areas of its impact was civil rights. A hint of what was to come occurred in 1984 when the Supreme Court, in the Grove City case involving women's rights, accepted the administration's position that substantially limited the application of civil rights laws barring discrimination in the use of federal funds by institutions. (Four years later Congress overrode a presidential veto and enacted legislation that effectively overturned the Grove City decision.)

The judicial turnaround in civil rights hit in full force during the Supreme Court's 1988–89 term. In *City of Richmond* v. *Croson*, the Court struck down, 6 to 3, an affirmative action plan that set aside 30 percent of city construction contracts in Richmond for minority-owned businesses.

That was followed by a series of rulings that undermined federal laws against employment discrimination aimed at women and minorities. In one, the Court said that minorities who sue for racial harassment on the job can no longer use an 1866 civil rights law. Others shifted the burden of proof on job-bias cases from employer to employee and opened the way for whites to challenge court-ordered affirmative action even when the challenges came long after acceptance of the Court remedies.

All of these were decided by 5 to 4 margins, with the majority consisting of the three Reagan appointees, plus Rehnquist and Byron White. In one of the cases, Justice Harry Blackmun wrote in dissent, "One wonders whether the majority still believes that race discrimination — or, more accurately, race discrimination against non-whites — is a problem in our society, or even remembers that it ever was."

Abortion was another area in which the Reagan Court turned back the clock. While the decisive case of *Webster* v. *Reproductive Health Services* in 1989 did not overturn *Roe* v. *Wade*, the Court upheld new limits on a woman's constitutional right to an abortion and opened the way to further legal challenges.

In a number of other cases, again often decided by narrow majorities led by Reagan appointees, the Supreme Court stripped or weakened individual rights. It upheld drug testing for certain government workers and ruled that states can execute murderers who are mentally retarded and those who were as young as sixteen when they committed their crimes. The power of police and prosecutors was expanded, while protections for defendants were weakened, including the "Miranda rule" that requires police to advise suspects of their rights. The High Court also gave prison authorities broad power to force mentally ill inmates to take antipsychotic drugs against their will.

When Earl Warren was chief justice, the Supreme Court strongly affirmed the power of federal courts to implement whatever actions were necessary to remedy situations in which majority rule stripped some individuals of constitutional rights. But as justices appointed by Presidents Nixon and Reagan moved the High Court to the right, both judicially and socially, it cut back on that vital authority of the federal courts. That is a devastating setback to millions who depend on the judiciary to safeguard their interests — and to all who believe that the rights of every citizen deserve to be protected in a democratic society.

The record made it clear to me that, for all his selective amnesia and his personal charm, Ronald Reagan knew precisely what he was doing to America and Americans. I would never find reason to forgive him.

CHAPTER TWENTY

The Shot Heard Round My World

THOSE SPRING DAYS of 1988, when I was a "president" and was hobnobbing with *the* president, were like dessert after a good long meal. Then fate came close to wiping out every honor I ever received and destroying me personally.

I told you at the very start of this book of my fear, and the frightful circumstances under which I shot in the wrist an intruder who was trying forcibly to enter my house. I have not told you of the many and profound ways a person's life can be changed by such an unexpected incident and the cruelties that followed it.

I had never in my life imagined that I would have to shoot another human being — not even one of those who frequently phoned in death threats. I had had, since arrival in Washington in 1961, an old .22 rifle that my boys and I had used to shoot tin cans off fences in Minnesota. Even when Carl Jr. left a revolver at my house for protection against the telephone nuts, I figured I would always find a way to safety without shooting anyone.

That is, until that moment on the morning of June 14, 1988, when Ben N. Smith, a strapping young man from the wealthy suburb of Bethesda, Maryland, tried to run through me and into my house, where I thought my wife would be in danger.

I still feel a sense of shock when I remember closing the patio door that Smith was trying to enter, putting down a security stick, putting down the gun, and walking out the northeast door where my wife and a policeman named Jasper Chatman were talking to a very frightened young white woman, who also had scaled my fence but had been abandoned by Smith when he thought the police were coming.

"I just shot a guy around there," I said, pointing toward the out-of-view area of my bedroom and family room.

Moments later, a tall white man walked around the corner, holding his bleeding wrist. He walked past the police and dipped his injured arm in my swimming pool. While the cops looked on in perplexity, he lay down beside the Jacuzzi, where Miss Laura Bachman, his companion, massaged him. Then he got up and *got back into my Jacuzzi.*

"What is this?" my wife complained.

"Maybe the heat will be good for him," a cop replied.

Officer Chatman had made an emergency call for an ambulance, but as so often was the case in the District of Columbia, nothing happened. Chatman called again, and this time got a rescue unit from the fire department and an ambulance. I went to the Fessenden Street gate and saw six police cruisers in front of my house.

About 3:30 A.M. a detective arrived. He showed me that a piece of the lock on the sliding door to my family room was freshly broken off. There were indications that someone had stood on the side of a ladder that was lying on the patio next to my bedroom window, which the intruder was trying to open when I was awakened.

After the police took Smith and Bachman away for booking on charges of unlawful entry, I continued to chat with the policemen, some of whom had been to my house many times because of intruders or death threats. I figured I was the victim, so I didn't need to clam up or hide behind the Miranda rule.

About 4:00 A.M. one of the officers said, "That gun could be a problem, Mr. Rowan."

"Why?" I asked.

"It apparently is not registered."

"Oh, my God," I said to myself, beginning to remember that the gun had some special registration or exemption from registration because it belonged to my son Carl Jr., a former U.S. marshal and FBI agent. I needed my son to remind me of the details, but he and his family were away on vacation.

Just before 5:00 A.M. I lay down to see if I could sleep for an hour, but this was impossible, so I got up and dressed for a tennis doubles match at the home of my friend Donald Brown. As I arrived I announced that there had been a terrible mess at my house and "I had to shoot a guy."

"I sure as hell hope the gun was registered," said Don.

"It's legal," I replied, then proceeded to humiliate myself on the tennis court. I couldn't hit the back end of a bull.

But I should have stayed on the tennis court. I got home to find that dozens of newspeople had called, and some already were staking out my house. I decided, foolishly perhaps, to talk to all of them. I still nurtured the illusion that I, as the victim of a crime, had nothing to hide or worry about. The following day I learned how naïve I had been.

I picked up the *Washington Times* and saw my picture at the top of page one with a big headline saying, ROWAN SHOOTS TEEN-AGE INTRUDER.

COLUMNIST SHOOTS TEEN SKINNY-DIPPER blared the headline in the *New York Post*.

A disc jockey was calling me "Rambo Rowan," and Wesley Pruden of the *Washington Times* was comparing me with Bernhard Goetz, ignoring the distinction that while Goetz went out with a gun looking for someone to shoot, I was fast asleep in my own bed when trouble came to me.

The first reporting was so erroneous that it pained my heart as a journalist. The public was led to believe that I went out to my pool, dragged a poor white "kid" out, and shot him. I learned painfully that a lie is, indeed, halfway round the world before the truth gets its boots on.

But I still was confident — again naïvely — that the truth would emerge and that no one would fault me for protecting my home and my wife. But I failed to understand or factor in several realities:

1. The National Rifle Association, which considered me one of its most worrisome foes, would sucker the media into swallowing the NRA argument that I was a hypocrite to write in favor of gun control when a gun was on my property.

2. That my blackness and my "celebrity" would send the media into a feeding frenzy.

3. That a *Washington Post* editorial writer would inexplicably

engage in a not-very-subtle campaign to pressure District officials to put me on trial on gun possession charges.

4. That I would become the focus of new and furious debates about all gun control laws, enacted or proposed.

The progun zealots in the NRA had a field day. They sold the line, pushed by the *Washington Times* and many other newspapers, that I was a "liberal writer, TV panelist, and former ambassador who has advocated a total ban of private ownership of handguns."

I had, indeed, favored a *national* law that would deny firearms to all but law enforcement people, and I still believe that that is the only way we will ever stop kooks and crazies from going on murder rampages. But we did not, and do not, have a national law of any consequence. I had never endorsed the D.C. gun law because I knew, first, that it was meaningless when the city was awash with handguns that District criminals and others could purchase legally just by driving into Virginia or Maryland and, second, that this supposedly "toughest gun law in the nation" refused to deal with the practice of law enforcement people's taking their service revolvers and other guns home when they retired. (It was a "secret," till now, that just before Police Chief Maurice T. Turner retired in the summer of 1989 he got a subordinate to register for him a Smith & Wesson .38-caliber revolver, a Remington rifle, and two sixteen-shot Glock 9-millimeter automatic weapons.)

The District gun law was a joke in the sense that almost every ex-lawman had an arsenal at his home, and the gun control office was saying that that was the way they wanted it. The District law was and is stupid in its interpretation that the owner of a store may own a gun and use it to kill a holdup man with no legal consequences. But if the owner goes to lunch and his store manager uses the gun to shoot a robber, the manager is to be prosecuted for using "an unregistered firearm" — or so the city prosecutor argued in my case.

So my advocating a national gun control law while permitting my son to keep a weapon in my home-office was not hypocritical. Still, the NRA sold eager enemies of mine a bill of goods, even as it had Senator Steve Symms send me an honorary membership in the NRA and as it asked if it could pay any of my legal expenses.

I was appalled when the NRA used my name to try to persuade

the black citizens of Maryland to vote for repeal of a recently passed law stopping the sale of the cheap and dangerously made handguns known as Saturday night specials. These sleazy NRA characters even suggested that somehow it would help me if the Congress refused to pass a "cooling off" amendment requiring a seven-day wait before a purchaser could take possession of a gun — the Brady measure, named after James Brady, the Reagan aide who was badly wounded in 1981 when John Hinckley, Jr., tried to kill the president. I favored a waiting period that gave authorities time to check up on those who may be mentally ill and out to shoot people at random.

The cowards in the Congress knuckled under to the NRA and refused to pass the Brady measure. But I took great joy out of the fact that even though the NRA spent some seven million dollars, the people of Maryland kept their law against Saturday night specials.

Two mornings after the incident at my house, the *Wall Street Journal* ran an editorial entitled "Frontier Justice," in which it suggested that I, "the famous liberal newspaper columnist and TV commentator," was a "vigilante." The *Washington Times* wrote an editorial lumping me with evangelists Jim Bakker and Jimmy Swaggart — "America's public moralists have been caught committing sins they have decried with fire-and-brimstone intolerance." You'd have thought that I'd sodomized my assailant instead of shooting him.

Some of the self-styled superliberal antigun people turned out to be nuttier than the NRA zealots. Colman McCarthy wrote in the *Washington Post* that I should have used "a baseball bat, a German shepherd, mace or perhaps a wild shriek. . . . Has he [Rowan] never heard of burglar alarms for the front door or barbed wire for the pool fence?"

Maybe McCarthy wants his home to look like Alcatraz with barbed wire and shards of glass on top of the fence, but I don't. And I doubt — slightly — that McCarthy is dumb enough to go at it in the dark with a baseball bat against a teenager who may have the temporary inhuman strength that PCP bestows, or a gun.

The newspaper barrage provoked hundreds of telephone calls daily. Letters came by the thousands.

From Virginia: "Niggers shooting white people! That's something we ain't gonna tolerate in this country."

From D.C.: "If that had been my black kids in David Brinkley's yard, my babies would be dead now."

From Maryland: "What's a nigger doing with a swimming pool and Jacuzzi anyhow?"

But some other letters came in — very interesting ones about Ben Smith from his neighbors. Agnes Portass, age eighty-one, wrote that Smith had harassed her family for years, once throwing two lighted rockets into her shower room. Andrew Nelson wrote that "Ben Smith is a trouble maker" who once had damaged the Nelson home. Maryland cops suggested I get "his juvenile record." I kept waiting for the newspapers and television stations to report on who Ben Smith really was. They never did, letting lie the canard that I had shot a "nice white kid" from the suburbs. In fact, the *Washington Post* ran an article about how "late-night trespassing at swimming pools is common. . . ." The implication was that I had gunned down someone who was merely out on a lark.

I could not believe that in a city where the White House and the media were demanding "zero tolerance" of drug abuse, the media, the U.S. attorney, and the D.C. corporation counsel would take such a permissive, cavalier attitude toward people who violated someone else's property to hold drug parties.

I realized how much my case had polarized the country when I got a letter from James B. Blackistone, Sr., of Hyattsville, Maryland, asking: "Can it be that the United States law is returning to the era of the Dred Scott decision that 'a black man has no rights that a white person is bound to respect'?"

I soon realized, though, that Ben Smith and Laura Bachman were unknowns, and *their* crimes meant nothing to the editors and news directors of America. Carl Rowan was the story — especially a Rowan some thought had been caught with his ethical and legal pants around his ankles. I had to live with grotesque caricatures and with being the victim of a hundred jokes.

"Who are the greatest pool shooters of all time? Willie Mosconi, Minnesota Fats, and Carl Rowan!"

The daughter of the Swedish ambassador whispered to me at an embassy dinner, "I'm coming over for a swim Saturday. I've bought a bulletproof swimsuit."

And at a roast of Senator Bennett Johnston, after Senator Alan Simpson had cut up the Louisianian with wicked wit, Johnston said: "Alan, I thank you for those remarks, and I am duty bound to reciprocate. I'm inviting you to a pool party at Carl Rowan's house. If you get there before I do, just crawl over the fence and wait."

The marvelous thing is that during this torrent of bad publicity, none of my business associates believed that I was anything other than the victim of a criminal intrusion — and a man who did what a man must do under the circumstances.

But you do find out, in cases like this, who your friends and enemies are, and who is a good or bad journalist. James J. Kilpatrick and I have disagreed on a thousand issues over almost two decades, but he bothered to get the facts and write two supportive columns. Godfrey Sperling, Jr., of the *Christian Science Monitor* and Georgie Anne Geyer of the *Chicago Sun-Times* were especially supportive.

And while I cannot remember all the supporters, I remember well the most irresponsible of the journalists. None was worse than Pat Buchanan, who, despite my statements and official evidence to the contrary, printed the lie that Ben Smith "climbed out of Rowan's pool, dripping wet in his underpants, after a midnight swim with his girlfriend, when Rowan wordlessly shot him, and scurried back in the house to hide."

Buchanan then proved that he could sink deeper into untruth and irresponsibility. Noting that I had said, "As long as the authorities leave this society awash in drugs and guns, I will protect my family," Buchanan wrote: "The 'society' Carl Rowan describes as failed is a society Carl Rowan helped to create. The 'authorities' who run Washington are, after all, Marion Barry & Co., Rowan's candidates and Rowan's friends."

Even an irresponsible flamethrower like Buchanan could have taken a couple of minutes to discover that Mayor Barry had never been my "friend" or "candidate" and was in fact plotting to humiliate me with a public arrest, handcuffs, and a two-year prison term.

But Barry was having trouble with Police Chief Maurice Turner, who warned that I ought not be prosecuted and that the city could never convict me; with a superior court judge who would not play his game; and with the fact that Barry himself had accepted a handgun in violation of the District's laws.

After I shot Ben Smith, I realized that the U.S. attorney, Jay B. Stephens, could charge me with a felony of assault with a dangerous weapon. I'd written a lot of columns criticizing President Reagan and Attorney General Ed Meese, and it occurred to me that here was a chance for "the white folks" to get even. But Stephens's office was a model of fairness and professionalism. I told my lawyers, Raoul Carroll and former U.S. attorney Joseph DiGenova, to invite the federal prosecutors to my house so they could see what had happened. The prosecutors came on a Sunday afternoon, with the senior member expressing surprise that a candidate for indictment was so open and willing to talk without his lawyers' intervention.

I walked my potential prosecutors from my bedroom through the whole course of the terrible events of June 14. They saw that Smith's blood was on the outdoor carpet four or five feet from the sliding door to my family room. Investigators cut out two bloody sections of the carpet. There was a trail of Smith's blood from my door to the swimming pool, where he doused his injured wrist, and to the Jacuzzi.

On June 23 the U.S. attorney announced that no charges would be pressed against me. The *Washington Times* sank to a new journalistic low. After having made me page-one copy for days, it put that story inside. On the front page it ran a picture of Ben Smith with a caption, "Rowan's victim."

All of a sudden my legal problem was not with white officials in the White House or the Justice Department, but with black leaders of the District of Columbia government. Especially Marion Barry. Would he insist that I be prosecuted on the misdemeanor charge of possession of an unregistered gun and ammunition? Barry knew that I regarded him as a terrible model for black kids, because of the myriad stories about his alleged use of cocaine, his liaisons with women who were not his wife, the convictions for corruption of his top aides and advisers.

I had been told a year earlier that Barry was angry about a column I had written urging black people to stop their "knee-jerk defenses" of black officials who were accused of bribery, theft, rape, drug deals, and other violations of law. I had said:

Consider the nation's capital. Enough members of the administration of Mayor Marion Barry have pleaded guilty and gone to jail to make it clear that corruption exists — corruption that cheats and dishonors black people. Why should any self-respecting black leader cry "racism" here when it is obvious that whites are not being shielded from assaults on official corruption?

I knew what Barry's intentions were when one of his aides and key police officials confided to me that the mayor and his crony on the police force, Isaac Fulwood (now chief), had conspired to get a warrant to have me arrested at my home, handcuffed, with cameras grinding, and then taken to the jail for a mug shot and finger-printing. Cops were sent to the courthouse to get a warrant, but the U.S. attorney's office intervened and stopped the scheme. Later, policemen were sent to the chambers of Judge Joseph Hannon, a white conservative the Barry people thought would be eager to "get Carl Rowan." They were shocked when Hannon refused to sign the warrant, describing me as a "distinguished citizen who isn't about to run away." I was never arrested, mug-photographed, or finger-printed.

Barry now would not be able to humiliate me except through the open filing of charges and a court trial. But would he take this route? To my dismay, the *Washington Post* seemed to be pressuring him to do so. While it carried its own stories and editorials asking "What about the Rowan gun?," the *Post* showed its colors on July 13 when it reprinted an editorial from the *Richmond Times-Dispatch* comparing me with Goetz and noting that "Mr. Rowan . . . has not volunteered to go to jail for this alleged violation of law."

Barry was a street-slick operator. On June 15, long before he or Corporation Counsel Frederick D. Cooke had any facts, Barry criticized me before the press for "going out and shooting someone." With this erroneous statement, Barry took the decision as to whether to prosecute away from Cooke, virtually leaving this subordinate no choice. Still, my case never would have gone to court but for the anger of Barry and his lawyer-confidant Herbert O. Reid, Sr., when they were rebuffed and rebuked in their efforts to extort from me a commitment not to criticize corruption in the Barry administration.

On June 16 my son Carl telephoned Barry to ask why he would "convict" me before the media without any facts. Reid called back, suggesting that the mayor disliked some things I had written and that the mayor would view the issue of prosecution in a friendlier light if I would "lower my voice." My son expressed his outrage, saying that Barry and Reid would "drop dead" before I would cut any such deal.

Twelve days later Barry called my son, ostensibly in response to the June 16 telephone call that led Reid to suggest that I "lighten up" in my criticism. Barry told my son that "Fred Cooke won't make any decision [regarding prosecution] without my input."

I got a tip, confirmed later in TV news reports, that Barry had told Cooke to hold up charging me until after the national NAACP met in Washington and the Democratic National Convention had ended in Atlanta. Barry did not want to face criticism when he showed up at those two gatherings. Benjamin Hooks, NAACP executive director, made a point of seating me at the head table at every NAACP event that I attended. He asked who was behind efforts to prosecute me and seemed shocked when I said, "Marion Barry."

July became the crucial month, with the city letting me twist in the wind until it seemed politically safe to level gun charges against me.

And my family and I were being tormented in other ways, especially by harassing and threatening telephone calls around the clock. Finally I authorized the telephone company to install equipment to "trap and trace" telephone calls to my listed home number. Their investigators traced the calls to the home of Congressman John Miller, a Washington State Republican, where twenty-three-year-old Michael Brown allegedly was house-sitting. Miller called me from Washington to apologize profusely and assert that Brown had lost his job and been thrown out of his house. Policemen told me that there were two telephones at the Miller home, and one was listed in Brown's name.

"You ever hear of a house-sitter with his own telephone?" a detective asked me.

I was too besieged even to think about that question, especially when the U.S. attorney's office told me that there were so many murders and drug cases in the District that no one had time to prosecute Brown.

I was outraged. The two people who invaded my property would be given a clean record on the promise that they would do forty hours of unspecified community service. Four of their pals who got away were known to the police, but no charges were filed. Brown was going scot-free. But I was to be prosecuted because I defended my property from 2:00 A.M. invaders.

Ben Hooks was furious. On August 3 he issued a statement calling the decision to prosecute "a grievous mistake." In asking Barry to withdraw charges against me, Hooks said: "Carl Rowan is not, and never has been, a lawbreaker. To the contrary, he has spent 40 years as a distinguished journalist, trying to force presidents, governors, Congress and others to obey the Constitution, to enforce decent laws, so that black people might be free."

I was grateful beyond words that Hooks would speak up. Just as the Reverend Jesse Jackson had. But a lot of timid blacks had run for the tall grass. I shook my head in despair when Barry, the mastermind of the prosecution, lied and said that while he could fire Corporation Counsel Cooke, he "didn't have the authority" to overrule his decision, as Hooks had requested.

City council member Nadine Winter called the decision to prosecute "unconscionable." The black ministers of Montgomery County, Maryland, assailed it as "persecution by prosecution." But there would be no reversal by Cooke and Barry.

Meanwhile, the media continued to hold stakeouts at our home. I asked my wife, "Where were the sons of bitches in April and May when I was raising over $208,000 for scholarships for black high school seniors and needed some publicity?"

To my surprise, the police acted with far greater integrity in my case than did the media. My defense was based on a legal principle called entrapment by estoppel — meaning that since D.C. gun control officials had specifically told my son that his guns were exempt from registration because he was a former law enforcement officer, and because my son had been specifically told that he could legally leave the gun at my house, the District could not prosecute either him or me. Police Inspector James Lee admitted to me and my lawyer well before the trial that my son's gun was exempt and that the advice he got was what the Gun Control Unit had always given former law enforcement people.

When the corporation counsel's prosecutors approached Lee, he said flatly: "I will not lie for you in court." They put enough pressure on Lee to constitute obstruction of justice, but Lee refused to lie.

Then things got worse for Cooke and Barry. A city official passed to me information indicating that I was a victim of "selective prosecution." I was given documents showing that from January 1, 1983, to June 27, 1988, 4,301 cases involving unregistered guns were presented to superior court in the District of Columbia, and that 82 percent of those cases were not prosecuted. I got from the police department a report that in 1987 the police had confiscated 1,996 handguns and 487 long guns, but there were only 393 arrests.

"The prosecution of you is clearly malicious and political," one police authority told me.

Then came a bombshell. "The city that is trying to jail you recently sold more than five hundred .38 specials to high officials and other citizens for $375 apiece, and those guns are out there, unregistered," I was told.

I got that gun list and was shocked that the city had passed out *962 guns* without registration numbers.

President Reagan got handgun AUF8518. George Bush got a pistol with the serial number AUF8534. Marion Barry got a .38 special with serial number AUF9178. Former police chief George R. Wilson was listed as receiving at least five handguns. The head of the Gun Control Unit who told my son it was legal to leave a gun at my house got at least two of these .38 specials. And in the city where it supposedly is impossible to buy or register a handgun, I counted perhaps one hundred people who got *two* guns in the "ceremonial" caper. When it leaked that Barry had a gun, he lied and said it was a gift to the city. One of his bodyguards told me that the day the story broke, Barry gave the gun to his chief security man and ordered him to lock it in a safe.

Viv was a model of strength, even when a Virginia woman called on a Sunday morning to tell her that a "contract" had been put out on my life "running till 1989." My wife calmly jotted down the time, and the FBI immediately identified the caller.

But the mental and physical toll on both of us was greater than we understood.

I got up especially early the morning of September 8, because I had to write a column for Sunday, confer with my lawyers about the court case, and give a speech at 8:00 P.M. before American University's Kennedy Political Union. I had worked seven hours before my wife insisted that I stop and eat bacon and eggs. I then worked until the lawyers arrived, soon followed by Mike Menchel of the Washington Speaker's Bureau, who would escort me to American University.

The meeting hall was packed, and dreadfully hot. I spoke for thirty minutes, answered questions for about twenty minutes, and then signed autographs for what seemed an eternity in a room that felt like an inferno. I left the Ward Circle Building, climbing a set of steps, and realized that I had to walk a couple of blocks to where Menchel had parked the car. I knew that I couldn't make it.

"I can't answer any more questions," I said to the clamoring students. I leaned against what I remember as a huge garbage can and said, "Mike, I feel like I could faint."

The next thing I knew, Menchel was leaning over me as I lay on the sidewalk.

A student used his cellular phone to call the District's emergency ambulance bureau — and got a busy signal.

I sat up on the sidewalk, overhearing one student say "chest pains." Another said, "Does anyone know CPR?" — cardiopulmonary resuscitation. I knew that whatever privacy I had left was gone.

I had no chest pains — just a roiling gut that told me I needed to get to a bathroom.

An ambulance arrived with efficient, caring people. They decided that I suffered from hypoglycemia from not eating, except for two eggs and bacon, for more than seventeen hours. They rushed me to Georgetown University Hospital. Menchel telephoned my wife, and by the time Viv got to the hospital, television crews had already staked out the emergency entrance.

Doctors ran tests and quickly decided that I had not had a heart attack. But Viv and Hector Collison, my family doctor, engaged in a little conspiracy and acquiesced in the hospital's desire that I be kept overnight. "As long as we have him in the hospital, let him get the thorough physical he's been dodging," Viv said.

I never saw so many doctors, interns, nurses, and others administering so many stress tests, blood tests, and probing into so many places. I had entered the hospital at 9:58 on Thursday night. On Saturday morning I staged a "jailbreak." I told Viv to come and get me. I walked out and waited on the sidewalk, laughing at the number of people who stopped to offer me a lift.

I got home to find a signed letter saying: "You gutless sonofabitch. You'll fake illness or do anything to avoid conviction."

I never worried about conviction. My lawyers told me that there was a good chance that the judge would throw the case out. "Judge Arthur Burnett has this case, and he's a solid intellectual," one lawyer said. "He isn't afraid to make a decision."

But I learned some things that I hated to see when we presented our case for dismissal. The rules of evidence and the procedural mumbo jumbo make it nearly impossible, even with the highest-priced lawyers, to put all the facts before a judge or jury. I credit Judge Burnett for allowing me to tell in detail what happened at my home in the wee hours of June 14. The city's lawyer argued vociferously that what happened was immaterial — that I had an unregistered gun and ought to be convicted — period.

But, as my wife expected, on September 16 Burnett ruled that a jury, not he, should decide on matters of fact. We were bitterly disappointed.

I didn't hear about Burnett's refusal to dismiss the case from the court or my lawyers. I arrived at WUSA-TV just before 1:00 P.M. to tape "Inside Washington." Into the parking area rushed one of the most obnoxious men I have ever met, Jim Upshaw, of WRC-TV, channel 4.

"The judge has rejected you," he shouted. "How does it feel to have to go on trial? How does it feel to have to face a jury?"

I went inside TV-9 and made a couple of telephone calls and learned that Burnett had indeed decided that I would have to go to trial.

Hard as I tried, I could not focus on Gordon Peterson's questions on "Inside Washington." I knew that I was in for another long round of public exposure and vilification, and that I would have to spend tens of thousands of dollars more if I wanted vindication.

Carroll, DiGenova, and I decided that if the city wanted a trial we would let everything we had hang out. I was appalled to see the extent to which prosecutors can use legalisms to prevent juries, and even judges, from knowing the truth. We tried to subpoena Kenneth L. Hutson, the court's director of data processing, so he could testify about who got prosecuted on unregistered gun charges and who did not. I wanted him to reveal that the drug peddlers just threw their guns out in a pile when the cops arrived, and Cooke and his colleagues didn't prosecute on grounds that they "don't know who owns which gun." We tried to subpoena Barry and Cooke to let them tell the jury who really made the decision to prosecute me, and why. We tried to subpoena Herb Reid to ask him some questions about the attempt to extort from me, through my son, a promise to "lower my voice" about corruption in the Barry administration. We tried to subpoena the chief of police and have him bring to court the list of those who got those 962 handguns. The city moved to quash every one of these subpoenas, and the judge went along with the city. He said in a discussion at the bench that he "didn't want to drag all those celebrities in."

So my fate was in the hands of a jury that never knew a tenth of the truth about the law and handguns in the District of Columbia. A jury that could not hear how Barry had corrupted the office of the corporation counsel. Or how a reportedly drugged-up Barry had berated Police Chief Maurice Turner, blaming him for "leaks that help Carl Rowan." Or how City Council Chairman David Clarke had written a letter to Police Chief Turner, badgering him about the honest testimony of Inspector Lee. A jury that could not hear Cooke explain that he didn't even know that charges had been filed against me because "There was a glitch, a breakdown in the system," to use his own words uttered on television.

God, how I wanted the jury to see that list of 962 people who had just gotten new unregistered guns! But judges sometimes worry more about appeals and being overruled than they do about hearing the whole truth, so it was easy for Burnett to conclude that even if Barry, the police chief, and others were violating the gun law, it was immaterial to the question of whether Carl Rowan had violated it.

So the poorly informed jury became crucial. More so than I realized when the jury was being selected. Raoul Carroll warned me that my case was so celebrated that very few potential jurors would admit to any bias when the judge questioned them. "They all want

to sit on this case so they can say, 'I freed Carl Rowan,' or 'I put that
TV blabbermouth in jail.' "

Raoul was right. During the voir dire examination, a remarkable
number of those first in line to become jurors had no views on the
right to keep firearms for self-protection. They had no friends or
relatives who belonged to the NRA. They apparently had never
been robbed, never had a relative who had been mugged or bur-
gled, never thought about the rightness or wrongness of capital
punishment, had no thoughts about whether to believe a policeman
instead of another witness.

Voir dire was, I realized, a legal joke. Raoul and I would have to
fathom out who on that jury panel was faking ignorance and independence, and for what reason.

Of the two white people in line to become jurors, one was a
woman with solid gray hair who was the spitting image of Frances
Criss, the woman who was my secretary during my four and a half
years in government.

"That woman hasn't responded to anything," Raoul said to me.
"Should we use a peremptory challenge to throw her off?"

I looked at her again and said to myself, "Fran Criss would never
do anything to harm me."

I later learned from the jury foreman that that woman, Janet M.
Keyser, walked into the jury deliberation room shouting, "Fathers of
FBI agents should not have any exemptions. I vote guilty! And the
one I'd really like to put in prison is his son." The lone white man on
the jury promptly joined her.

"We'd have been out of there with a not-guilty verdict in twenty
minutes if it hadn't been for that woman," said the foreman, the
Reverend William C. Bartee. He said the white man got "cozy" with
a young black female juror "who was wearing his coat, and gave him
her telephone number and address," and she joined in the guilty
vote. Mr. Bartee said that after the judge was asked to reread the
instructions, the three saying "guilty" declared that "we can stay
here till Christmas, but we won't change our minds."

"Well, you'd better call and tell them to send your Christmas gifts
here," Bartee recalled saying, "because I'll walk through hell bare-
foot before I'll vote to convict."

This kind of argument went on for hours, and into the next day, while I stood in a courthouse corridor with my family, my lawyers, and all those reporters.

I knew that if that jury stayed hung, Mayor Barry would in part be the master of my fate, because he would tell Fred Cooke whether to retry me. If only to try to bankrupt me.

"There is a law against prosecuting people with the intention of inflicting financial harm," one of my lawyers said.

"Is that one of the laws that Barry obeys?" I asked.

In the end I had reason to feel good about a 9 to 3 vote. It was clear that no jury was going to convict me. Furthermore, some of Barry's most powerful supporters were saying that "it is time for the D.C. government to get off Carl Rowan's back." Bishop Smallwood Williams, who spoke those words in a sermon, called my prosecution "a grave mistake because the so-called D.C. gun registration law is certainly a colossal, miserable failure. . . ."

On October 5 Fred Cooke made a grudging and unprofessional announcement that although he still thought me guilty, he was dropping charges.

I said to my lawyers, "Thank you. The gag rule is off. Now I speak for Carl Rowan."

So on October 6 I held a press conference around the celebrated swimming pool and Jacuzzi, permitting reporters to see where Ben Smith was shot, and the 150 feet of concrete and stone between that spot and the Jacuzzi.

On October 7 I was on the front pages — again — because I had dared to tell the truth about a corrupt administration. COLUMNIST UNLEASHES TORRENT OF CRITICISM OF BARRY, PROSECUTORS, the *Washington Post* headline said. But on the editorial page, this newspaper, which had made a pretense of trying to nail Barry for years, called my attack on Barry "intemperate," and said my "outburst" was "a most sorry reaction." I knew that crooks in any city would always prevail if the media called truth telling "intemperate."

Later that day, I got a telephone call from President Reagan, who congratulated me on winning my case. He said the prosecution was "outrageous," and that it was a shame that I had to spend so much money on lawyers when I could have given it to kids who want to go to college. A nice call — inspired by his wife — from a man whom I had criticized so often, so angrily. I was appalled to read four days later that in the eyes of Richard Cohen of the *Washington Post* I had committed another crime — getting a congratulatory call from Mr. Reagan. In Cohen's eyes, that made me a soul brother of Ed Meese, Michael Deaver, Lyn Nofziger, and other cronies of President Reagan. I wrote a column blasting Cohen.

I had learned, the painful way, about the dishonesty, the irresponsibility, that permeates my own profession. And I know that if I died tomorrow, for much of the media my accomplishments would not mean as much as the fact that I was tried for allegedly shooting a "skinny-dipper" with an "unregistered" gun.

Change might come about if the citizens of the District of Columbia will take to heart my statement about why I paid so much in money and time to fight city hall:

> I have learned over four decades as a journalist that "City Hall" becomes more and more corrupt as more and more citizens lose the guts to fight. The crooks in the Barry administration have become emboldened by their belief that no one dares to stand up to them.
>
> None of us can be proud to live in a city that wallows in incompetence. . . . Who can be happy to see Washington become the "dope" capital of America? We look ridiculous when handguns are all over the District and there is a murder a day and more, even as buffoons boast about having "the toughest gun law in the nation."
>
> I have survived this political prosecution at a great cost, but it will be worth it if the people of the District wake up and understand that they need new and honest leaders.
>
> I have paid dearly, as has my family, for the right to say this to the people of the capital of this great nation: You deserve a government that is competent; that is not a sanctuary for the drug cartels; that does not blink at record numbers of homicide funerals. You deserve a mayor and other city officials whom your children can regard as inspirations to great achievement. What you have now is venality, ignorance, lack of couth and an absence of conscience at the top.
>
> I hope the citizens of the District will "see the light" that is radiating from a sad episode where intruders came to my home in the darkness.

In January 1990, Mayor Barry's troubles made my trial in the gun episode seem trifling. The FBI had caught Barry in a "sting" — a sordid videotaped affair in Washington's Vista Hotel in which Barry was seen by an astounded nation smoking crack.

Barry was indicted on fourteen charges of illegally possessing and using cocaine, of conspiring to buy, use, and distribute illegal drugs, and of perjuring himself by lying to a grand jury about his years of using dope.

His sensational trial wound up with a jury finding the mayor guilty of one count of illegal use of cocaine, acquitting him on a similar count, and declaring itself unable to agree on the twelve other charges. A handful of blacks on the jury must have said: Barry may be a cocaine junkie, a crack addict, a scoundrel in his sexual exploits, but he is *our* junkie, *our* scoundrel, and we don't want you white folk to jail him.

Although he faced a possible year in prison and a $100,000 fine, Barry held a "victory" celebration and announced that he was running for an at-large seat on the D.C. City Council.

My beloved city was tragically polarized between blacks and whites. Yet there were some whites — usually contract holders and city employees — who professed to support Barry, and many blacks who just wanted to get a mayor who had lied to and betrayed their children out of their lives.

I have had few sadder moments than on the day in 1986 when a black woman doctor came to me and said, "My thirteen-year-old is on drugs. I confronted him and he said, 'Momma, the mayor does drugs.' What can I do, Mr. Rowan?" I didn't know what to say. What I do know is that black people walk into self-imposed genocide if they do not understand the crisis in the life of that agonizing mother.

Barry's trial and its lurid disclosures, and the jury verdict, set back for many years any hopes of home rule, statehood, adequate federal financial support of this nation's capital. It undermined a drug war in which the U.S. is asking Colombian and Mexican officials to die.

I warned America about Barry in the mid-1980s. I was punished on that bogus gun charge. History will determine whether, in a time when racial passion often overrules reason, we can rise above this kind of destructive abuse of the criminal justice system.

CHAPTER TWENTY-ONE

A New Vision for America

I KNOW THAT MILLIONS of Americans blame the Marion Barrys of America for the rise in crime, drug abuse, and the other horrors of life in the cities of America as we move toward a new century. But as much as I deplore the Barry record, I know that neither he nor other black elected officials are responsible for America's decline in education and worldwide economic competitiveness or for high infant mortality, the breakdown of family solidarity, and other problems. No black mayor alone imperiled America's cities. No black street dealers alone magnified the curse of drugs. No blacks brought on a devastating recession or crippling budget deficits in the 1980s or turned America into a debtor nation, living to a shameful degree off loans from Japan, Saudi Arabia, West Germany, and other nations.

The rise in crime and the decline in the stability of the traditional American family have been going on for a long time. Only a fool would try to assess blame, racially or individually, for the fact that one black man out of every four aged twenty to twenty-nine is either behind bars, on parole, or on probation. (That compares with one Hispanic man out of ten and one white man out of sixteen in the same age group.)

The issues of overriding concern now are where can America go, and how does it get there.

Get there from where?

"Where" is not easy to write about. This country is in more peril today than it was in the thirties and forties when Hitler had his

Luftwaffe and Panzer divisions and Japan had thousands of men willing to commit suicide to win the war they started at Pearl Harbor.

As of now, we Americans are incredibly strong in terms of our military arsenals; but we are woefully weak internally in terms of ethics, racism, lack of commitment to universal education, official corruption, vulnerability to drugs.

We are at the brink of becoming the great "we give up" society of all time. Whether it is the "rising tide of mediocrity" in education across the land, the decline of the middle class among minorities and the rise of a permanent underclass, the plague of crack, cocaine, heroin, and other drugs, the crippling rise in our national debt as other nations assume primacy in the sales of automobiles, TV sets, videocassette recorders, and more, Americans have become the great surrenderers.

You can trace a large measure of the social malaise within America to the fact that the federal and state governments are literally *forcing* the poorest women in the land to deliver babies they do not want — babies brain damaged in wombs, babies whose mental and emotional development is stunted in infancy; children who will become victims of such mind-warping neglect, abuse, exploitation, that their lives will be dominated by hopelessness and the rage that provokes criminal outbursts against everything and everyone around them.

Poor children are at risk from the moment they are born, partly because they are seen as inherently dumb and ineducable lifetime welfare burdens, sometimes even by black teachers, and they are scorned by America's elitists who think education and opportunity are meant only for a privileged few.

I remember interviewing a former child of the Bronx and Brooklyn, the son of Jamaican immigrants, who recalled that when he was in the fourth grade his teacher wrongly wanted to put him in a remedial course because *she* thought he was "a little slow." That kid, of whom so little was expected by a bad teacher, went on to become a White House Fellow, Ronald Reagan's national security adviser, and the youngest chairman of the Joint Chiefs of Staff in the history of the U.S. military. He is General Colin Powell.

So the first step by government, corporate America, black

churches, social and civil rights groups, is to *intervene early* in the lives of youngsters who have been imperiled by recent court decisions and budget allocations.

If you deny a poor woman an abortion, you must not endanger the fetus you pretend to protect by refusing to give the mother adequate nutrition, medicines, vitamins, and prenatal care. To do so is to bring on the heavy costs of special education, lifelong medical care, institutionalization, and the rage and criminal behavior of some who have been retarded by maternal neglect during pregnancy or gross societal neglect in infancy.

These are the realities of maintaining national greatness, perhaps even of surviving, that Reagan and those around him never understood.

The Head Start program is a perfect and dismaying example of what can be expected by the poorest of the 10,200 babies who are born in this country every day. Head Start was begun a quarter of a century ago as a way of giving poor children something closer to an equal chance. Special attention to youngsters ages three through five has been extremely successful, even in the eyes of conservatives who see almost nothing good about the programs of Lyndon Johnson's Great Society.

But this year only one poor child out of twenty who is eligible for Head Start will get a place in that program. That is because Reagan never asked or allowed the Congress to appropriate enough funds. The current Head Start appropriation, adjusted for inflation, is less than the allotment for 1978.

President Bush proposes to add $500 million in fiscal 1991 to the current Head Start budget of $1.38 billion. That will mean that one of every eighteen eligible three-to-five-year-olds will find Head Start within their reach.

Those are not the figures of a nation trying to regain the competitive edge against the other industrialized nations of the world.

Would Japan, West Germany, Korea, or any other nation aspiring to economic, technological, or even military primacy deliberately consign 90 to 95 percent of its poor children to ignorance so great that they will never be able to cope, let alone compete? Obviously, no.

Former Japanese prime minister Yasuhiro Nakasone told us a truth, even though he got his tail in a crack for doing so. He said the

United States has so many blacks and Mexicans who are not properly educated that the country can never compete with Japan. Nakasone could have said, "We are a nation of peoples of homogeneous origins, and we benefit from the tranquility that brings. You are a melting pot, and you will always suffer from racial and ethnic conflicts that make for destructive politics and stupid allocations of your resources."

Nakasone told us why America's leaders are "tanking" it without much of a fight: because most politicians from the Oval Office to the statehouses to the city councils tremble before the irresponsible phrase, "*No new taxes.*"

"You can't solve problems just by throwing money at them" has become the great cop-out cliché of American life. I rarely attend a business convention, a conference of educators, a meeting of antidrug officials, or even sit on my television panel for "Inside Washington" when I don't hear that banal pretense of wisdom.

It's obviously true, as a general, out-of-real-life's-context discussion of how to change or save a complex, troubled society, that money alone is no panacea. But that cliché becomes a stifling expression of mindless conservatism, even greed, when what is at issue is a national problem that begs for application of a variety of funds and other resources.

The nation's leaders of the past several terms have been comparable to a group of doctors standing over a patient with a bad heart and a liver infection saying: "Well, you don't cure patients by throwing costly heart bypasses and liver transplants at them." Something costly gets thrown, or that patient will die.

A spin-off of the "don't throw money" cop-out, one used mostly by Republicans who denounce Democrats for their alleged "tax and tax, spend and spend" philosophy, is the canard that "social programs didn't work."

The unbendable troglodytes carry this argument all the way back to FDR as they seek to undermine Social Security and wage war on Medicare, Medicaid, and any reasonable federal program to protect families from catastrophic illnesses. But the obdurate foes of "socialism" cannot hide the reality that Social Security *does* work, and while some twenty-seven million Americans still have no medical insurance and millions more get virtually no medical care,

Medicare and Medicaid have taken a lot of cruel darkness out of the lives of millions of our people.

Roosevelt's people set up the Civilian Conservation Corps, and I know beyond doubt that the CCC camps worked infinitely better than reform schools. The Job Corps of the Johnson years is maligned today by know-nothings, but we would be infinitely better off with a couple million young men in job-training programs — kids hoping to be responsible citizens — than to have so many men in jails, prisons, reform schools, learning mostly about how to wreak revenge once they escape or are paroled.

The social programs of the Kennedy and Johnson years worked by lifting the level of life of black families to the point where, in the mid-sixties, they had sixty-four dollars for every one hundred dollars available to white families, a rise from only fifty-six dollars per black family in 1960. The tragic truth is that Johnson's Great Society never got a chance, because it was sabotaged by Nixon, Howard Phillips, and others who were commissioned to wage war on the War on Poverty. The Nixonites had the power to undermine every program that Johnson, Kennedy, Humphrey, and people of their views ever devised, and the Nixon toadies used their power ruthlessly. But they could never fool some of us children of the Great Depression.

I know that social programs *do* work. I am a product of the greatest welfare program this nation ever put forth: the GI Bill of Rights. The sinews of America, in any way you describe them, are buttressed today by the men, and some women, who got their educations from the GI Bill.

Don't tell me that it wasn't "welfare" because we are former soldiers, sailors, marines, who "earned" a GI Bill by fighting for our country. Many millions of other citizens have earned a chance at an education, an opportunity to rise and contribute, because they or their mamas and papas have made the ammunition, guarded the missile depots, swept the floors of the Pentagon, carried the messages from the State Department to the White House, plowed the fields of corn, or picked the cotton that was essential to winning any war.

Still, the nation is burdened by racist pap about who is and who is not educable.

That prevalent attitude is why, to pick just one city, the schools are so lousy in the ghettos of Washington, D.C. Children of almost unlimited potential have every bright horizon shut off every day by teachers who think they are riffraff; they are shunted off to the dead end of a school where even black principals, teachers, counselors, just want to say "good riddance" as quickly as they can by letting kids drop out or giving them a meaningless diploma.

For a nation of greatness, hoping to retain it, to give up on anything of potential value is foolish. For such a nation to give up on millions of its children is suicidal. For it to give up on children on the basis of their race, ethnic heritage, or financial condition is insanity bordering on criminality.

Yes, clearly, this society raised the white flag with speed on the issue of taking racism out of education, public and private. Yes, American officials in recent years gave a wink to the ghettoization of America by tolerating racism in private and public housing patterns; racial discriminations by sleazy savings and loan associations that were robbing people of all races blind; racial redlining by banks that believed it was more profitable to them to leave blacks in one neighborhood and whites in another. Despite the Fair Housing Act of 1968, the bureaucrats didn't want to tangle with Jim Crow–minded realtors and mortgage lenders.

Worst of all, the nation had for eight years, as secretary of the Department of Housing and Urban Development, a black man who didn't seem to give a damn about whether poor people of any race got decent housing — Silent Sam Pierce. I am certain that if it were not for the integrity and the clout of the new HUD secretary, Jack Kemp, the Bush administration would now be saying: "We tried to provide housing for the poor and miserable, but the money always gets stolen!"

Kemp has for a decade or more been an evangelist for enterprise zones, areas of cities that would be rebuilt by corporations that would get special tax breaks from Uncle Sam. Nixon endorsed enterprise zones as a way to give minorities "a piece of the pie." Reagan endorsed the concept. Bush has said he likes the idea. But nothing happens!

Corporate America knows that neither the federal nor the state governments will do enough to revitalize America's cities and inspire youngsters now mired in hopelessness. Joseph Antonini, the chairman of K mart who also is chairman of the National Minority Suppliers Development Council, laid the problem on the line in an interview with me last summer.

"I think tax incentives are a start, but I'm not sure that's ever going to be enough," he said. "I think what it takes is a true commitment by corporate America to make a strong effort to go into these cities and build various businesses."

"What about urban crime and drugs?" I asked Antonini. "Will big business come back to the cities despite these problems?"

Antonini was not deterred by the twin scourges of crime and drugs in our cities. "I'm one of those that say you'll never solve problems unless you get the money back, and you have got to start somewhere," he told me. "If we waited for things to get better, they may never get better, but things will always start to improve. Our job as corporate America and all the various organizations across America is to get involved, to help our cities, to help our minorities, to help our youth through education, through work programs, so important today."

K mart, he said, had built a huge store in a rundown area of Los Angeles, providing jobs for a lot of people who needed them desperately. The worst predictions for that store have not come true. Antonini says K mart will now move more boldly in taking jobs and easy shopping to neighborhoods where people are most in need.

If all the Fortune 1000 companies would make a commitment to our cities, we could cheer the damnedest urban renewal and revitalization ever known to any society. But so many of these corporations have been preoccupied with avoiding hostile take-overs, trying to take some company over, protecting themselves from their leveraged buyouts and junk-bond deals, that corporate social responsibility hasn't been on their agendas.

To put it bluntly, black social behavior in the toughest neigh-borhoods of our cities scares the hell out of the most decent of whites and certainly constitutes no welcome mat to anyone looking for a place to invest capital. A dismaying number of black city leaders are so prone to try to shake down potential investors, or to slash them with racial demagoguery, that even the most socially responsible corporate leaders are inclined to say, "Who the hell needs this?" I know that this is true because of my knowledge of what companies have faced in trying to do honest business with the Barry administration.

But there is no area of urban life that causes more well-meaning people to say "we give up" than the proliferating curse of drug abuse. In my city, children are killing children, peddlers are wiping out nonpaying junkies, girls are bartering their bodies for dope, entire neighborhoods are imprisoned in fear of the gunshots that deliver more than a corpse a day. In my suburbs the teenagers and young adults of affluent white families are taking in tens of thousands of dollars per night selling crack, marijuana, and other illicit substances. In the rural areas hardly an hour from my home, country boys are running labs that produce, not the moonshine of two generations ago, but Quaaludes, PCP, and a deadly assortment of mind-bending, life-shortening drugs.

Still, a destructive notion that we ought to legalize the drugs that are devouring America creeps slowly into the minds of more and more "important" people — judges, journalists, mayors, a former secretary of state. *Surrender* is becoming the American password.

Legalization advocates, like Nobel Prize–winning economist Milton Friedman and Mayor Kurt Schmoke of Baltimore, seem to think that with legalization some cosmic market forces would take over, the profit incentives for the Colombian and other cartels would vanish, and *drug-related crime* would become a term of the past.

Legalization is bound to lead millions more Americans to try, and get hooked on, crack, cocaine, heroin, and other mind-altering drugs. Who's going to supply all the drugs needed to meet the demand? You can bet your sweet bulletproof vest that if the Medellín cartels of Colombia, the gangs of Los Angeles, the mobsters of Washington, D.C., do not remain the suppliers, they will aim their automatic guns and target their car and truck bombs on anyone else who seeks to grab the market.

The new druggies will shoplift, rob convenience stores, sell sex (and intensify the problems of AIDS, syphilis, and other venereal diseases in the process). Those on horrible drugs like PCP will commit more gruesome crimes.

Legalization of these drugs will give America a crime problem beyond anything it has experienced.

Those arguing legalization want to stop fighting in the belief that we have "lost the war." The truth is that there hasn't been any real war against the drug merchants, and especially not against the armies of illicit drug users across this land. A handful of prominent people are cloaking cowardice in intellectualism and asking you and me to cave in.

I know that I, as a liberal or civil libertarian of sorts, am not expected to write this truth: The only way America will ever escape the abominations of imported and locally produced designer drugs is to wipe out the U.S. demand for such dope. And that requires medical help and education for the lower-class kids who are vulnerable day to day, and a draconian sledgehammer wielded against the middle-class and wealthy Americans whose drug purchases enrich and embolden the Medellín and Cali cartels of Colombia and the drug lords of New York, Los Angeles, Detroit, Washington, D.C., Miami, and a dismaying number of other cities.

The Bush administration and Drug Czar William Bennett keep dabbling in futile notions that somehow they can cut off the *supply*, and there won't be any crack to smoke or cocaine to snort. They have put Drug Enforcement Administration (DEA) agents into Mexico, Colombia, Peru, Bolivia, and other countries — fatal assignments for some. The United States has used diplomatic threats, poisonous insecticides against poppy fields, payoffs to peasant farmers, and a silly scheme to unleash ravenous caterpillars on the coca crops of the Andean nations. The Pentagon announced last March that it will spend $850 million this year and $1.2 billion next year to deploy 40 percent of this nation's AWACS (Airborne Warning and Control System) planes and a substantial number of E-2 reconnaissance, P-3, and other aircraft to enhance efforts to intercept the mammoth cargoes of illicit drugs that continue to come into the United States from the Caribbean, Central and South America.

You and I should applaud this belated action by the Pentagon. I have never understood the Pentagon's claim that it was spending $300 billion to protect America's shores from its enemies, such as the Soviet Union, when that same Pentagon could not close the borders to drugs. But we ought not fall suckers to the suggestion that the Pentagon can wipe out the drug curse.

The seemingly insatiable American *demand* for marijuana, crack, heroin, cocaine, and other drugs is the overriding abomination. The American demand is so high that farmers will grow poppies and coca, cartels will kill to protect their production facilities, and U.S. sheriffs, bankers, street cops, judges, and others will take bribes.

The Feds and other antidrug law enforcers could lock up ten million drug purchasers tomorrow, and I would never write a word saying that they have some constitutional right to subsidize the drug culture that is devouring so many children and weakening America in so many critical ways. So I have a vision of an America where rich people use their money to give hope to children at risk rather than to commit chemical suicide.

You look back over six decades and you see a lot of people, groups, individuals, political parties, that you think have let America down. In every year of breaking barriers I have thought innumerable times about how we black people have let ourselves down. I still see myriad ways in which we imprison ourselves.

I almost weep when I see what has happened to the civil rights movement, the bloody struggles for racial justice for blacks, Hispanics, and other minorities, and governmental and private compassion for the poor, the hopeless of this land. So much that was won over the bites of police dogs, the truncheons of bigoted cops, has been diluted — or lost.

Money magazine pointed out in November 1989 that

> the black middle class, a symbol of progress and possibilities for both blacks and whites, is in reality "fragile and shrinking" under the continuous assaults of racial discrimination. . . .
>
> For black households with annual incomes of $24,000 to $48,000 ("middle class"), median net worth is only $17,627, compared with a net worth of $54,644 for white families in the same income bracket.
>
> The message is clear: Unless we narrow that gap in the '90s, race will remain the most critical issue on the nation's agenda of unfinished business.

So, yes, white leadership playing to white racism is largely responsible for America's crime, drug, unemployment, education, and other woes. But I cannot exhort white America to a new agenda for this nation without first telling my fellow blacks how they have contributed to the malaise within this society. And there is a malaise, even greater than the sickness of spirit that Jimmy Carter cited, to his political peril.

We black people must get away from ceremony and memories and self-congratulations for deeds done a quarter century ago and deal with the problems of today.

I watched on television a black reenactment of the outrages in Selma a generation past. There were Jesse Jackson and a host of others, in Reagan-type photo opportunities, saying, "Look what we did." Tote up the costs of the airplane tickets and hotel rooms of those who put on that exercise of self-applause and see that the money could have provided hundreds of college scholarships to black kids who were abandoned by Reagan.

That reenactment in Selma didn't change a city government that is still driven by notions of "white power forever." Spending that money on bright young blacks could change another generation.

But that Selma celebration tells us how much self-idolatry and narrowness of vision permeates black leadership in these times.

Attribute it to disappointment, mindless rage, or whatever, but the record is clear that millions of blacks have wallowed in a revival of their own racism over the last two decades. We have seen it manifested in black women hating white women "who steal our men." We have seen racism of the Mississippi vintage I used to hear from Klansmen and White Citizens Councilmen — racism articulated by black social workers who are arguing that no white couple ought to be able to adopt a black child because black youngsters need the special protections they can get only from parents who share their culture and racial heritage.

I ask, How the hell does this differ from the white bigots of forty years ago saying that white children needed to have their culture and racial heritage protected from incursions of blacks into their schools, skating rinks, theaters, and neighborhoods?

The brutal reality is that in this country there are thousands of black kids who are up for adoption (plus thousands more in foster homes, halfway houses, reform schools) who are totally ignored by black adults. There are nonracist, compassionate, loving white families across the land who are willing to adopt these black youngsters and lavish on them the love, the educational opportunities, the inspiration without which these children will become victims of the ghouls who spread crime, drugs, sexual abuse, across the neighborhoods within which these unadopted children surely will languish.

Many blacks rejoiced in the exposures of evangelists Jim Bakker, Jimmy Swaggart, and others as tools of the devil. Few blacks in Washington, D.C., faced the fact that Mayor Barry had co-opted numerous preachers by giving their churches city money. Blacks get up in the early morning and sit up way past bedtime to take pride in, listen to, the new black darlings of television. And these black audiences seem so undiscerning that they never ask which of these sudden black millionaires have used their money to lift up black America, and which have in arrogance joined whites in saying, "Let the niggers eat cake."

Bill Cosby and Oprah Winfrey have been wonderfully notable in giving millions of dollars to institutions that seek to give young blacks the enduring asset of trained intelligence. But you look at the array of black superstars from Broadway and Hollywood and the music recording studios in between, and you will find a lot of blacks who are takers, but rarely givers.

I beg these newly powerful blacks in entertainment and other industries to wake up to the reality that a dreadful form of schizophrenia has become rampant in black America in recent years.

Blacks could go unthinkingly with the voices of black separatism, the hate-whitey hustlers, the trash-the-Jews demagogues such as Minister Louis Farrakhan, the ambitious young black politicians who still believe that they can climb to power by declaring that the new breed is *blacker* than the blacks who struggled before them.

In November 1989 I listened to a Black Entertainment Television (BET) program on which a Georgia legislator made numerous pejorative remarks about black leaders who no longer lived in black ghetto neighborhoods. The self-serving suggestion was that since he lived exclusively among blacks, he was a true supporter of black people, while those who had moved to the suburbs or affluent areas of cities were phonies, cop-outs, Uncle Toms, or worse.

This is the way in which some minorities have crippled themselves most destructively. Blacks with powerful public forums who dispense this ambivalence regarding integration and racial isolation confuse millions of other blacks. They give heart to the never-vanishing hordes of whites who prefer apartheid in America.

I know black men who urged LBJ to push through the Fair Housing Act of 1968; who demanded that the Department of Housing and Urban Development put housing for poor and middle-class families in previously all-white neighborhoods; who ranted against banks that limited mortgage loans and redlined certain areas to ensure that they would always be black ghettos. I know that some of these same blacks who demanded housing integration in public went to their barbershops and club dances and assailed their black brothers who had made a modicum of housing integration a reality by moving their families into areas that afforded them the advantages of first-class citizenship.

"Joe wants to be white!" some would say.

But even today the black racists and haters refuse to acknowledge that it takes guts, financial risk, personal bravery, for a black man or woman to take on a housing loan, buy a house in an all-white area, and then say to the haters, the egg throwers and cross burners: "Fuck you! This is my house and this is where I'm going to live. Challenge me at your peril."

How does any black person worthy of leadership mouth the demagogic propaganda, which white racists love, that only those who remain poor ghetto dwellers can care sincerely about impoverished people in our center cities? That is as stupid as saying that a surgeon has to have cancer himself to really relate to a cancer patient.

Whitney Young used to deflate the spreaders of this idea by explaining why he hobnobbed with white millionaires at the best watering holes and resorts.

"I've got to find out whether this goal of integration, of living like well-to-do whites do, is really worth achieving," he would say. "I never promised I'd come live with you and the rats. I said I'd make it possible for you to come live with me and these rich people."

I have been asked often over the last decade or so whether the decline of the civil rights movement resulted from the untimely death of Young, the murder of Dr. King, the passing of Roy Wilkins, Ralph Bunche, and others. I have no doubt that these are partly reasons for hard times on the still-rocky road to justice. The current leaders *are* a few cuts below those great black warriors of the 1960s, in terms of vision, commitment, and influence in the power circles of America.

I think the greater tragedy within black America is that we lost a sense of direction. King, Abernathy, Young, Wilkins, Thurgood Marshall, and the other towering figures of the fifties and sixties had it easy in the sense that black people and their white friends were driven toward one goal: the elimination of legally sanctioned racism in America. Every black person could understand the hatred of having to ride in the back of the bus. But once the legal basis for racial separation was wiped out, a lot of blacks walked into fogs of confusion about what the next goals ought to be.

Busing kids to school had been a great American institution for years as rural communities decided to give up the little red schoolhouse and join in building a modern emporium of education in some cornfield or pasture that was convenient to all the little towns. Americans were busing some nineteen million kids to school before the 1954 Supreme Court decision outlawing Jim Crow schools.

But when prosegregationists coined the phrase "busing for racial balance," that word *busing* became dirty, and more than a few blacks helped to make it so.

"I don't want my kid bused to South Boston where white bigots might kill her."

"I've seen enough to know that the white man ain't never gonna let a black man be an equal, integral part of this society. So I'll be satisfied if they just give our school the same books and equipment that they give the white kids."

As those litanies of black surrender cascaded around the land, I figured the confusion within black America couldn't get worse. But it did. People with significant followings began to talk of black separatism. It reached the absurdity in the 1970s of blacks asking for a group of southern states that they could turn into a separate black nation. Farrakhan now wants blacks to go to Africa. I'm staying here, fighting.

After establishing the civil rights to eat in dignity in restaurants, ride in self-respect on buses and trains, the black goal became the gaining of political rights. This has been probably the area in which blacks have achieved greatest success.

When Gus Courts, King, the Reverend George Lee, and Wilkins were carrying out their crusades, no one would have imagined that there would be some eight thousand black elected officials today, controlling most of America's greatest cities, and governing Virginia. But even in the gaining of incredible power, black America is burdened by the jealousies and absurd ambitions of a few.

The Reverend Jesse Jackson obviously reshaped the landscape of American politics by energizing millions of black people to register and vote. Every black elected to anything has been a beneficiary of Jackson's efforts. Jackson is the most ambitious, ubiquitous, irrepressible politician that I ever met. But it is obvious for any politically aware American to see that Jackson scares the hell out of millions of white people. He may run again, but he will never win the Democratic nomination or be elected president.

L. Douglas Wilder knew this, which is why he asked Jackson not to come into Virginia to speak for him in the historic campaign against J. Marshall Coleman. Jackson knew the old line, "I can praise you or attack you — whichever will help." He accepted Wilder's request.

Both Wilder and Mayor David Dinkins of New York resented Jackson's repeated public efforts to take credit for their election, but only Wilder had the guts to say, with Jackson beside him, "Doug Wilder won Doug Wilder's election as governor of Virginia."

Jackson moved his official residence to Washington, D.C., and went on for months with a charade in which he postured as a potential candidate for mayor. He telephoned me to say that "if Barry stumbles again" he would have to run "because the people will demand it." Barry stumbled into the FBI sting where he allegedly smoked crack with one of his mistresses, but the political draft that Jackson expected didn't materialize.

That made it easy for Jackson to decide that being mayor of a woefully troubled city wasn't worth what former FDR vice president John Nance Garner called "a warm bucket of spit." Jackson snubbed the mayoral race and loped off to South Africa, to Selma, and to everyplace else where he saw a photo opportunity and a headline. Jackson's obvious goal was to run again for president in 1992, a decision that spread dismay within the Democratic National Committee.

Jackson is an immensely popular American among blacks, unemployed whites, farmers who struggle for survival, laborers who find no real support among their now-affluent and, in some cases, toady white union bosses. I say to Jackson in this book, as I have said to him in person, that his leadership is no leadership if he does not dare to disprove Barry's assertion to a *Los Angeles Times* interviewer that "Jesse don't wanna run nothin' but his mouth."

In 1992 Jackson must show something other than his ability to run the Democratic party . . . into the ground.

Jackson could help to heal a long-bleeding wound, the schism that has existed for more than two decades between blacks and American Jews. If he can privately deal with Syrians, Iranians, and others on the humanitarian issues of American hostages and broader measures of peace, he ought to be able to move in ways to ensure that people who need to be allies do not go on as closet enemies during the most dangerous social times that America has known for generations.

Two groups of Americans whose fates have been so closely intertwined for generations have gotten caught up in self-destructive conflict over such issues as "affirmative action," as blacks call it — or "quotas," as some Jews call it. We have seen obscene Jew-bashing by Farrakhan and his followers and Jewish cries of "anti-Semite" hurled against blacks of integrity who just happen to disagree with some of Israel's policies in the Middle East, especially its occupation of Gaza and the West Bank.

The devastating funk in black-Jewish relations began to boil up in the summer of 1979 when some Jewish organizations successfully demanded the resignation of Andrew Young as the U.S. ambassador to the United Nations because Young had met with a member of the Palestine Liberation Organization. (It should be noted that ten years later, U.S. officials everywhere were talking to PLO members, but the Bush administration held the line on anything resembling recognition of the PLO as the genuine representative of Palestinians.)

On August 22, 1979, representatives of almost every black group of consequence met in NAACP national headquarters, then in New York, to pass a resolution about Young's ouster by Jimmy Carter under pressure from Jews. To understand the depth of the rift between blacks and Jews, read just a few paragraphs of the statement unanimously adopted by black leaders:

> There is no question that individual Jews and Jewish organizations and their leaders have worked as part of a liberal coalition with blacks and organized labor to form a powerful political force for social and economic reform in the United States. It is also clear that Jewish organizations and leadership have done so when it is in their perceived interest to do so as we do. It is reasonable to believe that they will continue to work with blacks when they believe that it is in their interest to be allied with blacks and our aspirations.
>
> However, it is a fact that within the past 10 years some Jewish organizations and intellectuals who were previously identified with the aspirations of black Americans for unqualified educational, political, and economic equality with all other Americans abruptly became apologists for the racial status quo. They asserted that further attempts to remedy the present forms of discrimination were violative of the civil rights laws.
>
> Beyond that, some Jewish intellectuals gave credence and policy substance to such concepts as "reverse discrimination" and "quotas" as reason for restricting further attempts to continue to seek remedies for discrimination against blacks. The term "quota" which traditionally meant the *exclusion* of Jews was now being used by many Jews to warn against attempts to *include* blacks in aspects of our society and economy from which we were previously excluded. To many blacks this seems to be a most perplexing Orwellian perversion of language.
>
> Black America is also deeply concerned with the trade and military alliance that exists between Israel and the illegitimate and oppressive racist regimes in South Africa and Southern Rhodesia. That relationship, in our view, imposes upon Jewish organizations in this country an obligation to insist that the State of Israel discontinue its support of those repressive and racist regimes.
>
> These causes of black-Jewish tension could only give aid and comfort to those who previously were as anti-Semitic as they were anti-black. It is also possible that it completed the circle of black separatism and bitterness.

I read that statement with a sense of impending social tragedy. I watched black-Jewish conflict widen over the years, due to the vulgar attacks on Jews by Farrakhan, or the loose-mouthed racism of "comedian" Jackie Mason as he tried to get New York Jews to vote against David Dinkins for mayor.

These are compelling and obvious reasons why we all must dare to denounce the divisive dribblings of the Farrakhans and Masons. The greatest reason should be that we understand that a terrible history of slavery in America, a Holocaust in Europe, and myriad antiblack and anti-Jewish discrimination in our towns and neighborhoods have created a special bond between blacks and Jews.

That bond was unbroken when racists in Philadelphia, Mississippi, in 1964, put two Jewish and one black civil rights volunteers — James Chaney, Michael Schwerner, and Andrew Goodman — in a common grave covered by a bulldozer.

I have always said and written what I felt proper about Israel, its invasion of Lebanon, its playing footsie with South Africa, but I have never sunk to the level of blaming every American Jew for every action of Israel. Just as I've never accepted the notion that every criticism of Israel was synonymous with *anti-Semitism.*

I wish with passion that we had no black anti-Semites, no Jews who seem to want to keep black people "in their place," but I know that in a free society we will never know such an idyllic state. I remember my little school in McMinnville that would not have existed but for Julius Rosenwald's vision and generosity and feel sure that the many generations of an alliance between blacks and Jews will endure for all time. I believe, because I see in 1990 the vulgar assaults on synagogues and cemeteries, and I see the neo-Nazis, the Skinheads, the modern Ku Klux Klanners, trying to establish an "Aryan nation." I see the new generation of bigots moving successfully to elect in Louisiana and elsewhere people with the mentality of Germany's Hitler and Goebbels, Birmingham's police chief Bull Connor, and Alabama's governor George Wallace, reminders of a time when racial and religious bigotry ruled more of America and the world than most people want to admit today.

We must face that ominous truth that blacks and Jews are still too much in the gunsights of the conscienceless haters for them to abandon each other.

Blacks and Jews cannot blind themselves to the truth that in most every area, Anglo-Saxons control America today as much as they did when Richard Wright wrote his books *Native Son* and *Black Boy*, and Laura Z. Hobson stung the economic elite with her novel *Gentleman's Agreement*.

I have called upon black Americans to accept their measure of blame, to rise up to new levels of responsibility in trying to solve the grave problems of this society. Do not seek comfort for a moment in my challenges to my fellow blacks.

White people control this nation, and I am not so foolhardy as to dispute the suggestion that they always will. That is why I have never accepted the arguments of black radicals that somehow America can be changed permanently by black rioting or walking away from efforts to invade and redirect the white man's system. So *white people* bear the greatest blame for what I, and others, see as the decline of America.

We are living through the decaying of what could be in perpetuity the greatest society in human history. But this is a nation that lacks the presidential, congressional, and media leadership to move against the chronic problems of greed and racism, to meet the requirements of education and training, to ensure the worldwide respect and security of this society.

Everyone has read either Arnold Toynbee, Edward Gibbon, Oswald Spengler, William Shirer, or all of them about the reasons for the fall of the Roman Empire, Greece, the Third Reich. Every one of these societies fell into decline partly because of what Spengler calls, in *The Decline of the West*, "race-suicide."

I offer these solutions:

• First, the federal government should set a national standard of the amount of money that is required to educate an American child properly if we are ever to reach the goals in math, the sciences, and other areas that President Bush and other officials have now set.

• Second, every state should say, "This is all the money we have for public education, including what rich and poor districts can do on the basis of property taxes. We are going to tote up all the state money and average it out per pupil and ensure that every child benefits from an equal allocation of state education money, rich and white, poor and black, or whatever."

• Third, the federal government will then say, whereas Michigan, California, and other states may be near or over the national spending goal per pupil, and Mississippi, Alabama, and other states may be below it, the federal government will allocate such funds as are needed to make educational opportunities equal from McAllen, Texas, to Montgomery County, Maryland, and from Selma, Alabama, to Scarsdale, New York.

If you think this is a radical proposal, look at the lawsuits that already have been filed in efforts to wipe out the disparities in spending and opportunity between rich and poor school districts. Montana, Kentucky, Texas, and New Jersey have struck down school-financing systems on grounds that there was unconstitutional discrimination against children who lived in areas of low property values, as against those who lived in wealthy neighborhoods. Similar costly challenges to school-financing schemes are pending in several other states.

Kentucky's entire school system recently was ruled unconstitutional by the state supreme court because it failed to offer anything close to an equal education for all the state's children. Kentucky is struggling to meet the complaints of its highest court. But even if Kentucky finds a way to provide parity of opportunity within its borders, a child in Kentucky, black or white, will still get shortchanged in the national scheme of learning.

That is why the federal government must step in with more money and leadership — not dominating, not meddling or controlling every community decision, but setting national goals and providing funds without which no state can meet standards that will ensure American competitiveness in an increasingly technological world.

The shameful truth is that most Americans have adopted this policy: If you can't educate 'em, and you can't find jobs for 'em, and you can't protect 'em from drug peddlers, throw 'em into prison.

The General Accounting Office says the population in federal prisons has doubled since 1980 and that the seventy institutions that were designed to handle a maximum of 30,860 prisoners are now crammed with 48,017 inmates.

What's worse, says GAO, the Federal Bureau of Prisons is going to spend $51,340 per bed to build prison space to accommodate 64,400 inmates.

Can you imagine the federal government spending $51,340 per ghetto youngster to improve schooling opportunities, to pay their teachers, to ensure them a chance to learn a trade or go to a junior college or even Oberlin or Yale? This lunacy of pouring billions into the sinkholes of prison must end. America must put its money into trained intelligence — and hope.

I look back to 1951 when I wrote: "I do not believe that man was born to hate and be hated; I cannot believe that the race problem is an inevitable concomitant of democratic life." I know now that I was naïve, just plain wrong. Thirty-nine years ago I thought it an absurdity that Benjamin Disraeli had written that "no man will treat with indifference the principle of race. It is the key of history. . . ." For all the white bigotry that I had encountered in my boyhood and youth, I was not ready to endorse the 1890 Senate speech in which J. J. Ingalls said: "The race to which we [white people] belong is the most arrogant and rapacious, the most exclusive and indomitable in history. It is the conquering and the unconquerable race, through which alone man has taken possession of the physical and moral world. All other races have been its enemies or its victims."

Ingalls's philosophy lives like a tumor on the collective brain of the hundreds of millions of white Americans who have institutionalized racism.

Americans who would never embrace racism in the specifics of persons and places will express bigotry ruthlessly in generalities. The very day that I began writing this chapter I read a letter in the *New York Post* declaring that the only way to have affirmative action is to lower job standards.

Not a journalist I know would have written specifically that "job standards" had been lowered when I entered the State Department, went to Finland, or directed USIA, but most of them could oppose, quietly or loudly, the broad idea of bringing more blacks, Hispanics, and women into the State Department to make the foreign service more representative of the America it serves. In the abstract, it was so easy to argue that to do this necessitated a dilution of the quality of the foreign service.

This was a reflection of the views held in thousands of American towns and cities, North and South, where school integration is still being resisted, that "mixing the races" inevitably means "lowering educational standards." I don't know whether or when America can rise above this stunting mentality where views of race control everything. I do know that the only escape from this prison of racial stereotypes is to infuse every institution of America, from the White House to the statehouses to the veritable outhouses of America, with a spirit of equality of honor and opportunity for those who earn it by displays of character and achievement.

I look at my country today and I see so little of the bravery of Harry Truman and Gus Courts, so little of the political vision of Hubert Humphrey and Whitney Young, so little of the social bravery of two men who never loved each other, Lyndon Baines Johnson and Martin Luther King, Jr. What I see are fakers who breathe every political breath in fear. They remind me of a story my mother told me over and over again in the 1930s in her way of inspiring me to go on — and upward.

Mama told me that the train whose arrival announced that it was time to go to school had to climb a steep hill to get to Sparta. She said that one morning there was a heavy frost, and the tracks were slippery, and the stationmaster in McMinnville said to the crew, "Please don't run halfway up that hill and fail, because you'll slide back into McMinnville and kill a lot of people."

My mother said that the train's engineer expressed no fear. "With this little engine, we always make it," he said.

But as the engine and boxcars got halfway up the hill to Sparta, the engineer sensed a frightful drag.

"Throw another load of coal in," the engineer commanded the fireman, as he jerked one valve and pushed another and, in the moment of utmost crisis, nudged that train over the top of the hill, rolling it into Sparta.

As my mother told it, the engineer turned to his brakeman and said, "What happened? I never had such panic in trying to climb that hill."

"Well," said the brakeman, "I got so scared we'd roll back down that hill and kill a lot of people in McMinnville that I put the brakes on halfway up the hill."

Reagan put the brakes on halfway up America's hill. Bush doesn't seem to know how to take the brakes off.

And a lot of poor children are dying needlessly in the McMinnvilles and Spartas of America.

Index